LAW AND SOCIETY

An Interdisciplinary Introduction

**Lee S. Weinberg
Judith W. Weinberg**

106846

UNIVERSITY
PRESS OF
AMERICA

LANHAM • NEW YORK • LONDON

For Daniel, Jennifer, Bim, Arnold,
Ruth, Helen, and Roland

We are grateful for the support of the University of Pittsburgh External Studies Program in the development of these materials. We particularly wish to thank Charles Lyons and Diane Davis for their suggestions and criticisms. In addition, the entire staff of the External Studies Program have been most helpful in producing this book. Finally, we want to thank Richard E. Vatz of Towson State University for his enormous contributions to the content, organization, and editing of the final manuscript.

Lee S. Weinberg
Judith W. Weinberg

Contents

To The Instructor

This book was developed after I taught a course entitled "Law and Society" for a number of terms and concluded that no textbook existed which was interesting and readable for undergraduates. The few possible books available tended to be collections of readings whose contents was too difficult for undergraduates to understand or small paperbacks which focused on specific issues, but did not offer a broad, straightforward introduction to the field. More out of frustration than a burning desire to put together a text, I set out to structure, write, and edit a book for my course.

The result is a unique and, I hope, an effective text which is neither a comprehensive encyclopedia of law and society nor an unrelated collection of journal articles. I have used the concept of Mini-lectures to set forth information which students need to know and I have reprinted relevant excerpts of a number of articles where appropriate. Study questions and Discussions follow each of these.

While, obviously, other instructors will wish I had included topics of special interest to them and omitted some of those included, I believe that this book can be used successfully and creatively by a great many teachers of law and society. The book is not intended to be exhaustive or deeply analytic. It is intended for students who seek an introduction to the field of law and society. I have used other smaller books along with this one quite effectively. Of these, Schur's Law and Society (Random House, 1969) is the most compatible. However, others would be quite useful as well.

Finally, if others struggling to teach students a first course in this area find this text effective in their courses or have suggestions for improving it, I would hope that they would contact me with their ideas. I am certain that this text will not fit every instructor's needs; I am hopeful, however, that it will offer an alternative to others who share my view of the weaknesses of the books in this field.

To The Student

Rationale and Goals

Law and Society: An Interdisciplinary Introduction is designed
to explain and review basic ideas concerning the role of law in society.
Because law and legal institutions daily impinge upon our lives, it is
valuable for all students to become familiar with how society affects the
development and administration of law and how law, in turn, affects social
life. For example, social theories which explain law as a reflection of
social structure are presented in Unit 3 and empirical studies of how
effectively law can produce social change are presented in Unit 6.

This book assumes no previous knowledge of the field on your part
and will hopefully be of interest to you whether you are a pre-law student,
a police officer, or a social science major. The pre-law student will find
that the fundamental questions of legal philosophy, discussed in this book,
are at the heart of the practice of law and will learn some of the limits
of law as a means of resolving disputes and maintaining social order. Police
officers, who work on the 'front lines' of the law, should be interested in
the political, economic, and sociological views of law as well as the role
of law in achieving and maintaining order. The discussion of law and psychiatry
also should be of interest to officers, faced daily with psychiatric/legal
issues. For political science, sociology, and other social science majors,
the text offers an opportunity to focus on the role of law from a social
scientist's point of view, that is, the theoretical and empirical dimensions
of law in society.

The overall goals of this text, for all students, are:

a. to increase your awareness of law in American life;

b. to enable you to examine the nature and function of law
    from a variety of disciplinary perspectives;

c. to encourage you to relate the knowledge and skills
    acquired in this course to the legal phenomena unfolding
    around you; and

d. to provide the basic concepts, general background, and
    analytic skills necessary for more specialized course-
    work in the study of law and society.

Organization

There are nine units of work in this book. Units 1 and 2 provide you with a variety of approaches to the problems of law and society. Units 3-6 deal with the relationship of law to social structure and with the three most significant functions of law: resolving disputes, maintaining social control, and achieving social change. Units 7-9 examine the role of law in American society and include more detailed discussions of two issue areas: law and psychiatry and reverse discrimination. Below is a brief overview of each of these units:

UNIT 1 JURISPRUDENCE

This unit is devoted to a summary of the philosophical roots of the efforts to study law as a social phenomenon. You will study many different definitions of law to demonstrate to you the difficulty of really capturing the essence of 'law'. Recognizing the problem of defining law is important to an understanding of many of the controversial legal issues of our day. Also it is important to realize that law may be defined differently for different purposes.

UNIT 2 INTERDISCIPLINARY PERSPECTIVES ON LAW AND SOCIETY

Unit 2 offers you an opportunity to study the ideas of economists, political scientists, sociologists, anthropologists, psychologists, and rhetoricians as they are brought to bear on the problem of law and legal systems. You will find that the perspectives of each enables you to see different aspects of legal problems. You will be able to see the many facets of law and realize that different interpretations of the role of law and different solutions to various problems may result from the application of different disciplinary perspectives.

UNIT 3 LAW AND SOCIAL STRUCTURE

This unit views law as a dependent variable, that is, a reflection of underlying social organization. While recognizing that law can help to bring about social change, the focus here is on law's role in maintaining the status quo. Developmental theories of law and social structure are presented, including those of Maine, Marx, Durkheim, Galanter, Weber, and Nonet and Selznick. To begin to understand the role of law, you must deal with the fact that law and legal institutions cannot solve all social problems because legal institutions are, to some degree, the creations of the same social situation which they are supposed to change. These theorists discuss law from this point of view.

UNIT 4 LAW AND DISPUTE RESOLUTION

Here the function of law as a means of dispute resolution
is examined and the possible alternative means of non-legal dispute
resolution are presented. The concepts of negotiation, avoidance,
mediation, arbitration, judging, and others are developed to give
the ability to conceptualize the problem of dispute resolution.
Finally, the small claims courts, the citizen dispute centers, and
the community moot are offered as possible alternatives. One of
the central functions of law in all societies is to provide a
means for settling disputes. The various methods of resolving
disputes which are described here suggest to you that perhaps
better legal and non-legal methods can still be developed.

UNIT 5 LAW AND SOCIAL CONTROL

The second function of law to be discussed is that of
social control. The unit attempts to deal with the nature of
social control, the distinction between legal and non-legal
control, the problem of legal deterrence, and the relationship
between law and other social controls such as family, church,
and psychiatry. While you are all familiar with the coercive
powers of the legal system, you will be encouraged here to
critically think about whether law is capable of achieving
all of the goals for which it is employed. It will be possible
for you to better explain the failure of law to deter crime and
to analyze the relationship between law and other types of social
controls.

UNIT 6 LAW AS AN INSTRUMENT OF SOCIAL CHANGE

The function of law is studied primarily through the eyes
of the impact theorists who attempt to study the impact of Supreme
Court decisions on lower courts, political elites, and the public.
Examples from the literature on impact are presented and analyzed.
You are undoubtedly aware that the mere announcement of a Court
decision does not assure immediate changes in society. By
focusing on the other instituons whose cooperation is necessary
for Courts to successfully order social change, you will be able
to analyze current Court decisions and assess the likelihood of
their success.

UNIT 7 LAW IN CONTEMPORARY AMERICAN SOCIETY

The focus here is on the American legal culture, legal
mobilization, and the heavy reliance on legal forms and legal
solutions to problems. Reading from Alvin Toffler's "The Future
of Law and Order," and Glazer's "Toward an Imperial Judiciary"
offer you two perspectives on the consequences of our reliance
on law. In addition, the inherent incapacities of the judicial
process are explored. You will see from this unit that American
law has expanded into an ever increasing range of issues and you
should begin to think about the desirability of this trend.

UNIT 8 LAW AND PSYCHIATRY

The use of psychiatry as an alternative means of social control is explored in depth with special attention to the work of Dr. Thomas Szasz and the implications of his work for the role of law versus the role of psychiatry in maintaining a minimum level of social control.

UNIT 9 A CASE STUDY: REGENTS OF THE UNIVERSITY OF CALIFORNIA vs. ALLAN BAKKE

The famous reverse discrimination case is presented and an annotated summary of parts of the opinions are included to provide you with the legal background necessary to an understanding of the case. In addition to exploring the legal and philosophical dimensions of the Bakke case, an attempt is made in this unit to apply all of the learning from the earlier units to an analysis of the reverse discrimination problem.

Study Directions

The materials in the book include mini-lectures written by me, and readings reprinted from a variety of sources.

Each unit begins with a Rationale explaining the importance of the unit to the overall text and its relation to the other units. The Overview in each unit summarizes what you will be studying and is intended to help you to begin to organize your thoughts before reading the various readings in each unit. Objectives are listed for each unit. You should pay close attention to them and be certain that you can meet each of them. To help you be sure that you have completed all of the Tasks in the unit, a Unit Task Checklist is provided for each unit. As you complete each task, simply check it off in the box.

Reading selections reprinted from other sources and included in the study guide are called Readings. Those which I have written are called Mini-Lectures. Following every reading and mini-lecture you will find Study Questions which are designed to focus your thinking on the major issues contained in the reading selections. These questions will be most helpful to you if you attempt to answer them yourself in the space provided. Following each set of Study Questions you will find my Discussion of Study Questions which you are to compare to your own answers. These Discussions review the central points to be studied and should be read as carefully as the reading material upon which they are based.

UNIT 1

Jurisprudence

Rationale

Underlying all studies of law and society are certain assumptions about the nature of law, the nature of justice, the justifications for disobeying law, and many other questions involving value judgments. Legal philosophers have explored alternative answers to such questions for centuries. Philosophy of law is also called jurisprudence, a term which is derived from the Latin name for those who were "wise in the law" (juris prudentes). This unit undertakes an examination of the jurisprudential roots of the modern study of the role of law in society. As you will see, social scientists, while placing great emphasis on data collection and analysis, still must deal with certain philosophical arguments and assumptions which cannot be resolved by research methods. As Edwin M. Schur states,

> individuals and groups within a society, including legal
> functionaries themselves, find it necessary to make ethical
> choices regarding legal matters, to assess in whatever
> terms they choose to adopt the meaning of 'law' and
> 'justice' and to decide what stand they will take when a
> proposed legal policy is advanced or decision suggested.
> These choices--which, in turn, influence the actual shaping
> of the legal system and hence help to determine that which
> we are concerned with empirically--are not easy to make . . .
> From a variety of philosophical perspectives and expressed
> or inarticulate premises, jurisprudence provides a rich
> storehouse of responses. (Schur, 1968, p. 18)

1

Objectives

After you have completed all the tasks in this unit, you should be able to do the following:

1. Define and/or distinguish:

    a. conventionalist and essentialist views of the definition of law

    b. natural law and positive law

    c. cultural and historical schools of thought

    d. good law and valid law according to Austin, Kelsen, Savigny, and Bentham

    e. positive law and living law

    f. sociological jurisprudence and legal realism

    g. utilitarianism

    h. procedural natural law

    i. Malinowski's, Hoebel's, Hart's, and Bohannon's definitions of law

2. Given a sample case, describe the nature of the uncertainty of law by analyzing the basic arguments of each judge in the case.

3. Describe the relationship between jurisprudence and the sociology of law.

4. Given a legal dilemma, analyze alternative solutions based on each of the major philosophical perspectives by incorporating the concepts of legal positivism, natural law, procedural natural law, utilitarianism [and any other concepts discussed in Unit 1].

Overview

This unit consists of an examination of the jurisprudential roots of the social scientific study of law and society. Mini-Lecture #1 summarizes various philosophical perspectives, such as natural law, legal positivism, cultural and historical jurisprudence, utilitarianism, sociological jurisprudence, legal realism, and procedural natural law. Each of these schools of thought highlights a different aspect of the nature of law, and you should try to see the advantages and disadvantages of each point of view.

The organization and major points in Mini-Lectures #1 and #2 are drawn primarily from Schur's (1968) excellent discussion of these issues. While they are summarized here, you might wish to read Schur (especially pages 17-24, 26-58, 70-79, and 110-116) for a more detailed analysis.

2

Mini-Lecture #2 is presented here because it adds some additional definitions of law from a social scientific perspective. As you will see quite quickly, it is difficult to capture the entire nature of law in any single definition or from any particular philosophical stance.

There is, in fact, no one accepted definition or philosophical description of the nature of law. Many different philosophical notions are used in the study of law and society and will be reflected in the views of the social scientists that will be studied in this course.

There are three amusing, but significant imaginary cases presented to you in the unit. "The Case of the Speluncean Explorers" is presented in Mini-Lecture #1. The unusual facts of the case lead to five fascinating judicial opinions on what the solution should be. In "The Problem of the Grudge Informer" you become the decision maker and prepare an opinion in another hypothetical case. A close reading of the unit materials will help you to prepare your written opinion. Finally, an optional reading is included, "Son of The Speluncean Explorer," which will provide additional food for thought for those of you who begin to find yourselves wrapped up in the problem of jurisprudence.

Finally, the second optional reading is provided for those students who want to pursue the issues raised in this unit in greater depth. This is a difficult reading and, therefore, I have given you a few study questions and answers to help in summarizing the substance of the reading.

Study Task Checklist

The following is a list of all of the activities that you will need to complete for this unit. It has been set up as a checklist so that you can keep track of your progress, should you need more than one sitting to complete the unit. You may also find it useful to keep track of the time you spend on each task so that you can begin to budget your time over the term.

You will find a checklist such as this at the beginning of every unit.

☐ 1. A. Read Mini-Lecture #1, "Jurisprudence and Sociology."

☐ 1. B. Answer Study Questions for the mini-lecture and compare your answers with the Discussion of them.

☐ 2. Answer Study Questions for Readings #1 and #2 and compare your answers with the Discussion of them.

☐ 3. A. Read Mini-Lecture #2, "Alternative Definitions of Law."

☐ 3. B. Answer Study Questions and compare your answers with the Discussion of them.

☐ 4. Complete the Unit Review Matching Exercise.

☐ 5. Complete the Unit Assignment using Reading #1.

☐ 6. Optional: Study Reading #2, "Son of the Speluncean Explorer," by Burton F. Brody.

☐ 7. Optional: Study Reading #3, "More Thoughts on Hart, Kelsen, Fuller: An Epistemological Comment," by Lee S. Weinberg and Richard E. Vatz.

☐ 8. Optional: Answer Study Questions and compare your answers with the Discussion of them.

JURISPRUDENCE AND SOCIOLOGY

To hope to answer the central question of jurisprudence, "What Is Law?" in a brief essay would be absurd! To ignore the question in a course about law and society would be inexcusable! Accepting these limitations, I am convinced that you can acquire some awareness of the nature of law by a close reading of this mini-lecture.

The Problem of Definition

Before examining the jurisprudential roots of the modern study of law and society, it is useful to point out that there are two schools of thought on the nature of definition, conventionalism and essentialism. Conventionalists believe that it is ultimately not possible to arrive at the 'correct' definition of law. For them, "Definitions of law are, in short, conventional. They are good or bad, adequate or inadequate, depending on the purpose of the definition" (Friedman, 1977, p. 3). Therefore, if our purpose in defining law is for use in a course on law and society, Friedman would argue that our definition need only be a convenient one for referring to the subject matter to be studied. He suggests, therefore, that "'Law' for us, then, is what other people call by that name" (Friedman, 1977, p. 3). His point is that most people would agree that police conduct, court trials, and statutes are examples of the behavior, process, and content of law. To simply define an area for study requires no more precise boundaries to be established for the concept of law.

Essentialists, on the other hand, argue that the law has an essence and that it is possible to specify the conditions which must be met in order to assert that law or a legal system exists in a particular society (Golding, 1975, p. 8).

The Speluncean Explorers

Lon Fuller, the late Harvard philosopher of law, to illustrate the problems of understanding the nature of law, created a hypothetical set of facts concerning five cave-explorers trapped by a landslide for thirty-two days (Fuller, 1949). After being advised by radio that they did not have enough food to survive until the rescue team would reach them, they cast lots to select one of their group who would be killed and eaten in order to allow the others to survive until the rescurers could reach them. Following their rescue, the four were convicted of murdering their companion and sentenced to death. They appeal their convictions to the mythical Supreme Court of the jurisdiction and the five justices of the Court write opinions about what should be done. Each of these opinions highlights some aspect of the problem of understanding the nature of law and of legal reasoning.

A. The Chief Justice approaches the defendants' appeal in a highly technical manner. Having examined the language of the statute defining murder, he concludes that the act of the defendants constitutes murder. Had the legislature not intended such a case to be included, it presumably would have written the statute to read: "Whoever shall willfully take the life of another, except where trapped in a cave and about to starve, shall be put to death." The Chief Justice believes that respect for the law would be undermined if any other decision were made. He seems to believe that strict reading of statutes encourages general respect for law. Recognizing the tragic result of following the law in this particular case, he recommends executive clemency, hoping both to retain general respect for the law and to avoid an unpleasant result in this case.

B. Justice Foster makes two arguments in support of his vote to overturn the conviction. First, he claims that the situation involved in this case was outside of the legal order to which the statute was addressed. That is, the murder statute did not apply because the killing took place in the state of nature, not within the jurisdiction of the legislature. Alternatively, he argues that even if the statute did apply to this case, a self-defense claim by the defendants would

6

justify a reversal of their conviction. In other words, the need to defend their lives against starvation justified their conduct even under the murder statute.

C. Justice Tatting, upset because the state even prosecuted these defendants, withdraws from the case in bewilderment. Agreeing with the Chief Justice that the murder statute does apply and disagreeing with Justice Foster that self-defense would justify the killing, Justice Tatting cannot reconcile the competing demands of upholding the law and providing a just and merciful result.

D. Justice Keen, arguing that the role of courts is to give effect to the decisions of the politically sensitive legislature, votes to uphold the conviction.

E. Justice Handy attempts to deal with the case from a 'common sense' point of view. Indicating that public opinion heavily favors a pardon, but that no pardon will be forthcoming, he concludes that overturning the conviction is the only sensible course of action. He further adds that the defendants have already paid a terrible price and have suffered enough. (NOTE: Didn't we hear the argument that "he has suffered enough already" raised by Richard Nixon's defenders who sought to spare him further punishment following his resignation?)

This intriguing case serves to illustrate vividly the fluid and problematic nature of law. Each of the Justices has touched upon an important legal dimension. The Chief Justice reminds us that courts are supposed to apply legislative enactments, not to change them by adding exceptions not included by the legislature. Yet the problem remains, how should courts do this? Should they assume that the absence of a particular exception demonstrates that the legislature thought about and then rejected the exception? Should they assume, on the contrary, that the legislature never imagined such a situation ever arising under this statute and, therefore, infer what the legislature would have done if it had addressed the issue? He also brings up the critical question of whether citizens will continue to accept a legal system which ignores the language of the statutes. But, then, we might ask the Chief Justice if he thinks that the citizens will continue to support a legal system which holds rigidly to the rules even when totally unacceptable decisions are the result.

Justice Foster's opinion suggests that law, a set of general rules written to cover general categories of future events, must be interpreted so as to produce fair results. Because no general rule can ever anticipate every set of circumstances to which it might be applied, the court must recognize which circumstances are beyond the intended coverage of the law.

Justice Tattings position highlights the difficult position in which judges are often placed. The courts cannot easily control which decisions they will have to make. Here, Justice Tatting's solution to the problem created by an overzealous prosecutor is to decide NOT to decide. The United States Supreme Court similarly exercises its right to decide not to decide when it denies a writ of certiorari (a writ requesting that the Court hear a case). It is essential to remember, however, that it is impossible to avoid a decision.

A refusal to decide a case leaves the appellant (the dissatisfied party who seeks a reversal of a lower court decision) in the same position as a negative decision. In Fuller's case, Justice Tatting's refusal to vote has the same effect as a negative vote. Remember, the result was 2 votes to overturn the conviction, 2 votes to uphold the conviction, and 1 abstention. The result: the conviction stands.

Justice Keen's reasons for upholding the conviction raise the issue of the unrepresentative nature of the courts. The judges, being appointed or elected for long terms, are far removed from the electoral pressures which confront the legislature. Since the legislature, therefore, is the more democratic branch of government, shouldn't the decisions of the legislative process be deemed superior to those of the elitist judicial process? Justice Keen apparently thinks so. He might also agree with the Chief Justice on the pragmatic ground that failure to accept the superiority of the legislature will result in a revolt against the unrepresentative judiciary. Surely, Keen and the Chief Justice must agree, it is better to make some difficult decisions than to lose the authority to make decisions at all! The problem to bear in mind, however, is what should be done about an incompetent or evil legislature? Should the courts defer equally to its superiority?

Finally, Justice Handy's views remind us of Holmes' (1881) famous comment, "The life of the law has not been logic, it has been experience" (p. 5). Common sense has enabled the law to change, survive, and remain useful in organizing social, economic, and political life. This sounds convincing enough. But how would you feel if you were told by a court that the technical language of the law upon which you rest your claim of right supports your position; but common sense supports your opponent! The difficulty, of course, lies in the fact that 'common' sense is rarely 'commonly' agreed upon! Of what use is the law if it can be overridden by common sense? Alternatively, of what use is the law if it cannot be overridden by common sense!

As Fuller hoped, the Speluncean Explorer case is designed to draw your attention to some problems associated with the nature of law. The answers, unfortunately, are not as easy to point out as the questions!

Influences From Legal Philosophy

In the remaining part of this mini-lecture you will read a sketch of the philosophical underpinnings of the modern study of law and society. While a full discussion of the natural law influence on sociology of law will be deferred until the other positions are described, it is important to grasp the basic difference between the natural law approach and the legal positivist approach. By oversimplifying the problem somewhat we can say that in the natural law view the validity of law is a matter to be determined by reference to some external standard of evaluation. In other words, whether a 'law' is a valid law must be decided after measuring that 'law' against a higher standard. In one version of this natural law position. "(Aquinas) insists that human laws are means to ends and that they should be reasonable means to those ends. Whether a purported law has the 'force of law' depends on its being a reasonable direction toward the attainment of a given end" (Golding, 1975, p. 31). In addition, of course, the ends being pursued by the law must not themselves be in violation of the higher law, or natural law. In sum, natural law theorists assess the validity of

9

law on the basis of the extent to which the _content_ of law conforms to the requirements of some higher moral standard.

At the opposite end of the philosophical spectrum are the _legal positivists_ who argue that the validity of law is primarily a function of its _source_ rather than its _content_. If the political state lawmaking institutions enact 'laws' according to the practices of that state, then such 'laws' are valid laws. Whether they are good or bad laws is an entirely separate matter from whether they are valid or invalid laws. In John Austin's famous words, "the existence of law is one thing; its merit or demerit is another" (Quoted in Golding, 1975, p. 25).

A. Analytical Jurisprudence

The British legal positivist John Austin's position may be described as an example of analytical jurisprudence. It was analytical in that it sought to lay out "a formal, logical, closed system of legal rules" (Schur, 1968, p. 26). Reducing Austin to a few simple propositions undoubtedly does him an injustice, but it is necessary in order to give you a rough idea of his philosophy of law.

Austin maintained that law is the _command_ of the _sovereign_. A command is an indication of desire for a person to act or not to act in a particular fashion. In addition, a command is accompanied by a threat of harm for failure to comply with the announced desire. For Austin, then, "commands are orders backed by threats" (Golding, 1975, p. 26). The commands of the sovereign, according to Austin, impose upon the commanded a duty to obey. The duty to obey is not a function of the goodness or badness of the command, but of the _source_ of the command. The _sovereign_ in a particular state is the person who is habitually obeyed and who habitually obeys no one else. The commands of the sovereign, then, are the laws of the state. The question of whether these commands are moral or immoral is an important question for Austin, but not a _legal_ question.

A second example of this formalistic approach is Hans Kelsen's "Pure Theory of Law." As Schur states, "Kelsen views the legal system as a hierarchy of norms, with legal acts and rules of any level traceable to norms at still higher levels, culminating in the 'basic norm'" (Schur, 1968, p. 27). The validity of any law, for Kelsen, is determined by reference to another law whose validity, in turn, depends upon another law and so on. Thus, "the laws of a legal system . . . form a hierarchical structure, and the validity of a lower legal norm is justified by appeal to a higher legal norm, either because the content of the former conforms to the latter or because the creation of the former is authorized by the latter" (Golding, 1975, p. 40).

For both Austin and Kelsen, the validity of law and the morality of law are separate issues. The impact of this position upon efforts to study law and society has been great (Schur, 1968, p. 29). Most social scientists have been comfortable with the view that what the law 'is' and what the law 'ought' to be are to be carefully distinguished. While the focus on the formal, logical, coherent, consistent set of rules has been left primarily to legal scholars, the positivist distinction between the "is" and the "ought" has been widely accepted by students of law and society. (NOTE: Philip Selznick, a sociologist of law discussed in Unit 2, is a major exception.)

B. Cultural Jurisprudence

While the formalistic jurisprudence of Austin and Kelsen emphasized the need to examine law as a closed system which existed independent of social context, the cultural and historical orientations emphasized "that a legal system is but part of a larger social order, the various elements of which are interdependent" (Schur, 1968, p. 30). The position of the leading spokesman for this school of jurisprudence, Friedrich Karl von Savigny, was that law was

> . . . not a deliberately created product of some artificially contrived legislator, but was a slow organic distillation of the spirit of the particular People (volksgeist) among which it operated . . . such a law must be understood as the product of a long and continuing historical process and its validity depended on the fact that its traditional character was rooted in the popular consciousness and was thus a true national law in accordance with the spirit of the people. (Lloyd, 1976, p. 252)

The validity of law for Savigny, therefore, depended upon the extent to which the law conformed to the 'spirit of the people.' Mere legislative announcements might or might not qualify as valid law. Law which emerged out of customary practices of the people was preferred over

11

legislative enactments. The contrast between Savigny's notion of validity and that of Austin or Kelsen should be apparent: for Savigny there is a blurring of the validity and morality of law; for Austin and Kelsen, there is a strict separation.

Savigny was sensitive to the idea of viewing law as a social product; however, he excluded the possibility that law might also be a social force. He also muddied the distinction between the validity of law and the morality of law. How are we to determine the validity of a given law? We apparently must compare it to the 'spirit of the people' and decide if it accurately articulates the popular will. The inability to do this in an objective fashion raises obvious problems in assessing the validity of law.

Additionally, Savigny's concept of the volksgeist, or spirit of the people, is an ambiguous and mystical idea which can easily be used to refer to a racial or national group of people whose collective wisdom is presumed to be superior. Once such an idea takes hold, it can become a dangerous tool in the hands of skillful demagogues. Keep in mind, however, that the formalism of Austin or Kelsen could likewise become a dangerous tool in the hands of an evil 'sovereign.' For if all of his commands are valid despite their immoral content, law could be used to oppress and exploit some for the benefit of others. The very idea that the 'people' even have clear preferences on most matters of legal interest is highly questionable, and the need for judges and legislators to take decisive action before such preferences develop seems clear.

Despite these questions Savigny's contribution of sensitizing us to to the fact that law reflects the changing attitudes and desires of society remains important to the study of law and society.

An historical approach was taken by Sir Henry Maine whose study of the history of law revealed a pattern of legal development among all 'progressive' societies. Maine argued that in all those societies in which law was not fixed or static, there was a movement away from a status based definition of rights and duties to a contract based definition of rights and duties. As Schur (1968) states, "relationships determined solely on the basis of the social positions of the individuals involved gradually gave way to systems of rights and duties determined through contractual arrangements grounded in the consent of the parties" (p. 32).

For Maine, the idea of determining rights and duties by freely negotiated agreements was a tremendously progressive step. It was not possible in the nineteenth century for him to foresee the need to limit the freedom to make contracts in order to protect the party who was in an unfair bargaining position. For example, to say that a landlord and a tenant freely negotiate their mutual rights and duties might not be accurate in a situation where housing is scarce and all landlords use the same printed lease! In this situation, the prospective tenant in fact has only two choices: rent from a landlord on the landlord's terms, or refuse to rent on his terms. Refusal, of course, is not a viable alternative if one likes to sleep under a roof rather than the stars. Therefore, legislatures might impose duties on landlords not to raise rents. Wouldn't this be a return to status based definitions of rights and duties? Wouldn't the minimum wage law also violate the principle of freedom to contract on any agreeable basis? Maine, therefore, did accurately identify the trend toward a contract based society, but did not foresee that limits would have to be placed upon the freedom to contract in order to protect those with no bargaining power.

While identifying what he believed to be an evolutionary development in the law, Maine was not as totally historical or backward looking as Savigny. Whereas Savigny was suspicious of legislative efforts to interfere with the development of customary law which expressed the volksgeist, Maine urged the legislators to be creative in dealing with the increasingly complex problems facing the modern state. As one scholar put it, Maine recognized that,

> . . . though we cannot ignore the extent to which [the]
> present state is historically conditioned, history must
> not be used as a strait-jacket to impose traditional
> attitudes upon the needs of a new age" (Lloyd, 1976,
> p. 255)

C. Utilitarianism

Another philosophical perspective which influenced the later study of law and society was utilitarianism. Bentham applied utilitarian thought to the legal system: "Most notably the proposition that men act in such a fashion as to maximize pleasure and minimize pain, and the ethical rule that an assessment of the happiness produced by a human act should be the major criterion for approving or disapproving of it" (Schur, 1968, pp.

33-34). The influence of Bentham's view can be seen in the economic approach to law which you will read about in the next unit. Thus, Bentham argued that the goodness or badness of a law was to be determined by reference to this principle of utility. Like the positivists, Bentham believed that the validity of law was a separate question from the merits of the law as measured by the utilitarian yardstick.

Bentham attempted to create a legislative science which could be used to reform the legal system. Through a systematic study of the various social effects of alternative legislative policies, he hoped to advance the cause of achieving the greatest amount of happiness for the greatest number of people.

D. Sociological Jurisprudence

The views of Eugen Ehrlich and Roscoe Pound are best described as illustrative of sociological jurisprudence. Ehrlich is most widely known for his distinction between the 'positive law' and the 'living law'. The distinction reflects Ehrlich's belief that behind formal laws were the actual norms which people followed. They were not synonymous with the formal laws. For Ehrlich, " every society had an inner order of the associations of human beings which composed it, and this inner order dominated life itself, even though it had not been posited in legal propositions of the positive law" (Lloyd, 1976, p. 209). Ehrlich was not willing to say that a lack of congruence between the positive law and the living law invalidated the positive law. He was, however, willing to say that the effectiveness of the positive law would be impaired by a lack of congruence with the living law. As pointed out by Schur (1968), "Ehrlich's work had the merit of directing the attention of legal analysts to the larger world" (pp. 37-38).

This broader view of law expressed in the sociological jurisprudence of Ehrlich took hold in America and was championed by Roscoe Pound. His emphasis was on the study of the 'law in action'. This meant looking to see if the positive law conformed to the living law, if the statements of the courts conformed to the actions of the courts, and if the aims of statutes were actually achieved in the implementation of statutes (Schur, 1968, p. 39). Pound saw value in empirical research to answer the above questions and to determine how best to create laws which would satisfy human social needs.

E. Legal Realism

The most recent development in this overview of the development of jurisprudence is legal realism as expressed in the writing of Llewellyn, Frank, and Holmes. The heart of the legal realists position is the contention that "judges make law rather than find it" (Schur, 1968, p. 43). Judicial decisions are made on grounds unknown to the observer and are then announced as being the logical result of the application of legal principles to factual situations. Holmes famous statement that "The prophecies of what the courts will do in fact, and nothing more pretentious, are what I mean by the law" (Schur, 1968, p. 44) expresses the view that law is nothing but a prediction of what judges will do. In the end, it is difficult to demonstrate whether judges do or do not actually feel compelled by legal rules to make certain decisions which they otherwise would prefer to decide differently. Legal realists can always argue that if judges strongly desire to decide cases on either side they will do so despite the law. Thus, the case where the judge _appears_ to be bound to the result "dictated" by the law may simply be the case in which he/she does not feel strongly that a contrary result would be better.

F. Natural Law and Sociology

You'll recall from an earlier part of this mini-lecture that the natural law view held that the validity of a law was determined by evaluating the content of that law against the permanent, absolute, universal standards of the natural law. Such a view has had a great impact on the development of American jurisprudence. From the Declaration of Independence to the more current debate over human rights violations around the world, Americans have found the idea of basic rights--whether recognized in the positive law or not--to be most appealing. American sociologist Philip Selznick has been in the forefront of a movement to reconcile natural law and empirical sociology through his assertion of the ideal goal of 'legality'. Further discussion of this question will be postponed until Unit 2 in which Selznick's normative sociology of law is described.

G. The Inner Morality of Law

In perhaps his most important book, The Morality of Law, Lon Fuller tries to state "the natural laws of a particular kind of human undertaking, which I have described as 'the enterprise of subjecting human conduct to the governance of rules'" (quoted in Schur, 1968, p. 55). You will recall the legal positivist, John Austin, who defined law as merely the "command of the sovereign." Fuller argues that the 'commands' might fail to achieve the status of 'laws' if they violate the 'inner morality' of law which is expressed in the following eight statements:

1. There must be general rules.

2. These rules must be known.

3. They must not be retroactive.

4. They must be reasonably clear.

5. Laws should not be contradictory.

6. Laws should not require the impossible or the unreasonable.

7. Laws should be constant through time.

8. Law and the administration of law should not conflict.

In other words, Fuller rejects Austin's position that any command of the sovereign constitutes law. But, on the other hand, Fuller does not accept the natural law position that a law whose content violates the natural law is not law. His position is somewhere between the legal positivists and the natural law theorists. His eight conditions for successful lawmaking are often interpreted as a form of 'procedural natural law'. This suggests that while there may not be absolute standards for the content of law, there are absolute standards for the procedure for making law. Thus, if the sovereign issues commands which violate this procedural natural law (e.g., secret rules, ad hoc rules, retroactive rules, contradictory rules, etc.), they are not law. This is analogous to a natural law theorist's argument that commands which violate the natural law are not law. It is different from the natural law theorist's position in that Fuller maintains that nearly any content can be consistent with the requirements of procedural natural law.

While Fuller tries to say that any content can be included as law so long as it meets the eight requirements, he also says that it is difficult to adhere to the eight principles and accomplish all ends. For example, unlike the positivists, Fuller is not willing to call Nazi Germany a legal system. But unlike the natural law theorists, his reason is not that what the Nazis did under the umbrella of law was horrible. Rather, he argues that much of the Nazi "law" violated his procedural natural law (inner morality of law) by being ad hoc, secret, retroactive, etc.

Perhaps reference to the Nazi example is the easiest way to summarize the distinctions between legal positivism, natural law, and procedural natural law: For positivists Nazi law is <u>bad law</u>; for natural law theorists it is <u>not law due to its content</u>; for procedural natural law theorists it is <u>not law due to its procedural defects</u>.

1. What are the conventionalist and essentialist views of the problem of definition?

2. How do the justices of the Supreme Court vote in the Speluncean Explorer's case and what reasons do they give?

3. What is the basic difference between natural law and positive law?

4. What are the advantages and disadvantages of Savigny's point of view?

5. What was Maine's contribution to historical jurisprudence?

6. What was Bentham's utilitarian principle for evaluating the content of laws?

7. In what way may Bentham be considered a legal positivist?

8. What are the basic facts of the case of the Speluncean Explorers?

9. What do you think Fuller wishes to illustrate about law by this example?

10. What is a valid law for Austin (a legal positivist)?

11. What is a valid law for Kelsen (a legal positivist)?

12. What is a valid law for Savigny (a representative of cultural/historical jurisprudence)?

13. What is the difference between 'positive law' and 'living law' according to Ehrlich's version of sociological jurisprudence?

14. What is the heart of the legal realist position?

15. List Fuller's eight criteria of 'procedural natural law' which he calls the "inner morality of law."

DISCUSSION OF MINI-LECTURE #1 QUESTIONS

1. Conventionalists believe that definitions are neither correct nor incorrect, but rather useful or not useful for a particular purpose. Essentialists believe that definitions must precisely specify the necessary and sufficient qualities of that which is being defined.

2. The vote of two for upholding the conviction, two for overturning the conviction, and one abstention results in the upholding of the conviction. The reasons for their votes include (in order): a strict reading of the murder statute, the irrelevance of law to this situation, disapproval of the original prosecution, legislative superiority, and common sense.

3. Natural law refers to "higher" law by which man-made law is to be evaluated. If man-made law violates natural law it is invalid and need not be considered law at all. Positive law is man-made law. Legal positivists adamantly maintain that positive law which is immoral or evil is still valid law. They believe that we are more accurate in our analysis if we say that the issue of whether law is valid is different from whether law is good. To say that 'bad laws' are 'not laws' only confuses our thinking.

4. The advantage is that Savigny emphasizes that law was the result or product of social forces. The disadvantages are that it is not possible to conclusively demonstrate the popular will, that the popular will might itself be evil, and that the concept of volksgeist can be easily adapted to serve the needs of skillful demagogues.

5. Maine believed that there was an historical trend in the law of all progressive societies. He claimed that law based upon status or position evolved into law based upon contract or individual agreement.

6. Basically, Bentham argued that 'good' laws were those which tended to produce the greatest amount of good for the greatest number of people.

7. Yes, in the sense that he saw his utilitarian standard as a basis for determining the relative merit of a law rather than its validity.

8. Five amateur cave explorers became trapped in a cave following a landslide. Advised that they had insufficient food to survive until rescue parties would be able to reach them, they cast dice to determine which member would be killed and eaten by the remaining four. The four were subsequently tried and convicted of murder and are appealing their conviction to the Supreme Court.

9. Fuller seems to suggest: (a) law is not a mechanical, clear-cut set of rules to be applied; (b) Judges are human beings whose own views color their interpretations of the law; (c) legal systems require citizen support in order to function; (d) law on the books is modified by various ideas of 'higher laws'; and (e) the roles of the legislature and the courts overlap.

10. Austin says that a law is valid if it is a "command of the sovereign."

11. Kelsen says that a law is valid if it can ultimately be traced back to the basic norm.

12. Savigny saw validity as dependent upon a law's conforming to the dictates of the spirit of the people. Unlike Austin and Kelsen, Savigny was not willing to say that <u>all</u> commands of the sovereign were valid laws; only if their content accurately expressed the will of the people would Savigny accord them the status of valid laws.

13. Positive law, Ehrlich maintained, is the formal law on the books; living law is the law which actually guides human conduct. Positive law which was not in accord with living was likely to be ineffective, though valid, law.

14. Legal realists state that judges "make law rather than find it." It is difficult to refute this assertion because one can always argue that the judge who <u>appears</u> to be "finding the law" is actually only using the law as an excuse to achieve the desired results.

15. Fuller's criteria are as follows:

    1. There must be general rules.
    2. These rules must be made known.
    3. They must not be retroactive.
    4. They must be reasonably clear.
    5. Laws should not be contradictory.
    6. Laws should not require the impossible (or the extremely unreasonably).
    7. Insofar as possible, laws should be constant rhough time.
    8. Legal rules and administration of law should not conflict.

Mini-Lecture #2

ALTERNATIVE DEFINITIONS OF LAW

In addition to the philosophical definitions discussed in the first mini-lecture, there have been a number of other attempts to define law. As discussed earlier, we could avoid the philosophical entanglements by saying that "we all know what law is" and proceed to study its operations and relations to society. However, it appears desirable to be more precise and so a number of alternative definitions of law are presented here.

The Meaning of Law

The first question to examine is whether law is a necessary component of society. From a Marxist perspective, law may be seen as the tool of the capitalist class. Such a theory predicts the elimination of law as the true socialist state emerges. Law has not, however, disappeared in Marxist societies, though it can easily be argued that it will disappear once advanced stages of socialism begin to develop in these societies. It seems unlikely that rules of conduct will ever be unnecessary: "The idea that human society, on whatever level, could ever conceivably exist on the basis that each man should simply do whatever he thinks right in the particular circumstances is too fanciful to deserve serious consideration" (Lloyd, 1976, p. 24).

A well known study of two Israeli communities (Schwartz, 1954) suggests that there may be small, closely knit communities in which formal law is unnecessary due to effective informal means of social control. However, it is unlikely that the degree of intimacy and shared values and expectations achieved in the Kvutza community could ever be duplicated in an entire society. The central point of this study is not that society without law is possible, but that formal law is likely to develop when informal law fails.

The issue of identifying which social norms qualify as legal norms brings us back to the problem of definitions of law.

The broadest definition of law imaginable is offered by Malinowski in his study of the Trobriand Islanders. Where yam growers and fisherman adhered to the norm of exchanging yams and fish, Malinowski was able to see 'law'. The nature of this primitive law was the reciprocal expectations of the fishermen and the yam growers. Each believed he had a duty to provide his product and a right to receive the other product in exchange. If either side in the exchange violated the expectations, they would be denied the exchange. To define this reciprocal relationship as law would exclude virtually no custom from the status of law! The custom of exchanging Christmas presents, under this view, might be seen as illustrative of American Christmas Present Law.

Anthropologist E. Adamson Hoebel attempted a distinction between social norms and legal norms in his definition of law: "A social norm is legal if its neglect or infraction is regularly met, in threat or in fact, by the application of physical force by an individual or group possessing the socially recognized privilege of so acting" (Schur, 1968, p. 75). Hoebel's three key elements of law, therefore, are physical force, official authority, and regularity. This definition of law emphasizes the coercive character of law. It distinguishes the use of force by requiring that official authority be possessed by those applying the force. Finally, repeated use of force in similar circumstances is a necessary component of law.

The advantages of Hoebel's definition are that it does not require a finding of particular institutions such as courts or police--it merely requires some socially recognized agent--and it permits us to distinguish customs from laws. Its disadvantages are that it makes law and government synonymous, thus rendering "the notion of a government subject to law meaningless" (Schur, 1968, p. 75), and that it places too much emphasis on the coercive side of law. Much law is not easily thought of in terms of coercion, i.e., there is no coercive effort to force people to make contracts or punish them if they don't. Contract law merely says to people, "If you want to make an agreement which the legal machinery will enforce, then you should do it in this fashion."

H. L. A. Hart's book, The Concept of Law, contains another influential effort to define law. Hart defines law in terms of the union of primary and secondary rules. Hart, a positivist, defines valid law as those rules which can be identified by reference to the 'rule of recognition'.

Paul Bohannon, another anthropologist, argues that laws are simply those rules or norms for which society provides an institutionalized method for dealing with violators. The 'reinstitutionalization' of custom idea is helpful in distinguishing customs from laws. For example, if it is customary not to eat with one's fingers and I do not adhere to the custom, there is no institution to which you can take me complaining that I have violated the rules! If, however, I fail to pay my rent, you can take me to a magistrate and complain.

Bohannon's definition makes it possible to find law in a variety of situations where perhaps Hoebel's definition would not. For example, if there is no recognized authority empowered to exercise physical force—as in the international realm—Hoebel might say no law existed. But Bohannon, finding re-institutionalization of custom in national and international institutions, is able to claim that a form of law is present at the international level.

1. Is law a necessary, inevitable component of society?

2. What does Schwartz's study of Israeli communities suggest about the nature of law?

3. What is Malinowski's basis for his claim that law existed in the Trobriand Island society?

4. How does Hoebel distinguish social norms from legal norms?

5. What did Bohannon mean by 'reinstitution' of norms?

DISCUSSION OF MINI-LECTURE #2 QUESTIONS

1. It appears that only Marxists maintain that law, being the mechanism for enforcing the self-serving rules of the capitalist class, will disappear as capitalism gives rise to socialism. Nonetheless, those states purportedly following Marxist doctrine continue to have law.

2. The comparison of the collectivist and private property communities suggests that formal law arises when informal social control is ineffective in maintaining social order.

3. He believes that 'reciprocal expectations' of the yam growers and fisherman warranted the conclusion that a primitive form of law was present.

4. Hoebel identifies physical force, official authority, and regularity as the criteria for distinguishing legal norms from social norms.

5. The 'reinstitutionalization of norms' is a concept designed to distinguish customs from laws by suggesting that society makes only the latter amenable to adjudication in another social institution.

UNIT REVIEW

In this unit, which is one of the longest units in this course, you have studied a number of new concepts and theoretical perspectives. These are important as a foundation to the rest of the course.

The following matching exercise has been provided to help you review these new ideas. It is important that you complete this exercise independently before you check your answers with the answer key provided on the following page. This should help you to prepare the unit assignment, which follows this review exercise.

MATCHING EXERCISE

Match the term or idea on the left with the appropriate definition or description on the right.

___ 1. positive law

a. the emphasis on law as a product of social forces

___ 2. conventionalist view of law

b. the Pennsylvania Criminal Code (law) is an example of _____

___ 3. legal realism

c. the principle of utility must be used to determine if a valid law is a good law

___ 4. Malinowski's definition of law

d. the rules people actually follow

___ 5. natural law view

e. the union of primary and secondary rules

___ 6. Bohannon's definition of law

f. retroactive criminal law does not constitute valid law

___ 7. essentialist's view of law

g. law is what other people call by that name

___ 8. Hart's definition of law

h. the belief that judges simply used the law to justify decisions they reach on other grounds

___ 9. Kelsen's definition of good vs. valid law

i. valid law is the command of the sovereign whether the command is a good one or a bad one

___ 10. legal positivists view of law

j. laws which are not congruent with the will of the people may be invalid

___ 11. Bentham's definition of good vs. valid law

k. it is necessary to define law with great precision

___ 12. utilitarianism

l. the argument that certain human rights are possessed by all people regardless of the law of the land reflects

_____

___ 13. Savigny's definition of good vs. valid law

m. the reinstitutionalization of norms

___ 14. cultural and historical schools of thought

n. the value of a law depends upon the degree to which it produces more pleasure than pain

___ 15. Hoebel's definition of law

o. valid law is traceable to the basic norm and may be good or bad law

___ 16. procedural natural law

p. law exists whenever there are reciprocal expectations violations of which results in some sanction

___ 17. Austin's definition of good vs. valid law

q. while the Supreme Court ban on Bible reading in the public schools is immoral, it is still valid law

___ 18. living law

r. the regular application (or threat) of force by official authorities

Unit Review--Answer Key

1. b

2. g

3. h

4. p

5. l

6. m

7. k

8. e

9. o

10. q

11. c

12. n

13. j

14. a

15. r

16. f

17. i

18. d

Directions for Unit Assignment:

A.   After reading "The Problem of The Grudge Informer," analyze each of
     the recommendations for dealing with the "problem" using the elements
     of legal positivism, natural law, procedural natural law, utilitarianism,
     or any other concepts discussed in this unit. For example, you might
     want to consider these _types_ of issues in your analysis:

     1.   What is the significance of the First Deputy's argument that the
          reported acts were unlawful at the time they were committed?

     2.   What is the significance of the Second Deputy's view that "A
          legal system does not exist simply because policemen continue
          to patrol the streets . . ."

3. Is it significant that the constitution was <u>not</u> repealed by the Purple Shirts?

4. What view does the Fifth Deputy espouse when he opposes enacting a statute to resolve the problem?

B. In addition to your analysis of the recommendations of each deputy, state <u>which</u> recommendation <u>you</u> would accept and explain your reasons.

Reading #1

READING FOR UNIT ASSIGNMENT

*THE PROBLEM OF THE GRUDGE INFORMER

By a narrow margin you have been elected Minister of Justice of your country, a nation of some twenty million inhabitants. At the outset of your term of office you are confronted by a serious problem that will be described below. But first the background of this problem must be presented.

For many decades your country enjoyed a peaceful, constitutional and democratic government. However, some time ago it came upon bad times. Normal relations were disrupted by a deepening economic depression and by an increasing antagonism among various factional groups, formed along economic, political, and religious lines. The proverbial man on horseback appeared in the form of the Headman of a political party or society that called itself the Purple Shirts.

In a national election attended by much disorder the Headman was elected President of the Republic and his party obtained a majority of the seats in the General Assembly. The success of the party at the polls was partly brought about by a campaign of reckless promises and ingenious falsifications, and partly by the physical intimidation of night-riding Purple Shirts who frightened many people away from the polls who would have voted against the party.

When the Purple Shirts arrived in power they took no steps to repeal the ancient Constitution or any of its provisions. They also left intact the Civil and Criminal Codes and the Code of Procedure. No official action was taken to dismiss any government official or to remove any judge from the bench. Elections continued to be held at intervals and ballots were counted with apparent honesty. Nevertheless, the country lived under a reign of terror.

Judges who rendered decisions contrary to the wishes of the party were beaten and murdered. The accepted meaning of the Criminal Code was perverted to place political opponents in jail. Secret statutes were passed, the contents of which were known only to the upper levels of the party hierarchy. Retroactive statutes were enacted which made acts criminal that were legally innocent when committed. No attention was paid by the government to the restraints of the Constitution, of antecedent laws, or even of its own laws. All opposing political parties were disbanded. Thousands of political opponents were put to death, either methodically in prisons or in sporadic night forays of terror. A general amnesty was declared in favor of persons under sentence for acts "committed in defending the fatherland against subversion." Under this amnesty a general liberation of all prisoners who were members of the Purple Shirt party was effected. No one not a member of the party was released under the amnesty.

The Purple Shirts as a matter of deliberate policy preserved an element of flexibility in their operations by acting at times through the party "in the streets," and by acting at other times through the apparatus of the state which they controlled. Choice between the two methods of proceeding was purely a matter of expediency. For example, when the inner circle of the party decided to ruin all the former Socialist-Republicans (whose party put up a last-ditch resistance to the new regime), a dispute arose as to the best way of confiscating their property. One faction, perhaps

*
    From Lon Fuller, The Morality of Law
    (New Haven: Yale University Press, 1964).

40

still influenced by prerevolutionary conceptions, wanted to accomplish this by a statute declaring their goods forfeited for criminal acts. Another wanted to do it by compelling the owners to deed their property over at the point of a bayonet. This group argued against the proposed statute on the ground that it would attract unfavorable comment abroad. The Headman decided in favor of direct action through the party to be followed by a secret statute ratifying the party's action and confirming the titles obtained by threats of physical violence.

The Purple Shirts have now been overthrown and a democratic and constitutional government restored. Some difficult problems have, however, been left behind by the deposed regime. These you and your associates in the new government must find some way of solving. One of these problems is that of the "grudge informer."

During the Purple Shirt regime a great many people worked off grudges by reporting their enemies to the party or to the government authorities. The activities reported were such things as the private expression of views critical of the government, listening to foreign radio broadcasts, associating with known wreckers and hooligans, hoarding more than the permitted amount of dried eggs, failing to report a loss of identification papers within five days, etc. As things then stood with the administration of justice, any of these acts, if proved, could lead to a sentence of death. In some cases this sentence was authorized by "emergency" statutes; in others it was imposed without statutory warrant, though by judges duly appointed to their offices.

After the overthrow of the Purple Shirts, a strong public demand grew up that these grudge informers be punished. The interim government, which preceded that with which you are associated, temporized on this matter. Meanwhile it has become a burning issue and a decision concerning it can no longer be postponed. Accordingly, your first act as Minister of Justice has been to address yourself to it. You have asked your five Deputies to give thought to the matter and to bring their recommendations to conference. At the conference the five Deputies speak in turn as follows:

FIRST DEPUTY. "It is perfectly clear to me that we can do nothing about these so-called grudge informers. The acts they reported were unlawful according to the rules of the government then in actual control of the nation's affairs. The sentences imposed on their victims were rendered in accordance with principles of law then obtaining. These principles differed from those familiar to us in ways that we consider detestable. Nevertheless they were then the law of the land. One of the principal differences between that law and our own lies in the much wider discretion it accorded to the judge in criminal matters. This rule and its consequences are as much entitled to respect by us as the reform which the Purple Shirts introduced into the law of wills, whereby only two witnesses were required instead of three. It is immaterial that the rule granting the judge a more or less uncontrolled discretion in criminal cases was never formally enacted but was a matter of tacit acceptance. Exactly the same thing can be said of the opposite rule which we accept that restricts the judge's discretion narrowly. The difference between ourselves and the Purple Shirts is not that theirs was an unlawful government—a contradiction in terms—but lies rather in the field of ideology. No one has a greater abhorrence than I for Purple Shirtism. Yet the fundamental difference between our philosophy and theirs is that we permit and tolerate differences in viewpoint, while they attempted to impose their monolithic code on everyone. Our whole system of government assumes that law is a flexible thing, capable of expressing and effectuating many different aims. The cardinal point of our creed is that when an objective has been duly incorporated into a law or judicial decree it must be provisionally accepted even by those that hate it, who must await their chance at the polls, or in another litigation, to secure a legal recognition for their own aims. The Purple Shirts, on the other hand, simply disregarded laws that incorporated objectives of which they did not approve, not even considering it worth the effort involved to repeal them. If we now seek to unscramble the acts of the Purple Shirt regime, declaring this judgment invalid, that statute void, this sentence excessive, we shall be doing exactly the thing we most condemn in them. I recognize that it will take courage to carry through with the program I recommend and we shall

THIRD DEPUTY. "I have a profound suspicion of any kind of reasoning that proceeds by an 'either-or' alternative. I do not think we need to assume either, on the one hand, that in some manner the whole of the Purple Shirt regime was outside the realm of law, or, on the other, that all of its doings are entitled to full credence as the acts of a lawful government. My two colleagues have unwittingly delivered powerful arguments against these extreme assumptions by demonstrating that both of them lead to the same absurd conclusion, a conclusion that is ethically and politically impossible. If one reflects about the matter without emotion it becomes clear that we did not have during the Purple Shirt regime a 'war of all against all.' Under the surface much of what we call normal human life went on—marriages were contracted, goods were sold, wills were drafted and executed. This life was attended by the usual dislocations—automobile accidents, bankruptcies, unwitnessed wills, defamatory misprints in the newspapers. Much of this normal life and most of these equally normal dislocations of it were unaffected by the Purple Shirt ideology. The legal questions that arose in this area were handled by the courts much as they had been formerly and much as they are being handled today. It would invite an intolerable chaos if we were to declare everything that happened under the Purple Shirts to be without legal basis. On the other hand, we certainly cannot say that the murders committed in the streets by members of the party acting under orders from the Headman were lawful simply because the party had achieved control of the government and its chief had become President of the Republic. If we must condemn the criminal acts of the party and its members, it would seem absurd to uphold every act which happened to be canalized through the apparatus of a government that had become, in effect, the alter ego of the Purple Shirt Party. We must therefore, in this situation, as in most human affairs, discriminate. Where the Purple Shirt philosophy intruded itself and perverted the administration of justice from its normal aims and uses, there we must interfere. Among these perversions of justice I would count, for example, the case of a man who was in love with another man's wife and brought about the death of the husband by informing against him for a wholly trivial offense, that is, for not have to resist strong pressures of public opinion. We shall also have to be prepared to prevent the people from taking the law into their own hands. In the long run, however, I believe the only course I recommend is the one that will insure the triumph of the conceptions of law and government in which we believe."

SECOND DEPUTY. "Curiously, I arrive at the same conclusion as my colleague, by an exactly opposite route. To me it seems absurd to call the Purple Shirt regime a lawful government. A legal system does not exist simply because policemen continue to patrol the streets and wear uniforms or because a constitution and code are left on the shelf unrepealed. A legal system presupposes laws that are known, or can be known, by those subject to them. It presupposes some uniformity of action and that like cases will be given like treatment. It presupposes the absence of some lawless power, like the Purple Shirt Party, standing above the government and able at any time to interfere with the administration of justice whenever it does not function according to the whims of that power. All of these presuppositions enter into the very conception of an order of law and have nothing to do with political and economic ideologies. In my opinion law in any ordinary sense of the word ceased to exist when the Purple Shirts came to power. During their regime we had, in effect, an interregnum in the rule of law. Instead of a government of laws we had a war of all against all conducted behind barred doors, in dark alleyways, in palace-intrigues, and prison-yard conspiracies. The acts of these so-called grudge informers were just one phase of that war. For us to condemn these acts as criminal would involve as much incongruity as if we were to attempt to apply juristic conceptions to the struggle for existence that goes on in the jungle or beneath the surface of the sea. We must put this whole dark, lawless chapter of our history behind us like a bad dream. If we stir among its hatreds, we shall bring upon ourselves something of its evil spirit and risk infection from its miasmas. I therefore say with my colleague, let bygones be bygones. Let us do nothing about the so-called grudge informers. What they did do was neither lawful nor contrary to law, for they lived, not under a regime of law, but under one of anarchy and terror."

law dealing with it. We shall not then be twisting old laws to purposes for which they were never intended. We shall furthermore provide penalties appropriate to the offense and not treat every informer as a murderer simply because the one he informed against was ultimately executed. I admit that we shall encounter some difficult problems of draftsmanship. Among other things, we shall have to assign a definite legal meaning to 'grudge' and that will not be easy. We should not be deterred by these difficulties, however, from adopting the only course that will lead us out of a condition of lawless, personal rule."

FIFTH DEPUTY. "I find a considerable irony in the last proposal. It speaks of putting a definite end to the abuses of the Purple Shirtism, yet it proposes to do this by resorting to one of the most hated devices of the Purple Shirt regime, the ex post facto criminal statute. My colleague dreads the confusion that will result if we attempt without a statute to undo and redress 'wrong' acts of the departed order, while we uphold and enforce its 'right' acts. Yet he seems not to realize that his proposed statute is a wholly specious cure for this uncertainty. It is easy to make a plausible argument for an undrafted statute; we all agree it would be nice to have things down in black and white on paper. But just what would this statute provide? One of my colleagues speaks of someone who had failed for five days to report a loss of his identification papers. My colleague implies that the judicial sentence imposed for that offense, namely death, was so utterly disproportionate as to be clearly wrong. But we must remember that at that time the underground movement against the Purple Shirts was mounting in intensity and that the Purple Shirts were being harassed constantly by people with false identification papers. From their point of view they had a real problem, and the only objection we can make to their solution of it (other than the fact that we didn't want them to solve it) was that they acted with somewhat more rigor than the occasion seemed to demand. How will my colleague deal with this case in his statute, and with all of its cousins and second cousins? Will he deny the existence of any

reporting a loss of his identification papers within five days. This informer was a murderer under the Criminal Code which was in effect at the time of his act and which the Purple Shirts had not repealed. He encompassed the death of one who stood in the way of his illicit passions and utilized the courts for the realization of his murderous intent. He knew that the courts were themselves the pliant instruments of whatever policy the Purple Shirts might for the moment consider expedient. There are other cases that are equally clear. I admit that there are also some that are less clear. We shall be embarrassed, for example, by the cases of mere busybodies who reported to the authorities everything that looked suspect. Some of these persons acted not from desire to get rid of those they accused, but with a desire to curry favor with the party, to divert suspicions (perhaps ill-founded) raised against themselves, or through sheer officiousness. I don't know how these cases should be handled, and make no recommendation with regard to them. But the fact that these troublesome cases exist should not deter us from acting at once in the cases that are clear, of which there are far too many to permit us to disregard them."

FOURTH DEPUTY. "Like my colleague I too distrust 'either-or' reasoning, but I think we need to reflect more than he has about where we are headed. This proposal to pick and choose among the acts of the deposed regime is thoroughly objectionable. It is, in fact, Purple Shirtism itself, pure and simple. We like this law, so let us enforce it. We like this judgment, let it stand. This law we don't like, therefore it never was a law at all. This governmental act we disapprove, let it be deemed a nullity. If we proceed this way, we take toward the laws and acts of the Purple Shirt government precisely the unprincipled attitude they took toward the laws and acts of the government they supplanted. We shall have chaos, with every judge and every prosecuting attorney a law unto himself. Instead of ending the abuses of the Purple Shirt regime, my colleague's proposal would perpetuate them. There is only one way of dealing with this problem that is compatible with our philosophy of law and government and that is to deal with it by duly enacted law, I mean, by a special statute directed toward it. Let us study this whole problem of the grudge informer, get all the relevant facts, and draft a comprehensive

need for law and order under the Purple Shirt regime? I will not go further into the difficulties involved in drafting this proposed statute, since they are evident enough to anyone who reflects. I shall instead turn to my own solution. It has been said on very respectable authority that the main purpose of the criminal law is to give an outlet to the human instinct for revenge. There are times, and I believe this is one of them, when we should allow that instinct to express itself directly without the intervention of forms of law. This matter of the grudge informers is already in process of straightening itself out. One reads almost every day that a former lackey of the Purple Shirt regime has met his just reward in some unguarded spot. The people are quietly handling this thing in their own way and if we leave them alone, and in-struct our public prosecutors to do the same, there will soon be no problem left for us to solve. There will be some disorders, of course, and a few innocent heads will be broken. But our govern-ment and our legal system will not be involved in the affair and we shall not find ourselves hopelessly bogged down in an attempt to unscramble all the deeds and misdeeds of the Purple Shirts."

As Minister of Justice which of these recommendations would you adopt?

Optional Readings

The following are optional readings.

Reading #2

SON OF THE SPELUNCEAN EXPLORER*

Burton F. Brody**

IN THE SUPREME COURT OF NEWGARTH, 4321

ABNER, G. Acting Chief Justice. The appellant seeks reversal of an order by the Stowfield County Board of Election Commissioners denying him the right to register to vote in the Newgarth Special Senatorial Election in November of this year. The Board decision was affirmed by the Stowfield County Court of General Instances and the Twelfth Circuit Court of Appeals. Under the Administrative Review Act (N.C.S.A. Chapter 172 Section 56.6 g) this court is required to review administrative determinations affecting rights guaranteed by the Charter. The Board denied registration to the appellant under a local ordinance because he is "the lineal descendant of a person convicted within the County of a crime of violence." (S.C.E.I. § 2).

The Newgarth Civil Liberties Union, The Newgarth Lawyers Committee, The Newgarth League Of Women Voters, and The Concerned Parents of Newgarth all supported the appellant as amici curiae. Amicus briefs in support of the Board were filed by the Newgarth and Stowfield Bar Associations, the Mother's March League and the Newgarth Watchdog Committee For A Wholesome Environment. My Brother Justices have instructed me to express our most profound gratitude for the excellent and instructive briefs and arguments presented by each counsel. The volume of these efforts is second only to their quality in demonstrating the universal interest of our people in this most provocative of questions. However, it must be noted at the outset that regardless of how intellectually inviting it may be to explore the charterality of visiting the sins of the father upon the son, it has been the longstanding policy of this Court to avoid Charter interpretation if other means of resolving the problem exist. To be direct, we disavow any intent to determine the charterality of section 2 of the Stowfield Election Law; we are convinced this question may be disposed of without disturbing the delicate balance between the

County's vital interest in the election process and the appellant's right to vote as guaranteed by the Charter.

The appellant's father was one survivor of an exploration group accidentally imprisoned in a cave. After a miraculous rescue effort taking over a month, the nation was horrified to learn that those saved had maintained their lives by slaughtering and eating the flesh of one of their group, one Roger Whetmore by name. The appellant's father and his fellow survivors were indicted, convicted, and, after an appeal to this Court, hanged for their act. The execution was called for by section 12-A of the N.C.S.A, which endures unchanged, and provides only the death penalty for the willful taking of a life. The appellant was *in esse* at the time of the conviction and appeal, but was born prior to the execution. The prison records show that the appellant was viewed by his father only once, and there can be no question of any paternal influence in the appellant's upbringing. However, the appellant's genealogy is also of unquestionable certitude. Nevertheless, quibbling about such questions of statutory interpretation is unnecessary to our opinion which is directed at the father's conviction and thereby resolves the son's current dilemma.

The overwhelming difficulty of judging the father's guilt or innocence is best observed from the record of his conviction. That record is replete with universal regret, dismay, and sorrow over deciding such a perplexing question. A closer inspection of that record reveals that little, if any, objective human wisdom was ever applied to that tragic homicide. That the defendants acted was never questioned; only the societal significance of their act had to be assessed. The conditions under which the defendants and their victim reached their agreement were, to say the least, not conducive to a reasoned evaluation of the social impact of their contemplated act. The record discloses that they were fully aware of their legal, as well as physical, plight; they sought advice from some observers at the scene whose faculties were not hampered by being trapped beneath the earth's surface without food or water. A doctor at the sight would not give the benefit of his counsel, nor could any clergyman or government official be found to help in reaching an answer.

The paucity of objective intellectual analysis at the scene is surpassed by its total absence, once the judicial system assumed the burden of decision—which, as will be soon seen, it never really did. At trial, the defendants' counsel permitted a lawyer to sit on the jury. This lawyer-juror, acting as foreman, gained for the twelve good men and true the right to render a special verdict. Thus insulated, the jury passed only on the uncontested facts without a determination of guilt. The special verdict was the jury's escape from its responsibilities. That this practice was unusual even twenty-one years ago goes

---

*The famous *Case of the Speluncean Explorers*, 62 HARV. L. REV. 616 (1949), brought together certain philosophies of law and government and analyzed them by applying them to the same very difficult problem. Professor Brody attempts to present his difficulties with the philosophies, add the influence of contemporary social thought, and finally tender a possible stepping stone to further analysis.

**Visiting Associate Professor, University of Denver College of Law, on leave I.I.T./Chicago-Kent College of Law 1970-71; B.S.C., J.D., DePaul University.

The opinions in the original case—or rather what they omit—begin to suggest a reason, other than extreme difficulty, for the judicial inability to evaluate the question. The Court's attack swerved from the essence of the problem and devoted itself entirely to periphery or tangential questions. The inevitable result was that the Court was hamstrung and hogtied without getting within striking distance of a solution.

Nowhere in any of the opinions is there any discussion of what is law, as distinguished from the question of what is *the* law. Our predecessors were too involved in whether it was *the* law that an act of cannibalism for survival was a justifiable homicide, to see that law is merely one means of social control. The failure to see law as simply one means of social control had at least two distinct ramifications. On the one hand, as pointed out earlier, this Court failed to recognize their societal duty to evaluate the act and thereby doomed the explorers to death without disapprobation. On the other hand, by pursuing a tangential question, the opinions groped in search of an answer their writers somehow sensed was not at hand. As a result of each opinion grasping at an answer, every opinion was validly criticized by the others. It is no wonder doubt reigned supreme.

For example, the beloved Mr. Justice Foster sought a just solution by arguing that jurisdiction is territorial. It is, he stated, based to a large extent on the authorities' ability to gain physical control over the defendants. Therefore, he reasoned, since the civilized world was so dramatically unavailable to the explorers, the obverse was equally true; the defendants had been beyond the jurisdiction of the state at the time of their act.

The late Justice Tatting characterized the Foster opinion as "shot through with contradictions and fallacies." He quickly disposed of the fictional territorial jurisdiction argument by considering all its facets. By thus mocking the artificiality of the fiction, Mr. Justice Tatting exposed it for the fiction it was, and by that forensic ploy drove it from belief!!!! Tatting, perhaps mirroring the plight of us all, withdrew. He could not accept Foster's logic, but be found Keen's result equally abhorrent.

It would appear helpful to set forth a summary of the original opinions. Such a synopsis would provide a framework for analyzing conclusions reached by our predecessors in their quests along spurious paths. The first opinion, that of Chief Justice Truepenny, reaches no conclusions because it seeks none. He simply rationalized that executive clemency was the appropriate solution. By judicious use of the executive power, Truepenny rationalized, "justice will be accomplished without impairing either the letter or spirit of our statutes and without offering any encouragement for the disregard of law."

without saying; but today, in the light of present understanding of the jury function, that questionable decision by defense counsel becomes crucial. It is now understood that the jury performs psychological as well as legal functions. The jury brings to its determination of guilt the community moral standards. Moreover, it is thought that the jury's decision is also an expression and expiation of the community's guilt. If these theories of modern psychology have any degree of validity, it becomes obvious that the appellant's father and the other defendants did not receive the full measure of protection our jury system contemplates.

Further examination of the record shows that the jury's escape was duplicated at the appellate level. This Court split evenly, the tie-breaking Justice refusing to participate because of the difficulty of the question. Our predecessors either urged the Prosecutor to grant clemency or chastised the Prosecutor for taking the matter to the Grand Jury. The irony of those protestations was that this Court asked of individuals a decision that it, in its collective wisdom, could not reach. It can be further observed that this demand for decision was directed at officials with less responsibility for making it than this Court. At each step in the legal system, responsibility was relinquished. Surely there is some truth in the thought that hard cases make bad law, but must Herculean ones destroy the legal system?

Thus, tragically, men were put to death without the benefit of any direct evaluation of their act. At each plateau of officialdom the obligation to judge before execution was neatly avoided and some other level of the hierarchy called upon. In this manner, the actual fate of the surviving explorers was left to the wisdom contained in thirteen words set forth in our statute book (N.C.S.A. § 12-A). Therefore we are now confronted with the stark truth that the only detached, objective human evaluation our society ever gave the appellant's father's act was the thought behind the drafting of that statute. There is little need here to discuss the quality of thought embodied in such a statute. Suffice it to say that we are convinced that the legislature did not by any stretch of the imagination consider any circumstance such as the one in question, when it enacted section 12-A. Thus, we are faced with the awful verity that the appellant's father was put to death, and now the appellant faces denial of a basic freedom, for an act so essentially singular in difficulty that our society refused to judge it because it feared it could not. This Court cannot permit such a state of affairs to continue. We are agreed that a primary responsibility of government is to resolve such matters as a part of the duty to maintain domestic tranquility. Further, we feel that our civilization has evolved a legal system capable of fulfilling this obligation.

arisen when the courts had gone too far in supplementing legislative edicts.

The irony which undermines Mr. Justice Keen's intense defense of legislative supremacy is that the doctrine of legislative supremacy is itself a matter of judicial interpretation! The Charter merely creates each of the three branches of government and articulates their powers and duties; it does not establish, or even hint at which, if any, of the branches established shall take precedence. The doctrine of legislative supremacy is inherited from an ancient ancestor of our civilization. It was created in response to a state of affairs extant in that civilization which, because of our revolutionary beginnings and the careful planning of the Founding Forefathers, never arose in our Nation. That ancient government began as an absolute monarchy with the judicial system merely an extension of the monarch's omnipotence. Through a number of centuries of social and political struggle, the legislative branch emerged and prospered. The doctrine of legislative supremacy merely recognizes the outcome of that struggle. The doctrine of legislative supremacy was a counterpoise to first neutralize and eventually overcome the throne. As such, the doctrine has less meaning in our government where the three branches have, by Charter, existed independently since the very beginning. It seems that Mr. Justice Keen's devotion to the doctrine exemplified a school of judicial thought which cloaked the abdication of judicial social responsibility in the dignity, and seeming humility, of a doctrine of judicial restraint, i.e. legislative supremacy. We are convinced that by recognizing the doctrine of legislative supremacy as an anachronism surviving from an era beset by problems quite different than this nation has ever faced, the true role of the judicial branch becomes clear.

There have been too many successful instances of what Mr. Justice Keen would pejoratively describe as judicial legislation to drive the judiciary from an active role in our government. Admittedly, not all judicial edicts are rousingly accepted; many are fought—mostly by the doctrine of legislative supremacy, we might add—before they are accepted. In too rare a moment of judicial humility, this Court is constrained to admit that it knows all too well that judge-made law may be ignored, if not repealed. Nevertheless, any honest appraisal shows judicial legislation is a valuable part of our government. Furthermore, we are convinced the drafters of the Charter envisioned just such a government. They fully intended, we believe, three *equal* branches of government; each branch essential to the operation of government, but none supreme. Our Charter divided the governmental functions among the the three branches because all were, as all now are, aware of the abuses which can flow from too great a concentration of power. As the Founding Drafters foresaw it, the immense strength of our Nation

This pontifical evasion of duty typifies the bureaucratic buckpassing condemned earlier.

The next opinion, Mr. Justice Foster's, after removing the spelunkers from any earthly jurisdiction, offers two additional bases for their acquittal. Their legal freedom from the rules of our society, he reasoned, placed them in a state of nature and they were, at the time of their act, subject to "those principles appropriate to their condition." Without articulating what he thought those appropriate principles might be, Justice Foster did not hesitate in reversing the murder conviction. He then relied on the antiquated dogma of the social contract theory of government and expounded a mini-social contract for his mini-society of nature. This ground for reversal is totally dependent on the fictional "extra-territoriality" rationale and is thereby equally untenable.

The third rationale for reversal offered by Foster was based on statutory interpretation. He said a judge must first find the purpose or purposes the legislature sought in enacting a statute. Then, with those purposes uppermost in mind, a judge must decide how the statute reasonably applies to the facts. He supported this technique with precedent and by pointing out the ludicrous results possible from extreme literalism. He garnered additional intellectual support by articulating the truism that the legislature could be wise in its view of the future, but clairvoyance was beyond even that august body. Anticipating, no doubt, Mr. Justice Keen's statements—for theirs was a longstanding, hotly contested dispute—Justice Foster conceded the legislature's supremacy over the judiciary, but expressed the belief that even the most absolute monarch would appreciate intelligent, informed, and sympathetic protection from "obvious legislative errors or oversights."

After closer inspection, one is driven to agree with Tatting that Foster's opinion, while reaching an appealing conclusion, was based on the frailest premises. Even Mr. Justice Keen, who was most vocal in his disapproval of Foster's beliefs, opted for freeing the survivors. Keen's reasoning, however, is at least as open to question as was Foster's.

The logical bedrock of Mr. Justice Keen's opinion was also a dogma. His dogma was not the social contract theory, but rather pertained to matters rising after a government came into existence. Justice Keen deeply believed that of the three branches of government, the legislative branch was supreme. He therefore condemned Foster for engaging in—what one receives the definite impression was considered treasonous by Keen—judicial legislation. The firm faith in legislative supremacy was supported by an allusion to the civil strife which had

should only be released as law (except in extraordinary emergencies) when all three branches concurred. Our Charter did not contemplate legislative supremacy, nor for that matter any sort of hierarchy. Rather it contemplated and set forth three branches—none supreme, each essential. As created by the Founding Forefathers, our system requires unanimity among the branches to operate. Although none is supreme, each has a veto.

The remainder of Keen's opinion attacks the means Foster employed to accomplish his judicial legislation. He pointed out the inherent intellectual weakness in having to "divine" some single statutory "purpose." Then, Keen pointed out, Foster went through the process of finding and filling statutory "gaps" or finding and correcting legislative "oversights." Keen condemned these filling and correcting processes as judicial legislation to accomplish that most perverse governmental goal—legislating morality.

We must disagree with the eminent Justice Keen's condemnation of the corrective processes available to a judge called upon to apply a particular statute. This disagreement results primarily from the more fundamental disagreement about the dogma of legislative supremacy. However, our disagreement is reinforced by our understanding of what Mr. Justice Keen saw as the function of a judge called upon to interpret a piece of legislation. Keen said it was the duty of a judge "to enforce faithfully the written law, and to interpret that law in accordance with its plain meaning without reference to our personal desires or our individual conceptions of justice."

It cannot be disputed that judges must not follow their "personal desires," nor may they follow their personal concept of justice. However, if Mr. Justice Keen is to be read with the same literalism he would have us read statutes, then the Bench is for grammarians, not lawyers. He would have his judges consult only dictionaries and would consider as bordering upon radicalism any judge consulting a thesaurus or work on semantics. Such a restricted view of a judge's role is totally inconsistent with the traditions of our legal system. Moreover, it might well be added that it was just such an approach—linguistic chicanery—that contributed much to past social unrest.

As we view it, the function of a judge in statutory interpretation under our Charter transcends that of legislative translator. While we quite agree that no judge may inject his "personal code of justice," we believe that he can hold the statute up to the light of some code of justice. The standards of justice it is incumbent a judge use are surely not his own, but rather those set out in the Charter and those we have as a nation worked out as we have progressed. Our nation has recognized fundamental concepts and traditions of justice and these must be applied to each and every case. That is the reason experienced lawyers, well schooled in the law and our tradition of justice, are on the Bench instead of linguists. Furthermore, it seems to me the Charter envisioned just such a role for the judiciary when it established it as an independent branch of government.

Our agreement with Justice Keen's disdain for moralism in the law is also qualified. We wholeheartedly concur in the belief that the law cannot be used to secularize a special-interest group, sectarian, or personal moral code. We have seen too many experiments of this kind fail. However, we have also seen instances where statutes have been enacted, or judicial decisions propounded, which guarantee for particular groups fundamental charter rights. These edicts, although strictly legal in their intent and primary effect, have over the course of time profoundly influenced our national morality. Further, at still another level, my experience is such that I must state that there have been moral precepts so widely and deeply held that they have in some way precipitated legal action. For example, the statute prohibiting willful homicide that troubles us here.

Thus, the total and absolute separation of law and morality demanded by Justice Keen is an altogether too great extension of a narrow fear. The justifiable fear that government power will be used to impose particular moral codes upon an unwilling nation has blinded many from the true relationship of law and morality. True, the government must be eternally vigilant to prevent its rightful power from being used for special purposes. This vigil, however, should not be carried to the extreme Justice Keen would carry it. He would either ignore or repeal any valuable statute because it also conforms to some moral code. Still more tragically, he would automatically reject a proposed statute because if flows from some sort of widely held moral precept. The law should not actively pursue particular moral principles—the differences of opinion on matters of this kind are too volatile for government. Nevertheless, the government should not, and in fact cannot, reject expansions or particularizations of fundamental Charter rights which also reflect so-called moral principles. Further, when the populace is influenced by moral teachings to such an extent that legislation results which mirrors that moral growth, the government cannot reject it, unless the law violates the Charter.

For all these reasons Keen's opinion does not satisfy us. Its bedrock is legislative supremacy, a dogma without support in this society, and it reaches conclusions we find unrealistic. What he felt was a line of reasoning establishing the validity of his position was only a forensic attack laying bare the flaws of Foster's. If Justice Keen's arguments established nothing, Justice Handy's created the specter of a monster.

The sage Handy wanted to escape from what he described as the "tortured ratiocinations" of his brothers. He viewed the problem as one of "human realities," "not of abstract theories." We find his use of the concept of reality appealing—as you will soon see—but what he felt was efficient government we can only describe as expedient rule by rabble.

Justice Handy spoke of many realities, but the one which seemed uppermost in his mind was that the first duty of government was to perpetuate itself. He justified (?) this by pointing out that in a state of anarchy, neither Keen's literalism nor Foster's law of nature would mean anything. He believed that the best means of fulfilling the governmental duty to survive was by being responsive to the wishes of the masses. He pointed out that more governments have fallen and more misery has resulted from a lack of responsiveness on the part of the rulers to the desires of ruled than for any other reason. However true this observation may ring, we can only offer that the calamitous failures to respond were over demands of real, active, personal concern to far greater numbers than were involved in the *Explorers'* case. Fallen governments, like fallen women, were open to the private blandishments of those few who got near; but neither, because of the very nature of things, could respond to more widely held needs. Governments which fell failed to respond on matters such as taxation, starvation, or war. They were not brought to their knees over the outcome of a nonpolitical criminal trial of widespread vicarious interest. They failed on national issues. The responsiveness by rulers called for by Handy is too close to the practice of the ancient Caesars who let the roaring circus crowds determine the fate of the gladiator. Governance by expedient, passive populism has little attraction. Our respect and affection for Justice Handy and his widow prevents further comment.

We have seen our predecessors argue amongst themselves. Each was able to find an answer, but none was able to maintain that answer against his brethren. Foster's consummate goodness was weakened by an artificial substructure holding up layers of speculation. Keen's strict devotion to the written word is based on a dogma from the primitive past and builds a conclusion he himself does not like. Finally, Handy's opinion is based on a most cynical approach to government. Each of these opinions is wanting either in reasoning or result and one of them falls short in both.

It is altogether proper to question our conclusion that these three preeminent scholars of the law were each in error in the same case. Our analysis supports that conclusion, and we believe each of them supports us in our analysis of the others. The more rewarding question is how these brilliant men erred; we believe it is a matter of where they went wrong. They marched right past the question that demanded an answer—without so much as a nod of recognition—and pursued a secondary question which was of necessity not ready for answer. They wanted to know what was *the* law without first deciding what is law. They sought to determine whether it was legal to commit an act of cannibalism without first determining the import of the concept of legality. We are confident that had they viewed the problem from this more basic vantage point, they would have written opinions satisfactory both in reasoning and result—at least we hope so because we are about to attempt it. Before we plunge into that effort, however, honesty demands that we temper our critique of our predecessors. Without their incisive analysis of the issues they saw, this Court would not have the fundamental ideas with which to attempt our analysis. Our apparent criticism is simply camouflage for our awe. We mean to question, not to condemn, because to continue the search is the greatest tribute we can pay these men.

Law is simply one means of creating a given pattern and quality of life within some given social unit. The purpose of law (this purpose is not to be confused with the narrower statutory purpose Justice Foster sought) and the administrative system created to effect it is to implement some basic criteria of conduct which the community finds necessary. This assertion is so fundamental that it borders on a truism; however, within it is contained much which bears on this case. Let us explore the social role of law as an abstract principle, before we attempt to see the principle's applicability to the plight of the appellant's father.

Recognizing law as a means to social order requires the denial of the law as an end in itself. Many, particularly those in the legal profession or government, think of law only in the sense of a particular rule or set of rules. We give that rule a stature, bordering on gospel, by referring to it as the law (or better still, THE LAW). As such, the rule gathers an existence of its own, independent of the societal goal it was created to achieve. It thus becomes deified and too often it is worshipped without regard for the true reason for respect. In this manner, law or THE LAW is viewed as—and thereby tends to become—a set of abstract principles totally removed from any sort of human environment. Then a second principle of social inertia comes into play, and THE LAW rolls on and on creating social situations never contemplated.

The most serious result of viewing the law as an end in itself is not that we lose control of it, but rather that this flaw is an obstacle to wise control. This poor perspective causes us to squander opportunities for improvement because we fail to see the true problem. Thus we attack THE LAW when we really mean to attack the societal decision which precipitated the edict. This misdirection in attack results in the condemnation and alteration of an innocent instrument of social will (a legal rule), but it permits the evil wielder of that instrument to escape detection. By raising law to an end in itself and thereby overlooking it as a mere means to some end, we have subjected law to unwarranted criticism and forgone the real opportunities for progress.

Therefore, failing to see law as a means to social order and instead seeing it as an end in itself has had two distinct effects. First, it tends to put law on a higher level than other human endeavors. This results in the law wrenching itself free from humanity. Secondly, and more harmfully, it insulates the true problem from attack and solution.

The role of law (and the legal system) in any society is to create and administer an outline or framework for conduct within that society. Depending on the political structure of the society, these standards of acceptable conduct either will be imposed by a few or consented to by many. However, the particular political structure of a society is less significant than the recognition that the society is unique.

This political structure is less significant than the unique nature of the society for two reasons. First, because history proves that even the most powerful tyrant is subject to some restraint, be it only the capacity of the people to endure his caprice. Secondly, the political structure itself is a creature of those unique qualities which caused the particular social unit to evolve. The far more illuminating quest is for those things which cause the society to form and flourish.

A society or governmental unit is, after all, merely the banding together of many individuals with some common interest. These interests may result from one or more factors. History teaches that geography, economics, religion, politics, fear, or any one of a thousand reasons will cause individuals to form some sort of social unit. These persons, because they share some common plight, will also share some beliefs as to what life ought to be like. They band together in pursuit of that ideal and use that collective strength in furtherance of their pursuit. These similar beliefs when immersed in a social unit become the goals—generally inarticulated—of the unit. The unit then begins adopting rules aimed at achieving those goals—and, because the unit has replaced individuals, modified goals for the modified group reality. These rules become THE LAW of the unit. However technical and abstract the rules may become, we must not forget their humble origins as goal-oriented instruments of our social unit.

To conclude this particular discussion we might add that to our way of thinking a "bad" law is one which does not contribute to attaining the goals of the society which promulgates it, or one which prevents the attainment of those goals. Laws which do not comply with the standards of some *other* society are still law within their own area. Inhabitants of the *other* society cannot say such a rule is not a law nor even that it is a "bad" law. The most they can say is that such a rule re-

flects a society seeking different things for itself. The other society then may assess those goals *from its own point of view* and condemn them. The point is that law cannot itself be good or evil; it can only reflect the virtue (or lack of it) of the society it serves.

Now that we have established that law is a means of achieving societal goals, and as such is not much different from other tools, we can address ourselves to that horrifying act of twenty-one years ago. We can, for the first time, evaluate the social impact of that act, as the law demands we must. We can meet our obligation because we see the law (section 12-A) as a means to that end, rather than as some idol before which we must genuflect.

A note of caution should be sounded, however, so that no one will misinterpret these words. Law is to be seen as a means to an end, but these particular social tools are not to be treated in a cavalier manner. Laws are delicate instruments, painstakingly manufactured. Literally thousands of years go into their making; fortunes are invested therein, and lives lost in their creation. They are powerful devices capable of achieving astounding results. They are implements deserving the greatest degree of respect for their power and reverence for their heritage. As such they can be modified only in rare circumstances. Situations permitting modification or abolition of rules are changes in social goals, discovery that the present rule cannot achieve the goal, or changes in the environment (either physical or social) which caused the society to create the rule in the first place.

As a servant of the social unit, law must confront the environment in which the unit finds itself. Any law, to be effective, must have a viable relationship with reality. If it does not, it is a poor servant. The cries we are now hearing for "relevance" in our society are simply a demand that our laws mold themselves to our present living conditions. Law must be relevant in that it must seek to control activity which is actually taking place. Law that has no or little relationship with reality because it addresses acts not taking place or conditions not truly extant is meaningless and is generally treated as such.

One of the most significant realities for all Western societies, if not all societies, is the human instinct to survive. This instinct is so overwhelming that it is recognized throughout the law. Section 12-A, if it attempts to control homicide without recognition of the particular reality of the survival instinct, is "bad" law because it does not contribute to achieving a goal of our social unit. We seek individual safety by prohibiting willful homicide *in a social unit where the instinct to survive is strong*. We do not, because we know we cannot, prohibit every such homicide. However, for us to hold section 12-A does not apply to the reality in which the spelunkers found themselves would be too much like Justice Foster's "extra-territoriality" rationale to justify this discussion. Rather, we hold that section 12-A does not seek to proscribe homicides resulting from the survival instinct. The self-defense exception demonstrates that.

From the judicial point of view, therefore, the question becomes simply a matter of determining the manner in which section 12-A, with its implicit understanding of the survival instinct, applies to the homicide.

We could find that as a matter of law a homicide resulting from a valid exercise of the instinct to survive is not willful and therefore the appellant's father was wrongfully convicted. By definition, the exercise of an instinct is spontaneous, automatic, impulsive, unreflecting, and *involuntary*. Thus, we could hold that even though the facts make it appear that the spelunkers understood their plight and seemingly discussed it in a rational manner, their pain, fear, and anguish were such that these apparently rational acts were not rational in the sense section 12-A contemplates. Their physical suffering placed them in a condition where their fundamental instincts as living organisms took control of their intellectual capacities, and they were thereby disabled from the understanding and evaluating their act so that it could be deemed willful within the meaning of section 12-A. The survival instinct is so strong, it deprived them of the rationality the law requires.

There are other grounds upon which the conviction of the spelunkers may be questioned. It can be said that because of the unusual procedure of permitting a special verdict, without a finding of guilt, the surviving spelunkers were denied their right to trial by jury. And it can be said that because their lawyers permitted that most extraordinary procedure, there is reason to believe that the spelunkers were not represented at trial by competent counsel. These related beliefs both are a consequence of our earlier expressed positions about the function of a jury, the relationship of law and morality, and the absolute necessity for a viable relationship between reality and the law.

We were quite clear (we hope) in expressing the firm conviction that law (including the administrative structure implementing it) should not seek to secularize any particular moral code. It was conceded, however, that certain fundamental moral beliefs could be so uniformly held throughout the social unit that they could not help but somehow be reflected in the law. (Please notice that we have said "moral beliefs uniformly held" and not "moral tenets so correct that they *should* be universally held." The failure to make this distinction contributes mightily to the raging dispute over the relationship of law and morality.) The law cannot reasonably impose any given moral precept as such on society, but it cannot help but reflect the moral code society already accepts. The law should be the passive recipient of existing, actual moral standards, not the active agitator for hoped-for standards.

It seems to us that the jury, as a cross section of the social unit, can through its finding of guilt or innocence apply the existing moral standards of the community to the case. We believe that this is a vital role of the jury in our system and that the permission for a limited verdict prevented the spelunkers from receiving the full and fair trial that was their right under the charter. They did not receive the full benefit of our legal system because this function of the jury is fundamental to the operation of that system. Therefore, by permitting the jury to render its limited verdict, the trial court denied the appellant's father his charter right to a trial by jury.

Much the same reasoning can be applied to the function of the jury in establishing the relationship of the law to reality. The jury, through its finding of guilt or innocence implicitly determines the "relevance" of the law. It determines whether the reality contemplated by the statute exists, or whether the statute truly reflects the goals of the social unit or if those goals remain the goals. The special verdict denied the spelunkers their right to have society's decision about willful homicide as set forth in the statute, reviewed by society (as mirrored by the jury) in the light of the unique circumstances. Thus the decision by the trial court to permit the special, limited verdict is a flaw, fatal to the conviction of the spelunkers.

Regardless of which line of reasoning is adopted, the result is the same. We reverse the decision of the Twelfth Circuit affirming the Stowfield County Election Commissioner's refusal to permit the appellant to register. The appellant is the lineal descendant of a person convicted of a crime of violence, but there is enough weakness and defect in that conviction to refuse to perpetuate it, if not to reverse it.

SCHWEITZER, A. I must dissent. My inclination, as is true of everyone

CADWALLADER, J. A. Concurs.

who has come in contact with this most unfortunate event, is to find the survivors not guilty. The attempt to reopen that festering sore by denying to the son his right to vote only intensifies my inclination. Furthermore, I must admit that I concur wholeheartedly with the Acting Chief Justice's analysis of the role of law in a western civilization. I am especially in agreement with his call for relevance — the failure of law to be relevant, in the manner he described, has led to too much unrest for me to disagree. It is the conclusion he reached about what may be excused by the passion for survival that I must respectfully, but most strongly, deny.

Life is too precious a treasure to be taken for any reason other than to immediately protect another life. It seems to me that the spelunkers, instead of taking Whetmore's life as they did, were obligated to each other and to our society, to wait until the first of their number perished from the deprived conditions they were in. The others could have then had their required nourishment as scavengers rather than as murderers. It is the interruption of the life process that must be condemned. The same reality that dictates the survival instinct dictates the survival of the fittest. The crime for which the appellant's father was convicted was the act of molding reality to his purposes rather than accepting it as it was.

It is my opinion that Mr. Justice Abner misapplied his own impeccable analysis of the relationship of law and reality. He gave the spelunkers the benefit of the reality of the instinct to survive but he erred in not charging them with the equally real fact of survival of the fittest. Therefore, I must dissent from the opinion of the Court.

I am authorized to report that Mr. Justice Gabriel joins me in this dissent.

Former Chief Justice Boedel heard the arguments in this matter, but did not participate in the decision because his unforeseen resignation took place during our deliberations.

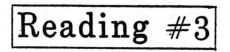

MORE THOUGHTS ON HART, KELSEN, AND FULLER:

AN EPISTEMOLOGICAL COMMENT

Lee S. Weinberg

Richard E. Vatz

For positivists Kelsen and Hart a central goal is to think about law in such a way as to separate questions about the validity of law from questions about the morality of law. In their efforts to achieve this goal, both of them have paid insufficient attention to the vital question of how duties can be said to arise from the mere validation of rules as laws.

For Kelsen, the problem relates to the sharp distinction which he draws between validity and effectiveness. A legal norm is valid if it is derived from a higher valid norm which ultimately is itself derived from the Basic Norm. A valid norm, however, need not always be efficacious since, for Kelsen, efficacy is a quality of behavior--what "is"--while norms possess only the quality of validity or invalidity. Yet he does not maintain that efficacy and validity are entirely independent of one another. The Basic Norm itself must constitute a by and large efficacious order. Hence, ". . .effectiveness is a condition for the validity, but it is not validity."[1] In the absence of a generally effective legal order, there would be no validity; but the reason (as opposed to the condition) for validity of legal norms is the presupposed Basic Norm according to which the validity of all other norms may be tested.

Kelsen argues that, ". . .the answer to the question why the norms of this legal order ought to be obeyed and applied - is the presupposed Basic Norm, according to which one ought to comply with an actually established, by and large effective, constitution."[2] So Kelsen maintains that the Basic Norm not only tells us which norms are valid legal norms, but also answers the question of why we ought to obey them. While this is somewhat ambiguous and confusing, it appears to be Kelsen's position. This confusion is aggravated by his attempt to equate the validity of a legal norm, the existence of a legal norm, and the duty to obey a legal norm. He specifically says that, "By the word 'validity' we designate the specific 'existence' of a norm."[3] . . ."To say that a norm is 'valid'. . .means that it 'ought' to be obeyed."[4] Thus, the fact that a legal norm is valid is somehow equivalent to the idea that one has a duty to obey it.

One critic of Kelsen focuses in on this tendency to confuse the notions of existence, validity, and binding force and argues that the question of "whether a given legal rule 'L' belongs to some legal system 'S' is quite different from the question 'Ought I (or anyone) obey 'L'?"[5] Certainly Kelsen's "pure theory" contains a major impurity if he fails to separate these two questions. As Golding points out, the anarchist can easily identify which law is valid within the legal system and still reject the legal system itself.

Kelsen further attempts to explain how a duty is imposed on a member of a legal system in terms of his reconstructed form of the legal rule. By taking the legal norms themselves and rationally reconstructing them into the form, "If A is, then B ought to be," he claims that that the citizen's duty may be implied. This form of the legal rule is simply a direction to an official to apply a sanction upon the occurrence of a condition--namely, the commission of a delict. Kelsen's legal rule does not, by its own terms, however, impose a duty upon the citizen. The duty arises by implication from the negation of the delict. Thus, if "delict = A", then "duty = not-A." For Kelsen, it is not meaningful to talk of what the citizen "ought" to do. He states,

> "Legal obligation is not, or not immediately, the behavior that ought to be. Only the coercive act, functioning as a sanction, ought to be. If we say: 'He who is legally obligated to a certain behavior ought to behave in this way according to the law, we only express the idea that a coercive as a sanction ought to be executed if he does not behave in this way."[6]

Since the reconstructed form of the legal rule simply imputes to certain non-legal conduct an official sanction, it is hard to see how the individual has any "duty" since he cannot "break the law;" he can only act in such a fashion as to have the law direct officials to apply sanctions against him.

While it is difficult to see how Kelsen seeks to impose a "duty" on sub-jects who are _only_ subjects, it is not so difficult to see how he imposes "oughts" on subjects who also function as officials. For the form of the reconstructed legal rule itself directs officials to apply sanctions. But even this is clouded somewhat by Kelsen's including in the word "ought" "per-mission","authorization", and "command".

The problem takes on a slightly different form in Hart's version of positivitism. Hart's problem comes in trying to distinguish the situation in which "X (actor) _ought_ to do A (action) in C (circumstances)" from one in which "X has a _duty_ to do A in C." It appears that "X _ought_ to do A in C" whenever there is a social rule to that effect. There is such a rule if and only if there is a generally known practice, deviation from which causes and justifies critical reactions. In Hart's terms, both the external and internal aspects are needed for a rule to be said to exist. If it does exist, then any member of the class of "X's" referred to in the rule "ought" to follow it.

But Hart clearly does not want to imply that merely saying "X ought to have done A in C" can be taken as equivalent to "X had a duty to do A in C." Hart argues that to say that one "ought" to do something implies that a rule exists; however, ". . .it is not always the case that where rules exist the standard of behavior required by them is conceived of in terms of obligation."[7] Hart recognizes his distinction between "ought" and "duty" is a weak one when he admits that ". . .the line separating rules of obligation from others is at points a vague one, yet the main rationale of the distinction is fairly clear."[8] In fact, the point of separation is quite vague and the rationale barely clear. Hart's position is that we can say "X has a duty to do A in C" if and only if three conditions exist over and above those necessary to assert that "X ought to do A in C," namely that 1) the demand for conformity is "insistent" and the social pressure or critical reaction is "severe,"[9] 2) the individual does not wish to do what the rule requires of him, and 3) that the rule is believed to be ". . .necessary to the maintenance of social life or some highly prized feature of it."[10]

The central question about Hart's additional conditions is whether or not they are really "additional" or merely represent an effort to require that the deviation be socially detrimental before he is willing to say that a duty has been imposed. For to say that the critical reaction is severe and that the rule deviated from is perceived as protecting a highly prized feature of social life is simply to say that the deviation is socially detrimental.

The lack of clarity in the "ought" v. "duty" distinction of Hart can be highlighted by use of examples. Suppose, for example, that a social rule exists which states, "All persons present in the courtroom shall rise when the judge enters." Can we say that person "X" has a duty to rise or only that he ought to rise? Applying Hart's tests leaves us unsure. After all, "X" obviously does not want to rise or presumably (if able) he would do so. Certainly the critical reaction would be severe--he might even be ordered to leave the courtroom. Without doubt, the belief underlying the rule--that all must show respect for judges and the judicial system--goes to a prized feature of society. Do we want to say that "X" has a duty to rise? Is this in some way different from Hart's own example of baring one's head in Church? There, Hart says only that "X" ought to bare his head. Should we treat rising in the courtroom differently merely because the judge may order "X" to rise? We find Hart unhelpful in answering these questions because we find the three conditions which he proposes to add to "ought" to impose a "duty" are frequently present in situations in which even he would not want to impose a duty, i.e. churches and, perhaps, courtrooms. Thus, we are left with the distinct feeling that Hart's three conditions mainly serve to achieve implicitly that which Kelsen achieves explicitly, namely, that the deviation or delict be socially detrimental before the notion of duty becomes relevant.

This discussion of Hart's attempt to get from "ought" to "duty" in the case of social rules brings us to the question of how a duty is imposed in the case of legal rules. For Hart, a rule is a valid legal rule when it ". . . satisfies all the criteria provided by the Rule of Recognition."[11] He simply states that a necessary condition to having a legal system is that, ". . .where laws impose obligations or duties these should be generally obeyed."[12] Apparrently, once a legal rule is established as being valid, the duty to obey follows. Yet using Hart's own conditions which turn "ought" into "duty" we can argue that it is possible to have a valid legal rule, but not "duty" to obey it; one simply "ought" to obey it. Where deviation does not produce severe critical reactions (organized sanction in this case) and the valid legal rule does not pertain to a prized feature of social life, then there can be no duty to obey it. Thus, any particular legal rule can be regularly disobeyed and no sanction be applied, but still remain a valid legal rule which one "ought" to obey. But it could hardly be said that one had a "duty" to obey since the tests for converting "oughts" into "duties" have not been met.

Hart's Rule of Recognition and Kelsen's Basic Norm

Kelsen and Hart share the central positivist premise that rules or norms which can properly be called laws can be identified by reference to their origin or "pedigree" rather than to their content. The validity of a rule or norm is based upon its meeting the criteria of validity as contained in the Basic Norm and the Rule of Recognition.

For Kelsen, the validity of every norm is derived from a higher norm--never from a fact. Ultimately, all valid norms can be traced to the Basic Norm, whose validity cannot be derived from a superior norm. Put simply, nothing in the legal system can do for the Basic Norm what the Basic Norm can do for the other norms of the system. Its validity is presupposed.

This presupposition notion, Kelsen admits, grows out of his Kantian epistemological assumption that one cannot know and interpret the empirical world without ". . .recourse to meta-legal authorities."[13] Thus, to make meaningful the positive legal order, we presuppose a Basic Norm which, though itself not a part of the legal system, confers validity on a constitution which in turn can confer validity on the entire heirarchy of legal norms. By bringing this presupposed Basic Norm to the coercive order, we infuse into that order a legitimacy or validity. Apparently this is intended to distinguish the sheer coercive order of Austin from the legal order. It is not clear, however, at what point the Basic Norm is presupposed or even _who_ does the presupposing.

The legitimacy which the legal order derives from our presupposition of the Basic Norm is ". . .limited by the principle of effectiveness."[14] In other words, when the system no longer is by and large efficacious due, for instance, to a revolution, then the Basic Norm has simply been changed. When the new constitution and the resulting new "legal" order have become established, we then impose on them, or presuppose, a new Basic Norm which creates the legitimacy.

Kelsen's idea is that the positive "legal" order of its own nature is never a "legal" order. It is not anything understandable at all until we bring to it a conceptual framework within which we can interpret it. By our own mental acts, we infuse meaning into phenomena which our senses tell us are present. If that is what Kelsen means by "presupposing" of a Basic Norm, we find it useful in explaining why we "label" a particular coercive order such as the United States a "system of law." It is only by the mental act of presupposing the Basic Norm that we are able to say "this is a legal system."

Hart's Rule of Recognition is similar to Kelsen's Basic Norm in that it sets the criteria of validity for all other rules or norms in a purely dynamic sense; there is no reference to content. Its function for Hart is also similar to the Basic Norm in that it distinguishes the legal order from the pure coercive order. However, Kelsen is more persuasive in that the Basic Norm is something which we impose on the coercive order to "transform" it into a legal order. But the Rule of Recognition is a part of the legal system as a matter of social fact--much like Austin's sovereign is a matter of social fact. The Rule of Recognition provides the criteria by which we may determine the validity of a given rule, but the Rule of Recognition, since it is part of the system, cannot help us determine if the system as a whole is valid. For Hart, of course, this is not an important question since he claims to be simply describing how legal systems operate--not when they are valid. He essentially takes the view that where there is a union of primary and secondary rules and the masses generally obey the primary rules while the officials take an internal view of the secondary rules, there is a legal system.

The Rule of Recognition ultimately reduces to a matter of social fact. Officials who "accept" the Rule determine the validity of rules by "using" it.[15] The Rule of Recognition, while it is within the legal system, cannot be valid or invalid; it can only be ". . .accepted as appropriate for use."[16] For Hart, then, the Rule of Recognition either exists or it does not. For Kelsen, the Basic Norm is either presupposed to be valid or it is not. Thus, while Kelsen talks of "validity" of the Basic Norm, Hart only talks of "existence" of the Rule of Recognition.

Hart's reason for distinguishing his Rule of Recognition from Kelsen's

Basic Norm in this way is that only by doing so can we talk about whether or not a legal rule exists--it exists when it is valid ". . .given the system's criteria of validity."[17] Hart argues that when one says, "This statute is valid", he is _using_ the Rule of Recognition which, in fact, is generally used in this legal system. Whether or not the statute meets the criteria of the Rule of Recognition is _factual_ and whether the Rule of Recognition is generally used is also _factual_. Thus, Hart argues, it is not accurate to describe this process in terms of presupposing the validity of the Basic Norm as Kelsen does.

It would seem that Hart and Kelsen are talking about two different things. Hart is talking about what we mean when we assert that a particular rule is a valid one within a particular legal system; Kelsen is talking about how we determine whether or not a particular coercive order can properly be interpreted as being a legal system. Thus, the fact that the Basic Norm is _outside_ the legal system and the Rule of Recognition is _inside_ is the key to the differences between the concepts.

The Basic Norm as Inner Morality of Law

From another perspective, Kelsen's Basic Norm may be interpreted as a substantially diluted version of Fuller's inner morality of law in that the Basic Norm requires the application of the ". . .principle of exclusion of contradictions . . .to rules of law describing legal norms and, therefore, indirectly also to legal norms."[18] It is odd on the one hand, that Kelsen includes this requirement in what he puts forth as a "pure" theory of law, and odd on the other hand, that he includes _only_ this requirement. For if he can fit the non-contradiction condition into the pure theory, why can he not also fit Fuller's other requirements? Kelsen apparently elevates the non-contradiction principle to a position of primacy because of its relationship to the efficacy of the whole legal system. As Kelsen sees it, if one is subject to legal rules to the effect that, "If A is, then B ought to be" and "If not-A is, then B ought to be,"[19] he is faced with a meaningless utterance. If it is meaningless, it cannot be effective; if it cannot be effective, then it cannot be valid since effectiveness, while not the _reason_ for validity, is a _condition_ for validity.

In Kelsen's pure theory, then, it simply is not possible for the Basic Norm to be presupposed where rules are contradictory. But it is not clear to us why this should be so. Why should there be any restrictions on when the Basic Norm may be presupposed? To posit the principle of non-contradiction as he does is to invoke a variant of natural law as a condition for presupposing the Basic Norm. But this is inconsistent with his fundamental notion of a pure theory of law. Why doesn't Kelsen accept Fuller's (and Austin's) requirement of the generality of law?[20] Why doesn't he share Fuller's concern over retroactive laws?[21] Kelsen argues that if we do not excuse criminal behavior when the wrong-doer is unaware of the law, we should not be concerned about retroactive laws. After all, the wrongdoer does not know in either instance that his conduct is prohibited. Yet there are obvious differences, i.e. in the one case the wrong-doer _could_ have known the law while in the other he _could not_.

What is so puzzling in Kelsen's singling out one part of the inner morality and virtually making it a necessary, but not sufficient, condition to presupposing the Basic Norm is that Kelsen's reasons for doing so can be so easily applied to the other elements in the inner morality. For example, if laws are regularly enacted making punishable past conduct, the system will rapidly lose its effective-ness; if effectiveness is a condition for validity, Kelsen ought to put the principle against retroactivity on a plane with the principle against non-contra-diction. Kelsen is simply not convincing on the question of why one part of Fuller's inner morality must be assimilated into the pure theory, while the others may be safely disregarded.

An Epistemological Problem With Rules

For Hart, the notion of rules is essential. It is his focus on rules
which he feels constitutes his great step beyond Austin's commands issued by
the sovereign. A rule can be said to exist when there exists a practice,
deviation from which results in critical reactions. When we believe that there
are good reasons to justify our critical reactions, we can say that he "ought"
to have followed the rule, i.e. "do A in C." If one accepts the rule (in the
ordinary sense of acceptance), then merely finding that circumstances "C" exist
is sufficient to "do A."

But the problem is how do we know when we are "in C?" Much like Kelsen's
notion of a mental act which infuses validity into a particular coercive order,
we would argue that we must perform a mental act in order to infuse meaning into
a state of affairs which we wish to call "C".

When we say that we accept the rule "Do A in C", we gloss easily over this
problem. Fuller alludes to it in a footnote in which he states that we must
define the situation or circumstances.[22] However, political scientists, inter-
actional sociologists, and rhetoricians have devoted more thought to this problem
than have the legal philosophers. One rhetorician puts it this way:

> "No situation can have a nature independent of the per-
> ception of its interpreter or independent of the rhetoric
> with which he chooses to characterize it."[23]

Thus, we take it, the problem with rules is that we can never determine solely
by the nature of the situation whether or not we are "in C." To say, then, that
rules are the heart of the law raises problems not dealt with by Hart. How can
we "accept" rules if we cannot be certain we are "in C?" Perhaps the form of the
rule should be restated to account for this: X's shall do A when large numbers

of people believe the X's to be in C.

In a similar vein, political scientist Murray Edelman states:

> "Language does not mirror an objective reality, but rather
> creates it by organizing meaningful perceptions abstracted
> from a bewildering, complex world."[24]

In determining if we are "in C," we must perform certain distinct mental acts.
We must select from the bewildering world which elements to highlight in our
decision and we must infuse meaning into these elements. For Perelman, this
is not ". . .merely a simple choice, but also a creation, an invention of
significance."[25] This act of "creation" which Perelman focuses on is quite
similar to the act of "presupposition" which Kelsen focuses on. In the former,
our minds bring meaning to some elements of a situation so that we may assert
that we are "in C," and in the latter, our minds bring meaning to a coercive
order so that we may determine its validity.

An Epistemological Problem in Treating Like Cases Alike

Closely akin to the idea of a rule is Hart's notion that we must treat
like cases alike and different cases differently. How can a court know if the
case before it is like a prior case? Since no two cases are ever identical in
all particulars, it is always possible to distinguish the instant case from
one class and place it in another. If Perelman is right in arguing that this
is essentially an act of "creation", then the only problem lies in being able
to convince others that you have treated like cases alike. Whether, in fact,
like cases have been treated alike becomes a meaningless question!

Perelman suggests that there are criteria by which we can make the decision
of "likeness." Hart calls these the ". . .shifting and varying criteria used
to determine when, for any given purpose, cases are alike or different."[26]
But we have difficulty seeing what help this can be. For we then have to

determine when the facts fit the criteria by which "likeness" is determined and we do not have any way to do that. As we read Hart and Perelman on this point, they are saying:

1. All A's shall be treated in B fashion
2. X's shall be considered to be A's when they meet criterion Z
3. X meets criterion Z
4. Therefore, X is an A
5. Therefore, X shall be treated in B fashion

Step 3 is the crucial one, yet neither Hart nor Perelman adequately deals with it. It seems that on the one hand it is possible to set up sub-criteria by which we decide if criterion Z has been met; however, this reductionist position leads us nowhere. On the other hand, if we take the view that no X is by nature an A and no X can be shown by its nature to meet criterion Z, then it becomes important to see by whom and how X is depicted as being an A. In other words, whoever has the perceived authority to depict X as an A by virtue of first depicting X as having met criterion Z determines the ultimate meaning of "treat like cases alike."

Hart's emphasis on law as rules leads him to reject arbitrariness in the application of the rules, i.e., in treating like cases differently. In response, we have raised the question of how "likeness" is to be determined. Still, Hart would insist that merely because laws are not properly applied does not make them not laws. Moreover, while even fairly administered laws can be criticized as arbitrary and unjust, "it is plain that the law itself cannot now determine what resemblances and differences among individuals the law must recognize if its rules are to treat like cases alike and so be just."[27] For Hart, the criterion of relevance will vary and hence the assessment of the ". . .justice or injustice of the law may be met with counter-assertions inspired by a different morality."[28]

Fuller's emphasis on law as the purposive ". . .enterprise of subjecting human conduct to the governance of rules"[29] leads him to reject as arbitrary any rule which does not serve, in some way, the appropriate purpose of "law." If the rule does not fit Fuller's purposive definition, it must be arbitrary and cannot be considered law. Furthermore, in selecting the criterion of relevance by which like cases are identified, it is necessary that the criteria ". . .make sense, in some rational fashion, in some way that relates to the purpose of the rule."[30] But again, Fuller cannot answer the question of how it is to be determined that the purpose of the law in question serves or does not serve a legitimate purpose in "subjecting human conduct to the governance of rules." Similarly, he cannot answer the question of how it is to be determined if the criterion of relevance is rationally related to the purpose of the rule.

Whether arbitrariness is to provide a ground for criticism of the law (Hart) or a ground for refusing to call the rules a system of law (Fuller), it poses serious problems which need further examination. We have argued that arbitrariness in the application of rules, arbitrariness in the selection of criteria of relevance for determining "likeness", and arbitrariness in the content of the law itself as it relates to the purpose of law all present the same epistemological problem, namely, how to reconcile the notion of "created meaning" with the notion of arbitrariness.

At this point it is useful to re-phrase the important questions. The view we have been developing in this paper suggests that the major questions may not be:

1. Have we treated like cases alike and different cases differently?

2. Does the criterion of relevance rationally relate to the purpose of the rule?

3. Does the purpose of the rule fit within the proper purpose of the "law?"

67

Rather, these questions should be phrased:

1. How have we become _convinced_ that like cases are being treated alike and different cases differently?

2. How and why do we _believe_ that the criterion of relevance rationally relates to the purpose of the rule?

3. How and why do we _believe_ that the purpose of the rule comes within the proper purpose of the "law?"

Perhaps some confusion stems from the term "arbitrariness" itself. Our use of the term, unlike Hart, Fuller, and Pennock's, refers to the nature of meaning. Meaning is arbitrary in that it is not intrinsic. By arbitrary, then, we do not intend to suggest "utterly nonsensical." Meaning is arbitrary in that it depends wholly on a general acceptance of a particular version of reality. It is from this perspective that our questions about Hart and Fuller arise.

It might still be argued that we are trying to force law into the form of the logical syllogism when it would be more accurately interpreted as the subsumption of facts under rules. We would reject this criticism, however, on the ground that to talk of subsuming facts under rules assumes that facts have inherent meaning--the very point which we have sought to attack. Our position is that we must distinguish between an empirical phenomenon or occurrence and the language by which we articulate.

If one shares the view that ". . .language is always value-laden"[31], then to even _talk_ about events is an act of creation of meaning, a translation into words. While words may be more or less informative or evocative, they are never valueless. Bentham seems to be saying this when he distinguishes between eulogistic and dyslogistic terms used to describe the same event. Even Hart recognizes this to some degree in an essay in which he argues that ". . .sentences of the form 'he did it' have been traditionally regarded as primarily

68

descriptive whereas their principal function is what I venture to call <u>ascriptive</u>, being quite literally to ascribe responsibility for actions."[32] Our view of language simply extends this idea to encompass other values beyond ascribing responsibility.[33]

Conclusion

In this paper we have examined two basic questions arising out of the legal philosophies of Hart and Kelsen. First, we looked at how well each version of positivist theory logically moves from the identification of valid law to the imposition of a duty to obey such law, and second, we attempted to distinguish Hart's Rule of Recognition from Kelsen's Basic Norm. Beyond the problems of logic raised in our discussion of these issues, we have identified serious epistemological problems which point to the need for further analysis of the substantial rhetorical component of law and legal systems. In a subsequent paper we develop this rhetorical perspective by examining the symbolic life of the law and elaborating on the critical role of rhetoric in bringing about widespread adherence – both popular and scholarly – to the claim that courts are involved in the process of applying the "law."

[1] Hans Kelsen, The Pure Theory of Law (Berkeley: University of California Press, 1970), p. 213.

[2] Kelsen, p. 212.

[3] Ibid., p. 10.

[4] Ibid., p. 10-11.

[5] M.P. Golding, "Kelsen and the Concept of 'Legal System'," in Robert S. Summers, More Essays in Legal Philosophy (Oxford: Blackwell, 1971), p. 83.

[6] Kelsen, p. 119.

[7] H.L.A. Hart, The Concept of Law (Oxford: Clarendon Press, 1961), p. 83.

[8] Ibid., p. 84.

[9] Ibid.

[10] Ibid., p. 85.

[11] Ibid., p. 100.

[12] Ibid., p. 109.

[13] Kelsen, p. 202.

[14] Ibid., p. 211.

[15] Hart, p. 97.

[16] Ibid., p. 105.

[17] Hart, p. 107.

[18] Kelsen, p. 206.

[19] For Kelsen, while norms are neither True nor False, only valid or invalid, legal rules, which are only assertions about norms may be True or False.

[20] Lon L. Fuller, The Morality of Law, 2d edition (New Haven: Yale, 1969), p. 46.

[21] Ibid., p. 51.

[22] Fuller, F.N. 34, p. 224.

[23] Richard E. Vatz, "The Myth of the Rhetorical Situation," Philosophy and Rhetoric, Volume 6, No. 3, p. 154.

[24] Murray Edelman, Politics as Symbolic Action (Chicago: Markham, 1971), p. 66.

[25] C. Perelman and L. Olbrechts-Tyteca, The New Rhetoric, translated by John Wilkinson and Purcell Weaver (London: Notre Dame, 1969) p. 121.

[26] Hart, p. 156.

[27] Hart, p. 157.

[28] Hart, p. 158.

[29] Fuller, p. 106.

[30] J. Roland Pennock, "Law's Natural Bent", Ethics, Volume 79, No. 3, April, 1969, p. 225.

[31] Vatz, p. 157.

[32] H.L.A. Hart, "The Ascription of Responsibility and Rights," in Antony Flew, ed., Logic and Language (New York: Anchor-Doubleday, 1864), p. 151.

[33] While Hart apparently retreated later on from this position and admitted that to say "He is playing the piano" does not perform the ascriptive function, we would argue that it nevertheless is not valueless. It still represents a translation of an empirical event into meaningful language. For instance, we could also have "described" this event by saying, "He is banging on the piano" or "He is engaged at the piano" or "He is tickling the ivories." Each of these is different and, depending on the laws about pianos, each might have different legal significance.

1. What is the basic question addressed in the section entitled, "From Validity to Duty"?

2. How does Kelsen see 'duty' arising out of the demonstration of validity?

3. How does Hart see 'duty' arising out of the demonstration of validity?

4. Compare and contrast the 'basic norm' and the 'rule of recognition.'

5. In what sense is the 'basic norm' an example of the 'inner morality of law'?

6. What is the epistemological problem discussed by Weinberg and Vatz?

1. As you have read, the legal positivists Kelsen and Hart maintain a sharp distinction between the concept of a <u>valid law</u> and a <u>moral</u> or <u>good law</u>. The question addressed in this section is, why <u>do we have the duty</u> to <u>obey</u> a law <u>merely</u> because we can demonstrate its <u>validity</u>? More specifically, the question is, how do Kelsen and Hart find the duty to obey law arising out of the mere demonstration of the validity of law.

2. It appears that Kelsen's basic position is that the 'basic norm', which serves to validate all inferior norms, also is a <u>reason</u> for obeying such norms. For Kelsen, existence of a norm, validity of a norm and duty to obey a norm are all somehow equivalent.

3. Hart attempts to distinguish the idea that one 'ought' to act a certain way from the idea that one has a 'duty' to do so. Hart says that one 'ought' to act in a certain way whenever there is a social rule requiring such action. One only has a 'duty' to act when the demand for conformity to the rule is insistent, the social pressure severe, the individual does not wish to conform, and the rule is important in the maintenance of social existence.

4. The key difference between the 'basic norm' and the 'rule of recognition' is that the former is outside the system and the latter is inside the system. The 'basic norm' serves to identify whether a coercive order is a legal system; the 'rule of recognition' enables us to determine whether a particular rule is valid within a given legal system. The two concepts are similar in that they each "set the criteria of validity for all other rules or norms".

5. Kelsen argues that the 'basic norm' requires that no contradictory norms may be laws. This non-contradiction principle is one of Fuller's eight ways to fail to make law--or the criteria of the inner morality of law.

6. Epistemology is the study of knowledge. One of the problems with rules from an epistemological point of view is that we have to decide when two situations are sufficiently similar to warrant similar treatment. Weinberg and Vatz argue that 'likeness' is a matter of <u>creation of meaning</u> rather than <u>discovery of meaning</u>. Meaning, in the authors' view, is arbitrary and merely a matter of "general acceptance of a particular version of reality".

REFERENCES

Brody, B. F. Son of the speluncean explorer. 55 <u>Iowa Law Review</u>, 1969, pp. 1233-1247.

Cohen, C. <u>Civil disobedience</u>. New York: Columbia University Press, 1971.

Fuller, L. The case of the speluncean explorers. 62 <u>Harvard Law Review</u>, 1949.

Fuller, L. <u>The morality of law</u>. New Haven: Yale University Press, 1969.

Golding, M. P. <u>Philosophy of law</u>. Englewood Cliffs: Prentice-Hall, 1975.

Hart, H. L. A. <u>The concept of law</u>. Oxford: Clarendon Press, 1961.

Holmes, O.W. <u>The common law</u>. Boston: Little Brown, 1963.

Kelsen, H. <u>The pure theory of law</u>. Berkeley: University of California Press, 1970.

Lloyd, D. <u>The idea of law</u>. Baltimore: Penguin, 1976.

Schur, E. M. <u>Law and society</u>. New York: Random House, 1968.

Schwartz, R.D. Social factors in the development of legal control: A case study of two Israeli settlements. 63 <u>Yale Law Journal</u> pp. 471-491, 1954.

SUGGESTED READING

Barkun, M. (Ed.). *Law and the social system*. New York: Lieber Atherton, 1973.

Cohen, M., & Cohen, F. (Eds.). *Readings in jurisprudence and legal philosophy*. New York: Prentice Hall, 1951.

Cogley, J., *et al*. *Natural law and modern society*. Cleveland: Meridian, 1966.

Evan, W. M. (Ed.). *Law and sociology: exploratory essays*. New York: Free Press, 1962.

Frank, J. *Courts on trial*. Princeton: Princeton University Press, 1949.

Golding, M. *The nature of law*. New York: Random House, 1966.

Hart, H. L. A. *The concept of law*. Oxford: Clarendon Press, 1961.

Kert, E. A. (Ed.). *Law and philosophy*. New York: Appleton-Century-Crofts, 1970.

Summers, R. S. (Ed.). *Essays in legal philosophy*. Oxford: Basil Blackwell, 1968.

Summers, R. S. (Ed.). *More essays in legal philosophy*. Oxford: Basil Blackwell, 1968.

UNIT 2

Interdisciplinary Perspectives On Law And Society

Rationale

As you have seen in Unit 1, the two types of scholars traditionally involved in the study of law and the legal system are philosophers and lawyers. The philosophers are concerned with issues such as "What is law?" "What is justice?" and "Is bad law, law?" (Schur, 1968, p. 17) The lawyers are concerned with issues such as "What is the law in a particular situation?" and "How can the law be used to achieve a particular goal?"

While philosophical and legal questions about law remain significant and pressing problems, they hardly can be said to exhaust the possible ways of thinking about law. In Unit 2, you will be introduced to the concepts and comments of representatives of many branches of the social sciences and the humanities as they bring to bear the thinking of their disciplines upon the study of law.

The effective study of the role of law in society involves of necessity a sensitivity to a wide range of approaches. Law plays too deep and vital a role in human societies to be understood fully without reference to its political, social, economic, psychological, anthropological, and rhetorical dimensions. The multidisciplinary approach taken in this unit should provide

provide you with a framework for thinking about and evaluating legal issues and the role of law in society.

While it is apparent that each of the perspectives presented in Unit 2 might well be the subject of an entire semester of study, it is hoped that you will come away from this unit more alert to the multiple facets of law and society and more conversant with the contributions from various disciplines. In thinking about some law and society problems, you will find, for instance, that an economic approach is useful because it highlights particular relevant relationships; in thinking about other types of problems, you will likely be more impressed with the political or rhetorical perspectives. The overall goal of the unit is simply to provide you with a wide range of ideas from which you can draw in your efforts to better understand the role of law in society.

Objectives

After you complete this unit you should be able to:

1. Describe the central concerns of the sociology of law.

2. Contrast the normative sociology of law with the scientific sociology of law.

3. Explain the systems and stimulus-response models of how the legal system works using the concepts of demands, supports, and feedback and prior stimuli and subsequent responses respectively.

4. Summarize generally the analysis of the reciprocal relationship between law and politics, and specifically the effect of politics on the selection of federal judges.

5. Explain how economic approaches might be useful in understanding and reforming the law.

6. Summarize the anthropological framework and assumptions for studying law and society.

7. Summarize generally the psychologist's interest in law and society and specifically the concept of legal socialization.

8. Summarize the rhetorical or symbolic approaches to law.

9. Given a particular situation, predict the types of questions which might be asked by:

   a. sociologists

   b. systems theorists or stimulus-response theorists

c. political scientists
d. economists
e. anthropologists
f. psychologists
g. rhetoricians

Overview

The combinations of mini-lectures and readings in Unit 2 are intended to introduce you to the interdisciplinary character of the subject of this course. Sociology, political science, economics, anthropology, psychology, and rhetoric have all, in recent years, paid increased attention to the study of law and society. The various materials suggest to you the richness of the subject and indicate to you some of the concepts, approaches, and findings of scholars in these different academic disciplines.

After reading Schur's introductory section outlining his view of the field of law and society and his ideas on why it was, for so long, a neglected field, you will read a comparison of normative and scientific sociology of law. Following that is a brief section on "Law and Conceptual Models." This mini-lecture is fairly abstract and simply presents to you the concept of a systems model and a stimulus-response model of the legal process. These models have been used by social scientists as guides in their research on problems of law and society, and you ought to simply be familiar with them. The models may help you to organize your own thoughts and are likely to be useful to you should you take advanced courses in law and social science.

"Law and Politics" attempts to present to you some of the relation-ships between these two spheres, some of the differences between them, and some of the key approaches and findings of political scientists interested in law. Following the mini-lecture you will read a current account of the politics involved in the selection of federal court judges in order to il-lustrate for you one dimension of the law/politics relationship.

In "Economics and Law" I have briefly presented the way in which an economist approaches the problem of law and provided illustrations both in the mini-lecture and in Richard Posner's article of how one might apply economic theory to legal study.

"Anthropology and Law" and the article by anthropologist Laura Nader serve to introduce you to the field of legal anthropology and to provide you with a cross-cultural lens through which to examine law and society relationships.

"Psychology and Law" examines the contributions of psychologists to the study of legal phenomena and the Kohlberg application discussed in Linda W. Rosenzweig's article describes an important contribution of psychology to the study of legal culture. (See Unit 7 for a more detailed discussion of legal culture.)

Finally, Richard E. Vatz, the only non-social scientist included in this survey of interdisciplinary perspectives on law and society, offers the rhetorical perspective in which he suggests that law is most powerful as a symbol which is invokved to cloak what otherwise might be unacceptable actions. The notion of law as rhetoric is an intriguing one which social scientists have frequently overlooked.

Study Task Checklist

☐ 1. A. Read Mini-Lecture #1, "Sociology and Law," Part A: "Normative Sociology of Law".

☐ 1. B. Answer Study Questions and compare your answers with the Discussion of them.

☐ 1. C. Read Mini-Lecture #1, Part B: "Scientific Sociology of Law."

☐ 1. D. Answer the Study Questions for Part B and check your answers with those provided in the Discussion.

☐ 2. A. Read Mini-Lecture #2, "Law and Conceptual Models"

☐ 2. B. Answer Study Questions and compare your answers with the Discussion of them.

☐ 3. A. Read Mini-Lecture #3, "Law and Politics"

☐ 3. B. Answer the Study Questions and compare your answers with the Discussion of them.

☐ 4. A. Study Reading #1, "The Politics of Picking Federal Judges" by James Goodman.

☐ 4. B. Answer the Study Questions and compare your answers with the Discussion of them.

☐ 5. A. Read Mini-Lecture #4, "Economics and Law"

☐ 5. B. Answer the Study Questions and compare your answers with the Discussion of them.

☐ 6. A. Study Reading #2, Excerpts from "The Economic Approach To Law" by Richard Posner.

☐ 6. B. Answer the Study Questions and compare your answers with the Discussion of them.

☐ 7. A. Study Reading #3, "The Anthropological Study of Law" by Laura Nader.

☐ 7. B. Answer the Study Questions and compare your answers with the Discussion of them.

- [ ] 8. A. Read Mini-Lecture #5, "Psychology and Law".
- [ ] 8. B. Answer the Study Questions and compare your answers with the Discussion of them.

- [ ] 9. A. Study Reading #4, "Legal Socialization: A Cognitive Developmental Perspective" by Linda W. Rosenzweig.
- [ ] 9. B. Answer Study Questions and compare your answers with the Discussion of them.

- [ ] 10. A. Study Reading #5, "Rhetoric and the Law," by Richard E. Vatz.
- [ ] 10. B. Answer the Study Questions and compare your answers with the Discussion of them.

- [ ] 11. A. Answer the Unit Study Questions and compare your answer with the Discussion of it.

Mini-Lecture #1

SOCIOLOGISTS AND THE LAW

Before proceeding with this review of the perspectives of the various academic disciplines, it might be helpful to briefly summarize the views of a leading scholar in the field of legal sociology, Edwin M. Schur, on the issue of why the study of law as a social phenomenon has been generally overlooked by sociologists.

Given the importance of law in social life and the existence of a distinctively 'legal' set of institutions, it is strange how little interest there has been in the field of legal sociology. Schur (1968, pp. 5-8) identifies four factors which contribute to this relative lack of attention to law as a social phenomenon.

a. First, law is often seen by sociologists as a normative enterprise involved in establishing rules of proper conduct. Since many sociologists believe that, as social scientists, they must draw a firm line between what is (an empirical question) and what ought to be (a normative question) they have avoided the normative world of law.

b. Second, he argues that the social scientist has often been afraid to enter into the apparently foreign world of the law. The overwhelming body of law which exists has been a barrier to many social scientists.

c. Third, there is a tendency, says Schur, for American sociologists to perceive the study of legal phenomena as more appropriately within the domain of philosophers of law, the students of jurisprudence. In addition, many of these philosophers had also received legal training and were seen, therefore, as possessing a major advantage over American social scientists.

d. Finally, he suggests that the study of law as a social institution is often hindered by the lack of mutual respect among lawyers and social scientists. Hampered by different terminology and pursuing different goals, lawyers and social scientists have not cooperated fully with one another. Lawyers are advocates who must convincingly argue for certain results despite grossly incomplete information; social scientists are attempting to acquire knowledge, not fight battles and are likely to be tentative, indecisive and non-combative in their style.

Despite all of these problems, the growing importance of law will most likely provide the impetus for greatly expanded social science efforts in the study of law. As Selznick writes, "If society cannot depend on an informal, autonomous, self-reputating, person-centered order for the maintenance of social control, it will turn to more explicitly organized agencies and to more powerful instruments of surveillance" (Schur, 1968, p. 7). Such developments are already evident in American society and a corresponding growing interest in the social role of law is also evident.

As you have just seen from the summary of Schur's views, he offers a sociological view of law and society. He advocates studying the legal system as "sociologically important in its own right" (Schur, 1968, p. 4) and defines the legal system in terms of "a distinctive and more or less coherent (though continuously changing) set of legal roles, norms, and organizations, together with characteristic patterns of interrelation between the legal order and other institutional realms of society" (p. 4).

In this mini-lecture I want to draw your attention to two basic schools of thought within the field of sociology of law and to illustrate the way in which each of these is the outgrowth of a different jurisprudential root examined in Unit 1.

Part A: Normative Sociology of Law

One school of legal sociology grows out of the natural law tradition of jurisprudence and can be seen most clearly in the work of its chief contemporary proponent, Philip Selznick. Selznick basically maintains that the task of the legal sociologist is to study the nature of legality and the conditions which encourage its development. Selznick agrees with Fuller that 'rules' become 'legal rules' only when they meet the requirements of the 'inner morality of law'. All governmental rules and all social control structures do not qualify as laws and legal systems. For Selznick, the sociology of law cannot ignore the fact that some social control systems do not measure up to the requirements of 'legality'. In other words, the natural law view that there are certain absolute standards-- either substantive or procedural--by which actual laws and legal systems can be evaluated is incorporated into Selznick's version of legal sociology.

As Schur indicates, ". . .Selznick seems willing to determine the (relative) 'maturity' of a legal order in terms of its approximation of the idea of legality" (Schur, 1968, p. 57).

The obvious drawback to Selznick's approach parallels the drawback to the natural law school of jurisprudence, namely the inability to precisely define and demonstrate the content of 'legality'. Without any agreed upon measure of legality, the normative sociologist of law is faced with critics who argue that to call a legal system which we do not approve of an 'immature' legal system is not a scientific statement. Since we cannot prove that a particular legal system fails to meet the test of 'legality', we are saying nothing more that "I don't like that system" when we call it 'immature'.

The advantage, on the other hand, to Selznick's school of legal sociology, is that it does not require us to treat offensive systems, such as the Nazi system, as fully developed legal systems since we can simply argue that such a system does not meet the test of 'legality'. Therefore, Selznick implies, there is less or no obligation to obey the commands of such a system. For Selznick, then, some social control systems qualify as legal and some do not. Unlike political systems which can all be classified as 'political' whether we like them or not, 'legal systems' become only one variety of social control systems.

Selznick's views appear in condensed form in a section which he wrote for the International Encyclopedia of the Social Sciences (1968), entitled "The Sociology of Law." In this article, Selznick discusses his concept of 'legality.' He states that, "In a developed legal order, authority transcends coercion, accepts the restraints of reason, and contributes to a public consensus regarding the foundations of civic obligation. To the extent that law is 'the enterprise of subjecting human conduct to the governance of rules' (Fuller, 1964, p. 106), it can be said that law aims at a moral achievement; the name of that achievement is legality, or 'the rule of law.' It's distinctive contribution is a progressive reduction of the arbitrary element in positive law and its administration." (Selznick, 1968, p. 52)

Selznick believes that the study of legality can be carried on within a framework of four key issues: the transition from legitimacy to legality, the distinction between rational consensus and civic competence, the institutionalization of criticism, and the institutionalization of self restraint.

For Selznick, legitimacy simply means that those who exercise power in a society are justified in doing so because their power is derived from an accepted principle. In our society, for example, winning an election is an accepted principle for justifying one's exercise of power. However, mere justification for exercising power is only a step towards legality. Beyond this justification (legitimacy), there must be a critical evaluation of the specific decisions of those in power if legality is to be achieved. Once it is recognized that officials must not only justify their authority, but also must defend their decisions in a principled and reasoned fashion, there is a movement from <u>legitimacy to legality</u>. He believes that weak reasons ultimately weaken the authority of decision makers.

Rational consensus and civic competence are distinguished by Selznick. The former is seen as a prerequisite to the latter. <u>Rational consensus</u> refers to the freely arrived at general agreement of people in society that government must be restrained, that people must be free to exchange ideas, and that the world is complex, unclear, and often hard to understand.

The particular rational consensus which is needed to achieve legality

". . .entails deepened public understanding of the complex meaning of freedom under law. This goes beyond passive belief or even commitment. It is an extension of civic competence--the competence to participate effectively in the legal order." (Selznick, 1968, p. 54)

Selznick argues that a high degree of civic competence is necessary to support the professional decision makers if they are to achieve and maintain a system of legality.

As to the instituionalization of criticism, Selznick states, "If the ideas of legality are to be fulfilled, the capacity to generate and sustain reasoned criticism of the rules and of official descretion must be built into the machinery of lawmaking and administration." (Selznick, 1968, p. 54). In the American system, the adversary process provides the needed <u>institutionalization of criticism</u>.

Beyond criticism, however, he believes that those in power must themselves recognize the need to act with <u>restraint</u>. That is, the officials must internalize the proper values and respect for the rule of law if legality is to be maintained.

Utilizing these four general ideas, Selznick believes that we can assess the degree to which a particular system approaches the ideal legality.

1. What is the goal toward which law is moving in Selznick's normative sociology of law perspective?

2. List the four topics which Selznick believes to provide a useful framework for studying legality.

3. What is the relationship between legitimacy and legality?

4. Why are the concepts of rational consensus and civic competence important in Selznick's view of legality?

5. Why is institutionalized criticism central to the achievement of legality?

6. How does institutionalized self-restraint further the cause of legality?

DISCUSSION OF MINI-LECTURE #1, PART A QUESTIONS

1. Selznick believes that law has a purpose, namely, the achievement of 'legality'. He maintains, like Fuller, that law has a peculiar contribution to make to human social life. "It's distinctive contribution is a progressive reduction of the arbitrary element in positive law and its administration" (Selznick, 1968, p. 52). This belief in 'legality' as a standard against which positive law content and administration can be measured reflects Selznick's attachment to natural law theory.

2. a. The transition from legitimacy to legality;

   b. Rational consensus and civic competence;

   c. Institutionalized criticism;

   d. Institutionalized self restraint.

3. Legitimate power refers to an agreement in a political community on the right of officials to exercise control, to give orders, and to enforce orders. Legitimacy is established by appeal to an agreed upon source of authority, e.g. elections, divine right monarchy, etc.

   However, legitimacy only involves justification of the exercise power; it does not require officials to give reasons for their official decisions. The evaluation of official acts marks the transition from legitimacy to legality. "Most important, legality goes beyond a gross jusitifaction of the right to hold office" (Selznick, 1968, p. 53) Therefore, Selznick is arguing, legitimacy is a prerequisite to legality; but legitimacy alone does not demonstrate legality.

4. Rational consensus basically refers to a society's genuine agreement upon the value of free thought, the importance of self-restraint, and the acceptance of a certain amount of ambiguity. Rational consensus is necessary to the achievement of legality because legal decisions require the "exercise of discriminating judgment" (Selznick, 1968, p. 54) by professionals. However, public support for these judgments is required in order for legality to be maintained. Therefore, rational consensus supports legality.

   Civic competence is "the competence to participate effectively in the legal order" (Selznick, 1968, p. 59). Civic competence is the mature type of rational consensus necessary to sustain legality. The consensus which is needed to maintain legality, in other words, is of a special sort which requires a "deepened public understanding of the complex meaning of freedom under law" (Selznick, 1968, p. 54).

5. There is a great need to build into the legal system the ability to "generate and sustain reasoned criticism of the rules and of official discretion" (Selznick, 1968, p. 54). The adversary system in American law is designed for this purpose. The significance of this institutionalization of criticism is that legality can only be achieved if the lawmaking and law-administering systems are subject to constant re-evaluation.

6. Selznick argues that a system of legality requires more than institutionalized criticism. It requires self-restraint on the part of its officials. In other words, the society must inculcate proper values and proper respect for the rule of law if it is to sustain 'legality'. While officials in the legal system must exercise independent judgment, they must do so in a restrained manner. Only <u>self-restraint</u> can effectively guarantee the existence or continuation of 'legality'.

Part B: Scientific Sociology of Law

The scientific sociology of law, as articulated by Donald Black, is an outgrowth of the legal positivist school of jurisprudence. As you should recall, legal positivists argue that whether or not a law was good or bad was entirely separate from whether or not it was valid law. Thus, for Black's school of sociology of law, no effort is made to assess the 'degree of legality' present or to evaluate the goodness or badness of a legal system.

Unlike Selznick, Black would seem to agree that all governmental rules and all social control systems _are_ laws and legal systems. He defines law as "governmental social control" (Black, 1972, p. 1096), thereby including the social control efforts of _all_ political states. As you see in the following excerpt from Black, the proper goal of legal sociology is the creation of a sociological theory equally applicable to "the law of the Nazi's as well as American law, to revolutionary law as well as the cumbersome law of traditional China" (Black, 1972, p. 1097). Black summarizes his position this way,

> It is my contention that a purely sociological approach to law should involve not an assessment of legal policy, but rather, a scientific analysis of legal life _as a_ system of behavior. The ultimate contribution of this enterprise would be a general theory of law, a theory that would predict and explain every instance of legal behavior. While such a theory may never be attained, efforts to achieve it should be central to the sociology of law. By contrast, the core problems of legal policy making are problems of value. Such value considerations are as irrelevant to a sociology of law as they are to any other scientific theory of the empirical world. (Black, 1972, p. 1087)

The advantage of Black's approach is that it deals with the testing of empirical propositions, not the assertion of unprovable statements about 'mature legality'. Unlike Selznick, Black treats the concept of 'legal system' precisely like one might treat the concept of 'political system', i.e., there are good ones and bad ones but they are all 'legal' or 'political'.

The problem, of course, is that Black's view makes no distinction on the basis of the _quality_ of the legal system, and, like legal positivist jurisprudence, it is often difficult to grant the status of 'legal system' to some of the world's oppressive and horrifying social control systems.

Black's own words, which follow, should help you to grasp the essential reasoning of scientific legal sociology.

"THE BOUNDARIES OF LEGAL SOCIOLOGY"

V

The proper concern of legal sociology should be the development of a general theory of law. A general theory involves several key elements that may not at first be obvious. To say that a theory of law is general means that it seeks to order law wherever it is found. It seeks to discover the principles and mechanisms that predict empirical patterns of law, whether these patterns occur in this day or the past, regardless of the substantive area of law involved and regardless of the society. By contrast, the contemporary study of law is ideographic, very concrete and historical. Legal scholars tend to rebel at the suggestion of a general theory of their subject matter. Nevertheless, unless we seek generality in our study of law, we abandon hope for a serious sociology of law.

If the sweep of legal sociology is to be this broad, a correspondingly broad concept of law is required. I like to define law simply as *governmental social control*.[35] This is one possibility among many consistent with a positivist strategy. It is a concept easily employed in cross-societal analysis, encompassing any act by a political body that concerns the definition of social order or its defense. At the same time it excludes such forms of social control as popular morality and bureaucratic rules in private organizations. It is more inclusive than an American lawyer might deem proper, but more selective than anthro-

34. My critique of contemporary legal sociology arises from a very conventional conception of scientific method, a conception associated with the broader tradition of positivist thought. I have not made and do not intend to make a philosophical defense of this tradition. I wish only to advocate a sociology of law true to basic positivist principles as they have come to be understood in the history of the philosophy of science.

35. I mention this only as a means of delineating the subject matter of legal sociology. A definition of the subject matter is a prerequisite to any scientific inquiry. Just as a physicist must first define motion before he can describe its characteristics, a sociologist of religion, for example, must first define the pattern of social behavior that constitutes religion before he can proceed with his research. This does not mean that there is only one proper definition. Law itself has been defined non-normatively in a variety of ways. *See, e.g.*, M. WEBER, THE THEORY OF SOCIAL AND ECONOMIC ORGANIZATION 127 (T. Parsons ed. & transl. 1964):

An order will be called *law* when conformity with it is upheld by the probability that deviant action will be met by physical or psychic sanctions aimed to compel conformity or to punish disobedience, and applied by a group of men especially empowered to carry out this function.

I have chosen "governmental social control" as a definition of law for the reasons that follow in the text. I should add, however, that for me the choice of a particular sociological concept of law is not at all critical to my larger aim, since my ultimate interest goes beyond law per se to all forms of social control. For me, the study of law is preliminary and subordinate to the more general study of social control systems of all kinds. Therefore, if my concept of law is too narrow or too broad it does not matter *theoretically*, since it will in any case be relevant to a sociology of social control.

Reprinted with the permission of The Yale Journal Company and Fred B. Rothman & Company from The Yale Law Journal, Vol 81, pp. 1086-1087.

pological concepts which treat law as synonymous with normative life and dispute settlement of every description, governmental or otherwise. If we are to have a manageable subject matter, our concept must construe law as one among a larger array of social control systems. And if we are to have a strategically detached approach, our concept must be value neutral. We need a theoretical structure applicable to the law of the Nazis as well as American law, to revolutionary law and colonial law as well as the cumbersome law of traditional China. What do these systems share, and how can we explain the differences among them?

Ultimately a theory is known and judged by its statements about the world. These statements both guide and follow empirical research. They propose uniformities in the relation between one part of reality and another. Thus a general theory of law is addressed to the relation between law and other aspects of social life, including, for instance, other forms of social control, social stratification, the division of labor, social integration, group size, and the structure and substance of social networks. At the moment we have only a small inventory of theoretical statements, or propositions, of this kind. The relevant literature is sparse, and many of our leads must come from the classic works of Maine,[36] Durkheim,[37] Weber,[38] Ehrlich,[39] Pound,[40] and the like. Marx, too, should not be forgotten, though he gave law only passing attention.[41] Apart from classical sociology and comparative jurisprudence, anthropological literature, notably the work of such scholars as Malinowski,[42] Hoebel,[43] Gluckman,[44] Bohannan,[45] and Nader,[46] has contributed more than sociology to a general theory of law. Contemporary sociologists tend to limit their attention to the American legal system, and even there, disproportionate emphasis is given the criminal justice system. Rarely do they compare American law to governmental social control in other societies; yet if legal sociology is not comparative, its conclusions will inevitably be time-bound and ethnocentric.

36. *See, e.g.,* ANCIENT LAW (1861); VILLAGE-COMMUNITIES IN THE EAST AND WEST (1871).
37. THE DIVISION OF LABOR IN SOCIETY (G. Simpson transl. 1933); PROFESSIONAL ETHICS AND CIVIC MORALS (C. Brookfield transl. 1957); *Two Laws of Penal Evolution* (M. Mileski transl. 1971) (available in my files).
38. MAX WEBER ON LAW IN ECONOMY AND SOCIETY (M. Rheinstein ed., E. Shils & M. Rheinstein transls. 1954).
39. FUNDAMENTAL PRINCIPLES OF THE SOCIOLOGY OF LAW (W. Moll transl. 1936).
40. *E.g.,* SOCIAL CONTROL THROUGH LAW (1942); *The Limits of Effective Legal Action,* 27 INT'L J. ETHICS 150 (1917); *A Survey of Social Interests,* 57 HARV. L. REV. 1 (1943).
41. Marx did, however, inspire some interesting sociological work on law. *See, e.g.,* K. RENNER, THE INSTITUTIONS OF PRIVATE LAW AND THEIR SOCIAL FUNCTIONS (O. Kahn-Freund ed., A. Schwartzchild transl. 1949); Pashukanis, *The General Theory of Law and Marxism,* in SOVIET LEGAL PHILOSOPHY 111 (H. Babb transl. 1951).
42. The standard work is CRIME AND CUSTOM IN SAVAGE SOCIETY (1926). This study is considered the first ethnography of law.
43. THE LAW OF PRIMITIVE MAN (1954); K. LLEWELLYN & E. HOEBEL, THE CHEYENNE WAY: CONFLICT AND CASE LAW IN PRIMITIVE JURISPRUDENCE (1941).
44. *See, e.g.,* THE JUDICIAL PROCESS AMONG THE BAROTSE OF NORTHERN RHODESIA (1955). Gluckman provides a useful overview of legal anthropology in POLITICS, LAW AND RITUAL IN TRIBAL SOCIETY (1965).
45. JUSTICE AND JUDGMENT AMONG THE TIV (1957); *The Differing Realms of the Law,* in THE ETHNOGRAPHY OF LAW 33 (1965) (supplement to 67 AM. ANTHROPOLOGIST 33 (1965)).
46. *E.g., An Analysis of Zapotec Law Cases,* 3 ETHNOLOGY 404 (1964); *Choices in Legal Procedure: Shia Moslem and Mexican Zapotec,* 67 AM. ANTHROPOLOGIST 394 (1965).

MINI-LECTURE #1, PART B QUESTIONS

1. What does Black believe to be the proper concern of the sociology of law?

2. a. What is Black's definition of law?

    b. What does he feel are the advantages of so broad a definition?

3. What is the standard for evaluating the utility of a theory of law?

4. What is the essential difference between Selznick's and Black's point of view?

1. Black (1972), a spokesman for the scientific sociology of law, states that the goal of sociology of law should be to develop a general theory of law designed to ". . .discover the principles and mechanisms that predict empirical patterns of law, whether these patterns occur in this day or the past, regardless of the substantive area of law involved and regardless of the society" (p. 2.19).

2. a. Black (1972) defines law as "governmental social control".

   b. By defining law broadly, Black argues that he is better able to study law in many different contexts. His definition enables him to talk about Nazi law and American law as examples of the same phenomenon, that is, "governmental social control." He also maintains that his definition is useful because it excludes 'popular morality', rules of private organization, and various forms of dispute settlement which anthropologists see as part of the law.

3. Theories are useful if they enable us to make accurate statements about the world. We can test theoretical statements by reference to the empirical world and then accept or reject them. Thus, a good theory of law (which is, after all, what Black argues is the goal of sociology of law) would permit us to make accurate statements about the relationship between law and other aspects of social life.

4. Selznick, in the natural law tradition, seeks to evaluate legal systems in terms of an ideal standard--legality. Black, in the legal positivist tradition, refuses to make an evaluation of legal systems. He seeks to scientifically study all legal systems, both good ones and bad ones.

LAW AND CONCEPTUAL MODELS

In the following pages I want you to become familiar with two conceptual models which are used by social scientists in analyzing the legal system. They are quite similar in that they both emphasize that law must be viewed as both a <u>social product</u> (dependent variable) and a <u>social force</u> (independent variable). In other words, law both <u>reflects</u> the broader social and political context in which it operates and it <u>affects</u> that context.

Models are abstractions of reality; they are not reality themselves. It is necessary for you to recognize this fact before attempting to understand the models below and their potential value. In a sense, a model is like a road map. The road map is not the road! It is simply a model of the road which brings to your attention certain factors about the road, e.g., the location of exits off of highways, the terrain, and the location of service areas. Similarly, the models described in this mini-lecture simply highlight or draw your attention to certain relationships between law and society. The models serve only to provide you with some useful concepts for thinking about the interactions between law and society and to suggest some areas for inquiry.

Many social scientists have attempted to analyze legal systems from the perspective of systems theory or stimulus response theory. The language used in these two types of models differs; however, the overall value of them is similar. Each attempt to draw attention to the fact that law is best viewed as part of a wider social context. Interactions between inputs and outputs, or prior stimuli and subsequent responses both emphasize this interactive dimension.

Systems Model

The systems model (Easton, 1953) has been employed by social scientists from various disciplines in an attempt to organize their thinking about the social system, the political system, or the legal system. Basically, a system is defined by what it does.

LEGAL SYSTEM

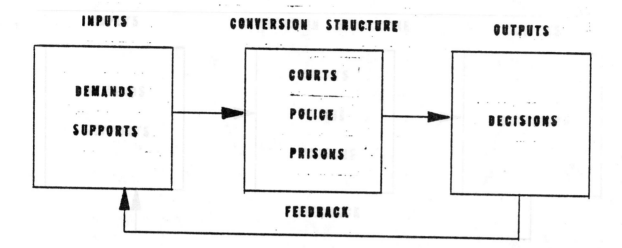

The legal system's job, for example, is to authoritatively distribute justice. It does this by converting various demands into legal decisions, or by converting system inputs into system outputs. A legal system, since it is defined by what it does, can continue to function only if it's decisions are authoritative, i.e., they are accepted as binding by those within the legal system's jurisdiction.

Inputs

Demands are one of the two types of inputs. Demands are the raw materials which are fed into the system. Without demands, the legal system would have nothing to do. In an ideal world in which the distribution of just results was not a matter of disagreement, there would be no need for a legal system since there would be no conflicting claims. Demands can take many forms, but typically they consist either of a claim that X has a right against Y (civil demand) or that the state should prosecute lawbreakers (criminal demand). The sources of such demands include individuals, victims of crime, other units of government, the press, pressure groups, etc.

Supports are the other type of input. Supports are necessary in order for the legal system to continue to do its job of authoritatively distributing justice. If the citizenry and the other governmental units do not accept the decisions of the legal system as binding and are not willing to comply with such decisions even when they disagree with the content of the decisions, then the legal system will cease to successfully do its job and will be replaced by some different legal arrangements.

This concept of support leads us to ask the question, "why do people support the legal system?" One answer, of course, is that people _fear_ the consequences of non-support. They recognize that if they do not comply with legal decisions, they face the coercive power of the State in terms of jail, fines, etc. However, it is unlikely that a legal system could long survive if it could obtain support only by coercive techniques. It seems that a degree of voluntary compliance and support must exist if the legal system is to survive.

A second reason, then, why people might voluntarily support the legal system is that they are satisfied with the outputs or decisions of the system. Plainly, we can see that the winners in legal battles would quickly support the system which has satisfied their demands. However, it is clear that there are losers each time there are winners and that today's winners might be tomorrow's losers! Again, therefore, the degree of support required to maintain a viable legal system must be the result of additional factors.

The third factor, _legal socialization_, accounts for the bulk of the supportive attitudes and behavior directed toward the legal system. Legal socialization (which is discussed further in Unit 7) can be defined as the process of acquiring legally relevant attitudes, or the process of internalizing the legal culture. Most people acquire strongly positive feelings toward the legal system at early ages, and this residual fund of supportive attitudes causes them to _believe_ in the beneficient quality of the legal system even when no coercive effort has been made against them and when their demands are not met by the legal system.

Conversion Structure

The legal system, more so than the political system, restricts access to its converting mechanisms, that is, while anyone can enter the political arena, there are restrictions on who can bring what cases to a courtroom. In the parlance of the systems theorists, there are _regime rules_ and _gate-keepers_ whose job it is to limit and screen out many of the demands. Regime rules refer to those rules which specify who can use the legal system and under what circumstances. For example, the notion of _standing to sue_ is a regime rule which requires that only the persons who themselves have suffered legal injuries may assert their legal rights in court. This rule eliminates demands made by one person for legal injuries suffered by another. Many such regime rules help to restrict access to the legal system. Gatekeepers are political actors who deliberately work to reduce demand on the system. Lawyers who pressure for out of court settlements and police and prosecutors who plea bargain are performing gatekeeping functions.

Decisions

After processing the demands, the system produces outputs in the form of decisions. Basically, these decisions emanate from courts at various levels, police, and other legal decision makers. When the policeman decides to arrest or not to arrest or when the court upholds or overturns a lower court ruling, the legal system has issued a decision.

After decisions are made by the legal system their effect on subsequent inputs is referred to as feedback. The systems model emphasizes the dynamic quality of the legal system. The inputs affect the outputs; the outputs affect the inputs. Decisions can affect levels of demands and supports in various ways. For instance, the satisfaction of demand may reduce future demands, i.e., some people may now have achieved their goals and cease to make further demands. Alternatively, the satisfaction of demands may intensify demands among those who past demands have been satisfied. Once the legal system has formally acknowledged that demands are legitimate, more demands may result. The desegregation decision in 1954, for example, led to more, not fewer, civil rights claims.

The systems model, then, focuses on law as decisions made in response to demands and on the effect of those decisions on subsequent demands. The value of this model, like any model, lies in the questions it causes us to ask about the legal system. For instance, we might be led to ask the following questions based upon a systems approach:

1. Who institutes litigation? (Makes the demands?)

2. How frequently do various people make demands?

3. Are some types of litigants more successful than others?

4. How do court decisions affect perceptions of court legitimacy?

5. Who complies and under what conditions?

Some of these questions are dealt with in later units. For now, they are raised to illustrate the way in which an abstract model can lead us to ask particular research questions about the role of law in society.

Stimulus - Response Model

Another common model (Nagel, 1969) employs slightly different concepts to achieve the same basic results. Nagel begins

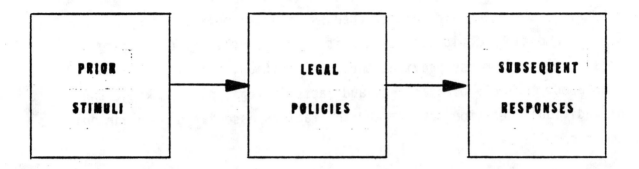

with the concept of 'legal policies' and suggests that they must be viewed simultaneously as responses to prior stimuli and as stimuli to subsequent responses.

Prior Stimuli

Prior stimuli which produce legal policies include normative standards, empircal facts, and the policymakers through which the standards and facts are filtered. The normative standards may be announced by government, such as in the case of statutes, regulations, and past cases, or not announced by government, as in the case of custom, scholarly articles, or shared values. The empirical facts may be legally admissable evidence at trial or legally inadmissable evidence, such as the race, age, or status of the litigants. Both standards and facts are then filtered through policymakers who have certain characteristics and attitudes which influence their perceptions of the standards and facts.

Legal Policies & Subsequent Responses

The legal policies, however, must also be seen as stimuli to subsequent responses. Various inhibiting and facilitating factors, such as the role of the press in reporting court decisions and the reactions of public officials, furthermore, influence the responses to legal policies. (The impact concept discussed earlier corresponds closely to the 'subsequent responses' in this model.) The legal policy and the various facilitating and inhibiting factors again are filtered through policy appliers (judges, administrators, police) and policy recipients (general public). The characteristics of the appliers and recipients will influence their perceptions of the policies. Ultimately, the responses to legal policies manifest themselves either as change or stability in behavior and/or attitudes. Legal policies may change behavior, but not affect attitude, or they may change behavior which in turn changes attitudes. Additionally, changes in attitude and/or behavior may stimulate further changes in legal policy. Many of th same type of questions would emerge--albeit with slightly different jargon--from this model as from the previous one. In addition, this model raises questions about the role of standards and facts in legal policymaking, the role of individual decision makers, and the factors associated with various degrees of compliance.

Summary

The purpose of outlining these two abstract models of the legal system has been to introduce you to some of the conceptual tools currently used by social scientists who study the relationships of law to society, to highlight the nature of law as both a social product and a social force, and to cause you to think about questions which need to be studied about law and society.

MINI-LECTURE #2 QUESTIONS

1. What are conceptual models and what purpose do they serve?

2. Summarize the elements of the systems model and identify some of the questions which it makes salient.

3. Summarize the elements of the stimulus-response model and identify some of the questions which it makes salient.

4. Identify the similarities between the two models.

DISCUSSION OF MINI-LECTURE #2 QUESTIONS

1. Conceptual models are abstractions from reality which help us to organize our thoughts about various aspects of social existence. They provide concepts which help in analyzing social life, and they suggest lines of inquiry for examining social life.

2. The systems model conceives of the legal system as a conversion mechanism which processes demands into authoritative allocations of justice. To continue to successfully distribute justice the legal system must receive adequate support from those within its boundaries. The decisions of the system have an effect upon subsequent demands; the legal process, therefore, is an ongoing interaction between inputs and outputs.

   A systems model suggests that we should ask:

   a. Why do people support the legal system?

   b. How does the legal system control the number of demands which it will process?

   c. How do court decisions alter perceptions of the legal system?

   d. How do court decisions affect levels of demand?

3. The stimulus-response model focuses on the idea that law, or legal policies, must be seen as a response to prior sets of stimuli and as a stimulus to subsequent sets of responses.

   This model leads us to ask questions such as:

   a. What effect do various normative standards have upon the development of legal policy?

   b. What facts are considered in legal policymaking?

   c. What role is played by the individuals who hold positions in the legal structure?

   d. What factors inhibit and facilitate the administration of legal policies?

4. Both models emphasize the interaction of law with other aspects of society. Whereas systems theorists talk about demands, the same basic idea is expressed as prior stimuli in the stimulus-response model. Whereas the systems theorists talk about feedback, the stimulus response theorists talk about law as stimulus to subsequent responses. The key difference is that systems theorists begin their analysis with the conversion process and stimulus response theorists begin with the legal policies. The results, however, are quite similar in that both stress the interactive nature of the elements of the models.

LAW AND POLITICS

Perhaps the most obvious of the various academic lenses through which the legal system has been observed is that of the political scientists. For most students it is intuitively sensible to think of law as a cousin to politics. In fact, pre-law students have traditionally majored in political science. In this mini-lecture, then, the relationship of law to politics will be described, the difference between law and politics will be highlighted, and the work of political scientists who have studied this relationhip will be summarized.

A Reciprocal Relationship

The political nature of law in American society is complex and reciprocal. Its complexity makes it difficult to clearly delineate the respective realms of law and politics, and this complexity is compounded by the fact that law is in some crucial ways dependent upon politics and politics is similarly dependent upon law. When political bodies such as legislatures enact statutes requiring or prohibiting certain conduct, the legal system provides for enforcement of these policies. Without such enforcement, legislative enactments would carry little weight. However, the authority of that legal enforcement mechanism is itself dependent upon prior political agreement on its legitimacy. Thus, political system decisions require legal system support, just as the legal system itself requires political system support.

More specifically, the relationship between law and politics can be expressed in a number of propositions. First, law poses limits to political authority. There exist a wide range of legal restraints on the exercise of political power. From constitutional restraints on governmental actions and the two-term limit for a President to the many statutes defining the proper scope of action for political leaders, we can quickly see that laws prevent the unfettered exercise of political power. Second, laws provide the rules within which political conflict is carried on. Laws define who is eligible to run, how the electoral machinery is to be operated, how much money candidates may spend during their campaigns, and so on. Third, laws provide a basic source of legitimacy for political decision making. Mass acceptance of political decisions of the Congress is readily produced so long as the laws which govern how Congress should operate have been followed. In other words, so long as people believe that legal procedures have been complied with, they generally are willing to accept the results as binding upon them, even if they disagree with the content of the law.

The complexity of the law and politics relationship, however, makes even these three propositions difficult to understand. For the laws which limit political power and provide the framework for political conflict are themselves the product of prior political decision making. We are, thus, left with a certain amount of ambiguity about the nature of the relationship. For, in the absence of law, political power can easily be abused; but in the absence of political support, law can easily become meaningless. As one observer has noted,

> The effectiveness of judicial decisions depends on the legitimacy of the courts; the legitimacy of the courts in turn depends, to a large extent, on their political autonomy. It is their very independence from the democratic political process that allows courts to decide those questions of fundamental political importance which cannot be resolved through political mechanisms deadlocked by irreconcilable differences of opinion and feeling. But it is the inevitable consequence of decisive judicial action in areas where basic political agreement is nonexistent that courts will be considered partisan, regardless of who won or lost. It is a paradox of the liberal system that the strength of political autonomy which allows courts to make divisive decisions will diminish as a result of such decisions. (Shattuck, 1974, pp. 152-153)

Distinctions Between Law And Politics

While, on the one hand, it is tempting to treat legal decision making and legal decision makers as mere subsets of political decision making and political decision makers, such a view can be misleading. For law is distinctive in certain ways. Legal fact-finding is different from political fact-finding. In other words, the evidence which Congress might gather in preparing legislation and the evidence which courts might admit in deciding cases are not the same. A vast number of complicated rules of evidence restrict the legal fact-finding process. What a Congressional Committee

107

investigating wrongdoing might inquire about may differ from what a court may inquire about.

The access to the legal process is different from that of the political process. Jurisdictional and substantive requirements limit access to the legal process in a way quite unlike the political arena in which money, votes, and charisma may guarantee access to decision makers.

Judges do not behave precisely like other decision makers. They are generally more insulated from politics and they present reasoned opinions in support of their decisions. By contrast, national and state legislators are always facing re-election efforts, and they may justify their decisions to voters in a much less rigorous fashion.

Nonetheless, despite these differences, the institutions which administer the law must operate in the concrete, highly political, real world and are not likely to be entirely beyond political influences.

The Contribution Of Political Scientists

In order to summarize the work of political scientists who have explored the interfaces between law and politics, their various works have been divided here into three categories, each of which deals with a different aspect of the relationship.

A. The Effect of Politics On Court Decisions

The first group of political science studies are concerned with the effect of politics on Court decisions--usually Supreme Court decisions. One approach to this problem examines the recruitment of judges. These studies are purely descriptive and provide information on the background characteristics of the people who sit on the bench. Typically, these characteristics include age, ethnic background, religion, prior career patterns, political party affiliation, and region of the country. The purpose of such studies is to demonstrate that the same type of people dominate both the political system and the judicial system.

A related type of study explores the Presidential appointments of federal judges, U.S. Attorneys, and Supreme Court Justices. In these studies it becomes readily apparent that Presidents overwhelmingly select from among their own political party to fill these positions. President Carter's pledge to select such people on merit, rather than politics, brought this

108

particular interface between law and politics to the attention of the
general public when the President dismissed a Republican U.S. Attorney
in Philadelphia who had pursued Democratic Congressional wrongdoers.
Carter responded that his campaign pledge had been misinterpreted. He had
not meant that he would cease the practice of appointing members of his
own party; he had merely meant that he would only select well-qualified
members of his party!

Another facet of the political scientists' effort to study the
effect of politics on the courts is the type of study which seeks to correlate
the background characteristics of judges with their decisions. Thus, for
example, Democratic judges have been found to be more sympathetic to claims
of injured plaintiffs; judges who had formerly been prosecutors have been
found to be less lenient in dealing with criminal defendants. Such studies
uniformly reject causal models, i.e., they do not claim that party identification
or career patterns cause judges to behave in particular ways. They merely
maintain that they can identify strong associations between party affiliation,
for instance, and certain types of decisions.

Finally, other political scientists interested in the effect of
politics on courts have studied the role of various interest groups.
The NAACP, Common Cause, the American Civil Liberties Union, The Environmental
Defense League, and many others have attempted to influence the outcome of
court decisions at all levels. Common strategies have included raising
money to finance long court fights, recruiting plaintiffs to bring suits of
interest to the general membership of the group, carrying out public campaigns
to generate support or opposition to pending cases, and preparing and filing
amicus curiae briefs. These are legal arguments presented to the Supreme
Court by interested groups who are not, themselves, parties in the case.
The Bakke case, which is the subject of Unit 10, stimulated the filing of
more amicus briefs than any case in the history of the Supreme Court.

In all of these examples, the focus was the same: how do a variety
of political factors help to explain the behavior of legal decision makers.

B. The Effect of Politics on the Implementation of Court Decisions

Turning away from the issue of the effect of politics on the legal
process, some political scientists have focused their efforts on the question
of how politics affects the implementation of court decisions. Once it is
recognized that court decisions are not self-executing, the issues of how

politics can affect the degree of compliance, what reactions are produced in other political institutions, and with what results become more significant.

The factors which affect the degree and manner of compliance with court decisions have been studied by political scientists who define their area of interst as 'legal impact' theory. Since these impact studies will be examined in Unit 6 in connection with a consideration of the role of law as an instrument of social change, they are only mentioned here as part of the review of the political science perspective on law and society.

The study of the reactions of other political institutions to Supreme Court decisions focused on the Congress, the President, lower courts, state and local officials, and the public. Studies of Congressional reactions reveal efforts by Congress to alter the jurisdiction of the Court, the personnel of the Court, and the Constitution itself. The well-known unsucccessful attempt by President Roosevelt to enlarge the Court and the equally unsuccessful attempt to remove Justice William O. Douglas (led by the then House Minority Leader, Gerald R. Ford) illustrate these reactions. Efforts to alter the Constitution itself in order to reverse the Supreme Court have been launched by advocates of Bible reading, opponents of busing, and opponents of abortion.

The reactions of lower courts to Supreme Court decisions vary from outright disregard of the high Court rulings to strict adherence to such rulings. While the hierarchical structure of American courts suggests that the decisions of the higher courts will 'trickle down' to and control the decisions of the lower courts, the actual operation of the courts reveals a greater degree of lower court autonomy. To get around Supreme Court decisions which they dislike, lower courts can find that the facts of the cases before them differ significantly from the facts in the Supreme Court cases which allegedly should control the result. The cost in time and money of an appeal from a defiant and/or erroneous lower court ruling often means that the erroneous decision will stand.

C. The Effect of Court Decisions on the Political Process and the Political Agenda

An interesting, but underdeveloped area of study of the interaction between law and politics involves the effect of court decisions on the political process and the political agenda. In recent years, a number of decisions touching on the electoral process have been handed down. For example, in <u>Williams v. Rhodes</u> (1968), the Supreme Court invalidated an Ohio statute, which would have prevented George Wallace's name from appearing on the ballot, on the ground that it was restrictive. While Ohio argued that it was simply trying to preserve the two-party system, the Court held that the statute unfairly restricted the choices available to voters. Clearly, any court decision which alters the access to the ballot will have vast consequences for the political party system and the political process generally.

A related case in California involved a challenge to the filing fee of $7000.00 which candidates were required to pay in order to be placed on the primary election ballot. The Court invalidated this fee arguing that it had the effect of barring poorer people from becoming candidates. Once again, any court decision which makes it easier--or harder--to get on the ballot will have an effect on the entire political process.

In 1974, Congress enacted the Federal Election Campaign Act in an effort to regulate the excessive expenditures of money in political campaigns. In a challenge brought by U.S. Senators Buckley (N.Y.) and McCarthy (Minn.) the Supreme Court upheld some portions and struck other portions of the act. The Congress placed a $1000.00 limit on the amount an individual could countribute to a candidate for federal office and a $1000.00 limit on the amount an individual could <u>spend</u> on behalf of such a candidate. The Court upheld the contribution limit, but struck the spending limit. The rationale offered in the opinion was that a contributor is not exercising <u>his/her</u> <u>own</u> right of free speech; rather the contributor is helping a candidate exercise <u>his/her</u> free speech right. In contrast, however, an individual who <u>spends</u> 5 million dollars to buy T.V. time to announce <u>his/her</u> <u>own</u> preference in an election is exercising his/her own right of free speech and cannot be limited to $1000.00 worth of free speech by Congress! Similarly, the Congressional attempt to restrict candidate spending on their own behalf was invalidated on the same ground, i.e., that Congress cannot limit free speech by placing a dollar limit on candidate contributions to themselves.

Once again, the effect of this court opinion is immediately felt in the political process where once again the so-called "fat cats" and wealthy candidates are free to outspend their opponents. The point here is not to determine if the Supreme Court was wise or foolish, right or wrong, in making these decisions. Rather, the idea to grasp is that there is a rippling effect of court decisions on the political process. In fact the entire structure of American politics could be quietly reshaped by Supreme Court decisions of the sort discussed here.

The effect of court decisions on the political agenda is an even more subtle type of influence. For example, the 1954 desegregation decisions, Brown v. Board of Education did far more than overturn the earlier 'separate but equal' standard in race relations. It fundamentally changed the political agenda; that is, it changed the subject matter about which political conflict was to revolve for the next 25 years. The successful use of the courts by civil rights advocates helped to set the stage for conflict over the rights of juveniles, homosexuals, students, mental patients, and women. The Brown decision resulted in the political controversy surrounding busing of children to achieve racial balance, new federal legislation guaranteeing equal opportunity in housing and employment, and the emotional political struggle over the issue of reverse discrimination (which is extensively covered in Unit 9).

Summary

While the full range of legal-political relations have not been explored here, various significant points of interface have been indicated and some of the contributions of political scientists to the field of law and politics have been described. In the end, the relationship of law to politics and the exercise of political power is still very much an open one. For, as one political scientist concludes,

> ". . .law is not only an instrument of rule; it serves also as an instrument to control the exercise of power. While law serves powerful economic interests, it is also available as a potential instrument to restrict economic exploitation. Whether law is, in fact and not only in theory, available to the ruled as well as the rulers, whether courts are accessible to economically and socially underprivileged groups and classes as well as to corporations, are questions which should be of considerable importance to political scientists." (Shattuck, 1974, p. 154)

1. Describe the reciprocal nature of the relationship between law and politics.

2. List key difference between law and politics.

3. Describe the three categories for classifying the work of political scientists in their study of the relationship between politics and law, and cite one illustration in each category.

1. Law, requires legitimacy for it to be effective; political consensus provides that legitimacy. Legal legitimacy, requires the belief that it is apolitical. Legislative politics also provides the laws for the legal system to apply.

    Law, however, provides legitimacy to political events as well as vice versa. Furthermore, law serves to restrain political power. The symbiotic relationship can be summarized this way: ". . .in the absence of law, political power can easily be abused; but in the absence of political support, law can easily become meaningless" (p. 2.33).

2. a. Legal fact-finding is different from political fact-finding.

    b. Access to the legal system differs from access to the political system.

    c. Legal decision makers, such as judges, are less vulnerable to political pressure and must often defend their decisions in written opinons.

3. a. The first category includes those studies which examine the effect of politics on court decisions. Examples include studies of pressure groups efforts to influence the court, studies, of the backgrounds of judges, and studies which correlate judges' background characteristics with decisions.

    b. The second category includes those studies which examine the effect of politics on the implementation of court decisions. Examples include impact studies, and studies of Presidential, Congressional, and public reactions to court decisions.

    c. The third group involves the study of the effect of Court decisions on the political process and the political agenda. The ballot access cases, the campaign finance case, and the effect of Brown v. Board of Education are illustrative of this category.

In the spring of 1976, Ross Sterling was a lawyer at John Connally's Houston firm. President Ford wanted Connally's help against Ronald Reagan. In April, Ford nominated Sterling to the U.S. district court. In July, Connally endorsed Ford. Ford beat Reagan, but lost in November. Now he plays pro-am golf. And Ross Sterling is still a federal judge.

Jimmy Carter's recent order creating citizen panels for appointment of federal judges to the 11 U.S. circuit courts of appeals is a first. Never before has a president attempted so boldly to remove federal judge selection from political backrooms. Never before has a presidential candidate's talk about merit selection been backed up by action. But President Carter's order is also a serious retreat from the merit selection he campaigned for last year. Then, Carter was holding up the Georgia merit plan for picking state judges as his model for federal judge selection.

That plan, created by Carter, applies to trial as well as appellate judgeships. Yet Michael J. Egan, a Republican who worked closely with Carter on the Georgia plan before he was appointed to his current position as associate attorney general in the Justice Department, says the president has "no present plans" to set up a merit system for federal district judgeships. The administration's strategy, according to Egan, is to see how the circuit merit plan works out before deciding to push merit selection of district judges on a reluctant U.S. Senate.

Surely, White House Press Secretary Jody Powell's "you-can't-always-do-everything-immediately" defense of the president's backstepping on his campaign promise must have left senators smirking. The old way of handing out the 398 U.S. district judgeships—the heart of senatorial patronage—was unshaken by the president's order. And the "blue-slip" system, which enables one senator to blackball a nominee, seems to have survived intact.

(Under the president's order, one of 13 citizen panels is "activated" whenever an opening exists for one of 97 circuit judgeships. (The number of circuit and district judges would increase substantially if a bill currently being considered by Congress passes.) The panels, all appointed by the

THE POLITICS OF PICKING FEDERAL JUDGES

by James Goodman

president, match up with the 11 circuit courts of appeals. The geographically large fifth (deep South) and ninth (far West) circuits each have two panels.

The president notifies the appropriate panel of any vacancy. Within 60 days the panel must recommend to the president, in confidence, the five persons it considers best qualified to fill the vacancy. While not bound to do so, the president makes his nomination from this list and then sends it to the Senate for confirmation.

While Carter's merit plan is new to the federal judiciary, on a state level—where it has been most difficult to separate the courts from politics—merit selection has a much longer history. Beginning with Missouri in 1940, 25 states, the District of Columbia, Guam, and Puerto Rico have adopted merit systems for state judge selection, says the American Judicature Society, a leading proponent of merit selection. Generally speaking, these merit systems rely on a commission, drawing from nonlawyers and lawyers alike, to submit a list of nominees to the governor for final selection. After a fixed time, the voters decide whether or not to keep the judge for another term.

Article II, Section 2 of the Constitution empowers the president to "nominate, and by and with the advice and consent of the Senate," to "appoint" federal judges. But behind the antiseptic sounding "nominate" and "appoint" is a mire of political push-and-pull. As Attorney General Griffin Bell told *The Washington Post*, "becoming a federal judge wasn't very difficult." The former fifth circuit court of appeals judge explained: "I managed John F. Kennedy's presidential campaign in Georgia. Two of my oldest and closest friends were the two senators from Georgia. And I was campaign manager and special, unpaid counsel for the governor."

Although the Constitution leaves the impression that presidents choose federal judges, Attorney General Bell was much closer to the truth when he said during his confirmation hearings that "selection" of district judgeships is in the hands of the senators. Joe Dolan, an assistant deputy attorney general (1961-1964) under Presidents Kennedy and Johnson, similarly told an American Bar Association conference last March that if one or both senators of a state come from the same political party as the president, the Constitution reads backwards. It should say: "the senators shall nominate, and by and with the consent of the president, appoint judges...."

Actually, federal judge selection is more complicated than senators simply deciding who should get the political plum. Presidents also try to take advantage of the political buying power of a judgeship. Throughout the nation's history, about nine of every ten judges appointed by the man in the White House have come from his own political party—a clear indication

Fearing a recurrence of the Haynsworth-Carswell fiasco, Mitchell got an ABA committee to review his prospects.

that presidents are not passive partners.

And the power of appointment has been used—or abused—by presidents of all parties. A disillusioned James Farley, the former postmaster general, quoted President Franklin Delano Roosevelt as saying: "We must hold up judicial appointments in states where the delegation is not going along. We must make appointments promptly where the delegation is with us. Where there is a division we must give posts to those supporting us...."

Federal judgeships were part of Lyndon Johnson's political wheeling and dealing, too. In *Judges*, Donald Dale Jackson tells of the time Johnson, as Senate majority leader in 1959, held up the confirmation of 13 judges until President Dwight Eisenhower okayed Johnson's candidate for a Texas vacancy. As president, Johnson kept federal judgeships close to his side. Unwilling to delegate authority even to his own Justice Department, he had White House staffer John Macy keep voluminous files to be used for presidential appointments, including judgeships.

Not surprisingly, President Richard Nixon had a highly politicized view of federal judgeships. This became most apparent when the Senate rejected his Supreme Court nominations of Clement Haynsworth and Harrold Carswell. As if Haynsworth's conflicts-of-interests and Carswell's segregationist past had nothing to do with it, Nixon lamented that "the real issue" behind the rejections was his nominees' "philosophy of strict construction of the Constitution," a philosophy the president said he shared.

In a subsequent letter to then Ohio Senator William Saxbe, Nixon further implied that the Senate had denied him the chief executive's right to choose Justices of his liking. He ignored the fact that the Senate has rejected almost one of every five Supreme Court nominees since 1789.

California Democratic Senators John Tunney and Alan Cranston found the Nixon Justice Department equally politicized when they approached Deputy Attorney General Richard Kleindienst in 1971 about resubmitting Cecil Poole's name for a California judgeship. Poole had been held in disfavor by conservatives because, as a U.S. attorney in 1967, he had persuaded a federal grand jury to drop charges against five anti-war demonstrators arrested for not having draft cards in their possession; Poole said the arrests were improperly authorized.

When Poole was considered for federal judge in 1968, and again in 1969, California Republican Senator George Murphy was able to stop the nomination. With Murphy gone in 1971 Poole backers thought he might make it through. But this time Kleindienst reportedly told Senator Tunney: "Poole said things about the administration which were unkind to the point where the attorney general [John

Mitchell] just would not give a recommendation."

Not until Gerald Ford was in the White House did Cecil Poole finally make it to the federal bench. Yet there is a footnote to this eight-year struggle. On May 5, 1976, less than six weeks before Poole was nominated for a district judgeship and scarcely a month before Tunney's Senate primary against Tom Hayden, Tunney reported receiving a $200 campaign contribution from Poole, who was then a practicing attorney. Tunney, by the way, was a member of the Senate Judiciary Committee, which handles all nominations for the federal bench.

During the Nixon years, even moderate Republican Senator Clifford Case ran into trouble when he sent the name of liberal Charles Clyde Ferguson to the Justice Department for possible nomination to the federal bench. By not acting on the New Jersey senator's recommendation—Case's office merely received a formal acknowledgment that Ferguson's name was received—the Justice Department made it clear that it did not want the former dean of Howard University Law School to be a federal judge. Senator Case submitted a new name.

President Gerald Ford did not use the Justice Department to block judicial appointments. On the other hand, twice during last year's heated campaign for the Republican nomination, Ford enhanced his political position in a state by making a timely judicial appointment. Hardly two weeks before the May 1 Texas primary, Ford nominated a member of John Connally's law firm, Ross N. Sterling, to the U.S. district court in Houston. At the time of the Sterling appointment, President Ford and challenger Ronald Reagan were vying for Connally's support. And sure enough, Connally shortly thereafter announced he favored Ford.

Then, in July, Ford nominated Donald Brotzman for a district court opening in Colorado. Brotzman had previously been appointed by Ford, his old congressional friend, to be an assistant secretary of the Army following his defeat in Colorado's 1974 Democratic landslide. More significant, among Brotzman's biggest backers for the federal bench was William Armstrong, an uncommitted delegate to the Republican convention.

It seemed that Armstrong was leaning towards Ford. Still, most of Armstrong's conservative colleagues, led by Joseph Coors of Coors beer, were in the Reagan camp. So Ford tapped Brotzman to be a federal judge, and Armstrong finally committed himself to the president. Ford got what he wanted, but another Republican, Colorado Supreme Court Justice William Erickson, was generally considered better qualified than Brotzman for the judgeship. Colorado's Democratic senators Floyd Haskell and Gary Hart were not receptive

he ABA pilloried a list of nominees, and Nixon exclaimed, '[Expletive] the ABA!' So went the agreement.

tulka

to Ford's choice, especially since a Democratic victory in November would increase their say in judge selection. When neither Colorado senator returned his "blue slip," the Brotzman nomination was killed.

While it has no statutory basis, the blue-slip system has managed to institutionalize senatorial patronage. Once the president formally nominates someone, the Senate Judiciary Committee sends each of the senators from the nominee's state a blue sheet of paper asking his "opinion and information concerning the nomination." In fact, the blue slip is asking whether the president's formal choice is the person the senator wanted or, in some cases, agreed to. If the senator approves, he returns his blue slip. If he disapproves, he holds on to the blue slip. Says a former congressional aide who worked close to this process, a withheld blue slip amounts to "a one-person veto," ending the nominee's chances.

If both blue slips are returned, confirmation hearings are scheduled. An informal subcommittee of the Senate Judiciary Committee, which until recently usually consisted of Senators James Eastland, John McClellan, and Roman Hruska (now retired), convenes for 15 or 20 minutes to ask the nominee a handful of perfunctory questions. Recommendation for approval is then sent to the full Senate, where confirmation is almost certain. But if the FBI's report on the nominee is negative, or if a bloc of senators, the ABA, or other outside groups oppose the nomination, it might be bottled up in the Senate Judiciary Committee.

In his studies of the appointment process to the federal bench, University of Minnesota Professor Harold W. Chase tells how conservative opposition nearly stopped liberals George Clifton Edwards and Thurgood Marshall from confirmation to U.S. circuit courts of appeals. Edwards, a former police commissioner of Detroit, had the support of both his Michigan senators and the Republican governor. Nevertheless, he faced stiff opposition because of his activist past and the fact that his father was a socialist. Even a representative from the Tennessee bar testified against the Michigan nominee. Despite that, Edwards still managed to win confirmation.

In Marshall's case, his long association with the NAACP Legal Defense Fund and the civil rights movement led the Judiciary Committee to drag its feet for almost a year. Because of a good deal of outside pressure, Marshall was finally confirmed.

At the other end, author Joseph Goulden (*The Benchwarmers*) found that the quickest confirmation was that of Richard McLaren, President Nixon's assistant attorney general in charge of antitrust. As White House tapes show, Nixon didn't want McLaren in the Justice De-

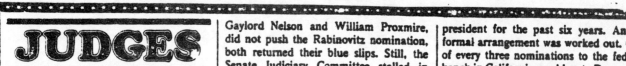

partment ("Get the son of a bitch out of here"), and a federal judgeship seemed like the most graceful exit. Yet the White House did not want McLaren's confirmation hearings to provide a forum for critics to question administration antitrust policies—especially since the ITT case was beginning to make news. By floating the inaccurate story that Illinois District Judge Julius Hoffman (the Chicago Seven judge) wanted immediate senior status, the White House managed to rush McLaren's name through the Senate Judiciary Committee without confirmation hearings. In record time, on December 2, 1971, McLaren was nominated and confirmed to the Illinois district bench.

Honorable as a federal judgeship might be, it is often difficult to fathom the politics behind a nomination. It has been suggested, for example, that Herbert J. Stern was nominated to the federal bench because as U.S. attorney in New Jersey he was going after corrupt politicians regardless of their political stripe and consequently stepping on too many toes.

Veteran Washington watcher George Reedy, Lyndon Johnson's former press secretary, says that "all the bitter divisions of a state come out during the selection of a federal judge." As Reedy sees it, internally divided states, such as Wisconsin, California, and Pennsylvania, are the most difficult for presidents to deal with.

The home of Robert LaFollette and Joe McCarthy, Wisconsin is a classic case. Twice in the past 15 years the state's conflicting traditions have clashed over federal judgeships. In September 1963, President Kennedy nominated labor lawyer David Rabinovitz to the federal bench in Wisconsin. Aligned with the liberal wing of the Democratic party since 1942, Rabinovitz had political roots going back to LaFollette's Progressive movement. He was instrumental in securing Wisconsin for John Kennedy in his drive for the 1960 Democratic nomination. This work had won Rabinovitz the favor of Attorney General Robert Kennedy, who pushed for his nomination to a Wisconsin district judgeship.

But Rabinovitz's labor background, particularly his representation of striking workers in the United Auto Workers' six-year strike against Kohler Plumbingware of Kohler, Wisconsin, aroused strong local opposition.

Despite added negative comments from the ABA, President Kennedy stood by Rabinovitz ("I'm for David Rabinovitz all the way"). So did President Johnson, who appointed Rabinovitz on an interim basis minutes before the second session of the 88th Congress began in January 1964. Though Wisconsin's Democratic senators, Gaylord Nelson and William Proxmire, did not push the Rabinovitz nomination, both returned their blue slips. Still, the Senate Judiciary Committee stalled in holding confirmation hearings. So Rabinovitz temporarily sat as a district judge in Wisconsin while his name was once again submitted to Congress.

In August 1964, without hearings, the Senate Judiciary Committee finally polled its members. The result: five to one against Rabinovitz. When Congress adjourned without taking further action on the nomination, Rabinovitz had to step down from the bench—this time for good.

The second Wisconsin controversy surfaced in 1971, when President Nixon nominated Wisconsin Congressman Glenn Davis to a district judgeship. Well-known for his conservatism, Davis is quoted as saying "every redblooded American is for Joe McCarthy," and he once referred to George Wallace as "a socialist." Liberals were not enthused about the choice, and Davis ran into strong opposition from minority groups because of a number of remarks he had made with anti-Semitic overtones. The ABA also came out against him, reportedly because he lacked sufficient trial experience.

The nomination dragged on for almost three years. Finally Senator Nelson revealed that he would oppose Davis, and the congressman withdrew. Interestingly enough, Senator Proxmire, the state's other liberal senator, said he would not stand in Davis' way.

If a senator is on an important congressional committee, his bargaining power with a president increases markedly—and more so if he is chairman. During the Kennedy administration, for instance, Oklahoma Senator Robert Kerr was able to push through Luther Bohanon for the federal bench despite widespread opposition. The reason was simple: As chairman of the Senate Finance Committee, the Oklahoma senator was in a position to block Kennedy's tax legislation.

Similarly, Mississippi Senator James Eastland, longtime chairman of the Senate Judiciary Committee, cleared the way for his law school roommate, W. Harold Cox, to wield a gavel in federal court. Eastland may well have more say than any other senator in judge selection. Besides Cox, four other judges with poor civil liberties records made it to the federal bench in Eastland's fifth circuit during the Kennedy years. While the Carter administration is reportedly about to change all this, Senator Eastland has hardly taken the lead in integrating the federal bench in the South, where not a single black judge sits.

How a senator's political affiliation matches that of the president and the other senator from a state is crucial in determining his influence in federal judge selection. California, for example, had two Democratic senators under a Republican president for the past six years. An informal arrangement was worked out. One of every three nominations to the federal bench in California would go to Democrats—though the nominee could not be too strongly identified with the Democratic party.

Now, with Republican S.I. Hayakawa having taken John Tunney's senate seat and a Democrat in the White House, the matrix has shifted and Democratic Senator Alan Cranston has the most say in California judge selection. But in an effort, according to a Cranston aide, "to remove politics and cronyism" from the selection process, Cranston has helped set up a nine-member commission to screen choices. Four commissioners are appointed by Cranston, three by the California state bar, and two by Senator Hayakawa.

Chaired by San Diego businessman Richard Silberman, the commission has been in existence only three months, has met only a few times, and has yet to choose anyone. But after screening possibilities, it will submit a list of three to five names to both senators, who will in turn designate their personal preferences. The complete report then will go to the White House for the final nomination.

Until President Carter's recent order, judges for the 11 U.S. circuit courts of appeals were usually selected by informal arrangements set up by the states in a given circuit. For the nine-judge second circuit, for example, New York was given six seats, Connecticut two, and Vermont one. In other situations, where the arrangements were less defined, the president had a greater say.

The success of different circuit court arrangements varied with the political situation. In *The Federal Courts as a Political System*, Sheldon Goldman and Thomas Jahnige tell of the time, in 1956, when Indiana's two Republican senators, Homer Capehart and William Jenner, could not agree on Indiana's choice for the U.S. court of appeals for the seventh circuit. Meanwhile, Indiana Congressman Charles Halleck, in high standing with the Eisenhower administration, pushed for his own choice. Both Republican senators considered this move an infringement on their patronage. Halleck was also aided by Robert Grant, a former congressman, who lined up eight Indiana Republican congressmen behind Halleck's choice.

The situation stalemated. And Illinois Senator Everett Dirksen was waiting in the wings with his own candidate. But a compromise was worked out.

Senator Capehart, up for re-election, had the chairman of the Citizens Committee for Capehart appointed to the circuit court opening; the next vacancy on that court went to Halleck's choice; and the nominee of Indiana's other senator, as well as Grant, received district-court appoint-

JUDGES

ments.

A more recent "package" helped former Connecticut Governor Thomas Meskill to the federal bench. First nominated by President Nixon on the eve of his resignation, Meskill was part of a three-judge deal put together by Connecticut's two senators, Republican Lowell Weicker and Democrat Abraham Ribicoff. Since a Republican was in the White House, Weicker got two choices to Ribicoff's one.

The package fit together as follows. Several years earlier, Ribicoff had supported Weicker's choice of Chief U.S. District Judge William Timbers for a circuit court of appeals appointment. Weicker in turn backed Ribicoff's choice of Jon Newman, a former Ribicoff aide and later U.S. attorney, for Timbers' vacant district-court spot. When a circuit-court opening next came up, it was Ribicoff's turn to back Weicker in his choice of Meskill, over the protests of Connecticut liberals and the ABA.

Since 1948, the ABA has consulted the Senate Judiciary Committee on federal judge selection. And beginning with Eisenhower, presidents have established a working relationship with the ABA.

Though it has no statutory authority, the ABA has more say about who will sit on the federal bench than anyone outside government. Its Standing Committee on the Federal Judiciary gives every nominee one of four ratings: "exceptionally well qualified," "well qualified," "qualified," and "not qualified." The standing committee does not like to recommend anyone over 63 and if over 60, the nominee should have a "well qualified" rating. The most common reason for a "not qualified" is lack of trial experience.

Last August, the ABA's governing House of Delegates expanded the standing committee from 12 to 14 members—one from each of the 11 U.S. circuits, a chairman, and the two new members from the large fifth and ninth circuits. All are selected by the ABA president, and no one on the standing committee can serve more than two successive three-year terms.

The standing committee has earned the reputation of representing only the elite of the legal profession. Not until last September was a black appointed to it, and there is not a single woman on it.

The standing committee functions on two levels. On the official level, it rates the nominee based on his or her answers to a lengthy questionnaire and telephone interviews.

But equally important are the informal contacts the president establishes with the ABA. Because it is bad politics to nominate people with low ABA ratings, presidents develop extensive contacts with the standing committee to head off embarrassing nominations. (Joe Dolan recalls that one year, while he was judge-scouting for President Kennedy, he spent 1,600 hours on the telephone with Bernard Segal, then standing committee chairman.)

Contacts between the ABA and the White House can backfire, as *The New Republic*'s John Osborne reported in 1970, following the Haynsworth-Carswell fiasco. Attorney General John Mitchell, trying to prevent future public confrontations over Nixon Supreme Court nominations, entered into an agreement with the ABA. All Supreme Court prospects would be reviewed by the standing committee before the attorney general sent them to the president. But when the ABA "pilloried" a list of nominees, Nixon exclaimed, "Fuck the ABA!" And so went the agreement.

With mixed success, a number of states have tried merit systems of their own for nominating federal judges. Democratic senators Lawton Chiles and Richard Stone of Florida established an independent nine-member judicial nominating commission. Each senator picks three members, as does the Florida bar. The commission publicizes a vacancy, screens and interviews 15 to 20 candidates, and presents a list of five in alphabetical order to the Florida senators. The senators then designate one candidate as their top choice.

Florida Republicans claimed this merit system was nothing more than a "power grab" by two Democratic senators seeking patronage during a Republican presidency. In any event, the effectiveness of the Florida system has been hampered by political infighting and, before January 20, direct dealings between Florida Republicans and President Ford, who did not feel bound by the recommendation of the Florida Democrats.

Illinois has been more successful in its move toward merit selection. Impetus for reform came from the 1,200-member Chicago Council of Lawyers. The council was formed in the late 60s because the Chicago Bar Association was so entrenched in local politics.

Although his influence will diminish considerably with a Democrat in the White House, Republican Senator Charles Percy, the mainstay of Illinois' merit system, brought the state and local bar associations into the selection process. Basically, Percy began choosing his nominees from a list of a half dozen candidates who had been selected and ranked by the bar associations.

But as the McLaren rush nomination indicates, it would be misleading to say politics has been removed from federal judge selection in Illinois. Since Percy became senior senator in 1969, only three of the 21 judicial appointments he has been involved in have been Democrats, and many of the Republicans Percy appointed, including the last two, had close ties to either the Republican party or Percy himself.

The argument has been made that improvement of the quality of our federal judges will require more than a system of merit selection. Salaries have to be raised, it is suggested, so that the best private lawyers will have an incentive for serving on the federal bench—or at least will not be financially penalized for doing so.

The recent rise of circuit court salaries from $44,600 to $57,500 and district court salaries from $42,000 to $54,500 should be seen in this context—though 44 judges who brought suit a year ago against their "compensation" being "diminished during their continuance in office" argued that the raise was only for cost-of-living.

Certainly, most federal judges could make substantially more as private attorneys. But that in itself raises another set of questions. As ACLU National Staff Counsel Richard Larson remarked in a paper prepared before the recent pay hike, "Judicial salaries, which have not been increased since 1969, have been frequently cited by the ABA and by the Justice Department as a deterrent to attracting qualified judicial candidates. If the marketplace is limited to the private corporate bar and to highly paid United States attorneys, that claim may have some merit. If the marketplace were expanded to include the public bar, however, the claim would be false. Many of the best lawyers in our country, practicing with civil rights and civil liberties organizations or teaching in our law schools, would receive substantial salary increases upon appointment to the federal judiciary."

The relationship between federal judge selection and money is a curious one, since most judges are not really in it for the money. Nor, for that matter, is the federal bench simply an outpost for Wall Street. Although a corporate lawyer is more likely to make it to the federal bench than a poverty lawyer, a study by Professor Sheldon Goldman indicates that a prosecutorial background might well be the outstanding characteristic of federal judges. Nearly half of the judgeships Goldman examined during the Johnson and Nixon presidencies went to onetime prosecutors.

But any attempt to diversify the background of federal judges, or to improve their quality, might become a futile exercise as long as political patronage continues to skew selections. President Carter has pointed in the right direction. But much more must be done, if judge selection is to be made responsive to the democratic process. □

James Goodman is the Washington, D.C., representative of the Committee for Public Justice. The views expressed in this article are not necessarily those of the committee.

1. Compare the old plan and the Carter plan for selecting federal judges.

2. How did Lyndon Johnson, Gerald Ford, and Richard Nixon use their power to appoint federal judges?

1. Under the old plan the U.S. Senator of the President's party from the state in which a vacancy on the federal bench occurs is consulted by the President and his or her recommendation is followed. Under the norms of Senatorial courtesy, the Senators will not vote to confirm a federal judge if the Senator from that state does not support the appointment.

   Under Carter's plan, citizen panels around the country, appointed by the President, recommend 5 candidates to fill a vacancy. The President then _may_ select one of these candidates and submit a nomination to the Senate. Note that the Senate norm of refusing to approve a nominee not supported by the Senator from the affected state is _not_ changed under the new system.

2. Johnson, as majority leader in the Senate, blocked Eisenhower's appointments until Eisenhower agreed to appoint Johnson's choice for a Texas vacancy.

   Mr. Nixon's Justice Department refused to appoint a number of people due to their outspoken anti-war positions.

   Mr. Ford didn't block appointments; rather he used them to strengthen his position. Ford nominated a member of John Connally's Texas law firm and Connally apparently 'reciprocated' by choosing to back Ford over Reagan in the 1976 Presidential race.

ECONOMICS AND LAW

An interdisciplinary view of law's role in society would not be complete without the perspective of the economist. The study of economics involves an examination of "how men and society choose, with or without the use of money, to employ scarce productive resources to produce various commodities over time and distribute them for consumption. . ." (Samuelson, 1966, p. 5). Economic theory begins with the assumption that people seek to rationally maximize their self-interests. Building upon that assumption, economists examine the behavior of this hypothetical, rational, 'economic person' under varying economic conditions and attempt to predict her/his behavior.

A basic proposition can be derived from this assumption that people alter their behavior in order to further their self interests in light of changing circumstances. A central economic axiom is that there is "an inverse relation between price charged and quantity demanded" (Posner, 1977, p. 4). In other words, as the cost of a desired good goes up, rational people will buy less of it. They will try to achieve their goals by other means or by purchasing alternative goods. Applied to the legal problems of crime and punishment, such a proposition suggests that an increase in the 'cost' of criminal conduct (more severe or certain punishment) will lead rational people to 'demand' less of that conduct. Perhaps they will seek alternative 'goods', i.e., conduct themselves differently so as to avoid the 'high price' to be paid for misconduct.

The application of some economic concepts to the law is the subject of the excerpted reading by Richard Posner which follows. Before you read that excerpt, however, think about these examples of economic approaches to law.

A. <u>Criminal Law</u>. Criminal law consists of prohibitions against certain types of conduct and punishments to be applied to violators. "The function of criminal law, viewed from an economic standpoint, is to impose additional costs on unlawful conduct where the conventional

damages remedy alone would be insufficient to limit
that conduct to the efficient level" (Posner, 1977,
p. 614). In other words, criminal law is interpreted
by the economist as establishing a 'price' which is
to be 'paid' by those 'consumers' who wish to 'purchase'
(engage in) the 'good' (conduct). Keep in mind, however,
that the cost of the punishment must also be considered
from an economic perspective. Therefore, "because
criminal sanctions are costly, it is wasteful to employ
them where they will not affect the level of unlawful
conduct" (Posner, 1977, p. 164).

B. Free Speech. The constitution prohibits the government
from abridging the right of free speech. To an economist,
this can be translated into "government may not limit
competition in ideas" (Posner, 1977, p. 541). Thus, if
the best way to determine the value of a product is to
rely on the marketplace forces of supply and demand, the
best way to determine the value of an idea is to rely
on the marketplace forces of supply and demand!

C. Negligent Torts. Negligent conduct or conduct which creates
an unreasonable risk of harm to others, can result in
legal liability if a person's negligent act does in fact
cause harm to another. From the economic perspective,
the precautions which should have been taken to avoid
the harm are seen as the "cost of avoiding the accident"
(Posner, 1977, p. 122). Depending on the likelihood that
such an accident might occur, the degree of harm such an
accident could be expected to cause, and the cost of taking
the necessary precautions, we decide whether or not a
particular defendant's conduct constitutes negligence.
This test of negligence is basically economic in nature.

Every area of law has been subjected to a similar economic interpretation.
These examples and the excerpt which you will read next should give you a
general notion of the economic perspective on law.

1. What is the basic assumption which economics makes about the nature of people?

2. What economic axiom can be derived from this assumption about the nature of people?

3. How can these basic economic concepts be applied to:

   A. Criminal Law

   B. Free Speech

   C. Negligent Torts

1. Economics is based upon the assumption that the 'economic person' will act rationally to maximize her/his self-interest. It is logical, therefore, to expect people to modify their behavior as circumstances are altered. Only by making different choices in different economic situations can people continue to maximize their self-interest.

2. Given the existence of the 'economic person' it is possible to argue that increases in the cost of desired goods will result in decreases in the demand for such goods. In other words, the rational 'economic person', faced with increased costs, will choose other less expensive goods, forego the goods altogether, or be satisfied with fewer of the same goods.

3. a. In essence, punishment or threat of punishment can be viewed as a 'cost' which the 'economic person' will take into account in deciding whether or not to 'purchase' prohibited behavior.

    b. The marketplace determines the value of goods; the marketplace might similarly be said to be the best way to determine the value of ideas.

    c. We hold a person liable for harm negligently caused to another when the cost of preventing that harm would not have been an excessive one. We then feel justified in saying that the price of prevention should have been paid.

Reading #2

EXCERPTS FROM:

THE ECONOMIC APPROACH TO LAW

II.

Although the product of only a few man-years, the "new" law and economics literature is already too rich and complex to be summarized adequately in the compass of this article.[21] I shall content myself with a few words on what it means to apply economics to law and indicate briefly the major findings that are emerging from current and recent studies.

The basis of an economic approach to law is the assumption that the people involved with the legal system act as rational maximizers of their satisfactions. Suppose the question is asked, when will parties to a legal dispute settle rather than litigate? Since this choice involves uncertainty—the outcome of the litigation is not known for sure in advance—the relevant body of economic theory is that which analyzes decision-making by rational maximizers under conditions of uncertainty. If we are willing to assume, at least provisionally, that litigants behave rationally, then this well-developed branch of economic theory[22] can be applied in straightforward fashion to the litigation context to yield predictions with respect to the decision to litigate or settle;

we discover, for example, that litigation should be more frequent the greater the stakes in the dispute or the uncertainty of the outcome. These predictions can be, and have been, compared with the actual behavior of litigants in the real world. The comparisons indicate that the economic model is indeed a fruitful one as applied to litigation behavior,[23] *i.e.*, it enables us to explain the actual behavior we observe.

It may be argued that if economic theory only involves exploring the implications of assuming that people behave rationally, then lawyers can apply the theory perfectly well without the help of specialists. In this view, the economic approach to law just supplies a novel and confusing vocabulary in which to describe the familiar analytical activities of the lawyer. There is indeed a good deal of implicit economic analysis in legal thought—a point to which I shall return—and a good deal of economic theory does consist of elegantly formalizing the obvious and the trivial. But it is not true that all of the useful parts of economic theory are intuitively obvious to the intelligent lawyer. The logic of rational maximization is subtle, frequently complex, and very often counterintuitive.[24] That is why the level of public discussion of economic policy is so low, and why the application of economics to law is more than the translation of the conventional wisdom of academic lawyers into a different jargon.

17. *See, e.g.*, G. Becker, The Economics of Discrimination (2d ed. 1971); Becker, *Crime and Punishment: An Economic Approach*, 76 J. Pol. Econ. 169 (1968); and his forthcoming collection of essays, The Economic Approach to Human Behavior. The scrupulous historian of economic thought would note, as has Becker himself, his debt to Bentham. *See* note 55 *infra*; *cf.* note 10 *supra*.

18. *E.g.*, Ehrlich, *The Deterrent Effect of Capital Punishment: A Matter of Life and Death* (forthcoming in Am. Econ. Rev.); Ehrlich, *The Deterrent Effect of Criminal Law Enforcement*, 1 J. Legal Stud. 259 (1972).

19. *E.g.*, Landes, *Legality and Reality: Some Evidence on Criminal Procedure*, 3 J. Legal Stud. 287 (1974).

20. Komesar, *Toward a General Theory of Personal Injury Loss*, 3 J. Legal Stud. 457 (1974).

21. The literature is summarized in R. Posner, *supra* note 16.

22. *See* G. Becker, Economic Theory 57-66 (1971).

23. *See, e.g.*, Landes, *An Economic Analysis of the Courts*, 14 J. Law & Econ. 61 (1971).

24. Sam Peltzman's recent study of the effects of automobile safety regulations provides a good example. Peltzman, *The Regulation of Automobile Safety* (forthcoming in J. Pol. Econ.). Intuitively, it seems obvious that a technically sound and reasonably well-enforced seat-belt requirement would reduce the number of deaths and injuries from automobile accidents. But as Peltzman shows, this intuition is unsound. By increasing the driver's safety, the seat belt, if used, reduces the cost of fast driving, which should, according to economic theory, lead to an increase in driving speed and therefore in the number of accidents, possibly offsetting the beneficial effect of the seat-belt requirement in reducing injuries to drivers and other vehicle occupants. In particular, there should be a sharp increase in pedestrian injuries, since their number will increase with faster driving and there is no offsetting effect from seat-belt protection. Peltzman's study found, as his analysis predicted, a relative increase in pedestrian injuries and in automobile deaths and injuries due to the seat-belt requirement. The economic theory that underlies his study is straightforward, but it is unlikely that a noneconomist would have reasoned to a similar conclusion.

As another example, while the implicitly economic proposition, "punishment deters," is intuitive, another important proposition derived from the economic model of crime and punishment is not: a 1% increase in the probability of apprehension for murder will have a greater deterrent effect than a 1% increase in the conditional probability of conviction given apprehension, which in turn will have a greater deterrent effect than a 1% increase in the probability of execution given conviction. *See* Ehrlich, *The Deterrent Effect of Capital Punishment: A Matter of Life and Death* (forthcoming in Am. Econ. Rev.).

than explicit) with promoting economic efficiency.[28] The rules assigning property rights and determining liability, the procedures for resolving legal disputes, the constraints imposed on law enforcers, methods of computing damages and determining the availability of injunctive relief—these and other important elements of the legal system can best be understood as attempts, though rarely acknowledged as such, to promote an efficient allocation of resources.[29] The idea that the logic of the law is really economics is, of course, repulsive to many academic lawyers, who see in it an attempt by practitioners of an alien discipline to wrest their field from them. Yet the positive economic analysis of legal institutions is one of the most promising as well as most controversial branches of the new law and economics. It seeks to define and illuminate the basic character of the legal system, and it has made at least some progress toward that ambitious goal. One byproduct of this research that has considerable pedagogical importance has been the assignment of precise economic explanations to a number of fundamental legal concepts that had previously puzzled students and their professors, such as "assumption of risk,"[30] "pain and suffering" as a category of tort damages,[31] contract damages for loss of expectation,[32] plea bargaining,[33] and the choice between damages and injunctive relief.[34]

A third important finding in the law and economics literature is that economic analysis can be helpful in designing reforms of the legal system. Obviously there is some tension between this finding and the

Now to some of the major findings of the "new" law and economics research. The first is that the participants in the legal process indeed behave as if they were rational maximizers:[25] criminals, contracting parties, automobile drivers, prosecutors, and others subject to legal constraints or involved in legal proceedings act in their relation to the legal system as intelligent (not omniscient) maximizers of their satisfactions. Like ordinary consumers, they economize by buying less of a good or commodity when its price rises and more when it falls. To be sure, the "good" and the "price" in the economic analysis of law are often unconventional, which is perhaps why it took so long for economists to claim the law as a part of economics. The "good" might be crimes to a criminal or trials to an aggrieved plaintiff, and the "price" might be a term of imprisonment discounted by the probability of conviction, or a court queue. But though the goods and prices may be somewhat unusual, and the purchasers may not fit one's preconceived idea of "economic man," there is a growing, and cumulatively rather persuasive, body of evidence supporting the proposition that the usual economic relations continue to hold in the formally noneconomic markets of the legal system. For example, it has been found that an increase in the expected punishment costs of crime—through an increase either in the severity of punishment or in the probability of its being imposed—will reduce the amount of crime[26] and that a decrease in the trial queue will increase the number of trials,[27] all in accordance with the predictions of economic analysis.

In the type of research just described, the legal system is treated as a given and the question studied is how individuals or firms involved in the system react to the incentives that it imparts. A second important finding emerging from the recent law and economics research is that the legal system itself—its doctrines, procedures, and institutions—has been strongly influenced by a concern (more often implicit

28. This insight is, of course, not entirely novel. *See, e.g.,* J. HURST, LAW AND SOCIAL PROCESS IN UNITED STATES HISTORY 4 (1972). What is novel is the rigor and persistence with which the insight is being applied in the recent literature.

29. The literature through mid-1973 is summarized in R. POSNER, *An Economic Analysis of Legal Rulemaking, supra* note 16. For some recent additions to the literature, see Ehrlich & Posner, *An Economic Analysis of Legal Rulemaking,* 3 J. LEGAL STUD. 257 (1974), and Landes & Posner, *supra* note 8. This literature is to be sharply distinguished from an older body of writings (summarized in 1 R. POUND, JURISPRUDENCE 199, 225, 228-31 (1959)) that argued that the rules of law were designed to promote the welfare of a particular economic class. *See, e.g.,* Bohlen, *The Rule in Rylands v. Fletcher,* 59 U. PA. L. REV. 298, 318-19 (1911). For an effective critique of that approach, see Pound, *The Economic Interpretation and the Law of Torts,* 53 HARV. L. REV. 365 (1940). *See also* R. POSNER, *supra* note 16, at 100-02.

30. *See* R. POSNER, *supra* note 16, at 72-73.

31. *See* Komesar, *supra* note 20.

32. *See* Barton, *The Economic Basis of Damages for Breach of Contract,* 1 J. LEGAL STUD. 277 (1972).

33. *See* Landes, *supra* note 23.

34. *See* Calabresi & Melamed, *Property Rules, Liability Rules, and Inalienability: One View of the Cathedral,* 85 HARV. L. REV. 1089 (1972); Michelman, *supra* note 12,

25. I say "as if" instead of "as" to indicate that the economist is not interested in the question whether and in what sense people may be said to be "rational." It is enough for purposes of economic analysis that the assumption of rationality has greater explanatory power than alternative assumptions. On the realism of economic assumptions, see M. FRIEDMAN, *The Methodology of Positive Economics,* in ESSAYS IN POSITIVE ECONOMICS 3 (1953).

26. *See* Tullock, *Does Punishment Deter Crime?,* PUB. INTEREST, Summer 1974, at 103 (summary of recent studies).

27. *See* Landes, *supra* note 23. Landes also finds that the number of trials is increased by an increase either in the amount of subsidization of legal services or in the stakes involved in the dispute, again as predicted by economic analysis.

while statistical studies of the legal system have ever been conducted by noneconomists. But the number of such studies is small, and in only a few years economists have produced a body of statistical studies that in number weighted by quality already, I believe, overshadows the non-economic quantitative work.[37]

Several reasons may be suggested for the greater success of the economists in studying the legal system quantitatively. First, economists tend to be better trained in modern methods of quantitative analysis than other social scientists, let alone lawyers. A second point, related but distinct, is that economists appear to be more resourceful in discovering and using existing statistics on the legal system, and also more sensitive to the qualitative problems involved in drawing inferences from statistical data. These are perhaps simply aspects of being better trained, but they are distinct from simply possessing more powerful mathematical techniques.

I shall illustrate these points with two celebrated examples of non-economic quantitative research on the legal system. One is the study by the University of Chicago Jury Project on the use of the jury in criminal cases.[38] Rather than attempt to mine the considerable existing data on the use of the criminal jury, the researchers conducted an elaborate mail survey to generate fresh data. Unfortunately, but typically, only a small fraction of the judges to whom the survey was mailed responded. No effort was made to establish the reasons for judges' not responding, and as a result there is no basis for a conclusion that the survey results are representative of the views of American judges. Moreover, the key question in the survey was a hypothetical one—how would the judge have decided the case if he, rather than the jury, had been the trier of fact—and the reliability of answers given to such questions is open to serious doubt.

My second example is Thorsten Sellin's study of the deterrent effect of capital punishment,[39] which was cited by a Supreme Court

previous one. Were the legal system systematically and effectively designed to maximize economic efficiency, the role of normative economic analysis would be very small. In fact what one observes is areas of the law that seem to have a powerful and consistent economic logic—for example, most common-law fields—and others that seem quite perverse from an economic standpoint—in particular, many statutory fields. Some effort has been made to explain what appears to be a systematic difference in this regard between judge-made and statutory law by analyzing the different constraints of the judicial and legislative processes.[35] This work is part of a larger effort to explain—in economic terms, of course—the behavior of political institutions.[36] But this is not a well developed area of law and economics, and many anomalies remain. For example, while civil procedure reveals many economizing features, the failure to require that the losing party to a lawsuit reimburse the winner for his litigation expenses appears to be highly inefficient, and no economic explanation for this settled feature of American procedure has been suggested or is apparent. The tendency of government to use queueing rather than pricing to ration access to the courts and to other government services is another puzzle, since pricing is a cheaper method of rationing. So long as there remain important areas of the legal system that are not organized in accordance with the requirements of efficiency, the economist can play an important role in suggesting changes designed to increase the efficiency of the system. Of course, it is not for the economist, *qua* economist, to say whether efficiency should override other values in the event of a conflict.

A fourth important finding in the law and economics literature is that the quantitative study of the legal system is fruitful. It may seem odd to ascribe such a finding to the economic approach to law. Surely, it will be argued, quantitative analysis of the legal system long predates the economists' interest in the system, and the methods of statistical research are independent of the theories that generate the hypotheses to be tested by those methods. These points are correct but misleading. Economists have raised the level of quantitative research in the legal system very markedly, to the point where it is now plain, as it was not previously, that the statistical study of legal institutions has much to contribute to our knowledge. This is not to say that no worth-

37. *See, e.g.*, Ehrlich, *supra* note 18; Ehrlich, *Participation in Illegitimate Activities: A Theoretical and Empirical Investigation*, 81 J. Pol. Econ. 521 (1973); Komesar, *A Theoretical and Empirical Analysis of Victims of Crime*, 2 J. Legal Stud. 301 (1973); Landes, *supra* notes 19 & 23; Landes, *The Economics of Fair Employment Laws*, 76 J. Pol. Econ. 507 (1968); Peltzman, *supra* note 24; Peltzman, *An Evaluation of Consumer Protection Legislation: The 1962 Drug Amendments*, 81 J. Pol. Econ. 1049 (1973).
38. H. Kalven, Jr. & H. Zeisel, The American Jury (1966) (no significant differences in fact-finding were found between judges and juries).
39. T. Sellin, The Death Penalty: A Report for the Model Penal Code

35. *See* R. Posner, *supra* note 16, at 327-32.
36. *See, e.g.*, Stigler, *supra* note 8.

Justice in *Furman v. Georgia*[40] for the proposition that capital punishment has no incremental deterrent effect.[41] The heart of Sellin's study was a series of comparisons of murder rates in groups of contiguous states, one of which had abolished the death penalty while the other had not. He found that the murder rate was no lower in the states that retained the death penalty and concluded that the death penalty does not deter murder. Sellin's procedure, however, was fatally flawed by his failure to hold constant other factors besides punishment that might influence the murder rate. Only if the death penalty is the only determinant of the murder rate, or if the other determinants are identical in states having different execution rates, would it be proper to infer from Sellin's evidence that the death penalty had no deterrent effect. Sellin was at least dimly aware of this problem: this was what made him compare murder and execution rates in contiguous states. But relying on contiguity to hold the other relevant variables constant is inadequate. There is no reason to expect that states, because they happen to have a common border, are identical in all respects relevant to the murder rate save the use of capital punishment. Suppose, for example, that the arrest and conviction rate for murder was higher in a state which had abolished capital punishment than in a state that retained the death penalty, so that while a convicted murderer was punished less severely in the former state, the chances of his escaping punishment were lower than in the neighboring retentionist state. The net expected punishment cost for murder might be higher in the former state, and, if so, this would explain the lower murder rate there in terms wholly consistent with the proposition that the independent deterrent effect of capital punishment—holding probability of conviction and all other relevant variables constant—is positive.[42]

Part of Sellin's problem, perhaps, was that he had no theory as to why people commit murders or other crimes. This brings me to the third reason why economists have an advantage in quantitative research: it is very difficult to conduct such research without a theoretical framework. If one has no notion as to why people commit crimes, it is very difficult to know what factors to hold constant in order to determine the independent significance of the test variable (punishment or whatever). The economist, viewing the decision to participate in criminal activity as a standard problem in occupational choice,[3] has a clear a priori idea of what factors influence the rate of criminal participation and should therefore be included in a model of criminal activity. The empirical researcher who does not proceed from theory to the construction of a model identifying relevant variables has great trouble measuring the independent significance of the variable in which he is interested.

PROJECT OF THE AM. LAW INST. (1959). It was presumably Sellin's work that led my distinguished colleague Norval Morris to conclude that "the existence or nonexistence of capital punishment is irrelevant to the murder, or attempted murder, rate. This is as well established as any other proposition in social science." N. MORRIS & G. HAWKINS, THE HONEST POLITICIAN'S GUIDE TO CRIME CONTROL 75-76 (1970). For empirical evidence to the contrary, see Ehrlich, *supra* note 18. A full critique of the Sellin study may be found in a forthcoming paper by Professor Ehrlich which presents additional findings from his study of capital punishment.

40. 408 U.S. 238 (1972).

41. *Id.* at 348-53, 373-74 (Marshall, J., concurring). Justice Marshall's opinion was one of several concurring in the judgment invalidating existing death-penalty statutes; no opinion (other than the brief *per curiam* opinion announcing the judgment of the court) commanded the support of a majority of the Justices.

42. Sellin also conducted some before-and-after studies of murder rates in states that had abolished the death penalty. Finding no increase in the murder rate in these states, he again concluded that the death penalty had no deterrent effect. But this pro-

1. How does economic theory help us to predict which parties will settle their disputes out of court and which will proceed to a trial?

2. Refer to footnote 24 and state why economic theory might help us to see a relationship which is non-obvious?

3. List the four major conclusions which emerge from the economic approach to law.

4. What research flaws are illustrated in the legal research of non-economists?

1. Since economic theory indicates that the <u>stakes</u> and the <u>uncertainty</u> are factors which affect a person's choices, Posner asserts that "litigation should be more frequent the greater the stakes in the dispute or the uncertainty of the outcome"

2. The seemingly obvious relationship between a requirement that all drivers wear seatbelts and a decline in the number of injuries or deaths in automobile accidents turns out to be inaccurate. The economic analysis suggests that the seat belt requirement, by increasing driver safety, "reduces the cost of fast driving, which should, according to economic theory, lead to an increase in driving speed and therefore in the number of accidents"

3. a. "Participants in the legal process indeed behave as if they were rational maximizers"

   b. "[T]he legal system itself. . .has been strongly influenced by a concern. . .with promoting economic efficiency"

   c. "[E]conomic analysis can be helpful in designing reforms of the legal system"

   d. "[T]he quantitative study of the legal system is fruitful"

4. NOTE: The Chicago Jury Project involved an attempt to compare the decisions of judges and juries by asking trial judges in jury cases to make decisions of guilt of innocence before the actual decisions were reached by the juries. Posner argues that an economist, being more sophisticated in terms of methodology, would have examined the question of why some judges failed to respond in order to assess the representativeness of the responses. I imagine that many other social scientists might well take issue with Posner's claim for the superior skills of economists!

   The Sellin study of capital punishment's effect on murder rates in contiguous states is faulted for failing to deal with the fact that <u>other factors</u>, in addition to the presence or absence of capital punishment, might have explained the results reported by Sellin.

THE ANTHROPOLOGICAL STUDY OF LAW

Laura Nader

Editor's Note

Oliver Wendall Homes, Jr. wrote in 1899, that, "If your subject is law, the roads are plain to anthropology," since "it is perfectly proper to regard and study the law simply as a great anthropological document" (p. 443). Cultural anthropology generally focuses on the distinctive cultural patterns of different socieities. It tends, more so than sociology and political science, to view society as an intergrated whole, rather than as a collectio of subsystems, such as law, politics, social structure, etc. Anthropology strives to avoid ethnocentricity (the belief that one's own cultural patterns are superior) and, therefore, seeks to comparatively examine cultural patterns in simple and complex society alike, making no judgment in favor of or opposed to any particular cultural pattern.

Legal anthropologist E. Adamson Hoebel (1958) argues that law is that part of culture which performs the following functions:

1. to identify acceptable lines of behavior for inclusion in the culture and to penalize contradictory behavior, so as to maintain at least minimal integration between the activities of individuals and groups within society;

2. to allocate authority and to determine who may legitimately apply force to maintain the legal norms;

3. to settle trouble cases as they arise; and

4. to re-define relationships as the conditions of life change, so as to keep the culture adapable. (p. 484)

This anthropological conceptualization of the functions of law corresponds closely with the materials in Units 4, 5, and 6. "Law and Dispute Settlement" deals with settling trouble cases, "Law and Social Control" explores how law defines acceptable lines of behavior and authorizes the authority to use force to maintain these norms, and "Law as an Instrument of Social Change" examines how law contributes to changing values and thus, keeps the culture adapable.

An excerpt from Laura Nader's article, "The Anthropological study of Law" which follows, outlines for you some dimensions of the field of legal anthropology. The general goal of legal anthrology has been "to identify the kinds of societies in which certain legal constitutions appear, and to examine the kinds of legal procedures, norms, principles, and rules, and concepts that are found under given social conditions" (Falk, 1969, p. 294). Nader's article summarizes a number of studies of law in different cultural settings, discusses the functions of law, and raises questions about the difficulties of comparing the role of law in different types of cultural contexts and of generalizing about legal phenomena cross-culturally. In addition, she outlines the basic assumptions of legal anthropologists and the type of questions which ought to be studied in the future.

PRESENT TRENDS AND NEW DIRECTIONS

During the past two decades the major contributions to the ethnography of law have been descriptive, functional analyses of systems both isolated and in contact situations. The tendency has been to treat the legal system as an institution virtually independent and isolated from other institutions in society, except insofar as 'society' is gleaned from the law materials. This last tendency is especially evident where courts are present, less so where the lack of court institutions virtually forces the anthropologist to elicit the whole life history of the case. Furthermore, we have not been interested in historical developments although the history of our civilization is rich in data (cf. Rheinstein 1963 and H. Kay in this volume). Nor have we pursued to any great extent the examination of hypotheses—either in the manner which Evans-Pritchard (1963) refers to as illustrative (the citing of examples in support of a thesis arrived at deductively), or by cross-cultural statistical studies, or by means of intensive controlled comparison. Our work for the most part has not been comparative.

If we are to develop a true ethnography of law the angle of vision of the ethnographer needs to be broadened in order to include descriptions that would explicate law as part of a many-threaded fabric. Furthermore we should look at both the latent and the manifest functions of the law. We need to understand what the generally agreed upon functions of the law are, as well as to note its other functions which may or may not be recognized in a society. Malinowski observed years ago, "An ethnographer who sets out to study only religion, or only technology, or only social organization cuts out an artificial field for inquiry, and he will be seriously handicapped in his work" (1922:11). A legal system reflects many facets of a society; because of this an ethnographic study of law is more than a study of judicial institutions. Law and politics are sometimes discussed together in anthropology—what about other aspects of social life that may be relevant to the "law," such an economics, language, ecology, or stratification and rank systems?

As a working frame I would like to reiterate what others have said before— namely that (1) empirical studies of law should be set in the general context of social control (although of course not equated with social control); (2) we should consider the possibility that the range of functions of a legal system may

this is as true of anthropologists as of other social scientists. Aubert (1963:17) states the essence of these functions: "Law seems to have two distinct although interrelated functions: to create conformity with norms, and to settle conflicts."

The oral tradition of the practicing American bar is full of examples which lead us to believe that the law performs many other functions. Every lawyer and perhaps most citizens could cite examples: A businessman may bring a competitor to court with the express purpose of ruining his credit rating. During political campaigns opposing candidates have accused one another of innumerable legal wrongs, usually ending with the filing of a lawsuit for libel, with the object of winning elections. Wives may demand or even initiate divorce actions with little intention of actually obtaining a divorce but rather to frighten the husbands into behavior more acceptable to them. Or an ex-husband may request a change of child custody to harass an ex-wife. Similarly arbitrary enforcement of vagrancy laws or Sunday "blue laws" provides an avenue by which "the law" may harass a less than ideal citizen. Selective application of obscenity laws may perform the function of witchcraft hunts in other societies.

Riesman (1954:448–449) brings two interesting novels to our attention: James West's *Plainville U.S.A.* and James Gould Cozzens' *The Just and the Unjust*. These novels provide examples of the trial as both a cohesive and divisive force for small towns, as in West's case of the garagekeeper and the undertaker—a trial that caused a factional split in town. Or, Riesman states, the trial may serve as a divisive point "in terms of a moral turning point, such as . . . the Western world experienced in the trial of Sacco and Vanzetti." A familiar example of the political function of judgeships is also quoted by Riesman (1954:442): "In the big cities . . . judgeships become part of the system of ethnic brokerage by which the party machines keep the urban peace— the rise of the Italian judge is a recent illustration." Riesman also comments on the entertainment value of the law as well as its socialization functions.

Thurmond Arnold (1935) adumbrates some of the latent functions of the law. He comments on the drama of the court as partly a socialization or enculturation agency—a place where values are tested, changed, or consolidated, and further notes that these may be "legal" values or other such as religious values. (Cf. Hoebel's paper in this volume as an example.) His observations on the ritual value of the trial should be of interest to anthropologists.

Ethnographic examples from other societies are not easy to locate in the literature although they are probably well known to most fieldworkers. In this volume Cohn states:

> The use of the courts for settlement of local disputes seems in most villages to be almost a minor one. In Senapur, courts were, and are, used as an arena in the competition for social status, political and economic dominance in the village. Cases are brought to court to harass one's opponents, as a punishment, as a form of land speculation and profit making, to satisfy insulted pride, and to maintain local political dominance over one's followers. The litigants do not expect a settlement that will end the dispute to eventuate from recourse to the state courts.

vary cross-culturally; and (3) we should aim at both empirical and explanatory generalizations.

It has often been stated that legal systems constitute only a part of a larger system of social control, and that sometimes the social control functions of law can be understood only when viewed as part of the larger system. Schneider (1957) provides us with one example of the way in which the legal and supernatural systems complement each other in the differential handling of fratricide and patricide on Yap. Nader and Metzger (1963) describe the procedures for handling husband-wife conflict in the court and family systems of two Mexican villages where an important variable is the amount of authority allocated to the court and kinship groups. However, in most of the recent monographs, Gulliver (1963) being a major exception, the law has been treated as isolated from other social control systems, and indeed in some monographs it has been left for the reader to place the law in its socio-cultural context. This is a criticism that Malinowski (1942:1253) leveled at Llewellyn and Hoebel as authors of *The Cheyenne Way*. It is also a criticism that can legitimately be made of most of the law monographs produced since *The Cheyenne Way*.

Furthermore it is not always clear whether the social control functions of law are to "clean up social messes" (Llewellyn and Hoebel 1941), or to maintain order (Malinowski 1942), although how the law handles the breach is usually clearer than how in fact it serves to maintain order. Law may settle conflicts by a variety of means (adjudication, mediation, arbitration, etc.); it may perform solely a punitive function; it may prevent or deter breaches of the law; it may maintain order in the fields of law, politics, and economics—or it may accomplish *all* these tasks. It is not always clear which of these functions the law in a particular society is intent upon performing. Our elaboration of these tasks is not always as precise as we would wish if we are to use ethnographic data for comparative ends, or even if we are to explore the relations between means and ends. In this context I would like to call attention to Aubert's example (1963:19) of the function of legislative formulations. In his discussion of the Norwegian housemaid law he noted that "the language of the law is shaped more profoundly by the function of solving conflicts than by the function of influencing the legally naive"; that is, it was directed at the legal professional rather than at informing the lay citizen of what the law was.

While we have assumed that there was a probable cross-cultural difference in the content and form of a legal system, we have at the same time ignored the variety of different functions a legal system may have. This is in spite of the fact that Riesman (1954:445) credits anthropologists with thinking otherwise:

> The anthropologist is not likely to harbor the naive assumption that the law, or any other institution, serves only a single function—say, that of social control—and that any other functions which in fact it serves are excrescences or "contradictions." The concept of ambivalence is part of his equipment; he tends to search for latent functions, transcending the ostensible.

The truth of the matter is, however, that (anecdotal exceptions to one side) the functions of law have generally been assumed to be universally the same, and

And as Cohn notes these were 'functions' of the court that the British failed to understand; the British system was in many ways at odds with traditional Indian procedures.

Beals (1955:91) reports: "After 1920, a number of individuals in Namhali used the [urban] law courts to acquire land or to bring about the economic ruin of their enemies." The law may function to bring about a more equitable distribution of resources or alternatively it may function to maintain an unequal distribution of power. Berreman (1963:270) gives an example of a typically false legal charge.

A villager's prosperity was envied by his caste-fellows. They had once tried unsuccessfully to get some of his land by bribing the government records officer to testify that he had acquired the land illegally. Failing in this, they obtained revenge by hiding liquor in his house and calling the police to say that he was dealing in illicit liquor.

Along these same lines Bailey (1958:106) mentions various measures taken by the village (i.e. the high castes) to insure that the village servants (i.e. the low castes) do not become too rich:

This particularly applies to the washerman since his eldest son has been working. He has been fined 2 or 3 times for letting his buffaloes stray into other men's gardens, and the fine has been demanded in cash while other offenders are penalized only by admonition or a demand for a small amount of paddy in compensation.

When a village servant shows signs of getting a lot of money, the village seems to resent this and penalizes him. In the dispute that follows, the victory goes always to the village, since the specialist castes are not organized to protect their members against these attacks.

Different sorts of models are brought to our attention by others. In discussing the therapeutic function of Kpelle moots, Gibbs (1963:6) notes: "Moot procedures are therapeutic in that, like psychotherapy, they re-educate their parties through a type of social learning brought about in a specifically structured interpersonal setting." Gluckman (1955a) illustrates the potential socializing effects of the judicial process. Armstrong (1954) considers the case of a Nigerian inquest into the death of a prominent politician. The inquest is shown to serve various functions in Senne Province: it enforces respect for the elders forming the council of the conclave, allows leaders to enhance their social position, serves to place the blame for the death, repair relationships among the living, excite public spectacle, and so on. Nader (n.d.) illustrates the use of Zapotec courts to increase the revenue of the town treasury.

The court sees itself as an institution which protects community interests at all times and places. Therefore they reason, the court may readily look for redress in situations where a party has not complained. . . . There are also practical considerations which have molded this court initiative, for in Talea laws governing personal behavior are being redefined with economic gain in mind. During one of my field stays when the Talean treasury needed replenishing for the big fiesta of the year, the president ruled that any individual echando un grito would be fined five pesos for each grito. Earlier in this century when the new municipio was still being built the presidente would send a regidor out on market day with money especially destined to get visiting Rincóneros drunk. The court would then jail them for drunkenness and the following day would fine them a day or two labor on the municipal building. Although Talean citizens easily discuss the economic motives of the court, the court officials insist that new laws are being created to impress the neighboring towns, as well as the citizens of Talea, with peace and orderliness.

That law courts should be used for purposes other than the maintenance of peace and order is not unique with the Talean Zapotec. Throughout the development of the British common law, the King's court was well known for defining property laws with economic gain in mind.

Colson's materials however, illustrate another way in which the law may be used for economic gain:

They [court councillors] claim that if a man brings his wife to court a third time on an adultery charge they will refuse to grant damages and will instead inform the husband that his only recourse is to divorce his wife and get back his bridewealth, that the woman is now making a business of adultery and is a professional woman of the road [1958:170].

Fathers refuse to listen to a suitor until after an elopement, for they realize that they can then collect both elopement damages and bride-wealth. They also disregard the legal limitations on elopement damages, and their demands for damages have steadily increased. The lover, if he wishes, can take the matter to court and refuse to pay more than the legal amount. If he does this, the girl's father will refuse to listen to his suit. He will then have to elope with another girl, and again pay elopement damages before he can hope to pay bridewealth and receive his bride [1960:112].

In terms of conflict theory the function of the breach varies. Disputes may serve to solidify groups or individuals in a society (Beidelman 1959:66, Nader 1965b); they may prevent the formation of political factions (Glasse 1959), or serve to intensify disharmony and cause the development of new factions (Lewis 1958:148, Beidelman 1959:66). And finally Frake (1963:221) reports on a Philippine group:

Litigation in Lipay, however, cannot be fully understood if we regard it only as a means of maintaining social control. A large share, if not the majority, of legal cases deal with offenses so minor that only the fertile imagination of a Subanum legal authority can magnify them into a serious threat to some person or to society in general. . . . A festivity without litigation is almost as unthinkable as one without drink. If no subject for prosecution immediately presents itself, sooner or later, as the brew relaxes the tongues and actions, someone will make a slip.

In some respects a Lipay trial is more comparable to an American poker game than to our legal proceedings. It is a contest of skill, in this case of verbal skill, accompanied by social merry-making, in which the loser pays a forfeit. He pays for much the same reason we pay a poker debt: so he can play the game again. Even if he does not have the legal authority's ability to deal a verbalized "hand," he can participate as a defendant, plaintiff, kibitzer, singer, and drinker. No one is left out of the range of activities associated with litigation.

Litigation nevertheless has far greater significance in Lipay than this poker-game analogy implies. For it is more than 'recreation.' Litigation, together with the rights and duties it generates, so pervades Lipay life that one could not consistently refuse to pay fines and remain a functioning member of society. Along with drinking, feasting, and ceremonializing, litigation provides patterned means of interaction linking the independent nuclear families of Lipay into a social unit, even though there are no formal group ties of comparable extent. The importance of litigation as a social activity makes understandable its prevalence among the peaceful and, by our standards, "law-abiding" residents of Lipay.

More examples can be found. However, for the most part the inclusion of such extralegal functions in the anthropological literature has been anecdotal. The previous series of examples are not meant to illustrate the law; rather they are examples of what should be included in any truly ethnographic study of the law.

And finally a word about comparison and generalization. One function of

marriage pattern? The comparative papers in this volume on law ask such questions. Whiting asks: Why is there more physical aggression resulting in legal wrongs in some societies than in others? Roberts queries: Why do only some societies have oaths and ordeals? Cohn pursues yet another question: What relation is there between coalition formation in villages and frequency of dispute? But if we are going to ask and answer such questions we need good descriptive data, which leads us back to questions of description.

If field studies of law are to result in comparable data what essential materials should be covered by the ethnographer?[5] First, several assumptions should be made clear: 1) there is a limited range of dispute for any particular society; that is, all societies do not fight about all the possible things human beings could fight about; 2) a limited number of formal procedures are used by human societies in the prevention of and/or settlement of grievances (e.g. courts, contests, ordeals, go-betweens, etc.); 3) there will be a choice in the number and modes of settlement (e.g. arbitration, mediation, compromise, adjudication, and so on). How people resolve conflicting interests and how they remedy strife situations is a problem with which all societies have to deal; and usually they find not one but many ways to handle grievances. In any society also there are various remedy agents which may be referred to when a grievance reaches a boiling point, and an understanding of all such agencies is necessary for a comprehensive analysis of social control and for a sophisticated contextual analysis of the court system, should one exist.

Having in mind the range of remedy agents (or agencies) in a society certain empirical questions come to mind: 1) What do people fight and argue about publicly, and how, when, and where do conflicts come about? 2) How do societies handle disputes and what is the outcome for the individual(s) involved as well as for the society? 3) Within what groups are disputes concentrated? 4) How do disputes at one group level (family, kindred, lineage, etc.) affect that at another (village, region, nation, etc.)?

Information on these four areas should enable us to provide answers to such developmental questions as: At what ages (speaking of biological and sociological age) in the life cycle, in what roles, at what rank, and under what conditions do citizens fit into the picture as parties to specific disputes? What is the relation between the composition of the family, the frequency of crime, and the use of the courts? The Gluecks (1950) and B. Whiting in this volume suggest a relation between the composition of the family and delinquent acts. A relation between family structure and the use of the courts is illustrated by the Zapotec situation where the absence of a father and/or brother often forced women to take recourse to formal law agencies as plaintiffs. Why should this be? What are the social and cultural correlates of sex and age-linked offenses? Among the Zapotec for example, women are rarely defendants in dispute cases involving assault and battery, while men on the other hand are rarely defendants in slander cases. These informations should also enable us to answer the question: 5) What are the manifest and latent jobs of the law and how are they related to the social structure?

comparative study is to identify uniformities and differences and to explain them. Although it is true that we have a healthy handful of excellent monographs on certain aspects of law, are they indeed comparable? In some respects they are. For example, the mechanisms for dispute settlement (the procedural aspects of law ways) could profitably be compared to isolate answers to questions such as those proposed by Kluckhohn (1960:136): first, "What is apparently incompatible with what else?" Endogamous dual organization villages are found to be incompatible with the development of a court system of judgemade decisions (Nader 1965a); second, "What is extremely likely to be found with what else?" The use of a go-between as an important mechanism of nonfamily dispute settlement will be characteristic of societies which are politically decentralized and bilateral in kin form; finally, "Are some concantenations of cultural features or elements indifferent as far as minimal necessary coherence of the system is concerned and hence found associated or not associated merely as a result of the accidents of the historical process?" Here, we may note that crime rates may or may not be related to any procedural characteristic of law, and some evidence for this is presented by Beatrice Whiting in this volume. Whiting compares the frequencies of assault and homicide in six societies and considers the differences in the light of the concept of "protest masculinity" and the status envy hypothesis of identification.

But there are problems inherent in comparison, even leaving to one side the difficulties of comparing total legal systems, which we believe to be a task not likely to yield much fruit. A major problem, common to all cross-cultural comparative studies, relates to the formulation of concepts or categories which will permit cross-cultural analysis without distortion of the "folk-system" of a particular society. Or phrased in another way, how do we reconcile "the new ethnography" and the importance of generalization in anthropology. Bohannan (1957) is correct in viewing the description of the folk and the analysis of the system as two separate tasks, but his threefold social action model (action, counteraction, correction) is much too general for comparative usefulness. So is Gluckman's (1955a) conceptual model used to describe the judicial process of the Barotse. Yet a comparison of the formal institutions used for settling disputes raises certain problems inherent in Hoebel's volume *The Law of Primitive Man* (1954), that is, the problems of comparing a court system, with a gobetween system, with an Eskimo song duel, or even the problems in comparing a grade D court among the Tiv with the *presidente's* and/or the *alcalde's* courts among the Zapotec. We get into further complications by comparing the functions of these formal systems. These problems are similar to those faced in kinship research. For example, we compare a kinship system based on lineage and clan principles with one based on the nuclear family. In kinship we never 'solved' the problem of comparable units and yet comparison was not ignored. Rather we started with certain assumptions about the regularity of kinship forms and with certain questions the answers to which were sought through comparison: Why is it that "marriage" is more brittle in some societies than in others? What aspects of social organization are intimately connected to the

A quantitative and qualitative sampling of dispute cases from each society could provide key material around which comparison would be made—provided that sampling problems are resolved or indeed that one could guarantee that sampling more than a handful of cases in some populations. The dispute case, unlike any particular form of adjudication or class of disputes or functions, is present in every society. Universally such cases share most of the following components depending on what stage the dispute is in: the dispute or grievance (property, custody, theft, homicide, marital obligations, or however the society may class such disputes); the parties to a grievance (sex, age, rank, status, relation between parties); presentation of the grievance (before a judge, go-between, lineage head); procedure or manner of handling a grievance; the outcome; the termination of the grievance; and the enforcement of a decision. Mapping the component parts of a case so that the sociological aspects of conflict can be systematically discerned has been attempted for the Zapotec material (Nader 1964a). The results are mainly descriptive generalizations which have proved useful as a springboard for comparative work (Nader and Metzger 1963).

In examining monographs that included case materials, certain neglected areas were noted: frequency estimates, sociological data on the parties such as age and status, detailed descriptions of the legal and extralegal factors determining the outcome. The decision-making process is often ignored or barely mentioned. Typically, for example, there might be a statement of a case, then a sentence declaring that "after much wrangling" the case was settled in such and such a manner. We need to know more about the "wrangling." If we are dealing with a society with courts we need to investigate the dispute case in the context of the range of social institutions which adults use in the resolution or prevention of trouble situations, that is, we should sample out-of-court cases as well as court cases. In this way we may reveal the intricate balance between the use patterns of various authority systems. See Schneider 1957, Nader and Metzger 1963, and Gulliver 1963.

But how do we arrive at an understanding of our last question: 6) What jurisprudential ideas are expressed in legal reasoning? If prior to field work we attempt to make a category listing of substantive areas of the law such as family law, tort law, property law, we run into difficulties. Who could say, at this stage of knowledge, what the major categories of family law would be when viewed cross-culturally? The range of possibilities in terms of substantive law are too great to be handled in the same way as procedure, given our present knowledge. Is inheritance, for example, a universal category of law? (Cf. Hoebel 1948 for an example of a comparative treatment of inheritance.) Llewellyn and Hoebel might suggest that we "find" substantive law by noting cases of breach, and this one can do in the field only. But there is another possibility, one which admittedly has its drawbacks. Field workers, both implicitly and explicitly, have described the law ways of preliterate and nonliterate groups usually against a backdrop of Western European law. Hence the familiar chapters of family, property, contract, torts, etc. This has been the subject of much criticism. While I do not believe that we can adopt wholesale Western jurisprudential categories of law for use in non-Western cultures, it is possible that we could explicitly state that we are using an outline of Anglo-American common law, for example, against which or from which we view exotic legal systems. At least we would be clear about what our biases were. Such straightforward comparisons might serve field workers at least as one system against which to contrast their materials. It would also enable us to provide answers to the question, What jurisprudential ideas are expressed in legal reasoning? We could thereby *test* a suggestion made most recently by Gluckman (1965a) that certain jurisprudential ideas found in English and Roman law are universal ideas.

For example, Gluckman (1965a:113) states as a universal legal distinction that

> Both developed and underdeveloped legal systems distinguish sharply between immovable and movable property. Basically the distinction is between immovables and movables. The Roman *res mancipi* included slaves, horses, oxen besides land. Maine cites Scottish law as ranking a certain class of securities with land, and Hindu law as grouping slaves with land.

He continues his discussion by accepting a more generalized version of this distinction:

> As Maine pointed out, the difference between the two types of property is not absolutely between land and chattels—between immovables and movables. Immovable property provides fixed positions which endure through the passing of generations, through quarrels, and even through invasions and revolutions, and many social relationships are stabilized about these positions (p. 116). . . . Chattels . . . break up the exclusiveness of corporations aggregate by drawing their individual members into other relationships [cross-linkages] (p. 133).

And he proposes an interesting hypothesis to explain what contributes to this dichotomy in classifying property:

> Immovable property and chattels have different functions in the maintenance, through time, of a social system as an organized pattern of relations. Immovable property provides fixed positions which endure through the passing of generations, through quarrels, and even through invasions and revolutions, and many social relationships are stabilized about these positions (p. 116). . . . Chattels . . . break up the exclusiveness of corporations aggregate by drawing their individual members into other relationships [cross-linkages] (p. 133).

Even disagreement with the universality of the dichotomy that Gluckman poses does not detract from the fact that Gluckman in these recent essays makes a distinctive contribution to an anthropological understanding of both Western and Barotse jurisprudence. His essays also clearly illustrate the stimulus value of Western jurisprudential ideas. However, another approach in the exploration of cognitive categories is illustrated in this volume by Black and Metzger. Their approach is a contribution to the methodology of description while Gluckman's essays provide an example of anthropological legal interpretation of given descriptive categories. At any rate it remains clear that aspects of law assumed to be universal by eighteenth-century intellectuals remain a matter of search for twentieth-century scholars.

NOTES

[1] In conceiving the original outline of this paper I have profited immensely from the papers and discussions at the Wenner-Gren Conference on law, April 1964. I am especially indebted to Paul Bohannan, Herma Kay, and Julius Stone for many stimulating interchanges at the Center

for Advanced Study in the Behavioral Sciences. For their critical comments and readings of earlier drafts I wish to thank Eugene Hammel, Mel Perlman, Penny Addiss, Carl McCarthy, John Rothenberger, and most of all Norman Milleron. Penny Addiss served as research assistant during the writing of this paper. Anne Brower kindly edited several drafts. My colleagues at Berkeley, especially Elizabeth Colson and C. Lancaster were helpful in directing me to African and Indian materials. The responsibility for the paper in its present form, alas, is solely mine.

[1] This paper is *not a survey* of the literature past and present. Such would be the subject for a book. The examples quoted are primarily in English; a few French references are included. There is a long German tradition totally ignored here. We have elsewhere (Nader, Koch, and Cox 1964) annotated the German literature but for the most part the German literature is not utilized here. It would be important to consider such obvious scholars as Kohler and Trimborn in any historical treatment of the subject. Most relevant work can be found in *Zeitschrift für Vergleichende Rechtswissenschaft,* but see especially Leonhard Adam (1937) "Ethnologische Rechtsforschung," still the best review article on the development of German legal ethnology.

[2] For a broad review of trends in American sociology of law see Skolnick 1965.

[3] Anthropologists have more commonly analyzed other institutions as having legal functions rather than legal institutions as having other than legal functions. See Kaberry 1941 and 1942 for example.

[4] The Berkeley project on comparative village law has been concerned with the problem of conducting comparable ethnographic field studies of law. This group met during 1963–64 to work on the formulation of a field guide. In its broadest scope the field guide was intended to cover the social relations and contexts in which breaches of the law tend to develop, the institutions and mechanisms which serve to prevent social conflict, and the systematic collection of dispute cases.

REFERENCES CITED

ADAM, LEONHARD
1937 Quellennachweis. *In* Lehrbuch der Völkerkunde. Konrad Theodor Preuss, ed., Stuttgart, F. Enke, pp. 302–306.

ALLOTT, A. N.
1953 Methods of legal research into customary law. Journal of African Administration 5(4):172–177.
1960 Essays in African law with special reference to the law of Ghana. London, Butterworths.
1961 The changing law in a changing Africa. Sociologus, Vol. II, pp. 115–131.

ANDERSON, J. N. D.
1957 Law as a social force is Islamic culture and history. Bulletin of the School of Oriental and African Studies 20:13–40.

ARMSTRONG, R. G.
1954 West African inquest. American Anthropologist 56:1051–1069.

ARNOLD, T.
1935 The symbols of government. New Haven, Yale University Press.

AUBERT, V.
1963 Researches in the sociology of law. The American Behavioral Scientist 7(4):16–20.

AYOUB, V.
1961 Review: the judicial process in two African tribes. *In* Community Political Systems, Morris Janowitz, ed., Glencoe, The Free Press.

BACHOFEN, J. J.
1861 Das Mutterrecht. Stuttgart, Krais and Hoffmann.

BACON, M. K., I. L. CHILD and H. BARRY, III
1963 A cross-cultural study of correlates of crime. Journal of Abnormal and Social Psychology 66(4):291–300.

BAILEY, F. G.
1958 Caste and the economic frontier. Bombay and Oxford, Oxford University Press.

BARNES, J. A.
1961 Law as politically active: an anthropological view. *In* Studies in the Sociology of Law, G. Sawer, ed., Canberra, Australian National University, pp. 167–196.

BARTON, R. F.
1919 Ifugao law. University of California Publications in American Archaeology and Ethnology 15(1):1–186.
1930 The half way sun: life among the headhunters of the Philippines. New York, Brewer and Warren.
1949 The Kalingas: their institutions and custom law. Introduction by E. Adamson Hoebel. Chicago, the University of Chicago Press.

BEALS, A. R.
1955 Interplay among factors of change in a Mysore village. *In* Village India: Studies in the Little Community, McKim Marriott, ed., Chicago, University of Chicago Press.
1964 Gopalpur: a South Indian village. New York, Holt, Rinehart and Winston.

BEIDELMAN, T. O.
1959 A comparative analysis of the Jajman system. Locust Valley, New York, Published for the Association for Asian Studies by J. J. Augustin.

BERREMAN, G. D.
1963 Hindus of the Himalayas. Berkeley and Los Angeles, University of California Press.

BLACKSTONE, SIR WILLIAM
1765 Commentaries on the laws of England. Oxford, Clarendon Press.

BOHANNAN, P. J.
1957 Justice and judgment among the Tiv. London, Oxford University Press for the International African Institute.
1960 African homicide and suicide. Princeton, New Jersey, Princeton University Press.
1964 Anthropology and the law. *In* Horizons of Anthropology, S. Tax, ed., Chicago, Aldine Publishing Co., pp. 191–199.

BOORSTIN, D. J.
1958 The mysterious science of the law. Boston, Beacon Press. First published 1941.

BERNDT, R. M.
1962 Excess and restraint. Social Control Among a New Guinea Mountain People. Chicago and London, The University of Chicago Press.

BURRIDGE, K. O. L.
1957 Disputing in Tangu. American Anthropologist 59(5):763–780.

BUSIA, K. A.
1951 The position of the chief in the modern political system of Ashanti: a study of the influence of contemporary social changes on Ashanti political institutions. London and New York, Oxford University Press for the International African Institute.

CARLIN, J. E.
1963 Lawyers on their own. New Brunswick, Rutgers University Press.

CARLIN, J. E. and J. HOWARD
1965 Legal representation and class justice. UCLA Law Review 12(2):381–437.

COHN, B. S.
1959 Some notes on law and change in North China. Economic Development and Cultural Change, Vol. 8, pp. 79–93.

COLSON, E.
1953 Social control and vengeance in plateau Tonga society. Africa 23:199–212.
1958 Marriage and the family among the plateau Tonga. Manchester, University of Manchester Press.
1960 Social organization of the Gwembe Tonga. Manchester, Manchester University Press.

DURKHEIM, E.
1960 The division of labor in society. Glencoe, Illinois, The Free Press. First published 1893.

EVAN, W. M., ed.
1962 Law and society. New York, The Free Press of Glencoe.

EVANS-PRITCHARD, E. E.
1963   The comparative method in social anthropology. London, University of London, Athlone Press.

FALLERS, L. A.
1956   Changing customary law in Busoga district of Uganda. Journal of African Administration 8:139–144.
1962   Customary law in the new African states. Law and Contemporary Problems 27:605–631.

FRAKE, C. O.
1963   Litigation in Lipay: a study in Subanun law. In The Proceedings of the Ninth Pacific Science Congress, 1957, Vol. 3, pp. 217–222.

FRAZER, SIR J. G.
1890   The golden bough; a study on magic and religion. London, New York, The Macmillan Co.

FUSTEL DE COULANGES, N. D.
1864   The ancient city: a study on the religion, laws, and institutions of Greece and Rome. New York, Doubleday and Co. Inc., 1956. First published 1864.

GIBBS, J. L., JR.
1963   The Kpelle moot: a therapeutic model for the informal settlement of disputes. Africa 33:1–11.

GLASE, R. M.
1959   Revenge and redress among the Huli: a preliminary account. Mankind (Sydney) 5(7):273–289.

GLUCKMAN, M.
1955a   The judicial process among the Barotse of Northern Rhodesia. Manchester University Press, for the Rhodes-Livingstone Institute.
1955b   Custom and conflict in Africa. Glencoe, The Free Press.
1959   The technical vocabulary of Barotse jurisprudence. American Anthropologist 61:743–759.
1962   African jurisprudence. The advancement of Science 75:439–454.
1965a   The ideas in Barotse jurisprudence. New Haven and London, Yale University Press.
1965b   Politics, law and ritual in tribal society. Chicago, Aldine Publishing Co.

GLUECK, S. and E. GLUECK
1950   Unraveling juvenile delinquency. Cambridge, Harvard University Press.

GULLIVER, P. H.
1963   Social control in an African society: a study of the Arusha, agricultural Masai of Northern Tanganyika. Boston, Boston University Press.

GUTMANN, B.
1926   Das Recht der Dschagga. Mit einem Nachworte des Herausgebers: Zur Entwicklungspsychologie des Rechts. Arbeiten zur Entwicklungspsychologie, F. Krueger, ed, siebentes Stück. Abhandlungen der Sachsischen Staatlichen Forschungsinstitute, Forschungsinstitut für Psychologie, Nr. 7.

HARPER, E. B.
1957   Hoylu: a belief relating justice and the supernatural. American Anthropologist 59:801–816.

HART, H. L. A.
1961   The concept of law. Oxford, Oxford University Press.

HAZARD, J. N.
1962   Furniture arrangement as a symbol of judicial roles. Etcetera 19(2):181–188.

HOBHOUSE, L. T., G. C. WHEELER and M. GINSBERG
1915   The material culture and social institutions of the simpler peoples: an essay in correlation. The London School of Economics and Political Science, No. 3 of the Monographs on Sociology.

HOEBEL, E. A.
1940   The political organization and law-ways of the Comanche Indians. American Anthropological Association Memoir 54. Contributions from the Santa Fe Laboratory of Anthropology, vol 4.
1948   The anthropology of inheritance. In Conference on Social Meaning of Legal Concepts, E. N. Cahn, ed. New York, New York University.
1954   The law of primitive man: a study in comparative legal dynamics. Cambridge, Mass., Harvard University Press.
1961   Three studies in African law. Stanford Law Review 13: 418–442.

HOGBIN, H. I.
1934   Law and order in Polynesia: a study of primitive legal institutions. Introduction by B. Malinowski. London, Christophers.

HOWELL, P. P.
1954   A manual of Nuer law. Being an account of customary law, its evolution and development in the courts established by the Sudan government. London, New York, and Toronto, Oxford University Press.

JAYAWARDENA, C.
1963   Conflict and solidarity in a Guianese plantation. New York, The Humanities Press.

JONES, JR., EDGAR H.
1964   Power and prudence in the arbitration of labor disputes: a venture in some hypotheses. UCLA Law Review 2(5):675–791.

KABERRY, P. M.
1941, 1942   Law and political organization in the Abelam tribe, New Guinea. Oceania 12(1):79–95; No. 3:209–225; No. 4:331–363.

KANTOROWICZ, H.
1958   The definition of law. Cambridge, Cambridge University Press.

KAPLAN, I.
1965   Courts as catalysts of change: a Chagga case. Southwestern Journal of Anthropology 21(1):79–96.

KEUNING, J.
1963   Customary law and customary courts in Yoruba-land. Read at the Nigerian Institute of Social and Economic Research in Ibadan. (Mimeo.)

KLUCKHOHN, C.
1960   The use of typology in anthropological theory. In Selected Papers of the Fifth International Congress of Anthropological and Ethnological Science, 1956. A. Wallace, ed., Philadelphia, University of Pennsylvania Press, pp. 134–140.

KROEBER, A. L.
1925   Principles of Yurok law. In Handbook of the Indians of California. Washington, D.C., Bureau of American Ethnology, Bulletin 78.

LEACH, E. R.
1954   Political systems of highland Burma: a study of Kachin social structure. London, G. Bell and Sons, Ltd.
1959   Letter to the editor: social change and primitive law. American Anthropologist 61(6):1096–1097.
1961   Rethinking anthropology. London, Athlone Press.

LEWIS, O.
1958   Village life in northern India. Urbana, University of Illinois Press.

LLEWELLYN, K. N. and E. A. HOEBEL
1941   The Cheyenne way: conflict and case law in primitive jurisprudence. Norman, University of Oklahoma Press.

McLENNAN, J. F.
1865   Primitive marriage. Edinburgh, A. & C. Black.

MAINE, SIR H. S.
1861   Ancient law: its connection with the early history of society and its relation to

modern ideas. London, John Murray. Paperback edition printed by Beacon Press, Boston, 1963.
1871 Village-communities in the East and West. London, John Murray.

MALINOWSKI, B.
1922 Argonauts of the western Pacific. New York, E. P. Dutton and Co., 1961.
1926 Crime and custom in savage society. London, Kegan Paul, Trench, Trubner & Co., Ltd.
1934 Introduction to law and order in Polynesia by H. Ian Hogbin. New York, Christophers.
1942 A new instrument for the interpretation of law—especially primitive. The Yale Law Review 51:1237–1254.

MARCH, J. G.
1956 Sociological jurisprudence revisited, a review (more or less) of Max Gluckman. Stanford Law Review 8:499–534.

MARX, K.
1960 Capital: a critique of political economy. Translated from the third German edition by S. Moore and E. Aveling, F. Engels, ed. Revised and amplified according to the fourth German edition by Ernest Unterman. New York, The Modern Library.
1948 The Communist manifesto. Centenary Edition. London.

MAUSS, M. and M. H. BEUCHAT
1906 Les variations saisonnières des sociétés esquimaux; étude de morphologie social. Anné Sociologique 9:39–132.

MEAD, M.
1961 Some anthropological considerations concerning natural law. Natural Law Form 6:51–64.

METZGER, D.
1960 Conflict in Chulsanto: a village in Chiapis. Alpha Kappa Deltan 30:35–48.

MONTESQUIEU, C. L.
1750 L'esprit de les lois. London, printed for J. Nourse and P. Vaillant in the Strand.

MOORE, S. F.
1958 Power and property in Inca Peru. New York, Columbia University Press.

MOORE, S.
1960 Marxian law in primitive society. In Culture in History: Essays in Honor of Paul Radin, Stanley Diamond, ed., New York, Columbia University Press, pp. 642–662.

NADEL, S. F.
1942 A black Byzantium. London, Oxford University Press.
1947 The Nuba. London, Oxford University Press.
1956 Reason and unreason in African law. Africa 26, No. 2:160–173.

NADER, L.
1964a An analysis of Zapotec law cases. Ethnology 3:404–419.
1964b Talea and Juquila: a comparison of Zapotec social organization. University of California Publications in American Archaeology and Ethnology 48(3):195–296.
1965a Choices in legal procedure: Shia Moslem and Mexican Zapotec. American Anthropologist 67(2):394–399.
1965b Communication between village and city in the modern Middle East. Human Organization, Special Issue: Dimensions of Cultural Change in the Middle East.
n.d. Variations in Zapotec legal procedure. In Homenaje al Ingeniero Roberto Weitlaner. Mexico. (In press.)

NADER, L., K. F. KOCH and B. COX
1966 The ethnography of law: a bibliographical survey. Stanford: Current anthropology, special supplement. (In Press)

NADER, L. and D. METZGER
1963 Conflict resolution in two Mexican communities. American Anthropologist 65:584–592.

NAGEL, S. S.
1962 Culture patterns and judicial systems. Vanderbilt Law Review 16:147–157.

NICHOLAS, R. W. and T. MUKHOPADHYAY
n.d. Politics and law in two West Bengal villages. Bulletin of the Anthropological Survey of India. (In press.)

O'GORMAN, H. J.
1963 Lawyers and matrimonial cases. New York, The Free Press of Glencoe.

POSPISIL, L.
1958a Kapauku Papuans and their law. Yale University Publications in Anthropology 54.
1958b Social change and primitive law: consequences of a Papuan legal case. American Anthropologist 60:832–837.

RADCLIFFE-BROWN, A. R.
1933 Primitive law. In Encyclopedia of the Social Sciences, Vol. 9, pp. 202–206. New York, Macmillan. Reprinted in Structure and function in primitive society: essays and addresses by A. R. Radcliffe-Brown, Ch. 12. Glencoe, Illinois, Free Press.

REDFIELD, R.
1950 Maine's ancient law in the light of primitive societies. Western Political Quarterly 3:571–589.

RICHARDSON, J.
1940 Law and status among the Kiowa Indians. American Ethnological Society. Monograph I.

RIESMAN, D.
1954 Individualism reconsidered and other essays. Glencoe, Illinois, The Free Press, pp. 440–466.

RHEINSTEIN, M.
1963 Problems of law in the new nations of Africa. In Old Societies and New States, Clifford Geertz, ed., Free Press of Glencoe.

ROTHENBERGER, J. E.
1963 Judicial process and political organization among the Lozi and Tiv. Ms.

SCHAPERA, I.
1938, 1955 A handbook of Tswana law and custom. London, New York, Cape Town, Oxford University Press for the International African Institute.
1943 Tribal legislation among the Tswana of the Bechuanaland Protectorate. London, Lund, Humphries, for the London School of Economics and Political Science.

SCHNEIDER, D. M.
1957 Political organization, supernatural sanctions and the punishment for incest on Yap. American Anthropologist 59, No. 5:791–800.

SCHUBERT, G. A.
1959 Quantitative analysis of judicial behavior. Glencoe, Illinois, The Free Press.
1963 Behavioral research in public law. American Political Science Review 57:433–445.

SCHWARTZ, R. D. and J. C. MILLER
1964 Legal evolution and societal complexity. The American Journal of Sociology 70(2):159–169.

SIEGEL, B. J. and A. R. BEALS
1960 Pervasive factionalism. American Anthropologist 62:394–417.

SIMMEL, G.
1956 Conflict and the web of group affiliations. Glencoe, Illinois, The Free Press.

SIMONETT, J. E.
1963 The common law of Morrison County. American Bar Association Journal 49:263–265.

SKOLNICK, J. H.
1965 The sociology of law in America: overview and trends. Social Problems (summer issue), supplemental monograph.

SIEGEL, E. O.
1964 The Wall Street lawyer. New York, The Free Press of Glencoe.

SMITH, W. and J. M. ROBERTS
1954 Zuni law: a field of values. With an appendix by Stanley Newman. Cambridge, Massachusetts, Peabody Museum Papers 43(1).

STIRLING, P.
1957 Land, marriage, and the law in Turkish villages. Part I. The Reception of Foreign Law in Turkey: International Social Science Bulletin 9:21–33. UNESCO.

STRODTBECK, F.
1962 Social process, the law, and jury functioning. *In* Law and Society, Wm. M. Evan, ed., New York, The Free Press of Glencoe, pp. 152–164.

TAPPAN, P. W.
1947 Delinquent girls in court. New York, Columbia University Press.

TURNER, V. W.
1957 Schism and continuity in an African society: a study of Ndembu village life. Manchester, England, Manchester University Press.

UCHENDU, V. C.
1964 Livestock tenancy among Igbo of Southern Nigeria. African Studies Quarterly Journal 23(2):89–94.

WEBER, M.
1954 Max Weber on law in economy and society, M. Rheinstein, ed., Cambridge, Harvard University Press.

WHITING, B. B.
1950 Paiute sorcery. New York, Viking Fund Publications in Anthropology, No. 15.

WHITING, J. W. M., *et al.*
1953 Field manual for the cross-cultural study of child rearing. Social Science Research Council, New York.

WINANS, E. V. and R. B. EDGERTON
1964 Hehe magical justice. American Anthropologist 66, 1:745–764.

1. According to Nader, what should be the guiding framework for the anthropology of law?

2. What assumptions must be made if comparable information is to be gathered on the role of law in different cultures?

3. Given these assumptions, what empirical questions should be examined by researchers who study law in various cultures?

1. Nader argues that anthropologists should:

    a. examine law as part of a larger system of social control, rather than us an isolated institution. Focusing on the way in which law is integrated into the broader social control system e.g., the supernatural element in social control, is typical of the anthropologist's desire to emphasize the integration of cultural patterns, rather than the unique qualities of particular cultural patterns.

    b. consider the possibility that the functions of law are different in different societies. For example, American law may perform the function of ruining credit ratings, winning elections, harassing ex-spouses, or rooting out evil! Nader cites with approval Thurman Arnold's view of the court as an "enculturation process--a place where values are tested, changed, or consolidated. . .". In Senapur, courts served the function of providing arenas for social, political and economic competition. Kpelle modts perform therapeutic functions. Zapotec courts perform the function of raising revenue.

        The point Nader is making is that the anthropologist must not assume that law performs standard functions in all cultural settings. Rather, the researcher must be alert to the wide range of functions which might be found being performed by law.

    c. attempt to generate empirical and explanatory generalizations. In order to go beyond mere descriptions of law in various cultural settings, Nader suggests that the same materials must be collected by all researchers so that comparable information will be available.

2. a. There are only certain matters disputed in each society.

    b. There are only a limited number of formal processes used in human societies to resolve disputes.

    c. There will be choices made in each society as to the frequency and style of dispute settlement.

3. The types of questions which Nader believes should be studied by legal anthropologists include:

    a. What do people fight about publicly?

    b. How, when, and where do conflicts arise?

    c. How do societies handle disputes?

    d. What is the outcome for individuals and for society?

    e. Within what groups in society are disputes most commonly found?

f. What are the effects of disputes at one group level (family, kindred) upon other group levels (village, region, nation)?

g. What are the manifest (intended) and latent (unintended) functions of the law?

h. How are the functions of law related to social structure?

i. What jurisprudential ideas are expressed in the categories employed in legal reasoning?

PSYCHOLOGY AND LAW

In a recent article entitled "Psychology and the Law: An Overture," June L. Tapp (1976) suggests that there are three major areas of interface between the field of law and psychology: a) the judicial process; b) the criminal justice process; and c) legal socialization. She states, "Topics of traditional interest to the psychologist such as socialization, decision making, information processing, perception, memory, cognition, attitudes, group dynamics, and interpersonal relations all have relevance for various aspects of the legal system" (p. 370).

The Judicial Process

Psychologists have been concerned with a number of issues involved in the judicial process including the psychological impact of the adversary system, the problems of eyewitness perceptions, and the behavior of jurors individually and juries collectively.

An interesting illustration of the psychologist's research on law involves the effect of questioning upon eyewitness recollection of event. In an experiment carried out at the University of Washington, psychologist Elizabeth Loftus (1975) showed a video tape of 8 students disrupting a class to a group of undergraduates. Following this presentation, one group of students was given a questionnaire in which "passive style questions were asked. Example: "Did you notice the demonstrators gesturing at any of the students?" The other group was asked "active" style questions such as, "Did you notice the militants threatening any of the students?" Both groups were shown the same tape one week later and then asked to describe it. The result was that "the subjects. . .who were interrogated with questions worded in an active, aggressive manner reported that the incident they witnessed was noiser and more violent, that the perpetrators of the incident were more belligerent, and that the recipients were more antagonistic (Loftus, et al, 1975, p. 164).

The obvious implication of this experiment for the legal process is that the first person to interrogate a witness may have a significant effect on what that witness is able to recall of an event when he/she is asked to testify about it in court!

Psychologists have also investigated the way in which individual jurors make judgments, the credibility of various types of witnesses and the interactions among jurors as they go about reaching decisions. In addition, in recent years psychologists have assisted lawyers in jury selection in an effort to use psychological profiles to choose favorable and eliminate unfavorable jurors.

Criminal Justice Process

The role of psychologists in the criminal justice process is the subject of serious disagreement within both the psychological and legal communities. As Tapp (1976) puts it, "The central questions are how, who, and what achieves justice and health best in 'correctional' settings" (p. 392). Since the concept of mental health as it relates to the legal system is the subject of an entire unit ("Law and Psychiatry"), these questions will be delayed until then. In addition, psychologists have attempted to describe the personality traits of both law breakers and law enforcement personnel. There is a growing literature on the issue of whether or not there exists a police personality.

Legal Socialization

The concept of legal socialization arose in the last decade to refer to "the process of dealing with the emergence of legal attitudes and behaviors and describes the development of individual standards for making sociological judgments and for using the law and legal systems for problem solving" (Tapp, 1976, p. 371). Because this is a recent and significant area of inquiry, we will look at it somewhat more closely.

The following article by Linda W. Rosenzweig presents the core of the theory of legal socialization which maintains that there is a pattern of development in the ability of people to use legal reasoning. The various cognitive stages of legal development are outlined and their theoretical implications are explored.

LEGAL SOCIALIZATION: A COGNITIVE
DEVELOPMENTAL PERSPECTIVE

Linda W. Rosenzweig
Carnegie Mellon University

The concept of legal socialization refers to the process by which children learn about law and rules, authority and punishments, and the norms of the legal culture. The research of developmental psychologists, who are concerned with the study of behavior changes throughout the life span, suggests that people acquire legal knowledge, attitudes, and behaviors in an organized progressive fashion. Scholars who work in this area of psychology investigate the emotional, attitudinal, cognitive, and social processes which individuals go through from conception to death; the majority of their research up to the present has focused on these developmental processes in infants, children, and adolescents. Hence the findings of developmental psychology have contributed significantly to our understanding of the complex phenomenon of legal socialization which incorporates elements of all of these processes.

Perhaps the most widely known contemporary developmental psychologist is Jean Piaget whose research on cognitive development has influenced the entire field. Piaget maintains that children's cognitive development proceeds through a series of age-related states from a sensorimotor level to a symbolic intuitive level to a concrete level and finally to a sophisticated abstract level. (Piaget, 1928; Piaget and Inhelder, 1969). His work on cognitive growth and his explorations of children's morality have particularly in-fluenced the work of Lawrence Kohlberg, a developmental psychologist whose main interest is the study of the development of moral reasoning, cognitive moral development.

During the past twenty years, Kohlberg has conducted extensive research to determine how individuals reason about moral questions. Building upon Piaget's theory that moral development occurs in stages just as cognitive development takes place (Piaget, 1965), he and his colleagues have implemented both longitudinal and cross-cultural research to investigate moral reasoning. They have found that individuals think about moral issues in six qualitatively different ways or stages, through which they theorize that people pass sequentially   (Kohlberg, 1968; 1971; 1972).

The concept of a cognitive stage describes an organized system of thought which reflectes an underlying consistent structure, regardless of specific content. In a sense, the structure of thought can be characterized as a system of rules for processing information or for connecting events that are experienced. (Kohlberg, 1969). For example, one person might support an action that another person opposes, but both might use arguments based on a concept of fairness as reciprocity. This common element--the notion of reciprocity as defining fairness--represents the structure of thought.

Kohlberg's states are defined in terms of three levels which he designates as preconventional, conventional, and principled. Each level consists of two stages   (Kohlberg, 1968, 1972). His data suggest that individuals develop naturally through the stages of moral reasoning, proceeding from a preconventional moral world-view based on punishment and obedience, through perspectives which focus on pragmatic reciprocity and the fulfillment of group expectations, toward more adquate conceptions of justice based on ideas of societal maintenance, law, social contract, human rights and welfare, and finally universal self-chosen ethical principles. The research evidence indicates that cognitive moral development occurs step-by-step in an upward direction, but all people do not develop to the highest stages. Up to this point, none of Kohlberg's subjects has regressed or skipped a stage; changes in the stages of moral reasoning employed by subjects who have been reinterviewed at three-year intervals have always been to the next higher stage   (Kohlberg, 1971).

Because both the nature and function of the law are implicitly and inherently moral, the development of moral reasoning encompasses the growth of ideas of law. Kohlberg's research indicates that individuals define a wide variety of concepts in stage-related terms   (Kohlberg, 1971,; Kohlberg and Turiel, 1971) Hence one's moral world view generates one's notions of law, legal authority, legal obligation, etc. A person who reasons at the lower stages of Kohlberg's scale which make up the preconventional level, views legal issues from a narrow perspective such as avoiding punishment or gaining rewards. However, an individual who reasons at the principled level regards the same issues from a broader more universal perspective such as notions of the social contract or fundamental human rights. The integral relationship between cognitive moral development and conceptions of law suggests that legal development occurs in structured cognitive stages analogous to the stages of moral reasoning.

In order to examine this relationship empirically, June L. Tapp of the University of California at San Diego conducted studies specifically designed to assess the applicability of Kohlberg's findings to concepts of law and legal justice. Tapp and her colleagues interviewed 115 white middle class subjects from kindergarden to college in the United States and 406 preadolescent middle school students in six countries representing seven cultures. An open-ended interview consisting of 79 questions dealing with law, justice, compliance, punishment, and authority was administered to the preadolescent subjects in the cross-national study and adapted for the primary and college level subjects in the United States (Tapp and Kohlberg, 1977; Tapp, 1970).

Using the data from these interviews, Tapp constructed a classification scheme and a model of legal development which is similar to Kohlberg's scale of moral development. Because her research utilized a different methodology from that employed by Kohlberg in his investigation of moral reasoning, their classification schemes cannot be considered isomorphic (Tapp and Kohlberg, 1977). However the Tapp studies clearly identified definite continuities between the cognitive theory of legal development and Kohlberg's theory of cognitive moral development. (See Table I on page 2.80).

Tapp categorized her data into three levels, preconventional, conventional, and postconventional, according to subjects' responses in three areas: the value and function of rules and laws; the dynamics of legal compliance; and the changeability and breakability of rules. She found that primary school children generally demonstrated a preconventional orientation. For example, they viewed laws as prohibitive, existing to prevent specific bad acts or crimes rather than serving any positive social good. They offered negative reasons for complying with laws, e.g., avoidance of punishment or deference to power, and they regarded laws as permanent, almost physical entities (Tapp and Kohlberg, 1977).

The majority of the preadolescent subjects in both samples and the college subjects in the United States sample reasoned at the conventional level. In contrast to the preconventional subjects, they viewed the value of law in terms of maintaining order and preventing antisocial behavior. This societal maintenance perspective also applied to their ideas on legal compliance. While they advocated changing or breaking the law in extreme circumstances, they identified systems of law as the core of social order and social welfare (Tapp and Kohlberg, 1977; Tapp, 1970).

A minority of the college students presented the postconventional position, viewing laws as norms mutually agreed on by individuals for purposes of personal and social welfare. From this perspective, the postconventional subjects argued that laws which violate fundamental rights or universal moral principles can legitimately be broken, and that universal rational criteria define the need for maintaining laws (Tapp and Kohlberg, 1977).

In summary, the Tapp studies demonstrated the applicability of Kohlberg's cognitive moral development theory for the study of legal development. The United States kindergarten to college sample provided evidence of a developmental age-related shift in concepts of law from a preconventional, law-obeying perspective to a conventional, law-maintaining perspective, to a more flexible perspective orienting to universal rational principles of morality and justice. The data generated by the cross-national, multi-cultural study supported these findings of changes in legal development characterized by a progression through organized stages or modes of thought. The conventional, societal-maintenance level was the modal level for the majority of subjects in both studies.

Data from later studies conducted by Tapp and research conducted by E.L. Simpson illustrate the predominance of conventional legal reasoning among adults. Tapp and her colleagues identified the conventional level as modal for a sample of graduating law students, elementary and secondary school teachers, and prison inmates (Tapp and Levine, 1977). Simpson, whose study of adult development utilized questions from Tapp's interview, found that conventional reasoning predominated among her subjects also (Simpson, 1973). All of these findings concerning legal reasoning are consistent with Kohlberg's studies which locate most people at the conventional level of moral reasoning (Kohlberg, 1975).

In addition to the extensive research by Tapp and her colleagues, research by Joseph Adelson of the University of Michigan also supports the cognitive theory of legal development. Adelson did not attempt to apply Kohlberg's model to legal socialization, but he and his colleagues traced the growth of the idea of law during adolescence. They found that the view of law shifts significantly between the ages of 13 and 15 as evidenced by changes from concrete to abstract conceptions of various aspects of law, including purpose, function, and changeability (Adelson, Green, and O'Neil, 1969). Their data are consistent with both Piagetian and Kohlbergian notions of age-related cognitive developmental processes, and hence, with the notion of sequential growth in legal development.

The cognitive theory of legal development provides a framework for organizing diverse legal cognitions sequentially. The research implies that socializing agencies such as the home, the school, and the community should be concerned with determining what procedures are effective in stimulating development toward principled legal reasoning since the data suggest that the postconventional, principled level is not modal for most of the population.   Psychologists believe that structured cognitive development or stage change represents a process of interaction between cognitive structures and environmental factors   (Piaget, 1970; Piaget and Inhelder, 1969; Kohlberg, 1969).

The predominance of the conventional level of legal reasoning among both children and adults studied by researchers suggests that socializing agencies must provide rich environments which offer diverse interactive experiences if individuals are to develop the capacity to make principled legal judgments. The available evidence regarding socialization strategies suggests that in addition to transmitting substantive legal knowledge, effective socialization must provide exposure to constructive cognitive conflict about law, opportunities for participatory experiences such as role-playing and cooperation, and experiences of rule- or law-making and -administering process in a wide variety of contexts to promote legal continuity (Tapp and Levine, 1977).

The cognitive developmental approach to legal socialization draws upon the Piagetian and Kohlbergian conceptions of development as the progressive restructuring of modes of thought from lower to higher levels. This approach embodies the notion that higher stages of thought are better for solving problems, distinguishing between values, integrating differences hierarchically, and incorporating universal principles   (Kohlberg, 1971a). Developmental psychology offers empirical evidence of an integral relation-ship between moral and development and legal development, as illustrated by the continuities between the Kohlberg & Tapp studies.   And the interactive aspect of cognitive development implies that legal socialization should involve purposeful attempts to facilitate the development of higher stages of thought.

TABLE I: LEVELS AND STAGES OF MORAL DEVELOPMENT

THE PRECONVENTIONAL LEVEL (Stages 1 and 2)

At this level, people consider the power of authority figures or the physical or hedonistic consequences of actions, such as punishment, reward, or exchange of favors. This level has the following two stages:

Stage 1: The Punishment and Obedience Orientation

At this stage, the physical consequences of doing something determine whether it is good or bad without regard for its human meaning or value. People at Stage 1 think about avoiding punishment or earning rewards, and they defer to authority figures with power over them.

Stage 2: The Instrumental Relativist Orientation

At Stage 2 right reasoning leads to action which satisfies one's own needs and sometimes meets the needs of others. Stage 2 thought often involves elements of fairness, but always for pragmatic reasons rather than from a sense of justice or loyalty. Reciprocity, a key element in Stage 2 thought is a matter of "you scratch my back and I'll scratch yours."

THE CONVENTIONAL LEVEL (Stages 3 and 4)

People at this level value matintaining the expectations of their family, group, or nation for their own sake and regardless of immediate consequences. People at the conventional level show loyalty to the social order and actively maintain, support, and justify it. This level has the following two stages.

Stage 3: The Interpersonal Sharing Orientation

At this stage, people equate good behavior with whatever pleases or helps others and with what others approve of. Stage 3 people often conform to stereotypical ideas of how the majority of people in their group behave. They often judge behavior by intentions, and they earn approval by being "nice."

Stage 4: The Societal Maintenance Orientation

Stage 4 thought orients toward authority, fixed rules, and the maintenance of the social order. Right behavior consists of doing one's duty, showing respect for authority, or maintaining the given social order for its own sake.

THE PRINCIPLED LEVEL (Stages 5 and 6)

At this level, people reason according to moral principles which have validity apart from the authority of groups to which the individuals belong. This level has the following two stages.

Stage 5: The Social Contract, Human Rights and Welfare Orientation

People at Stage 5 tend to define right action in terms of general individual rights and standards which have been examined critically and agreed upon by the society in a document such as the Declaration of Independence. Stage 5 people stress the legal point of view, but they emphasize the possibility of changing laws after rational consideration of the welfare of the society. Free agreement and contract bind people together where no laws apply.

Stage 6: The Universal Ethical Principle Orientation

At Stage 6, people define the right by the decision of their conscience guided by ethical principles, such as respect for human personality, liberty compatible with the equal liberty of all others, justice, and equality. These principles appeal to logical comprehensiveness, universality, and consistency. Instead of being conrete rules, they are abstract ethical principles.

REFERENCES

Adelson, J., Green, B., & O'Neil, R.P. The growth of the ideas of law in adolescence. Developmental Psychology, 1969, 1, 327-332.

Kohlberg, L. The child as a moral philospher. Psychology Today, September 1968, pp. 25-30.

Kohlberg, L. Stage and sequence: the cognitive developmental approach to socialization. In D. A. Goslin (Ed.), Handbook of socialization theory and research. New York: Rand McNally and Company, 1969.

Kohlberg, L. The concepts of developmental psychology as the central guide to education--examples from cognitive, moral, and psychological education. In M. C. Reynolds (Ed.), Proceedings of the conference on psychology and the process of schooling in the next decade: alternative conceptions. Minneapolis: University of Minnesota Department of Audio-Visual Extension, 1971.

Kohlberg, L. From is to ought: how to commit the naturalistic fallacy and get away with it in the study of moral development. In T. Mischel (Ed.), Cognitive development and epistemology. New York: Academic Press, 1971a.

Kohlberg, L. A cognitive developmental approach to moral education. The Humanist, November-December 1972, pp. 13-16.

Kohlberg, L. Moral stage and moralization. In L. Kohlberg, Collected papers on moral development and moral education (Vol. 1). Mimeographed, Center for Moral Education, 1975.

Kohlberg, L., & Turiel, E. Moral development and moral education. In G. Lesser (Ed.), Psychology and educational practice. Chicago: Scott, Foresman, 1971.

Levine, F. J., & Tapp, J. L. The dialectic of legal socialization in community and school. In J.L. Tapp F.J. Levine (Eds.), Law, justice, and the individual in society. New York: Holt, Rinehart, and Winston, 1977.

Piaget, J. Judgment and reasoning in the child. London: Routledge and Keagan Paul, 1928.

Piaget, J. The moral judgment of the child. New York: Free Press, 1965. (Originally published: London, 1932.)

Piaget, J. Science of education and the psychology of the child. New York: Orion Press, 1970.

Piaget, J., & Inhelder, B. The psychology of the child. New York: Basic Books, 1969.

Simpson, E.L. Teachers of justice: a preliminary report of politico-legal socialization. Paper presented at the annual meeting of the American Psychological Association, 1973.

Tapp, J.L. A child's garden of law and order. _Psychology Today_, December 1970, pp. 29-31; 62-64.

Tapp, J.L., & Kohlberg, L. Developing senses of law and legal justice. In J.L. Tapp & F.J. Levine (Eds.), _Law, justice, and the individual in society_. New York: Holt, Rinehart, and Winston, 1977.

1. How does Rosenzweig define "legal socialization?"

2. What is the relevance of developmental psychology to the study of law?

3. What does Kohlberg's theory of cognitive moral development suggest about the process of legal socialization?

4. How did June Tapp attempt to study the legal socialization and levels of thought among children?

5. What were Tapp's findings?

6. What is the value of the cognitive legal development theory?

1. She defines 'legal socialization' as "the process by which children learn about law and rules, authority and punishment, and the norms of the legal culture" (Rosenzweig, 1978, p. 1).

2. Developmental psychology's focus upon human behavior changes throughout life suggests that learning about law might also be a developmental process throughout life.

3. Kohlberg's theory states that people reason about moral problems in a developmental pattern proceeding from lower to higher stages. Since law is "implicitly and inherently moral" (Rosenzweig, 1978, p. 2), Kohlberg's theory seems to suggest that there may be a process of legal development quite similar to the process of moral development. In other words, by reference to Kohlberg's theory of moral reasoning, Rosenzweig argues that "legal development occurs in structured cognitive stages analogous to the stages of moral reasoning" (Rosenzweig, 1978, p.3).

4. Tapp interviewed a sample of American students, from kindergarten to college in the U.S., plus samples of children in six other countries. She used them questions designed to measure their attitudes toward law, justice, authority, and related issues.

5. Tapp built a classification scheme from the answers to these questions. Her scheme of cognitive legal development closely resembled Kohlberg's classification of cognitive moral development. She claimed to be able to identify preconventional, conventional, and postconventional oreintations toward law. Specific components of the three orientations are presented in Reading #5.

6. If the theory is correct, then efforts should be made by parents, schools, and the community to stimulate movement toward higher stages of legal reasoning. If reasoning about the legal conflicts at higher developmental stages is better (as the theory suggests), then it is important to further investigate how to most effectively raise the levels of legal thought through the socialization process.

RHETORIC AND THE LAW

Richard E. Vatz
Towson State University

Hans Morganthau has argued that ". . .all systems of government derive their legitimacy from a myth" (Morganthau, 1968, p. 111). The American system of government is no exception, of course. Perhaps one of our most prevalent and indomitable myths can be summed up in the abstraction, 'the law.' 'The law' to most citizens comprises a massively complex, but well ordered and ultimately equitable and fair system of adjudications of disputes and alleged law breaking by which all citizens benefit. One need not belabor the metaphors of balanced scales of justice to comprehend this widespread mythology. In this piece we shall take a look at the general causes, effects, and accuracy of the largely unquestioned public reverence for our complex system of justice, neatly summarized into the abstraction, 'the law.'

To understand the public's perceptions of 'the law' and the causes and effects of those perceptions one must have an understanding of rhetoric, the art of persuasive communication. Most of the following points concerning the rhetoric of law are distilled from the writings of Murray Edelman, Roberto Unger, and Thurman Arnold, three writers who have provided important insights regarding the confluence of law and rhetoric.

To one interested in communication, the question of how fair and certain is our system of jurisprudence is secondary to the rhetorical concern of how language and symbols work to create public confidence in the fairness and certainty of that system. The public can witness but a negligible amount of the labyrinthine functioning of our system of justice. In fact, as Thurman Arnold points out, there are few in the public who confront 'the law' with any regularity and even those who do, see only perhpas some day-to-day activities of lower courts (Arnold, 1962, p. 111). Consequently, public confidence in 'the law' comes not from experiencing 'the law' but from experiencing communications about the law which convinces them that 'the law' is functioning in a way worthy of the public's considerable reverence. Arnold concludes, in fact, that ". . .the function of law is not so much to guide society as to comfort it" (Arnold, 1962, p. 34).

Let us look at some of the communication about law which conveys positive impressions of 'the law' to the public. First, there is the general public discourse. As Stuart Scheingold argues, opinion leaders in the socialization process constantly assure the public that a highly efficient, fair, and competent legal process is at work at levels beyond the public's observation. The neatness of procedure, he argues, blinds us to the inequities of the substance and thus, the imperfection of 'the law.' Scheingold asks, "Is it not rather curious that the relatively petty crimes of Watergate and not the unspeakable horrors of Vietnam could bring a President to the brink of impeachment?" (Scheingold, 1974, p. 52) One might add that the expedition of the procedure also obscured the fact that other Presidents who committed acts for which Richard Nixon was investigated (cover-ups, misuse of federal agencies, etc.) escaped the constraints of legal procedures altogether.

This faith assumption engendered by this visible process, that somehow 'things are being taken care of' by the law is complemented by the belief that that process is guided by tomes of critical legal and meta-physical literature. That the public has little access and less desire to read such literature presents no obstacle to this belief. As Arnold observes, "all inklings of doubt or apparent inconsistency in 'the law' is reconciled by 'thinking men,' [who], unable to reason the thing out, simply throw up their hands and pretend that it has been reasoned out by someone else. This requires an act of faith which is more complicated than a belief in the mysterious acts of Providence" (Arnold, 1962, p. 65). Yes, it requires faith: that is, it requires uncritical thinking. And, to the True Believer, no amount of contrary evidence will vitiate the greatness of the ideal or deity: in this case, 'the law.' Even those within the system are not immune to its overwhelming mystery. As Arnold points out,

> For the layman, the entire body of legal literature
> represents jurisprudence, because it is here that he
> thinks that the fundamental principles of the law have
> all been worked out to be revealed to him piecemeal in
> the occasional decision which comes to his attention. For
> the lawyer, jurisprudence is that part of the law which he
> never gets time to read--the part adorned with learned names
> like Austin, Jhering, Pound, which is separate from, and above,
> the legal arguments which he uses in court. He assumes that
> in jurisprudence is found the bridge from one legal subject
> to another, the philosophy that law is a seamless web, that
> it is based on logical theories which are sound, that it
> governs society, that it is the product of ages of conscious
> thought consciously synthesized into a uniform system.
> (Arnold, 1962, p. 57)

This is not to imply that all within the legal system are naive concerning its arbitrariness. A well known apocryphal story has the judge justifying his decision against the young attorney by saying, 'That's the law.' to which the latter replies, 'It wasn't until you said it, your honor.' As French legal philosopher Chaim Perelman indicates, it is rarely difficult to adduce legal reasons to justify the decision of the judge's choice.

Again, the disorderliness and arbitrariness of 'the law' and its processes, and its violation of many of our ideals and values is not incompatible with maintaining public impressions to the contrary. Nor do we necessarily maintain that such myths are to be eschewed. For those who despair over public misperception, however, there is little to give hope for change. If, as Arnold maintains, the public faith in 'the law' is analogous to and no less than religious faith, the continuing drama of trials and appeals coupled with the functioning institutions of law schools and other legal programs will continue to provide sufficient proof to the public of a legal system orderly and rational in its composition and sure in its execution. Neither legal literature nor legal procedure stand in danger of being unmasked. Arnold states, regarding the former, ". . .faith in reason compels reasoning man to pin his faith on a mass of literature so complicated that he cannot see its contradictions" (Arnold, 1962, p. 66). Similarly, the unending orderly drama of legal processes, regardless of the judiciousness of their outcomes, communicates the certainty and fairness of 'the law', and the public is unlikely to let the substantive disappointments destroy its faith. And myths regarding 'the law', like all other myths, require faith, not proof.

REFERENCES

Arnold, T. The symbols of government. New York: Harcourt, Brace and World, 1962.

Morganthau, H. Foreword. In D.A. Graver, Public opinion, the president, and foreign policy. New York: Holt Rinehart, and Winston, 1968.

Scheingold, S. The politics of rights. New Haven: Yale University Press, 1974.

1. What does 'the law' mean to most Americans according to Vatz?

2. What is rhetoric?

3. What is the key issue in Vatz' rhetorical view of law?

4. What types of communication about law are cited by Vatz as sources of public perceptions about law?

5. What is the rhetorical function of law books?

6. Why does the fact that law does not operate in accordance with the myths about 'the law' not weaken public adherence to the myths?

1. 'The law' is an abstraction which Vatz says represents "one of our most prevalent and indomitable myths" (Vatz, 1978, p.1). His point is that most Americans believe that a beneficient system of law exists in America which fairly solves disputes and adjudicates and punishes lawbreaking.

2. Rhetoric is the study of persuasive communications.

3. The key issue from the rhetorical perspective is the examination of how various communications about law engender respect for law regardless of the actual workings of law. Vatz does not argue that law does not provide a certain amount of fair adjudication of disputes and lawbreaking. What he argues is that reverence for the law is a function of communications about law rather than a function of evaluating the actual operation of law.

4. Those who help form mass opinion (opinion leaders) tell the public that the legal system works well. The emphasis on procedure communicates a high degree of technical expertise and a commitment to fairness among the legal professionals. Such communications focus our attention on formalities while blinding us "to the inequities of the substance and thus, the imperfection of 'the law'" (Vatz, 1978, p. 2)

5. Vatz agrees with Thurman Arnold that the vast legal literature basically communicates to the masses that legal decisions are derived from or based upon principles found in law books. People simply assume on faith that lawyers and judges understand and are in fact guided by 'the law.'

6. Vatz maintains that public support for 'the law' is based upon the same type of faith which sustains religion. Therefore, so long as communications about law indicate a healthy, efficient, and fair system of law, contrary evidence will not likely cause people to lose faith.

Read the following factual situation and answer the questions that follow.

Facts

The United States Supreme Court has announced that prior to interrogating a suspect in custody, the police must warn the suspect of his/her right to remain silent, right to an attorney, right to have an attorney provided if the suspect cannot afford one, and notice that incriminating statements will be used against the suspect.

Questions

List questions that might occur, regarding this situation, to:

a. sociologists

b. systems theorists and stimulus-response theorists.

c. political scientists

d. economists

e. anthropologists

f. psychologists

g. rhetoricians

a. 1. Does the Supreme Court's decision move the criminal justice
        system closer toward legality? (Sociologists: Normative
        Sociology of Law)

    2. What does this court decision suggest about the nature of law?
        (Sociologists: Scientific sociology of law)

b. 1. What demands led to this decision? (systems theorists)

    2. What was the role of various prior stimuli and what subsequent
        responses were stimulated by the decision? (stimulus-response
        theorists)

c. 1. How does the decision affect perceptions of court legitimacy?
        (Political scientists)

    2. What interest groups played a role in the decision? (political
        scientists)

    3. What pressures affected implementation of the decision?
        (political scientists)

b-c.   Which judges sat on the court and who appointed them? (political
        scientists and stimulus-response theorists)

d. 1. Will confessions be less likely because there is a lower price
        to remaining silent? (economists)

    2. Will the cost of compliance to the police reduce the incentive
        to solve crimes? (Economists)

e. 1. How does the decision reflect our conception of the function of
        law? (anthropologists)

    2. Do other cultures similarly limit law enforcement officers?
        (anthropologists)

f. 1. Does the decision make it harder to rehabilitate offenders by
        creating adversary and hostile relationships? (psychologists)

    2. Do policeman differ in their compliance depending upon their
        stage of legal development? (psychologists)

    g. What does this decision communicate to the public about the
        fairness of our legal system? (rhetoricians)

        These are a few examples of the types of questions which might occur
to various scholars in the disciplines you have studied in this unit.
Obviously, you may have thought of many additional questions. Remember that
the central goals in this unit were to help you to see the many facets of
law and to use different perspectives where they were helpful in evaluating
or understanding the role of law. It is more important, therefore, for you

to be able to see the questions which might be formulated within these various frameworks than to be able to answer them. It is often difficult to formulate useful questions about law; yet good questions must be asked if good answers are ever to be provided. Hopefully, this Unit helped you to ask better questions.

REFERENCES

Black, D.J. The boundaries of legal sociology. Yale Law Journal, 1972, 81, 1086-1100.

Collier, J.F. Legal processes: Annual Review of Anthropology, 1975, 4, 121-144.

Easton, D. The political system. New York: Alfred A. Knopf, 1953.

Friedman, L.M. Law and society. Englewood Cliffs: Prentice Hall, 1977.

Hoebel, E.A. Man in the primitive world. New York: McGraw Hill, 1958.

Holmes, O.W., Jr. Law in science and science in law. Harvard Law Review, 1899, 12, 443.

Loftus, E.F. et. al. Effects of questioning upon a witness' later recollections. Journal of Police Science and Administration, 1975, 3, 162-165.

Moore, S.F. Law and anthropology. Biennial Review of Anthropology, 1969, 252-300.

Nagel, S. The legal process from a behavioral perspective. Homewood, Illinois: The Dorsey Press, 1969.

Posner, R. Economic analysis of law. Boston: Little Brown, 1977.

Posner, R. The economic approach to law. Texas Law Review, 1975, 53, 757-782.

Posposil, L. Anthropology of law. New York: Harper & Row, 1971.

Sales, B.D. (Ed). Psychology in the legal process. Jamaica, New York: Spectrum, 1977.

Samuelson, P.A. Economics: an introductory analysis. (6th ed.). New York: McGraw Hill, 1964.

Schoenfeld, C.G. Psychoanalysis and the law. Springfield, Illinois: Charles C. Thomas, 1973.

Schur, Edwin M. Law and society. New York: Random House, 1968.

Shattuck, P.T. Law as politics. Comparative Politics, October, 1974, 127-154.

Selznick, P. The sociology of law. International Encyclopedia of Social Science, 1968, 9, 50-58.

Tapp, J.L. Psychology and the law: an overture. Annual Review of Psychology, 1973, 27, 359-404.

Tapp, J.L., & Levine, F. Law, justice and the individual in society: psychological and legal issues. New York: Holt, Rinehart & Winston, 1977.

Thibaut, J., & Walker, L. Procedural justice: a psychological analysis. New York: John Wiley and Sons, 1975.

SUGGESTED READING

Becker, G.S. Crime and punishment: an economic approach. 76 Journal of Political Economy 169, 1968.

Black, D.J. The boundaries of legal sociology. Yale Law Journal, 1086, 1972.

Evan, W.M. Law and sociology: exploratory essays. New York: Free Press, 1962.

Friedman, L.M. Law and society. Englewood Cliffs: Prentice Hall, 1977.

Hoebel, E.A. Man in the primitive world. New York: McGraw Hill, 1958.

Holmes, O.W., Jr. Law in science and science in law. Harvard Law Review, 1899, 12, 443.

Lett, A.A. Economic analysis of law" some realism about nominalism. Virginia Law Review, 60, 451, 1974.

Loftus, E.F. et. al. Effects of questioning upon a witness' later recollections. Journal of Police Science and Administration, 1975, 3, 162-165, 1975.

Posposil, L. Anthropology of law. New York: Harper and Row, 1971.

Selznick, P. The sociology of law. International Encyclopedia of Social Science, 9, 50-58.

Stone, J. Social dimensions of law and justice. Stanford: Stanford University Press, 1966.

Tapp, J.L., & Levine, F. Law, justice and the individual in society: psychological and legal issues. New York: Holt, Rinehart & Winston, 1977.

Thibaut, J., & Walker, L. Procedural justice: a psychological analysis. New York: John Wiley and Sons, 1975.

UNIT **3**

Law And Social Structure

Rationale

In this unit the law is reviewed as a dependent variable, that is, a reflection of underlying social organization. While recognizing that law can help to bring about change in the social order, we focus here upon the law as a force supporting and maintaining the current social divisions in any society. The idea that legal institutions and processes reflect social institutions and processes is frequently coupled with the idea that law and legal systems follow a developmental pattern. The variations on these themes of the relationship of law and social structure and law as an evolutionary or developmental process form the core of this unit.

Objectives

After you have completed this unit you should be able to:

1. Describe the relationship between law and social structure according to:

   a. Maine

   b. Marx and Engels

   c. Durkheim

   d. Vinogradoff

   e. Schwartz and Miller

   f. Galanter

   g. Nonet and Selznick

2. Recognize and explain the premise that law is a reflection of social structure and that law develops in relation to the development of social structure.

Overview

The reading for this exploration of the relationship between law and social structure includes a mini-lecture which summarizes a number of theoretical statements about law and social structure, and a reading summarizing the Marxist position on this relationship. In "The Main Themes of Marx' and Engels' Sociology of Law," Professor Cain attempts to draw together the bits and pieces of commentary about law and society which are scattered through the works of Marx and Engels. While it is difficult to fully understand Marxian sociology of law exclusively from this essay, it serves as a good starting point.

Throughout this unit, remember that law and society relationships are multifaceted and reciprocal and that we simply are isolating these relationships here for the purpose of learning about them in an orderly fashion. Thus, to identify ways in which law reproduces social arrangements or follows a pattern of development is not to deny that law can and does also affect those social arrangements and, in some cases, drastically alters them.

The basic themes of this unit are that law can be seen as the mirror image of social relations generally and that development in social organization generates development in legal organization.

Study Task Checklist

☐   1. A.   Read Mini-Lecture #1, "Law, Social Structure, and Legal Evolution."

☐   1. B.   Answer the Study Questions and compare your answers with the Discussion of them.

☐   2. A.   Study Reading #1, "The Main Themes of Marx' and Engels' Sociology of Law," by Maureen Cain.

☐   2. B.   Answer the Study Questions and compare your answers with the Discussion of them.

LAW, SOCIAL STRUCTURE, AND
LEGAL EVOLUTION

In this unit we are examining the impact of society on law. The central issues concern the effect of social structure and social stratification upon the legal system. Once a legal system comes into existence, the question arises, "Do legal systems evolve or develop in relation to the evolution or development of social systems?" The various efforts to answer this question are summarized in this mini-lecture.

The Concept of Legal Evolution

The idea of legal evolution suggests that legal systems might develop from lower to higher stages, much like lower forms of life developed into higher forms. While movement from stage to stage need not occur, where such movement does occur, it must proceed in a stage by stage fashion. Therefore, lower forms of legal systems might always remain, but if they change, they would change in predictable directions. A problem with the idea of legal evolution is that it often carries with it a normative judgment about the stages of legal development. Lower stages tend to be seen as more primitive and, therefore, less desirable. Higher stages tend to be seen as more advanced and more desirable. There is a propensity to intervene in the affairs of other nations in order to 'help' them develop and 'modernize' their legal systems. It is worth noting that the most 'advanced', 'progressive', and 'modern' legal systems bear a striking resemblance to the legal systems of the Western world. You should at least consider the possibility that so-called 'lower' stages of legal evolution might be <u>better</u>.

Sir Henry Maine (1822 - 1888)

As indicated in Unit 1, Maine theorized that all societies evolved through stages, and law evolved to reflect these stages. The earliest social systems were described by Maine as 'archaic societies', in which society consisted only of various families dominated by their eldest male members. The father of the family controlled the other members, but, since the family had no interactions with other families, there was nothing really qualifying as law.

176

In the second stage, the 'tribal stage', various families began to merge into groups of families led by a chief or a king. The chief, modeling his role upon that of the father in an individual family, began to exercise a degree of control over the relationship among families who belonged to the tribe. As anthropologist Leonard Pospisil (1971) writes, "As far as the essential characteristic of law is concerned, namely its nature as a system of abstract principles, the chiefs of the late tribal societies . . . by pronouncing the same judgments in similar situations, were unwittingly creating a set of abstract principles" (pp. 145-146). The rights and duties, however, in the tribal societies depended primarily upon which family one belonged to and what position that family had in the tribe. Legal rights and legal obligations, in other words, depended upon status or position in the tribal society.

In the latter part of the tribal stage and the early part of the next stage, the 'territorial stage' (in which tribes became unified around the principle of a common territory as well as common family ties), the law emerged as a set of fully developed abstract principles governing behavior.

After the emergence of law, Maine continued, the development did not stop. Rather, the status principle for allocation of rights and duties was gradually replaced by the contract principle under which individuals freely agreed to undertake particular rights and duties. The individual, not the status of the individual, became the building block for legal decisions.

Karl Marx (1818 - 1883) and Frederick Engels (1820 - 1895)

The law, for Marx and Engels, is best seen as an expression of the capitalist ruler's interests. The state emerged as a mechanism for legitimizing the laws which they create. As the contradictions of capitalism inexorably lead to its demise, the socialist society which emerges will see a gradual withering away of the state (the coercive mechanism for law enforcement) and the law (the exploitative rules promulgated by capitalist rulers).

Law is clearly seen as dependent upon social structure which in turn is dependent upon economic structure. The evolution of the economic and social systems brings with it a corresponding evolution of the legal system.

The reading on Marxist interpretations of law will clarify these ideas further.

Emile Durkheim (1858 - 1917)

Durkheim's version of legal evolution was also tied to social evolution. He theorized that the type of law in a society would reflect the type of social organization or social solidarity in that society. He categorized legal systems according to the type of sanctions typically employed in the system, and he categorized social systems according to the relative degree of role differentiation present in the society.

Legal systems, said Durkheim, rely either on <u>repressive</u> or <u>restitutive</u> sanctions. Repressive sanctions emphasize punishment for deviant behavior and restitutive sanctions emphasize the offender's duty to compensate society or individual victims.

Social systems are either marked by <u>mechanical solidarity</u> or <u>organic solidarity</u>. Mechanical solidarity is defined by low role differentiation, or little division of labor. All members of society performed most functions for themselves, that is, there were not specialized food growers, clothes makers, dispute settlers, or illness curers. In <u>organic society</u>, there is a sharp division of labor, or high role differentiation, in which specialized persons perform specific functions and then exchange their goods and services with other specialized persons.

The relationship between social solidarity and legal systems was that the shift from mechanical to organic solidarity was reflected by a shift from repressive to restitutive legal systems.

Durkheim reasoned that in the mechanical solidarity society, where each person shared common experiences as a result of the low division of labor, common values would emerge and be strongly held. Consequently, those who violated the norms of the society were dealt with harshly. In such a society, the 'collective conscience' was strong and the desire to punish was correspondingly strong.

In the organic society where life experiences are far more varied as a result of the division of labor, violations or norms are not seen as so threatening to the 'collective conscience'. As a result, the desire to punish is replaced by a desire to restore equilibrium, or to restore the status quo before the violation.

Thus, Durkheim's theory attempted to relate legal systems to social structures and to identify the evolutionary patterns of each. Societies tend to move from mechanical to social solidarity and from repressive to restitutive law.

Sir Paul Vinogradoff (1854 - 1925)

Vinogradoff conveived of six stages of juridical thought: totemistic, tribal, civic, medieval, individualistic, and socialistic (Pospisil, 1971, p. 177). The first two stages occur in primitive social systems. In totemistic society there really is no law as we know it. In the tribal society, law is not created by the tribal leaders but is found by them by a reading of the collective wisdom. In other words, the leaders simply try to reformulate the desires of the tribesmen; they do not legislate.

In the civic law stage, the law reflects the emergence of the political community, e.g., the Greek city-states. Medieval law represented the merging of sacred law and feudal law. Individualism was the stage in which the rights, duties, and needs of individuals formed the core of the law. The final stage, socialism, was seen as just developing and not clearly defined as yet.

Richard D. Schwartz and James C. Miller

Schwartz and Miller (1964) attacked the problem of legal evolution from an empirical standpoint. Examining anthropological data from 51 societies, they sought to determine if legal institutions developed in any patterned manner. They specifically looked at the presence or absence of:

1. Mediation: the regular use of non-kin third parties to intervene in settling disputes;

2. Police: a specialized armed force used at least partially for enforcing norms;

3. Counsel (lawyers): the regular use of specialized non-kin advocates in the settlement of disputes.

They report a variety of arrangements ranging from the absence of all three to the presence of all three. The interesting finding was that there appeared to be an order in which the legal institutions evolved. Mediation appeared first, followed by police and lawyers. No society studied was found to have lawyers but not police and mediation; virtually no society had police without mediation.

Furthermore, they claim that the simpler societies were less likely to have police than were the more advanced societies. As they conclude:

> Superficially at least, these findings seem directly contradictory to Durkheim's major thesis . . . He hypothesized that penal law--the effort of the organized society to punish offenses against itself--occurs in societies with the simplest division of labor. As indicated, however, our data show that police are found only in association with a substantial degree of division of labor . . . By contrast, restitutive sanctions--damages and mediation--which Durkheim believed to be associated with an increasing division of labor, are found in many societies that lack even rudimentary specialization. Thus, Durkheim's hypothesis seems to be the reverse of the empirical situation in the range of societies studied here. (Schwartz and Miller, quoted in Friedman and Macaulay, 1977, p. 1039)

It could be that Durkheim's reasoning on the theoretical relationship between social solidarity and sanction systems was faulty. Reversing Durkheim's logic, we might argue that in organic solidarity systems marked by a great division of labor the role of law becomes more important in holding society together. In other words, where shared experiences and shared values are absent, laws are more necessary to permit social life to proceed. Consequently, breaches of those laws required penal or repressive sanctions because violating those laws threatens social existence. On the contrary, in the mechanical solidarity system, where there is a low division of labor and a greater degree of shared values, restitutive sanctions are more acceptable and more easily arranged. Such an analysis would be consistent with Schwartz and Miller's findings.

Marc Galanter

Galanter (1966) attempts to describe the qualities of 'modern' legal systems, that is, ". . . a cluster of features that characterize, to a greater or lesser extent, the legal systems of the industrial societies of the last century" (p. 152). Before reading briefly about these traits, you should again be cautioned about the 'loaded' term, 'modern'. To say that what we currently have is 'modern' amounts to more than identifying that it takes place in the present. It implies the judgment that what we now have is superior. Such an assumption should be made explicit and reasons for making it should be presented.

In essence, Galanter claims that as legal systems evolve into modernity they develop certain types of legal rules, institutions, and relationships between law and the state. He argues that modern legal rules are uniform in their application to all persons within their jurisdiction. Second, he says the rules are transactional, i.e., they refer to individual conduct and individual responsibility rather than to statuses of people. Third, they are universalistic in that they are meant to apply to all similarly situated persons. Fourth, they are arranged hierarchically, such that lower level decisions can be appealed to higher levels in order to guarantee consistency.

As to the modern legal institutions, Galanter states that they are bureaucratic, rational, staffed by professionals, structured to utilize lawyers, and amendable by set procedures.

The relationship of the modern legal system to the state is that of a monopoly. The political state alone has authority to exercise legal authority; no religious law, for example, can compete. Finally, the jobs of making law (legislative), carrying out the law (executive), and adjudicating disagreements about law (judicial) are performed by different sets of decision makers.

Philippe Nonet and Philip Selznick

A 1978 book by these authors (Law and Society in Transition: Toward Responsive Law, New York: Harper and Row) sets out still another evolutionary theory of law. They state that "repressive, autonomous, and responsive law are not only distinct types of law but, in some sense, stages of evolution in the relation of law to the political and social order" (Nonet and Selznick, 1978, p. 18).

Repressive law represents the earliest evolutionary stage in which law is nothing but the tool of the powerful segments in society for serving their own interests at the expense of the rest of society. Law is purely a function of politics and power. Autonomous Law, the next evolutionary stage, emerges once order has been established. At this stage, law becomes differentiated from and somewhat independent from politics, power, and social structure. In other words, law can now restrain and control the unbridled exercise of power by the dominant segments in society. Law can reduce repression at this stage of development. To a great degree, this represents the current evolutionary stage of American law. Finally, responsive law represents the stage

181

toward which we are striving. The procedural emphasis and institutional independence of law in the autonomous stage must, they argue, give way to a law which is more result oriented, that is, more concerned with achieving a noble purpose than with adhering to the narrow requirements of autonomous law. Responsive law would permit society to better achieve its purposes and to go beyond the technical emphasis of the rule of law. They state:

> In our model, repressive law is 'prior' in the sense that it resolves the fundamental problem of establishing political order, a condition without which the legal and political system cannot move on to 'higher' pursuits. Autonomous law presupposes and builds upon that achievment, just as responsive law builds upon the more limited but basic constitutional cornerstones of the 'rule of law' stage. (Nonet and Selznick, 1978, p. 25)

SUMMARY

We have examined in the unit a number of theories about how society affects law. It is interesting to note that despite many differences, there is widespread agreement among theorists as diverse as Durkheim and Marx on the proposition that law, indeed, does reflect social structure and evolve or develop along with social structure.

The idea that legal systems might develop in the same sequence in all societies has been examined by many social theorists. Needless to say that agreement is lacking on the precise nature of the sequence of development. As Schur (1968) notes, "If there is more or less agreement that societal and legal complexity have gone hand in hand, beyond that there is little consensus" (p. 108). The goal is that you become more knowledgeable on the possibilities that legal evolution or legal development can be identified and that alternative models exist for further examination and testing.

1. Define "legal evolution."

2. What was Maine's legal evolutionary theory?

3. What was Marx's and Engel's legal evolutionary theory?

4. What was Durkheim's legal evolutionary theory?

5. What was Vinogradoff's legal evolutionary theory?

6. What was Schwartz and Miller's legal evolutionary theory?

7. What was Galanter's legal evolutionary theory?

8. What was Nonet and Selznick's evolutionary theory?

DISCUSSION OF MINI-LECTURE #1 QUESTIONS

1. Legal evolution refers to the belief that legal systems develop according
   to a pattern of stages. Usually theories of legal evolution are tied
   to notions of social development.

2. Maine identified three evolutionary stages in the emergence of law:
   the archaic society, the tribal stage, and the territorial stage. He
   saw law developing as social relationships developed from the family,
   to the tribe, to the territorial unit. He further maintained that law
   developed beyond this point from status-based allocations of rights and
   duties to contractual-based allocations of rights and duties.

3. Marx and Engels saw law evolving as an ideological justification for
   the capitalist state. Economic and social evolution which resulted in
   the development of law will, they claim, ulimately result in its
   disappearance.

4. Durkheim argued that legal forms reflected forms of social solidarity
   and that the evolution of societies from mechanical to organic solidarity
   was accompanied by a corresponding evolution from repressive to restitutive legal systems.

5. Vinogradoff saw law evolving through six stages in relation to stages
   of social development. His six stages were: totemistic, tribal, civic,
   medieval, individualistic, and socialistic.

6. Based upon empirical observations, Schwartz and Miller claim that as
   societies become more complex, legal forms become more repressive.
   Their evolutionary theory, therefore, appears to contradict that of
   Durkheim.

7. Galanter attempts to describe the defining features of a modern legal
   system. As legal systems evolve from less to more modern they are
   marked by a tendency to possess these features: uniform, transactional,
   universalistic hierarchical rules administered by bureaucratic, rational,
   professional institutions and personnel.

8. Nonet and Selznick argue that law develops in stages beginning with
   repressive law (where law is subordinate to social and political power)
   to autonomous law (where law is above social and political power and
   restrains its exercise) to responsive law (where law is used to move
   society toward its goals without the constraining forces of the 'rule
   of law', i.e., results became more important than procedures for attaining
   them).

EDITOR'S NOTE

While Marx and Engels wrote little specifically on the sociology of law from a socialist perspective, their ideas profoundly affect their vision of the role of law. The following article represents an effort to distill from the writings of Marx and Engels the main themes running through their ideas on law and the evolving socialist society. While the goal of Unit 3 was not to enable you to fully understand the Marxist position on law and its relationship to social structure, this article will help those of you who are interested to pursue this line of thinking.

THE MAIN THEMES OF MARX' AND ENGELS' SOCIOLOGY OF LAW*

Little has been written about Marx' and Engels' approach to law. This is largely because Marx never fully developed his theory of the State although, as Sweezy points out,[1] his original intention as stated in the Preface to the *Critique of Political Economy* was to discuss "state, foreign trade, world market" at some length.[2] He died before he could do this. Thus in piecing together "Marx on law" one is forced to treat sections from different works as additive, as if their central concerns were the same. Sometimes, as in chapter X of *Capital*[3] or Engels' *Anti-Dühring*,[4] the extracts are sufficiently long to stand alone as statements about law. At other times there is merely an allusion to law in a text dealing with other matters. These snippets are more open to the abuse of being interpreted out of context. Because my aim has been to let Marx' and Engels' writings speak for themselves I hope I have avoided this. I began the research for this paper with no pre-conceived categories in terms of which to order the extracts. My method was to copy onto cards all the relevant passages (with notes on their contexts) and then to classify them in terms of what seemed to be important or recurring themes.

Although I do not have any particular Marxist or academic axe to grind, two approaches to "Marx on Law" worried and still worry me. These are the "worker bashing" interpretation and the criminological interpretation. The former view has been held by lawyers, the latter by sociologists. Neither does justice to the complexity and *potential* of Marxist thought. Although I cannot claim to know what Marx and Engels really meant, I hope to show at least that their theory of law was highly sophisticated and that it is still useful not only in analysing and comprehending present day society but also in sparking off ideas dialectically with contemporary theory and in guiding one to fruitful areas of research.

Previous Discussions of "Marx on Law"

The "putting down the workers" model of Marx' thought is epitomised in the work of Denis Lloyd,[5] who none the less recognized that Marx "made a major contribution to the foundation of legal as well as other forms of sociology." Lloyd stated that for Marx "Law was nothing but a coercive system devised to maintain the privileges of the property owning class." Alternatively, law

> was distilled out of the economic order which gave rise to it, and was an institutionalized form of the prevailing ideology whereby the dominant section of society coerced the masses into obedience.

This is close enough to be recognizably Marx, yet by its dangerous over-simplification it makes it possible to dismiss Marx as incapable of explaining those many laws which have

---

* An earlier version of this paper was presented to the British Sociological Association Study Group on the Sociology of Law in May, 1972.

[1] P. M. Sweezy, *The Theory of Capitalist Development* (1942 Monthly Review Press, New York).

[2] K. Marx, "Preface to A Contribution to the Critique of Political Economy" in K. Marx and F. Engels, *Selected Works* (1969 Progress Publishers, Moscow).

[3] K. Marx, *Capital* (1970 Lawrence and Wishart, London) Vol. 1.

[4] F. Engels, *Anti-Dühring* (1935 Chas. H. Kerr and Co., Chicago).

[5] D. Lloyd, *The Idea of Law* (1964 Penguin, Harmondsworth) 22, 205–7.

neither this coercive intent nor this effect. Yet in one of his major writings on law Marx, with Engels, comes close to arguing that the law has little to do *directly* with inter-class relationships, the main purpose of laws being to iron out differences *within* the dominant class, and so, *indirectly*, to consolidate their class position.[6] I discuss this more fully below: to mention it here is sufficient to indicate that there is oversimplification in the "worker bashing" view.

Three recent texts have examined Marx' work either to discover in it a radical criminology[7] or to take issue with the radical criminologists' interpretation.[8] These three papers develop from the first, which is more literal in its interpretation, through that of Hirst, which points out the force of Marx' irony and offers a political (and convincing) explanation of Marx' well-known distaste for the "vagabond" and "parasitical" ways of the lumpen-proletarians, to the third[9] which takes the point about irony and seeks to give it a contemporary relevance with the claim that Marx was ridiculing the functionalists (unborn).

My own view is that Marx as a writer is very funny, very bitter, and very passionate. The first two are expected elements of irony; the third, Marx' rage and passionate concern for the sufferings of people, gives way regularly to irony just before it reaches a peak. Having described the processes of dispossession he remarks "In the year 1835, 15,000 Gaels were already replaced by 131,000 sheep."[10] Later "flung on the sea shore, . . . they became amphibious. . . ."

Marx is at his funniest when castigating his philosophical rivals[11] and his powerful blend of anger and irony is most apparent when concrete cases of human suffering, – mangled mineworkers,[12] bemused rustics driven from the land,[13] those bearing heavy sentences for trumped up political offences[14] – are presented. His intellectual grasp is best shown as he moves from weaving and demonstrating patterns of relationships at the highest levels of abstraction to the specific concrete case which illuminates the whole. None of these literary or intellectual skills is demonstrated in his comments on crime.

The problem with Marx, and his interpreters, in his discussions of crime is that he lapses into absolutism. Even in the oft quoted section from *Theories of Surplus Value* Vol. 1,[15] Marx speaks of "the criminal" as a *type of person* and implies that crime is a way

6 K. Marx and F. Engels, *The German Ideology* (1965 Lawrence and Wishart, London) 349–83.

7 P. Walton, paper presented to B.S.A. annual conference, 1971; I. Taylor, P. Walton, and J. Young, *The New Criminology* (1973 Routledge and Kegan Paul, London).

8 Hirst, "Marx and Engels on Law, Crime, and Morality" (1972) 1 *Economy and Society* 28–56.

9 Taylor, Walton and Young, *op. cit.*

10 *Capital*, (1974 Lawrence and Wishart, London) Chap. XXVII, p. 683.

11 Two good examples are *The Holy Family* (1957 Lawrence and Wishart, London) and *The German Ideology*, *op. cit.*, both written with Engels.

12 *Capital*, *op. cit.*, Chap. XV, Section 9.

13 *Ibid.*, Chap. X and XXVII.

14 F. Engels, "The Late Trial at Cologne" in *Selected Works op. cit.*

15 Quoted at length by both Hirst, *op. cit.* and Taylor, Walton and Young, *op. cit.*

of life. These positive definitions lie behind and are intrinsic to the ironic web he weaves in statements such as

> Crime, through its constantly new methods of attack on property, constantly calls into being new methods of defence, and so is as productive as strikes for the invention of machines.

At his worst in discussing crime Marx is a narrow moralist with a veneer of liberal tolerance. Thus, people may have been driven to villainies of various kinds, for example by being rendered homeless and destitute; penalties for these villainies (as well as for being homeless and destitute *per se*) were undoubtedly brutally harsh, this being the best known way of encouraging the landless to value the opportunity to become wage labourers. But both the understanding of the cause and the disgust at the savage punishments carry the implication that the villainy simply exists in itself.[16] Similarly, Engels, when arguing that the bourgeois family causes prostitution by creating a demand for it, treats the prostitute and the prostitution as absolute and given in themselves – even in the course of a polemic to the effect that sexual and familial relationships should and will be *re*-formed.[17]

What Marx and Engels have to say about crime, therefore, may produce a wry smile, but the quality of potential, of being complete but not finished, is lacking. Unlike their remarks on law, these comments do not set the mind a-scampering, tantalised, identifying relationships with other theories, seeking contemporary applications, formulating research problems. And if they do not they should perhaps be spared resuscitation by donnish critics.

Law, the State and Ideology

Criminological interpretations of Marx, as Hirst has pointed out,[18] have crime as their focal concern. This in itself distorts what Marx had to say,[19] for his focus of interest was always the forces and relations of production, the social organisation of the means of life. Marx' and Engels' discussion of law, on the other hand, *arises out of* their more general work. Allusions to law form part of their theory of the State and their sociology of knowledge.[20]

Nowhere is law defined. The authors deal only with legislation in their discussions of how law is created. They comment on enacted law whether or not it is enforced; one can assume that rules actually enforced by the courts are subsumed under their general discussion. Thus by and large they build their argument on the common sense view that we all know what law means. In so far as in their discussions of ideology they are accounting for other people's constructions and understandings, this is legitimate: law *is* what we all know it means. Law as it exists in "massy" reality is an objectified ideological form. Marx and Engels are interested in *ideology*, a concept integral to their theory of the social order.

---

16 For a full discussion of these phenomena see *Capital, op. cit.*, Chaps. XXVII and XXVIII.

17 See Engels, "Origin of the Family, Private Property, and the State" in *Marx' and Engels' Selected Works, op. cit.*, Vol. 3.

18 Hirst, *op. cit.*

19 This would not matter if the distortion were in order to develop new theories: it matters when what is intended is a commentary.

20 I deal with this second aspect at greater length in a forthcoming article.

Law, religion, philosophy, doubtless even social science, are *theoretically equivalent* as manifestations of this. The distinctions between these forms, as their comments on education show,[21] are not given in the world but are created by it. The allocation of ideological areas for examination is itself an ideological form.

In order to understand ideology (and therefore law) either in general or, what interested Marx and Engels much more, in either a particular historical or an idealised epochal manifestation, it is necessary to look at the bases of power in society, at the formation of classes, and at the structure of the State. In a paper about law these remarks must be scant and oversimplified, creating merely the context for the later exposition.

The basic fact of man's past has been the thrust for survival, individually and as a species.[22] The "means of life" at a time are a function of geography, history, and current knowledge.[23] Thus they are social as well as physical creations. The organization of people in relation to them (relations of production) is the social phenomenon which gives rise to classes, groups of people who stand in a particular relation to the means of production, such as slaves, capitalists, peasants, proletarians, and housewives.

> To claim that pre-bourgeois history, and each phase of it, has it own economy and an economic base of its movement, is at bottom merely to state the tautology that human life has always rested on some kind of production – *social* production – whose relations are precisely what we call economic relations.[24]

Capitalist society, which is most relevant for the present analysis, is characterised by *private property*. This is a unique way of conceptualising the relationship between people and things, although it has its conceptual origins in the personal and private use of tools.[25] This mode of thought is embodied in a peculiarly comprehensive set of legal rights in relation to the use and disposition of real, or fictitious but legally and socially existing, things. Capital is private property which enables the owner to buy the labour power of another individual, and use it to create surplus value. Workers, to the extent that they do not receive the full value of the labour power they expend, are exploited.

So brief a description leaves out all the dynamics and most of the theory. My hope is that it will give the student new to Marx a grip on some basic terms to help him through the ensuing discussion, but he should bear in mind Marx' warning:

> The proletariat and wealth are opposites; as such they form a single whole. They are both forms of the world of private property. The question is what place each occupies in the antithesis. It is not sufficient to declare them two sides of a single whole.[26]

In order to maintain their position of dominance, capitalists *as a class* gradually create a set of linked organisations (the State) with the dual purpose of protecting their

---

21 K. Marx, *Pre-Capitalist Economic Formations* (ed. E. J. Hobsbawm, 1964 Lawrence and Wishart, London).
22 This does not involve Marx in a denial that men can choose, for example, to die for a cause.
23 Again, for Marx, this is not an absolute concept.
24 Marx, *Pre-Capitalist Economic Formations*, *op. cit.*, p. 86.
25 *Ibid.*, and also Engels, "Origin of the Family, Private Property, and the State" in *Selected Works*, *op. cit.*
26 K. Marx and F. Engels, *The Holy Family* (1957 Lawrence and Wishart, London).

common internal class interests, such as the establishment of clearly understood rules for commercial transactions, and of protecting them against external threats from other classes or States. Engels clarifies the theory as follows

> The modern state . . . is only the organisation which bourgeois society provides for itself in order to support the general external conditions of the capitalist mode of production against encroachments of the workers as well as of individual capitalists. . . .[27]

The State, for Marx and Engels, is always peopled, never a metaphysical entity – peopled with officials, gaolers, and, late on in its development, with policemen. And these officials are directed, one way or another, by members of the bourgeois class.

> If power is taken on the basis of right . . . then right, law, etc., are merely the symptom of other relations upon which state power rests. The material life of individuals . . . their mode of production and form of interest which *mutually*[28] determine each other . . . this is the real basis of the state. . . · The individuals, who rule in these conditions, besides having to constitute their power in the form of the state, have to give their will . . . a universal expression as the will of the state, as law. . . .[29]

The argument then moves on two important steps. First, the State develops a seeming independence of material conditions "Having public power . . . the officials now stand, as organs of society, *above* society."[30] Or sometimes

> . . . periods occur in which the warring classes balance each other so nearly that state power, as ostensible mediator, acquires for the moment a certain degree of independence of both. . . . In (a democratic republic) . . . wealth exercises its power indirectly but all the more surely. . . .[31]

Secondly, and similarly, politics and law, religion and philosophy develop a seeming independence both of material conditions and of the State.[32] The important point is that these seemingly autonomous ideological areas develop according to their own inner logic; their links with "massy" reality (in Marx' phrase) may indeed become tenuous.

> The state presents itself to us as the first ideological power over man. . . . Hardly come into being, this organ makes itself independent *vis-à-vis* society; and indeed, the more so the more it becomes the organ of a particular class . . . the consciousness of the interconnection between this political struggle (ruling v oppressed class) and its economic basis *becomes* dulled and can be lost altogether. . . . But once the state has become an independent power *vis-à-vis* society it produces forthwith an ideology. It is indeed among professional politicians, theorists of public law and jurists of private law that the connection with economic facts gets lost for fair. . . .[33]

Engels, in particular, struggles with the apparent contradiction between the notion of ideas as *really* determined, and ideas developing in accordance with the rules of logic which

---

[27] Engels, *Anti-Dürhing*, op. cit., Vol. 2, p. 290.

[28] My italics.

[29] Marx and Engels, *The German Ideology*, op. cit.

[30] Engels, "Origin of the Family, Private Property, and the State" *op. cit.*, p. 577. Engels goes on in the passage to note the special rules necessary for the protection of policemen as State officials because they are "forced to represent something outside and above" society. This point is taken up by Durkheim, *The Division of Labour in Society* (1964 Free Press, New York).

[31] *Ibid.*, p. 578.

[32] The advantages of this process for the ruling group are discussed in the next section.

[33] F. Engels, "Ludwig Feuerbach and the End of Classical German Philosophy" in Marx and Engels, *Selected Works, op. cit.*, p. 616.

members of the particular discipline regard as proper. In the Old Preface to *Anti-Dürhing*[34] he castigates those who regard logic or the laws of thought as "eternal truth, established once and for all". However, he also argues

> Every ideology, however, once it has arisen develops in connection with the given concept material, and develops this material further, otherwise it would not be an independent ideology . . . that the material life conditions of the persons inside whose heads this thought process goes on in the last resort determine the course of this process remains of necessity unknown to these persons.[35]

In *Origin of the Family* Engels indicates how the dilemma might be resolved. Changes in material conditions of existence are necessary before certain concepts, legal or otherwise, can be developed. There is bounded choice about how the material conditions of existence are understood – bounded in that the group which controls the means of production in the new conditions will be constrained to conceptualise and "explain" the situation in a manner supportive of its position. Material conditions can be affected by the way they are conceived but material conditions must be capable of existing in order to be thought about. Thus, appropriation of instruments of production for private use (by the male) necessarily preceded the elaboration of property "rights".

Marx had earlier made a similar point[36] in the well-known section[37] in which he argues that "the mode of production of material life *conditions*[38] . . . intellectual life process in general" and that "consciousness must be explained . . . from the contradictions of material life". The *dialectical* nature of this inter-relationship between thought and things comes out more clearly in the discussion of property.

Engels too indicates one way in which the legal ideology influences behaviour which otherwise would have been directly determined by the economic base. The law can set the ground on which struggles must be fought and by so doing may, in particular cases, influence the outcome.

> Since in each particular case the economic facts must assume the form of juristic motives in order to receive legal sanction, and since in so doing, consideration of course has to be given to the whole legal system already in operation, the juristic form is, in consequence, made everything and the economic context nothing. . . . *Fuerbach*, *op. cit.*, p. 619.

It is important to remember that it may be necessary to lose a battle to win a war; that it may be more important to uphold values fundamental to the capitalist order than to gain a particular legal victory, e.g., equality before the law is linked with freedom of the individual, the break up of feudal society and ascriptive rights, without which capitalism could not have developed. The ideology now has a second, symbolic consequence in legitimating the entire social structure. But this is pre-empting the discussion in the next section.

[34] In the three volume 1970 edition of *Selected Works*, *op. cit.*, Vol. 3, p. 60.
[35] "Ludwig Feuerbach and the End of Classical German Philosophy", *op. cit.*, p. 618.
[36] See "Preface to a Contribution to the Critique of Political Economy", *op. cit.*
[37] Discussed by Hirst, *op. cit.*
[38] My italics.

As far as the law is concerned, Engels argues that the particular legal form within which and in terms of which conceptual development takes place is not relevant. Renner, of course, has elaborated these developments, though he fundamentally confuses legal words and concepts with what he calls legal norms.[39] Max Weber made a similar point that in a two tiered legal system such as our own, full rationality, yielding above all predictability of outcome, is necessary only in the upper tier in order for capitalism to be able to develop.[40] Engels' remarks deserve full quotation.

> If the state and public law are determined by economic relations, so, too, of course, is private law, which indeed in essence only sanctions the existing economic relations between individuals which are normal in the given circumstances. The form in which this happens can, however, vary considerably. It is possible . . . to retain in the main the forms of the old feudal laws while giving them bourgeois content: in fact, directly reading the bourgeois meaning into a feudal name. But also . . . Roman Law, the first world law of a commodity producing society with its unsurpassably fine elaboration of all the essential legal relations of simple commodity owners (of buyers and sellers, debtors and creditors, contracts, obligations, etc.) can be taken as the foundation.[41]

The Functions of Law

If the law as ideology is the first of Marx' and Engels' themes, the second theme in their sociology of law concerns the three functions of law. The State develops after irreconcilable class antagonisms have arisen, when it becomes

> necessary to have a power seemingly above society, that would alleviate the conflict and keep it within bounds of "order", and this power, arisen out of society but placing itself above it and alienating itself more and more from it, is the state. . . .[42]

The State is the creation of the class wielding real power, i.e., control over the means of production. By creating a seemingly autonomous State (1) real power relationships are obscured; (2) the exercise of real power is legitimated. The second consequence requires the development of an ideology "explaining" the State together with the development of a further ideology based on this earlier explanation. This second, higher order, ideology explains the use of "State" power in certain situations. This second higher order ideology is jurisprudence, which, among other things, tells lawyers what the law is for.

Real power relationships are obscured because legal forms of power (the right to vote, the right to enter freely into contracts) are equally available to all. Engels inveighs against legal forms which "put both parties on an equal footing *on paper*." He continues

> The power given to one party by its different class position, the pressure it exercises on the other – the real economic position of both – all this is no concern of the law. . . . That the concrete economic situation compels the worker to forego even the slightest semblance of equal rights – this again is something the law cannot help.[43]

[39] K. Renner, *The Institutions of Private Law and their Social Functions* (1949 Routledge and Kegan Paul, London).

[40] M. Rheinstein (ed.) *Max Weber on Law in Economy and Society* (1954 Harvard U.P., Cambridge) Chap. VII.

[41] Engels, "Ludwig Feuerbach and the End of Classical German Philosophy", *op. cit.*, p. 616.

[42] Engels, "Origin of the Family, Private Property, and the State", *op. cit.*, p. 58.

[43] *Ibid.*, p. 500.

Marx puts the point even more succinctly

> The recognition of the rights of man by the modern state means nothing more than did the recognition of slavery by the state of old.[44]

This is probably familiar territory which needs little elaboration. One further example is relevant, given the improvements in the legal position of women. Men have, as Engels noted "a dominating position which requires no special legal privileges."[45] Thus, women can be liberated to fulfil a useful economic role and the dominant values such as equality can be reinforced while real power relationships remain unchanged except in so far as their greater obscurity may strengthen them.

Before leaving the parallel mystifying and legitimating functions of law it is important to note that both Marx and Engels were aware that by emphasizing the autonomy of the State and law it was possible to create the mythology of a "total society" in whose interests these institutions operated, coupled with the belief that the State and law by reason of their apparent autonomy are value neutral. This last point does not even follow in logic. However, that the State should operate in the interests of the mythical whole community is in fact written into is as a guiding principle.

> What is good for the ruling class should be good for the whole of society with which the ruling class identifies itself. Therefore the more civilisation advances the more it is compelled to cover the ills it necessarily creates with the cloak of love, to embellish them, or to deny their existence.[46]

The third function of law is of a rather different order. In *The German Ideology* Marx and Engels for the first time discuss law as representing the "average interests" of the ruling class – the interests of the class conceived as a whole rather than of particular sections or individuals.

> Their (the capitalists) personal rule must at the same time be constituted as an average rule. Their personal power is based on conditions of life which as they develop are common to many individuals, and the continuance of which they, as ruling individuals, have to maintain against others and, at the same time, maintain that they hold good for all. The expression of this will, which is determined by their common interests, is law.[47]

Within the ruling class the law, it seems, operates as systems theorists would have us believe. It irons out conflict in the best interests of the whole, and maintains the unity and integrity of the class. But to see law only this way is to fall prey to the mythology of a "total society" outlined above. Because of this characteristic of law, many studies, such as Joel Barnett's examination of Rent Act legislation,[48] will yield considerable information about the effectiveness of different pressure groups, about means of access to ruling élites and about the importance of early contact to define the ground, but little evidence of *inter-class* struggle. In the *German Ideology* Marx and Engels at times come close to seeing law

---

[44] Marx, *The Holy Family, op. cit.*
[45] Engels, "Origin of the Family, Private Property, and the State", *op. cit.*, p. 501.
[46] *Ibid.*, p. 582.
[47] Marx and Engels, *The German Ideology, op. cit.*
[48] M. J. Barnett, *The Politics of Legislation* (1969 Weidenfeld, London).

making as a middle class game, wholly irrelevant to proletarians. But they do not maintain this position elsewhere.

Finally it scarcely need be said that law can be used for instrumental short-term purposes. But its utility as a legitimator limits the extent to which this is possible, as has been demonstrated by the fate of the Industrial Relations Act which exposed the fact that law and legislation serve *particular* masters.

Law and social change

This third theme is most easily presented as four sub-themes: the development of private property, the relationship between social and legal change, the usefulness of law in the class struggle, and law as a means of social reform. Here, however, the danger of distortion arising from the extraction of quotable sections is greatest, since *all* Marx' and Engels' analyses were concerned with change, society was *conceived* in terms of motion.

I have indicated already Marx' and Engels' view of private property as a legal phenomenon, a "general juristic conception" which, true to the second function of law, presents property relations as relations of volition rather than "in their real form as relations of production".[49]

The discussion of property is difficult because the authors use the term to mean *both* the general appropriation of land and things by labour *and* the developing bourgeois forms arising from their historically particular conceptions of relationships between people and things. The law elaborates the distinction between ownership (private property) and possession, and by so doing may well create a gulf between common sense or working class understandings of what it means to say something is mine, and for example the conceptions of lawyers or upper class persons involved in holding companies. Horning has produced evidence of these varying conceptions.[50] Property, however conceived, has always been a social phenomenon. "An isolated individual could no more possess property in land than he could speak";[51] and "Only in so far as the individual is a member – in the literal and figurative sense – does he regard himself as an owner or possessor".[52]

The notion of *private* property is to be found in the appropriation of tools for personal use (which still exists in Horning's factory). This is perhaps the seminal notion, pre-existing, which is elaborated when material conditions change and personal appropriation on a wider scale takes place. As Marx points out, the original meaning of "capital" was "cattle"; taking by *vi et armis*, in feudal Britain the only form of theft, embodies the same idea.[53] In order for something to be *stolen* it has to be *owned*. (Differing conceptions of ownership may also in part account for differential rates of "stealing" between social classes). Thus criminal law developed alongside civil law and, through the eighteenth century in particular, buttressed with its own elaborations the conceptual developments of the notion of private

[49] K. Marx, "On Proudhon" (Letter to J. B. Schweitzer) 1865 in *Selected Works, op. cit.*, Vol. 1, p. 355.
[50] D. Horning, "Blue collar theft" in E. Smigal and H. Ross (eds.) *Crimes Against Bureaucracy* 46–64.
[51] Marx, *Pre-Capitalist Economic Formations, op. cit.*, p. 81.
[52] *Ibid.*, p. 69.
[53] See Jerome Hall's discussion of this in *Theft, Law and Society* (1952 Bobbs-Merrill, Indianapolis).

property in the civil law. In civil law, especially, such developments continue. We too ". . . might well reflect on the extent to which civil *law* is linked with private *property* and to what extent civil law determines the existence of a multitude of other relations . . ."[54] Property, of course, is not just in the mind "Actual appropriation takes place not through the relation to these conditions (material) expressed in thought, but through the actual, real relationship to them."[55]

It is, however, a dialectical relationship. This is what is so vital for sociologists of law about Marx' discussion of the development of property. The legal conception *shapes* the external reality, develops with it, and is *developed by* change within the new external world thus created. The hoary old question, which comes first, the law or social change, push or pull, chicken or egg, cannot exist for Marx. The conception *becomes* the material world as the material world gives rise to the conception.

My second question, that of the relationship between social and legal change, is already in part answered. In spelling it out the dialectic discussed above must not be forgotten. But the point I specifically wish to make is that for Marx and Engels a legal form cannot hold back developments if a change in the real economic conditions has taken or is taking place. Engels points out that, as feudal society was breaking up

> Where economic conditions demanded freedom and equality of rights, the political order opposed them at every step with guild restrictions. Local prerogatives, differential tariffs, exceptional laws of all kinds in commerce, not only affected foreigners or inhabitants of colonies, but also often whole categories of the State's own subjects.[56]

The demand for legal equality, for free labour, grew. This is the basis of Enlightenment philosophy. But this bourgeois ideology gave and gives the workers a handle, they can extend the same arguments to demand *equality* in other spheres. Material conditions give rise to an idea or an ideal: who can say where it will lead?

The other case of the legislators standing out against change, real economic power having already shifted to the bourgeoisie, occurs in one of Marx' many discussions of the creation of the proletariat.[57] He describes how a century and a half of legislation designed to prevent enclosures – such as the Act of 1533 which restricted the number of sheep for one owner to 2,000 – proved fruitless. When the bourgeoisie gained control of the *political* institutions, however, the policy was reversed, the forms of feudal land tenure were abolished. The aims were now to extend large scale agriculture, to increase the supply of masterless "free", proletarians, to increase the dependence of the new proletarians on the market for goods also, and to increase "efficiency" on the farm and so provide a surplus for the manufacturers. Thus Marx demonstrates, obliquely for it was not his central purpose, that legal noises when not backed by real power achieve nothing beyond irritation, but that legal institutions in the control of the economically powerful can undoubtedly facilitate and expedite real economic change.

[54] Marx and Engels, *The German Ideology*, op. cit., p. 350.
[55] Marx, *Pre-Capitalist Economic Formations*, op. cit., p. 92.
[56] Engels, *Anti Dürhing*, op. cit., Vol. 1, p. 105.
[57] The present example occurs in *Capital* Vol. 2, Chap. XXIV, *Primary Accumulation* (1930 Everyman, London).

In the light of this, what can proletarians hope to achieve by using legal institutions? Marx and Engels suggest that much is possible through such usage. In the first place, an alliance may be formed with some of those within the bourgeoisie who need their help to achieve a particular sectional aim. Marx suggests that this happened at times during the struggle for the shorter working day.

> However much the individual manufacturer might give the rein to his old lust for gain, the spokesmen and political leaders of the manufacturing class ordered a change of front and of speech towards the work people. They had entered the contest for the repeal of the Corn Laws, and needed the workers to help them to victory.[58]

The notion of the "average interests" of the bourgeoisie is apparent again here. Marx emphasises also the point that the death rate of wage earners was alarming, that it was in the "average interests" of the manufacturers, therefore, to take action to improve conditions. "It would seem, therefore, that the interest of capital itself points in the direction of the normal working day."[59]

Two other factors were at work:

> After the factory magnates had resigned themselves and become reconciled to the inevitable, the power of resistance of capital gradually weakened, whilst at the same time the power of attack of the working class grew with the number of its allies in the classes of society not immediately interested in the question.[60]

Moreover, the working class itself became more organized and more determined, so that "the Factory Inspectors warned the government that the antagonism of the classes had arrived at an incredible tension".[61]

The lessons of this for a politically conscious working class are first, that changes can be achieved if differences *within* the bourgeoisie are exploited. A united bourgeoisie, as in the case of the mines where landed and manufacturing interests were coincident,[62] is more difficult to persuade. However, (lesson two) if workers present a sufficient threat (as in the last extract) concessions can be achieved. The final lesson is that class alliances must be formed where possible. Let Engels have the last word:

> But if the laws were in the hands of a government dominated by or under pressure from the workers . . . it would be a powerful weapon for making a breach in the existing state of things.[63]

Marx leaves one major effect of this, the impetus given to technological development, dangling as an unintended consequence. This is unsatisfactory. Why should unintended consequences so fortuitously and so frequently have effects favourable to the dominant economic class? Unintended consequence is little more than a residual sociological category meaning "we don't know". Carson has attempted to go beyond this in the case of factory

[58] Marx, *Capital* Vol. 1, Chap. X, p. 281 (1970 Lawrence and Wishart, London).
[59] *Ibid.*, p. 266.
[60] *Ibid.*, p. 296.
[61] *Ibid.*, p. 292.
[62] *Ibid.*, p. 464.
[63] Engels, *The Holy Family*, *op. cit.*, p. 472.

legislation, pointing out *inter alia*, that those bourgeois operating with steam, the more advanced technology, initially favoured such legislation as a weapon against their less technologically advanced competitors, whose costs were lower.[64]

The final question to be raised is, can the law bring about social reform? Marx and Engels discuss this point not because it is raised by their theory (which largely precludes it) but because they are constrained to do so by those with whom they are arguing, especially Proudhon and his followers. Marx in 1865 inveighs against Proudhon for mistaking the "legal expression" of property relations (as relations of volition) for their "real form" as relations of production.[65] In the *German Ideology* he had remarked "such concepts (as right) if they are divorced from the empirical reality underlying them can be turned inside out like a glove".[66]

In 1872 Engels developed this critique further, arguing strongly against attempts to bring about piecemeal reform by legal changes (separate solutions for so called political questions) and in particular emphasizing the point that the *criterion* of reform which would be used (human rights, etc.) is itself contingent upon existing relations of production.[67] He recognized that such attempts do take place and argued that if they really operated against the interests of the ruling groups then the law would not be applied or would be only partially applied. (There is a great risk of circularity in actually working with this idea). More probably, such attempts lead to the improvement of the position of one section of the ruling class *vis-à-vis* another rather than to any improvement in the relative position of the workers. For example, in response to Proudhon's argument in favour of a legal limit on the rate of interest he says "the only difference will be that renters will be very careful to advance money only to persons with whom no litigation is to be expected".[68]

Because forms of law are ultimately dependent on relations of production, because the effects of law, in diverse and subtle ways are usually to maintain an existing set of such relations, because, therefore, legal "reforms" cannot really change the pattern of interclass relationships, improving the access of the poor to law is a doubtful advantage. In attacking Sue, a young Hegelian, Marx writes

> (According to Sue) the only failing of French legislation is that it does not provide for payment of the lawyers, does not foresee exclusive service of the poor, and makes the legal limits of poverty too narrow. As if righteousness did not begin in the very lawsuit itself and as if it had not been known for a long time in France that the law gives us nothing but only sanctions what we have.[69]

Conclusions

If the foregoing is to be more than another exercise in literary criticism, the question "where does that get us?" has to be asked. It takes us, I think, a very long way.

64 W. G. Carson and B. Martin, *The Factory Acts* (Forthcoming, Martin Robertson, London).
65 "On Proudhon", *op. cit.*, p. 357.
66 *Op. cit.*
67 Engels, *op. cit.*, pp. 495–574.
68 *Ibid.*
69 Marx and Engels, *The German Ideology, op. cit.*

Theoretically we now see that Marx' and Engels' work not only influenced Durkheim and Weber, as has long been known, but also that it has links through Durkheim with modern functionalism, and, through whom I do not know, with phenomenology. Marx' comments point up criticisms of each of these two contemporary approaches. By showing that a *schema* very like that of Parsons works within a class but not between classes they emphasize again that the systems approach's main weakness is its empirical lack of fit rather than its logical flaws. In their discussions of the role of the subjective in world creation they remind us that in the last resort there is a human body which needs water, however either is conceptualised, if it is going to go on being a creative subjectivity.

The stimulation to current research is as great as the intellectual delights. Briefly, their remarks about law, the State, and ideology give guidelines for research about State personnel, about their relationships with capital and capitalists, about their beliefs, the occupational pressures to which they are subjected, and their professional socialisation. We are encouraged to regard jurisprudence as a higher order ideology, explaining lawyers to themselves. Which lawyers are exposed to this, and which take it on board? What are the limits to the autonomous development of legal thought in terms of its own concepts and thought-rules? The ramifications are endless.

We move on to the functions of law. Here emergence studies come into their own, and are given direction. We can explore the dimensions of intentionality and unintended consequence. And what of those on the receiving end? Do laws really legitimate and mystify? How are they understood by their various enforcers?

Law and change should speak for itself. We have four ready made research topics. I would argue that the first, the role of legal concepts in world creation and its converse, is the most important. I would want to investigate how everyone's world comes to be shaped by the lawyer's world and that of his capitalist clients of the past, how commonly understood statements like "I bought a second-hand car" *came* to be commonly understood. And as I indicated in the text, we must also question the *extent* to which such understandings, for example of what it means to own something, *are* shared.

For the rest, the fact that a reading of Marx and Engels will incite to laughter and to anger should not put them beneath the dignity of the sociologist of law.

MAUREEN CAIN*

* Lecturer in Sociology, Brunel University.

1. What is the "worker bashing" interpretation of Marx's view of law, and what does Cain see as its inadequacies?

2. What is the criminological interpretation of Marx's view of law, and what does Cain see as its inadequacies?

3. What is the relationship between the state and law for Marx?

4. According to Marx and Engels' sociology of law, what are the functions of law?

5. In viewing law as an instrument of social change, what are the four sub-themes of Marxist thought?

6. How does law contribute to the development of private property?

7. What is the relationship between social and legal change?

8. What is the value of law to the proletariat class in the class struggle?

9. Can law, in Marx's view, bring about social reform?

1. The "worker bashing" interpretation suggests that for Marx, "Law was nothing but a coercive system devised to maintain the privileges of the property owning class" (p. 3.20). Cain sees this as a gross over-simplification of Marx and refers to a passage in which Marx seems to argue that "the law has little to do <u>directly</u> with inter-class relationships, the main purpose of laws being to iron out differences <u>within</u> the dominant class, and so, <u>indirectly</u>, to consolidate their class position" (p. 3.21).

2. Cain believes that those who try to read into Marx and Engels a radical theory of criminal behavior are mistaken. While Marx and Engels did see law as closely related to the problems of production, they did not direct their attention to the issue of crime. Therefore, the attempt to find a theory of crime within Marx's work is misguided.

3. The state is created by the capitalist class for the purpose of " . . . protecting their common internal class interests, such as the establishment of clearly understood rules for commercial transactions, and of protecting them against external threats from other classes or states" (Cain, 1974, pp. 3.23-3.24). The state then begins to appear independent from and above the material conditions which gave rise to it and produces an ideology to justify and defend it. Law is a major element in the ideology which arises to disguise the economic basis for the state's very existence. Like the state, the law comes to be seen also as independent "both of material conditions and of the state" (Cain, 1974, p. 3.24).

4. Law functions to:

   a. <u>obscure real power relationships</u>: law has the mystification function of obscuring real power relationships. Despite what rights are provided on paper, real power--the power of the capitalist class-- determines the outcomes of conflict situations.

   b. <u>legitimizes the exercise of real power</u>: law has the legitimizing function of justifying the exercise of such power as proper under the law.

   c. <u>express the interests of the capitalist class generally, rather than of particular individuals or sections of that class</u>: law performs the function of reconciling differences within the capitalist class itself in order to maintain the "unity and integrity of the class" (Cain, 1974, p. 3.27).

5. a. the development of private property.

   b. the relationship between social and legal change.

   c. the usefulness of law in the class struggle.

   d. law as a means of social reform.

6. Private property is a legal concept which masks the true basis for the relationship of people to things. The concept of ownership leads to the concept of theft since there can be no stealing of that which is not owned. As Cain explains the relationship between legal conceptions and private property, "The legal conception shapes the external reality, develops with it, and is developed by change within the new external world thus created" (Cain, 1974, p. 3.29).

7. For Marx and Engels, " . . . a legal form cannot hold back developments if a change in the real economic conditions has taken or is taking place" (Cain, 1974, p. 3.29). In other words, law which does not have the support of the economic elite, however, can be a useful tool for bringing about change.

8. Law can be used by the proletariat if alliances with segments of the capitalist class are developed. Where there are divisions within the capitalist class, these divisions can be exploited through the creation of alliances based upon law. The example cited is that of the struggle for the legal restriction on the length of a working day. Since workers were dying, it was generally in the interests of the onwers to form an alliance with the workers to shorten the work day.

9. Marx believed that relationships between classes could not be altered by law because laws which significantly threatened the capitalist class would be subverted, ignored, or avoided. "Because forms of law are ultimately dependent on relations of production, because the effect of law, in diverse and subtle ways are usually to maintain an existing pattern of such relations, because, therefore, legal 'reforms' cannot really change the pattern of interclass relationships, improving the access of the poor to law is a doubtful advantage" (Cain, 1974, p. 3.31).

UNIT SUMMARY

This unit has presented a number of theories expressing in various forms a central thought: that law is largely a reflection of social structure and organization and that developments in social organization bring corresponding developments in law. While the particular focal points of the theories described are different, all represent efforts to deal with the same issue: how does society affect law?

REFERENCES

Cain, M. The main themes of Marx' and Engels' sociology of law. British Journal of Law and Society, 1974, 1, 136-148.

Friedman, L. M. Law and society. Englewood Cliffs: Prentice Hall, 1977.

Friedman, L. M. The legal system. New York: Russel Sage, 1975.

Friedman, L. M, & Macauley, S. Law and the behavioral sciences (2nd ed.). New York: Bobbs-Merril, 1977.

Galanter, M. The modernization of law. In M. Weiner (Ed.), Modernization. New York: Basic Books:, 1966.

Nonet, P. & Selznick, P. Law and society in transition: toward responsive law. New York: Harper & Row, 1978.

Pospisil, L. Anthropology of law. New York: Harper & Row, 1971.

Schur, Edwin M. Law and society. New York: Random House, 1968.

Schwartz, R. D. Social factors in the development of legal control: a case study of two Israeli settlements. Yale Law Journal, 1954, 63, 471.

Schwartz, R. D., & Miller, J. C. Legal evolution and complexity. American Journal of Sociology, 1964, 70, 159-169.

Unger, R. M. Law in modern society. New York: Macmillan, 1976.

UNIT 4

Law And Dispute Resolution

Rationale

Units 4-6 explore in more detail three of the functions of law: dispute resolution, social control, and social change. As indicated in the course overview these are the three most important functions because all societies need to have some institutions to enable them to perform these functions. More often than not, it is legal institutions which they employ.

While all societies provide some means of processing and resolving disputes, they use a variety of alternative processes. It is important to recognize these alternatives in order to evaluate the current means of dispute resolution and the possibilities for introducing better means.

Objectives

After you have completed this unit, you should be able to:

1. Define the following concepts:

   a. dispute

   b. negotiation or reconciliation

   c. avoidance

d.　mediation

　　　e.　arbitration

　　　f.　adjudication or judging

　　　g.　one-shotters

　　　h.　repeat players

　　　i.　small claims courts

　　　j.　citizen dispute centers

　　　k.　community moot

　2.　Analyze the desirability and feasibility of establishing
　　　community moots in America.

　3.　Describe the kinds of problems that might best be handled
　　　by formal courts and by informal dispute centers or community
　　　moots.

Overview

Unit 4 focuses on law as a means for resolving disputes.　Mini-
Lecture #1, "Alternative Mechanisms For Dispute Resolution," defines the
nature of disputes, describes the alternative forms of dispute resolution,
and describes three examples of institutions established for the purpose
of resolving disputes.　Reading #1, an excerpt from an article by Richard
Danzig, describes in more detail the community moot, an idea adapted from
a dispute processing technique used by a number of African tribes.

Study Task Checklist

☐   1. A.   Read Mini-Lecture #1:   "Alternative Mechanisms for Dispute Resolution."

☐   1. B.   Answer the Study Questions and compare your answers with the Discussion of them.

☐   2. A.   Study Reading #1, "Toward the Creation of a Complementary Decentralized System of Criminal Justice," by Richard Danzig.

☐   2. B.   Answer the Study Questions and compare your answers with the Discussion of them.

ALTERNATIVE MECHANISMS FOR DISPUTE RESOLUTION

Defining 'Disputes'

As indicated in the Introduction, one of the key functions of law is 'dispute settlement'. A 'dispute' may be defined as "...the public assertion of inconsistent claims over something of value" (Friedman, 1977, p. 12). This definition has the advantage of enabling us to distinguish 'disputes' from 'mere factual disagreements' on the one hand and 'mere conflict' on the other. A disagreement on a matter of fact (for example, "Is Sociology 774 a required course for Administration of Justice majors?") is not a dispute because it does not involve 'conflict', i.e., inconsistent claims over something of value. Disagreements over fact would become disagreements over value if the disputants "...desired not only factual vindication but also an admission of intellectual superiority" (Abel, 1973, p. 227). Conflicting claims over something of value constitute 'mere conflict', however, until there is public assertion of the claims. Thus, this definition of 'dispute' requires two elements to occur: the 'public assertion' and the 'conflict', or the "inconsistent claim over something of value."*

Forms of Dispute Processing

In describing the various mechanisms for processing disputes we can distinguish those processes which involve third parties from those which exclusively involve the parties to the dispute.

Two processes which involve only the disputing parties are negotiation or reconciliation and avoidance. Negotiation basically refers to bargaining in an effort to reach a mutually acceptable resolution to

---

*This definition of 'conflict' refers to what may be called 'conflicts of interest' in which there is disagreement over the distribution of a scarce valued good. There may also be 'conflicts of values' in which parties disagree over principles or norms, rather than on the distribution of things of value. (See Aubert, 1963.)

a dispute. No particular institutional setting or legal authority is necessary for negotiation to take place. "By reconciliation is meant the process by which parties in the dispute confer with each other and reach a point at which they can come to terms and restore or create harmonious relationships" (Kawashima in Aubert, 1975, p. 191). Avoidance essentially refers to withdrawal from the relationship which has produced the dispute. As Felstiner (1974) puts it,

> By avoidance, I mean limiting the relationship with the other disputant sufficiently so that the dispute no longer remains salient. While such a process of dealing with disputes may not prove entirely satisfactory, it does terminate the dispute and it spares the disputant the time, money, and discomfort of using the law to deal with the dispute. (p. 70)

Disputes may also be handled by use of third parties in a variety of capacities. Generally, third party dispute processes vary in their level of formality, their degree of openness, their conception of relevance, and their decisional style (Sarat, 1976, p. 340). Third party involvement, in other words, can be more or less formal and rigid, more or less open for public scrutiny of the dispute, narrow or broad in their definition of what is relevant to the dispute, and can decide cases by reference to norms which result in winners and losers or by seeking to compromise and balance the resolution to avoid the impression that one disputant was right and one was wrong.

The least formal third party dispute process is mediation, or the effort to get disputants to solve their own problems by appealing to their self-interest. There is no authority in the mediator to force any particular resolution on the disputants. The mediator simply looks for "possibilities of resolution which the parties themselves have not discovered and try to convince them that both will be well served with his suggestion" (Eckhoff in Aubert, 1975, p. 171). As Felstiner (1974) sees it, "...since success-ful mediation requires an outcome acceptable to the parties, the mediator cannot rely primarily on rules but must construct an outcome in the light of the social and cultural context of the dispute, the full scope of the relations between the disputants and the perspectives from which they view the disputes" (pp. 73-74).

The role of laws or norms in mediation is limited. If the disputants agree that laws should generally be followed but that the laws do not adequately cover their particular dispute, then the mediator can at least use the laws as a point of departure in seeking a solution. If, however, each disputant believes that the norms or laws do cover the particular dispute and that the laws dictate a result in their favor, then the laws are of little value to the mediator because each disputant is convinced of the rightness of his/her position under the law which applies to this type of dispute. (See Eckhoff in Aubert, 1975, p. 173.) The point is that the mediator is not trying to determine which party is right; rather he/she is trying to help the parties adjust their differences regardless of who is right.

> The mediator, therefore, must try to 'deideologize' the conflict, for instance, by stressing that interests are more important than the question of who is right and who is wrong, or by arguing that one ought to be reasonable and willing to compromise. (Eckhoff in Aubert, 1975, p. 180)

Arbitration and adjudication are also third party processes. They differ from mediation in that the third party has the authority to impose a solution even if the parties are unwilling to accept it. The only distinction between arbitration and adjudication is that the arbitrator is not required to be a professional judge, while the adjudicator is a trained professional. In a sense, the arbitrator can be thought of as an 'amateur judge' and the adjudicator as a 'professional judge'.

Both, however, are involved in judging, an activity which differs significantly from mediating. Whereas mediation involves laws or norms only indirectly as a means of encouraging disputants to reach agreement, judging constitutes a direct application of laws or norms to factual disputes and results in the conclusion that one or the other of the disputants acted in violation of the law. While the mediator is likely to consider future relationships between the disputants in his/her search for a mutually satisfactory resolution, the judge looks primarily at the governing law and the facts of the dispute, reaching a conclusion without reference to future relationships between the parties.

There is an interesting problem posed by the choice to mediate or to judge in any dispute situation. If mediation is used, then the emphasis is on compromise, rather than on the laws defining correct behavior in such situations. If judging is used, then the emphasis is on who was right under the law, rather than on working out a compromise solution fair to both parties. Eckhoff (1975) concisely captures the paradox when he writes, "By mediating one may weaken the normative basis for a later judgement and perhaps also undermine confidence in one's impartiality as a judge; and by judging first one will easily reduce the willingness to compromise..." (p. 180). The difficulty is that reliance on judging reduces the willingness to compromise because if you're right, you should win; but reliance on mediating reduces the value of law because being right is less important than reconciling the dispute.

Dispute Processing Institutions

A. Small Claims Courts

One attempt to provide institutionalized mechanisms for individuals to assert legal claims in disputes which do not involve large sums of money are small claims courts. The process for filing claims is simple and the rules of evidence are relaxed somewhat in order to allow disputants to present their respective arguments. The courts are run either by judges or arbitration panels made up of lawyers, and, basically, they are judging, not mediating. While supposedly not needing an attorney, the disputant who chooses not to retain one is at a disadvantage. One study of the New York Small Claims Court concludes, "Parties represented by attorneys receive more favorable outcomes in both adjudicated and arbitrated cases" (Sarat, 1976, p. 370). Since it is difficult to deny the right to a lawyer in a legal proceeding, the party with a lawyer is likely to prevail. Since the judges and arbitrators are also lawyers, they find it difficult not to respond to technical legal arguments on rules of evidence and various trial procedures. The unrepresented disputant in small claims court, therefore, is probably not much better off than in any other court.

One unanticipated problem with small claims courts has been that, instead of providing a forum in which individuals could assert their rights when their TV's didn't work, their gardeners stepped on their tomato plants, and their automobile mechanics fixed the same parts of their cars monthly without removing the offending squeaks, small claims courts become collection agencies for businesses. A study of small claims court in Dane County, Wisconsin revealed that 93% of the small claims plaintiffs were businesses (Rapson, 1961, cited in Nader and Singer, 1976, p. 284).

Furthermore, the claimants who rarely use the courts tend to be less effective than those who regularly use the courts. The former, called 'one-shotters' are unable to compete with the latter, called 'repeat players' (Galanter, 1974, p. 97). One-shotters lack the experience, expertise, and personal connections which the repeat players build up over time. Some critics of small claims agrue that it is difficult for an unrepresented plaintiff claiming that a major discount store sold him/her defective merchandise to defeat the discount store's insurance company's lawyer who defends against similar claims 5 hours a day, 5 days a week! On the other hand, however, a recent survey of the literature on small claims courts argues that, while substantial numbers of businesses appear regularly as plaintiffs in small claims courts, consumers, who appear far less often as plaintiffs, are likely to succeed--especially if represented by an attorney. In fact,

> The studies reviewed [also] indicate [however] that plaintiffs win at least 74% of the cases going to judgment (and frequently more), irrespective of who brings suit. The only factor which seems to significantly influence the rate of plaintiff victory is the presence of an attorney on one side (Yngvesson and Hennessey, 1975, p. 225)

B. Citizen Dispute Centers

A new idea for dispute resolution has emerged in several cities, including Orlando, Florida and Columbus, Ohio. Citizen Dispute Centers represent an effort to move away from judging toward mediation for resolving minor disputes. Basically, a volunteer attorney serves as a mediator for disputes of any sort. A complaint is filed by a complainant and the other party, the respondent, is notified that a hearing will be held usually within a few days. At the hearing the parties are free to present their sides of the dispute free of technical rules. If the mediator succeeds in persuading the parties to reach an agreement, they sign a statement expressing the terms of their agreement. While the agreement is not enforceable and either party can always resort to traditional courts, there is some incentive to abide by the agreement in order to avoid the possible future court action. The program director in Orlando summarizes the program:

The purpose of this informal hearing process is not to
determine right or wrong or impose legal sanction. Rather,
the fundamental goal is to assist the complainant and
respondent to reach a mutually satisfactory settlement,
should that settlement be restitution or a promise to
discontinue the problem behavior (quoted in Conner and
Sarette, 1977, p. 37)

C. Community Moots

A more unusual suggestion for dispute resolution is the 'community
moot', an informal mediation process patterned after those found among
African tribes. One such process is described by James L. Gibbs (1963)
who studied an African society known as the Kpelle. Existing along with
a court system, the Kpelle moot provides a mechanism for processing disputes by mediation while working to maintain a friendly relationship
between the parties.

The mediator has no power to imprision, coerce, or punish severely.
The mediator does, however, have the power to "express the consensus of
the group" (Gibbs in Bohannon, 1967, p. 281). The resolution has a
therapeutic quality to it in which "The parties and spectators drink
together to symbolize the restored solidarity of the group and the rehabilitation of the offending party" (Gibbs in Bohannon, 1967, p. 283).
Gibbs describes the operation of the Kpelle moot:

> The complainant speaks first and may be interrupted by
> the mediator or anyone else present. After he has been
> thoroughly quizzed, the accused will answer and will also
> be questioned by those present. The two parties will
> question each other directly and question others in the
> room also. Both the testimony and the questioning are
> lively and uninhibited. Where there are witnesses to
> some of the actions described by the parties, they may
> also speak and be questioned. Although the proceedings
> are spirited, they remain orderly. The mediator may
> fine anyone who speaks out of turn by requiring them
> to buy some rum for the group to drink.
>
> The mediator and the others present will point out
> the various faults committed by the parties. After
> everyone has been heard, the mediator expresses the
> consensus of the group. [In a case involving a
> domestic quarrel, the mediator concluded,] 'The
> words you use toward your sister were not good, so
> come and beg her pardon.' (Gibbs in Bohannon,
> 1967, p. 283)

Following the apology, the 'winner' gives a gift to the 'loser' who, in turn gives a lesser gift to the winner and a celebration of group harmony ensues.

There is a current debate in the ranks of scholars as to whether or not more mediation--along the therapeutic lines of the Kpelle moot-- is desirable or possible in American. Reading #1 is an expression of the view that alternatives such as moots ought to be attempted. In the discussion which follows the reading by Richard Danzig, I will summarize the position of Danzig's critics and his response to them.

1. How is the term "dispute" defined in this unit?

2. Differentiate negotiation (or reconciliation) from avoidance.

3. Differentiate mediation from judging (or adjudication/arbitration).

4. What are some of the advantages and disadvantages of:

    a. small claims courts

    b. citizen dispute centers

    c. community moots

DISCUSSION OF MINI-LECTURE #1 QUESTIONS

1. A dispute is defined as "the public assertion of inconsistent claims over something of value" (p. 4.4). This definition implies that there can be conflict which is not a dispute and disagreement over fact which is not a dispute. Disputes must involve both conflict and public assertion.

2. Negotiation (or reconciliation) and avoidance are similar in that both involve only the disputing parties in the effort to resolve the dispute. They differ in that in negotiation the parties seek an agreement while in avoidance they simply cease to associate.

3. Mediation involves a third party who seeks to find a ground upon which the disputants can resolve their differences. Judging involves a third party who seeks to apply a rule or law to a dispute in order to determine which party was right and which was wrong.

4. a. Small Claims Courts theoretically offer an uncomplicated way to adjudicate minor claims. They are operated basically like courts, though there is less concern for formal rules of evidence or procedure. However, the individuals (as opposed to businesses) who appear in small claims courts are most likely to appear as defendants, rather than plaintiffs, thus reducing the ability of the courts to provide efficient, inexpensive solutions for individuals who have complaints. Furthermore, the individuals are likely to be one-shotters who lack the knowledge, experience, and connections of the repeat player defendants whom they sue.

   b. Citizen Dispute Centers provide mediators for resolving disputes. This is preferable to adjudication in some cases. People may be, however, unwilling to meditate disputes if they believe the law to be on their side.

   c. Community Moots also provide for mediation of disputes. They do not require professional mediators, emphasize future relationships between disputants, and aim at therapeutic rather than punitive results. Such a system may not work in a diverse society such as the United States.

EXCERPTS FROM:

TOWARD THE CREATION OF A COMPLEMENTARY

DECENTRALIZED SYSTEM OF CRIMINAL JUSTICE

RICHARD DANZIG

D. *A Community Moot*

Periodically there appears in the literature of criminal law—either in commentary on foreign legal systems or in a revisionist approach to our own—a glimmering of recognition that a court could do very different things from those we are accustomed to its doing. This perspective is of pressing relevance to decentralization.

1. *Need for a new court model.*

So long as we think of courts as adjudicators of guilt, they are extremely unlikely candidates for decentralization. At the outset of this Article it was acknowledged that there are some things the existing system does well and that these should be preserved. A prime example was the trial mechanism which affords due process to the accused. The courts, it may be conceded, do not give as many defendants the benefits of a due process trial as they should, but this only points to a need for more courts or for improving the workings of courts. If distance, professional objectivity, a "blind" treatment of all individuals as though they were alike, and a highly controlled, even rigidified, procedural system are the underpinnings of due process (it would seem that they are), then certainly reformers attempting to expand the opportunity for a due process trial should not call for decentralization of the court system. By these lights the last things we want are paraprofessionals as judges, community mores as standards, and a neighborhood as a forum.

At their best, then, courts should be responsive to higher principles than the sentiments of those who are judged or, most especially, those who do the judging. Where is there a role for community control in such a pure—and surely correct—vision of the process? Moreover, as commonly conceived, courts also seem irrelevant to decentralization because each case involves so little policy input once a legislative code has been framed, and each case (except for the most spectacular) yields so little of consequence to the political arena when it is resolved. What can the average citizen contribute, and what does he care?

These perspectives change radically, however, if we stop thinking of courts as adjudicators, and view them instead as parts of a therapeutic process aimed at conciliation of disputants or reintegration of deviants into society.[116] One author has labelled these contrasting conceptualizations as the battle model and the family model.[117] Another, writing as an anthropologist, compares the function and style of parallel court systems in Liberia in similar terms.[118] A court system, established by the British, was primarily adjudicative, while a tribal "moot" performed an integrative, conciliatory function. Whereas the court was characterized by social dis-

---

116. "For the most part, litigation is a way of viewing the past through the eyes of the present. But perhaps justice is best done by starting with the present—with present needs and present demands—and using the past only where it reveals equitable considerations which will provide guidance in shaping a remedy . . .

"We are still—in contract law, in domestic law, in landlord-tenant law, in tort law—engaged in a quest for fault, for 'who did what when' as a way of deciding how the risk should be borne and who should pay, perform or provide remedy. Yet, in domestic relations, industrial injuries, automobile accidents, we are finding that the quest for fault is time consuming, elusive and not particularly productive in terms of enabling human beings to get back on their feet and to cope with the present or chart a rational course for the future." Cahn & Cahn, *supra* note 96, at 932. The Cahns propose the creation of a "Neighborhood Arbitration Commission" and other institutions less relevant to this discussion.

117. Griffiths, *supra* note 28, at 359. Though Griffiths does not discuss the point he could fairly have argued that insofar as it has developed the tool of arbitration, modern labor law provides us with an extended and successful experience in the operation of the family model. *See generally* A. Cox & D. Bok, CASES AND MATERIALS ON LABOR LAW 518–23 (6th ed. 1969).

118. Gibbs, *The Kpelle Moot*, 33 AFRICA 1 (1963), *abridged and reprinted in* LAW AND WARFARE 277 (P. Bohannan ed. 1967); Gibbs, *Poro Values and Courtroom Procedures in a Kpelle Chiefdom*, 18 Sw. J. ANTHROPOLOGY 341 (1962). Though Gibbs' insights have been taken as the starting point for this discussion, the anthropological literature is not without other examples of the same system in other cultures. *See, e.g.*, in Mexico, Nader, *Styles of Court Procedure: To Make the Balance*, in LAW IN CULTURE AND SOCIETY 69 (L. Nader ed. 1969); in Africa, Harries-Jones, *Marital Disputes and the Process of Conciliation in a Copperbelt Town*, 34 HUMAN PROBLEMS IN BRITISH CENTRAL AFRICA 29 (1964); and in India, Cohn, *Some Notes on Law and Change in North India*, 8 ECONOMIC DEVELOPMENT & CULTURAL CHANGE 79 (1959), in P. Bohannan ed., *supra* at 139, and in L. RUDOLPH & S. RUDOLPH, THE MODERNITY OF TRADITION 254 (1967).

Comrades' Courts in the Soviet Union bear some resemblance to the moots here proposed, particularly in their encouragement of neighborhood participation and their emphasis on total examination of the situation of the offender. But they differ markedly from the moots chronicled above and here recommended because of their coercive power (either through punishment or recordkeeping), their adjudicative emphasis (guilt or innocence determined by a tribunal of judges), and their link with the centralized state machinery. *See generally* Lipson, *Law: The Function of Extra-Judicial Mechanisms*, in SOVIET AND CHINESE COMMUNISM: SIMILARITIES AND DIFFERENCES 144 (P. Threadgold ed. 1967); Berman & Spindler, *Soviet Comrades' Courts*, 38 WASH. L. REV. 842 (1963). Note also Stanley Lubman's contrast between the emphasis on "right and wrong" in present Chinese communist mediation proceedings and the lack of such emphasis in traditional Confucian efforts at

tance between judge and litigants, rules of procedure which narrowed the issues under discussion, and a resolution which ascribed guilt or innocence to a defendant, the moot emphasized the bonds between the convenor and the disputants, it encouraged the widening of discussion so that all tensions and viewpoints psychologically—if not legally—relevant to the issue were expressed,[119] and it resolved disputes by consensus about future conduct, rather than by assessing blame retrospectively.[120] The consensual development of solutions was aided by the fact that while the "court" emphasized the trappings of authority and coercive power, the moot "takes place in the familiar surroundings of a home. The robes, writs, messengers, and other symbols of power which subtly intimidate and inhibit the parties in the courtroom, by reminding them of the physical force which underlies the procedures, are absent."[121] While courts often proceed in a mysterious, almost Delphic fashion, obscure and therefore unpersuasive to the people caught up in the system, a moot has a better chance of molding consensus because it operates in an everyday manner as well as milieu.[122]

Despite the differences between a tribal culture and our own, isn't there a place for a community moot in our judicial system?[123] Such a moot might handle family disputes, some marital issues (*e.g.*, paternity, support, separation), juvenile delinquency, landlord-tenant relations, small torts and breaches of contract involving only community members, and misdemea-

---

mediation. Lubman, *Mao and Mediation: Politics and Dispute Resolution in Communist China*, 55 CALIF. L. REV. 1284 (1967).

Cuba's "popular tribunals," though performing conciliatory functions and "organized . . . in the neighborhood, so that neighbors and acquaintances of those being judged can attend the trials . . . and . . . judges sitting in these trials come from the same community in which they live and work," MANUAL DE LOS TRIBUNALES POPULARES DE BASE VI (1966), *quoted in* Berman, *The Cuban Popular Tribunals*, 69 COLUM. L. REV. 1317, 1318 (1969), are also constructed on the coercive adjudicative model. *See, e.g.*, Berman's description: "[T]he '¡A pie!' cry when the judges enter and exit. . . . coupled with the armed and uniformed crier, gives the Popular Tribunals an aura of formality and authority which is not insignificant." *Id.* at 1342.

The community institution recommended in this Article has been called a "moot" to emphasize that it is more like the Kpelle than the communist system.

119. M. GLUCKMAN, THE JUDICIAL PROCESS AMONG THE BAROTSE OF NORTHERN RHODESIA 51 (1955), notes the advantages of the same all-encompassing technique in Barotse courts.

120. Griffiths calls this a "distinction between a punitive and a best-interests proceeding." Griffiths, *supra* note 28, at 411. The Rudolphs write: "The village tribunal, because its members reside among the disputing parties and find their own lives touched by their discontents, is less anxious to find 'truth' and give 'justice' than to abate conflict and promote harmony." L. RUDOLPH & S. RUDOLPH, *supra* note 118, at 258. Nader quotes Professor Hahm's observation that "analogous Korean proceedings prefer peace to justice, harmony to truth, and mediation to adjudication." Nader, *supra* note 118, at 84.

121. Gibbs, *The Kpelle Moot*, 33 AFRICA 1 (1963), *abridged and reprinted in* LAW AND WARFARE 277, 282 (P. Bohannan ed. 1967).

122. Curiously Gibbs does not emphasize this point. *But see* Srivinas, *The Social System of a Mysore Village*, in VILLAGE INDIA 18 (M. Marriot ed. 1955): "I do not hold that the justice administered by the elders of the dominant caste is always or even usually more just than the justice administered by the judges in urban law courts, but only that it is much better understood by the litigants." Jesse Berman's comment on the Cuban Popular Tribunals is similar: "Perhaps it is not unfair to say that it is deemed more important that the people know the judges, than that the judges know the law." Berman, *supra* note 118, at 1335.

123. It should be noted that other writers have called for the creation of neighborhood courts, and that some institutions of this sort are actually operating in the United States, but the emphasis in these programs has been on an adjudicative rather than a conciliatory forum. *See, e.g.*, Elson &

nors affecting only community members. The present system does not, after all, perform the job of adjudication in most of these cases. Civil proceedings are generally avoided because the parties are too ignorant, fearful, or impoverished to turn to small claims courts, legal aid, or similar institutions.[124] Many matters which may technically be criminal violations will not be prosecuted because they are viewed by the prosecuting authorities as private and trivial matters. The criminal adjudicative model seems particularly insufficient and a system of conciliation correspondingly well advised when we know that due to institutional overcrowding and established patterns of sentencing the vast majority of misdemeanants and some felons are not likely to be imprisoned. For these defendants, the judicial process is not a screen filtering those who are innocent from those who will be directed to the corrective parts of the process. Rather, it is the corrective process; as such it fails to be more than a "Bleak House,"[125] profoundly alienating, rather than integrating.

The arguments for abandoning the adjudicative model have received some recognition in two of the functional areas of court work which a moot might assume: those related to juveniles[126] and to family disputes.[127] But New York's Family Court,[128] reorganized in 1962[129] and again nominated for reorganization in 1969,[130] retains the trappings of the adjudicative

---

Rosenheim, *Justice for the Child at the Grassroots*, 51 A.B.A.J. 341 (1965): "In essence, our proposal is to transplant a certain group of cases from the juvenile court itself to a community panel created by the court specifically to hear and dispose of those cases." *Id.* Note especially *id.* at 344–45, discussing operating prototypes of such panels.

See also the description of the East Palo Alto, California, Community Youth Responsibility Program in Hager, *Neighborhood Court Judges Its Own Juvenile Offenders*, L.A. Times, Dec. 25, 1972, at 1, col. 5, and (in more detail) Urban and Rural Systems Associates, Evaluation of the Community Youth Responsibility Program, undated.

124. *See generally* Eovaldi & Gestrin, *Justice for Consumers: The Mechanisms of Redress*, 66 Nw. U.L. Rev. 281 (1971). After surveying the present range of options for consumer litigation, the authors conclude that "new approaches are needed which can transcend the limits of our traditional legal framework," *id.* at 302, and urge experimentation with arbitration techniques which would circumvent traditional court procedures.

125. I have borrowed Dickens' phrase from Schrag, *Bleak House 1968: A Report on Consumer Test Litigation*, 44 N.Y.U.L. Rev. 115 (1969), who uses it to describe the delays encountered in litigating consumer protection cases in New York City's courts.

126. W. Stapleton & L. Teitlebaum, In Defense of Youth: A Study of the Role of Counsel in American Juvenile Courts 103 (1972), quote Jane Addams: "There was almost a change in *mores* when the Juvenile Court was established. The child was brought before the judge with no one to prosecute him and none to defend him—the judge and all concerned were merely trying to find out what could be done on his behalf. The element of conflict was absolutely eliminated and with it, all notion of punishment as such. . . ." The Stapleton and Teitlebaum discussion underscores ways in which a thrust toward legalization has undermined this orientation.

127. *See generally* Foster, *Conciliation and Counseling in the Courts in Family Law Cases*, 41 N.Y.U.L. Rev. 353 (1966).

128. A civil court, but one included in this Article because of the obvious relevance of its work to the criminal justice system.

129. *See* Family Court Act, N.Y. Judiciary-Court Acts §§ 111–1019 (McKinney 1963 & McKinney Supp. 1973). Association of the Bar of the City of New York, Children and Families in the Courts of New York City (1954), describes the operation of the New York system prior to 1962. The report prompted the 1962 Family Court Act.

130. *See* Directors of Administration of the Courts, First and Second Judicial Departments, A Study of the Family Court of the State of New York within the City of New York and Related Agencies and Recommendations Concerning Their Administration (1969);

model.[131] Judges, 30 to 40 years older[132] and of an entirely different social stratum from those who typically are summoned to appear before them,[133] preside in downtown courts from raised benches, deciding cases involving charges of juvenile delinquency,[134] assaults between family members, divorce and nonsupport. The physical, social, and psychological distance between a judge and the citizens before him cannot be overcome, nor can the circumstances of a situation be penetrated in the limited time available for each case; decisions by fiat rather than conciliation are therefore necessary.[135]

2. *Workings of the proposed moot.*

A neighborhood moot, however, might handle segments of this case load[136] in a different manner. Again, we are dealing with activities (assaults

---

REPORT OF THE JUDICIAL CONFERENCE, *supra* note 66, at 287–325. Recommendations accepted from the former report and planned changes are described in *id.* at 63–70.

131. In part this is a result of a constitutional mandate called into play wherever coercive detention of significant duration is a likely outcome of a procedure. *See In re* Gault, 387 U.S. 1 (1967); Hogan v. Rosenberg, 24 N.Y.2d 207, 247 N.E.2d 260, 299 N.Y.S.2d 424 (1969). In part it is due to the administrative ambiance which envelops a high volume bureaucratic operation. "Impersonal attendants perform their duties with clipped routine, underscoring alienation. In the waiting rooms of the larger New York Boroughs it is not unusual for fifty or sixty persons to be gathered. As each case is called the name of the respondent is shouted out in full voice by a court employee dressed like a police officer. The name of the youngster is likely to be called a second time if he does not leap forward immediately, lest a moment be wasted. Observers find it ironic to recall the words of the Illinois Family Court Act, which expressed the intended spirit of the New York Law as well: 'The children . . . as far as practicable . . . shall be treated not as criminals but as children in need of aid, encouragement and guidance.'" Paulson, *Juvenile Courts, Family Courts, and the Poor Man,* in THE LAW OF THE POOR 370 (J. tenBroek ed. 1966).

132. Only one of the 30 Family Court judges who listed a birth date in the 1970 *Martindale-Hubbel* was born after 1924. The average age of judges listed there is 59.

133. *See generally* Paulson, *supra* note 131, at 371.

134. The unfortunate individual and institutional impacts of this labeling are discussed in Langley, *The Juvenile Court: The Making of a Delinquent,* 7 L. & SOC'Y REV. 273 (1972).

135. The New York Family Court's failure as an instrument of conciliation is suggested by the fact that of the 44,675 new cases it received in 1968–69, exactly 10 were for conciliation in an effort to avoid divorce or separation. REPORT OF THE JUDICIAL CONFERENCE, *supra* note 66, at 288, 319. Statewide, the number of conciliation proceedings in family courts declined from 520 in 1963–64 to 163 in 1968–69—the only decline in cases received by Family Courts except for a marginal decrease in neglect cases. *Id.* at 288. This lack of activity is not a problem in itself because conciliation bureaus established in 1967 have actively offered conciliation services in divorce and separation cases. *See id.* at 50, 106. But the Family Court's incapacity to play this role in divorce cases suggests its inability to abandon the adjudicative model in dealing with juvenile delinquents or family offenses.

136. It is not proposed that the moot entertain either adoption or divorce proceedings. Other cases could be handled either by the moot or family court, according to the preference of the litigants. *See* text accompanying notes 140–43 *infra.* The moot's resolution of support or similar cases could be given force simply by framing agreed results in the form of a contract between the parties.

The distribution of the case load in New York City's Family Court is as follows:

Types of cases in New York City Family Court, 1968–69

Proceeding	*Percent*
Juvenile delinquency	20
Person in need of supervision	11
Neglect and permanent neglect	9
Adoption	2
Support	29
Family Offense	11
Paternity	17
Other	1

Source: REPORT OF THE JUDICIAL CONFERENCE, *supra* note 66, at 289.

between family members, juvenile delinquency which does not reach the level of felony, marital relationships other than divorce) which do not have significant externalities. Again, the bankruptcy of the professional in handling these problems has many times been noted, especially by the professionals themselves.[137] Here also the existing system is overburdened and undermanned.[138] If a less elaborate community-based system assumed a defined portion of the case load, it would leave the regular court time to function in cases where its professional skills were relevant.

The usefulness of nonprofessionals assembled through the forum of a moot is suggested by therapeutic practices which secure progress with personal and family problems by building a pattern of supportive conduct among friends and neighbors.[139] The family court only treats parties in the courtroom environment; a moot would begin with the recognition that people's problems may be resolved or intensified—if not caused—by the milieu in which they dwell. Operating in that milieu the moot is designed to stimulate emotional and tangible support from those on the block and in the tenement, the people among whom the disputants live and on whom they depend.

The method of operation of such a moot could vary experimentally with each community. Typically, however, it might draw its "business" from referrals by social agencies, the community police,[140] the neighborhood attorney, the municipal police, the existing court system, and from voluntary submissions by individuals who wished the services of the body. A salaried counselor accepting such requests for a moot might then arrange sessions at a time and place suitable to the participants: the complainant, the persons about whom he had complained, and those invited by these parties or the counselor. If a necessary party refused to attend, a counselor would simply refer the other parties to the municipal justice system. This possibility should often secure the cooperation of those who in the court system would be defendants.[141] A significant attraction to complainants is that the

---

137. See J. POLIER, A VIEW FROM THE BENCH (1964); Paulson, *supra* note 131; Tolchin, *Experts Wonder If Family Court Is Doing Its Job*, N.Y. Times, Jan. 18, 1964, at 24, col. 3. All the foregoing specifically refer to the Family Court in New York City. Griffiths remarks generally that "[t]here is common agreement that the juvenile court movement—measured against its initial ideals and expectations—is more or less a failure." Griffiths, *supra* note 28, at 399.

138. The Family Court, "still suffers from acute shortages of necessary personnel and auxiliary services. . . . [The shortage] not only adversely affects the quality of the Court's work, but is creating a backlog of cases awaiting hearing or disposition of near critical proportions." REPORT OF THE JUDICIAL CONFERENCE, *supra* note 66, at 287. During 1968–69 the city's Family Court disposed of 34,935 petitions, about the same number as in the previous year, but 44,675 petitions were received. *Id.* at 288.

139. *See* Davidson, *To Treat a Disturbed Person, Treat His Family*, N.Y. Times, Aug. 16, 1970, § 6 (Magazine), at 10; text accompanying note 143 *infra*.

140. The Family Crisis Intervention Unit referred 34.8% of the families it dealt with to the Family Court. F.C.I.U. REPORT, *supra* note 86, at 30.

141. Excellent cooperation from juveniles has been obtained in East Palo Alto, *see* note 123 *supra*, when the experimental system is described as an alternative to police and court processing.

moot holds promise of being more conveniently located, more considerate, and much faster in processing cases than the municipal system.[142] Moreover, there is evidence that a number of would-be complainants do not proceed through the regular police and court system because they do not want the offender to be "harmed" or because they think that the incident is a private, not a criminal, matter.[143] For such people, the informal, private, noncoercive style of the moot may be very appealing. Because the moot has no power of compulsion and does not preempt regular court action, a complainant has nothing to lose by turning first to it. Refusal to give the counselor power to compel attendance is not likely, therefore, to leave a moot without cases.

A moot might be public or private, held in the home of a party, in a community meeting hall, or in the counselor's chambers, with a presumption in favor of private meetings in the counselor's chambers, unless all parties agreed otherwise. Typically, moots might function by the counselor asking the complainant to state his grievances and his requested remedies, by having the person complained about respond, and then by allowing general discussion and questioning between all those present.[144] It would be hoped that through such open discussion a range of grievances running in both directions would be aired and better understood;[145] that the counselor might be able to suggest future conduct by both parties to reduce tensions; and that both friends and relatives invited by the participants might

---

142. "An enormous amount of time is wasted by the parents of children pulled into court. Little or no attempt is made to space appointments for court hearings. Everyone is told to come at 9:30 in the morning, and the reception rooms fill with employed mothers and fathers who lose more wages with each passing hour.

"Waiting to appear in the court is not only expensive for those the court must serve, but the waiting often proves to be futile. A case scheduled to be heard may not be ready and an adjournment will have to be ordered, with the consequent loss of another day's pay for parents." Paulson, supra note 131, at 373; see Ash, supra note 112.

The community moot might hold most of its hearings on evenings or Sundays. Without lawyers or forms, continuances would be much less likely than in Family Court. The speed with which hearings could be initiated by the moot would add to its therapeutic advantages. "[T]he hearing takes place soon after a breach has occurred, before the grievances have hardened." Gibbs, supra note 121, at 282.

143. A National Opinion Research Center Survey of 10,000 households in 1965 revealed that only about 50% of all crimes were reported to law enforcement authorities. Thirty-four % of those who did not report an incident explained that they did not want the matter treated as a criminal affair or the offender harmed. Ennis, Crime, Victims and the Police, in MODERN CRIMINALS 87, 94 (J. Short ed. 1970).

144. In the moot, the parties are encouraged in the expression of their complaints and feelings because they sense group support. "The very presence of one's kinsmen and neighbors demonstrates their concern." Gibbs, supra note 121, at 284.

Not every type of community will have a cultural milieu conducive to the expression of such grievances, nor could we expect every potential participant in any given community moot to be open to this approach. See the comments on cultural barriers to the expression of feelings, in J. Spiegel, Some Cultural Aspects of Transference and Countertransference, in INDIVIDUAL AND FAMILIAL DYNAMICS 160, 161–75 (J. Masserman ed. 1959).

145. "In the moot the parties . . . are allowed to hurl recriminations that, in the courtroom might bring a few hours in jail as punishment for the equivalent of contempt of court." Gibbs, supra note 121, at 286.

serve as "witnesses" and participants in the consensual solutions evolved, thus joining community officials in keeping the peace.[146]

It will be seen from this brief description that in some cases it is hoped that the moot will have effects beyond the judicial and even the correctional function. The moot as recommended would be unique in prompting *community discussion* about situations in which community relations are on the verge of breaking down. When the juvenile who loiters around a shop now receives a police record and warning,[147] antagonisms between him and his peers and the shopkeeper and police are increased rather than relieved. If the complaint were replaced by a moot discussion, to which the teenager brought his friends, the shopkeeper his associates (including his family, other shopkeepers, his employees), and the police their officers charged with working with juveniles, there would be a fair chance for the kind of interchange which has proved valuable when staged as a one-event "retreat" in other communities.[148] Depending, no doubt, on the passions and personalities involved, the skill of the counselor and the root causes of tension, there is reason to hope that such sessions would be useful.

No legislation would be necessary to initiate the moot; the cooperation of individuals associated with the existing court system would be the only prerequisite. Insofar as the moot might prove ineffective in some cases or areas, complainants could be expected to reinitiate their cases in the municipal courts. The alternative system is thus backed up by the established system.

---

146. Of course the impact of social pressure will vary greatly with the "culture" and structure of the community in which the moot is held. Schwartz, *Social Factors in the Development of Legal Control: A Case Study of Two Israeli Settlements*, 63 YALE L.J. 471 (1954), notes several factors relevant to the greater influence of informally expressed opinion in one kibbutz than in another. The kibbutz with less primary group interaction, agreed norm-definition, peer-group identification, and self-selection by emigration or immigration is more likely to rely on more formal legal mechanisms. This suggests some reasons why a moot might be less effective in a New York slum than in a more primitive, rural community. But whether subgroups within an urban slum share enough of these characteristics to a great enough degree to make a moot worthwhile or whether they are so lacking in them as to make it impractical, must, in the absence of experiment, be a matter of conjecture. *See also* Kawashima, *Dispute Resolution in Contemporary Japan*, in LAW IN JAPAN 41 (A. von Mehren ed. 1963), for a discussion of "social-cultural" factors prompting the Japanese to resolve disputes through reconciliation or conciliation rather than litigation.

147. In New York a YD-1 form records a complaint made to the police, but not processed by the courts (and therefore not confirmed by judicially examined and approved evidence). Taken collectively the forms create a dossier, later used by schools, welfare agencies, and courts (in sentencing) as though it implied guilt. At present the system faces legal challenge as an invasion of privacy and a violation of the constitutionally mandated presumption of innocence. I am here proposing that the community moot, which would compile no records suggesting guilt, replace the YD-1 in New York and like systems in other cities.

148. In the moot, "rewards are positive, in contrast to the negative sanctions of the courtroom. Besides the institutional apology, praise and acts of concern and affection replace fines and jail sentences." Gibbs, *supra* note 121, at 288.

1. What are the advantages of the traditional criminal court system for adjudicating guilt?

2. How does Danzig distinguish the idea of courts from that of moots?

3. For what types of problems does Danzig envision the community moot system providing solutions in modern society?

4. How would the proposed moot be structured?

5. Beyond the judicial and correctional functions, what might the
   moot system accomplish?

1. The criminal trial is well designed to protect the rights of the accused. Adherence to criminal procedure in conducting trials helps to treat individuals objectively according to law and avoid the imposition of narrow community standards of conduct.

2. Courts perform the function of adjudication; moots provide a "therapeutic process aimed at conciliation of disputants or reintergration of deviants into society" (Danzig, 1973). The courts represent a 'battle model' and the moots, a 'family model'. Unlike the courts, which emphasize status differences between the judge and the judged and which attempt to ascribe guilt, the moot is held in familiar surroundings, minimizes social distance between the judge and the judged, and attempts to resolve disputes "by consensus about future conduct."

3. Danzig believes that the difference between tribal and modern societies do not make the moot system less feasible. Specifically he advocates use of a moot system for family disputes, landlord-tenant disputes, and even felonies where the adjudicative model is inadequate due to prison overcrowding and wide use of probationary sentencing.

4. The moot would be tailored to the specific needs of the community. Danzig suggests that a salaried counselor receive requests for the convening of a moot and notify all interested parties of the precise time and place--preferably within the neighborhood in which the disputing parties reside. Parties would be told that failure to attend the moot would result in the case being referred to the court system. "Because the moot has no power of complusion and does not preempt regular court action, a complainant has nothing to lose by turning first to it." The proceeding itself would consist of open discussion by all aspects of the problem and the feelings of the parties toward each other.

5. Danzig argues that the moot would encourage community discussion and community effort to work out problems. Rather than simply deciding which individual was at fault, the moot aims at collectively fashioning creative approaches to solving problems

Comment

After Danzig proposed this alternative dispute processing mechanism based more upon mediation than judging, some of his critics argued that such a mediation scheme would be unsuccessful in a modern American context. Felstiner (1974) for example, claims that mediation flourishes only "...where mediators share the social and cultural experience of the disputants they serve, and where they bring to to processing of disputes an intimate and detailed knowledge of the perspectives of the disputes." Thus, in urban America where the organization of society "minimizes the importance of and the intertwining (multiplexity) of family and other group ties and maximizes social, occupational, and geographic mobility" (Danzig and Lowy, 1975), it is less important to meet with and work out disputes. Felstiner argues, therefore, that <u>avoidance</u> of disputes is a more feasible solution than mediating disputes in moots.

Responding to Felstiner, Danzig and Lowy (1975) argue that 1) Felstiner's emphasis on the requirements for an effective mediator miss the mark because the value of the moot lies <u>not</u> in the skill of the mediator, but in the very process of coming together and discussing disputes, and 2) the psychological costs of avoidance rather than mediation are significant and underestimated by Felstiner. In their words, "we think that Professor Felstiner overlooks the extraordinary costs that the members of our society are now paying because of the paucity of interpersonal dispute resolution mechanisms in America" (Danzig and Lowy, 1975).

If one agrees that current court mechanisms for resolving disputes are rigid and ineffective in many types of disputes, then the moot offers an interesting possibility. Do you find Danzig's proposal and his defense of it convincing in light of Felstiner's criticisms?

UNIT SUMMARY

Unit 4 highlighted the dispute resolving capability of law and described a number of institutional alternatives for employing the law in this fashion. Processes involving only the disputants--negotiation and avoidance--and processes involving third parties--mediation and judging--were described. Small Claims Courts and Citizen Dispute Centers were evaluated as current examples of dispute processing institutions, and the community moot modeled upon the African moot was introduced as an alternative not yet attempted in the United States.

Probably it is accurate to conclude that some combination of formal courts which adjudicate disputes and informal dispute centers or community moots which mediate disputes provides the flexibility needed to handle various types of disputes. For example, where civil rights guaranteed by the constitution or by statutes have been violated, formal adjudications are probably necessary. It would be inconsistent to resolve such claims by mediation. It would be inadequate and unfair to find that one community felt that the alleged violation of civil rights was important while another felt it to be trivial. On the other hand, many minor criminal violations are never prosecuted, and the private disagreements of millions of Americans are not conveniently handled by the formal system of courts. For these matters, the alternatives described in the unit might be valuable additions to our dispute processing institutions.

REFERENCES

Abel, L. A comparative theory of dispute institutions in society. Law and Society Review, 1974, 8 (2).

Aubert, V. Competition and dissensus: two types of conflict and conflict resolution. Journal of Conflict Resolution, 1963, 26.

Aubert, V. Sociology of law. Baltimore: Penguin, 1975.

Connor, R.F., & Surette, R. The citizen dispute settlement program: resolving disputes outside the courts. American Bar Association, 1977.

Danzig, R., & Lowy, M. Everyday disputes and mediation in the United States: a reply to Professor Felstiner. Law and Society Review, 1975, 9 (4), 675-694.

Eckhoff, T. The mediator and the judge. Acta Sociologica, 1966, 10, 158-166.

Felstiner, W.F. Avoidance as dispute processing. Law and Society Review, 1975, 9 (4), 695-706.

Felstiner, W.F. Influences of social organization on dispute processing. Law and Society Review, 1974, 9 (1), 63-94.

Friedman, L. Law and society. Englewood Cliffs: Prentice Hall, 1977.

Galanter, M. Why the haves' come out ahead: speculations on the limits of legal change. Law and Society Review, 1974, 9 (1), 95-160.

Gibbs, J.L. The Kpelle moot. Africa, January 1963, pp. 1-10. (reprinted in Bohannon, P. Law and warfare. Austin: University of Texas Press, 1967.)

Kawashima, T. Dispute resolution in Japan. In Aubert, V. Sociology of law. Baltimore: Penguin, 1975.

Nader, L., & Singer, L.R. Dispute resolution. California State Bar Journal, July 1976, pp. 281-320.

Sarat, A. Alternatives in dispute processing: litigation in a small claims court. Law and Society Review, 1976, 10 (3), 339-376.

Yngvesson, B., & Hennessey, P. Small claims, complex disputes: a review of the small claims literature. Law and Society Review, 1975, 9 (2), 219-274.

SUGGESTED READING

Abel, R. A comparative theory of dispute institutions in society. Law and Society Review, 1974, 217.

Alper, C. The practice in the small court of the city of New York. St. Johns Law Review, 1934, 9, 24.

Aubert, V. Competition and dissensus: two types of conflict and of conflict resolution. Journal of Conflict Resolution, 1963, 7, 26.

Carlin, J., & Howard, J. Legal depresentation and class justice. U.C.L.A. Law Review, 12, 381.

Foller, L.L. Mediation--its forms and functions. Southern California Law Review, 44, 305.

Gellhorn, W. When Americans complain. Cambridge: Howard University Press, 1966.

Litigation and dispute processing, part I. Law and Society Review, 1974, 9 (1).

Litigation and dispute processing, part II. Law and Society Review, 1975, 9 (2).

McGonogle, J.J., Jr. Arbitration of consumer disputes. Arbitration Journal, 27, 65.

Small claims courts as collection agencies. Stanford Law Review, 1952 4, 237.

Statsky, W.P. Community courts: decentralizing juvenile jurisprudence. Capital University Law Review, 1974, 3, 1.

Yaffe, J. So sue me! The story of a community court. New York: Saturday Review Press, 1972.

UNIT 5

Law And Social Control

Rationale

A primary function of law is to establish and maintain a system of
social control. Yet social control is a broader notion than law. In this
unit, therefore, it is important to focus your attention on the issue of
social control generally and to distinguish legal from non-legal methods
of social control. In addition, the effectiveness of law as a means of
social control--especially the use of the criminal law--is a major concern
of this unit. However, because it is so important to think clearly about
the question of whether the criminal law does control behavior by deterring
potential offenders, the focus is upon conceptual problems, not empirical
problems. It is first necessary to know what questions must be asked about
deterrence before the answers can even begin to be discovered.

Objectives

After you have completed all of the tasks in this unit, you should
be able to do the following:

1. Define the following terms
   a. social control
   b. deterrence
   c. net deterrent effect

233

2. Distinguish legal from non-legal social control.

3. Compare and contrast the following styles of social control:

    a. penal

    b. compensatory

    c. therapeutic

    d. conciliatory

4. Describe the relationship between law and other social control according to Donald Black.

5. Describe the general relationship among all forms of social control according to Donald Black.

6. Summarize alternative versions of how the process of deterrence works.

7. Summarize the factors believed to make some people more deterrable than others.

8. State three errors often made by those who study deterrence.

Overview

This unit includes a reading excerpt in which law is defined in terms of social control and the concept of formal social control is defined. The mini-lectures are attempts to describe the relationship between law and social control and to clarify the issues surrounding the deterrent effect of the criminal law.

Study Task Checklist

☐ 1. A.   Read Mini-Lecture #1, "Law and Social Control."

☐ 1. B.   Answer the Study Questions and compare your answers with the Discussion of them.

☐ 2. A.   Read Mini-Lecture #2, "The Theory of Deterrence."

☐ 2. B.   Answer the Study Questions and compare your answers with the Discussion of them.

Mini-Lecture #1

LAW AND SOCIAL CONTROL

Introduction

In Unit 4 we examined law as a mechanism for settling disputes and in this unit we will look at law as a mechanism of social control. Social control generally has been defined as ". . . the process by which subgroups and persons are influenced to conduct themselves in conformity to group expectations" (Davis, p. 39). Therefore, there are many types of social control, some of which are formal and some of which are informal. F. James Davis argues that formal social control involves explicit rules of conduct, planned use of sanctions, and specific officials to enforce these rules. (See Davis, pp. 39-40.) Formal social control might be exerted by any institution which makes rules and enforces them according to explicit sanctions. When the _state_, however, is the source of the rules, sanctions, and officials, Davis claims, we have the phenomenon of "law." Law, therefore, is only one type of formal social control. And formal social control is only one type of social control.

Donald Black similarly defines social control in general as

the normative aspect of social life. It defines and responds to deviant behavior, specifying what ought to be:
What is right or wrong, what is a violation, obligation,
abnormality, or disruption. (Black, 1976, p. 105)

As you read in the excerpt from Donald Black in Unit 2, law can be considered to be 'governmental social control'. In that discussion the
issue was how to _define_ law. Here we are concerned with that _function_
law performs. Therefore, it is useful to accept this definition in
order to distinguish _legal_ social control from other forms of social control.

Social control involves normative expectations which people hold
about one another's behavior. All normative expectations, including definitions of politeness, customary behavior (e.g., removing one's hat in

236

church) ethical expectations, and definitions of normal and abnormal behavior, involve rules of conduct. Violation of these rules may result in
informal sanctions such as 'dirty looks', criticism, mockery, gossip,
shunning, or formal sanctions, such as fines or imprisonment. The point
is that "social control is found wherever and whenever people hold each
other to standards, explicitly or implicitly, consciously or not: on the
street, in prison, at home, at a party" (Black, 1976, p. 105).

Styles of Social Control

A recent typology developed by Donald Black attempts to
categorize the various styles of social control as penal, compensatory,
therapeutic, or conciliatory. He suggests that there is a distinctive
style of law which corresponds to each of these general social control
styles. Each style defines deviant behavior and the proper responses
to it differently.

FOUR STYLES OF SOCIAL CONTROL

	PENAL	COMPENSATORY	THERAPEUTIC	CONCILIATORY
STANDARD	PROHIBITION	OBLIGATION	NORMALITY	HARMONY
PROBLEM	GUILT	DEBT	NEED	CONFLICT
INITIATION OF CASE	GROUP	VICTIM	DEVIANT	DISPUTANTS
IDENTITY OF DEVIANT	OFFENDER	DEBTOR	VICTIM	DISPUTANT
SOLUTION	PUNISHMENT	PAYMENT	HELP	RESOLUTION

SOURCE: Donald Black, The Behavior of Law (New York: Academic Press, 1976, p. 5)

For each style there is a different standard, a different definition of the problem, a different process of initiating action, a different definition of the deviant individual, and a different type of solution to the problem. Note on the chart, for example, the penal and the therapeutic styles of social control. In the penal style, standards consist of <u>prohibitions</u> on certain conduct. If these standards are violated, a <u>punishment</u> of the <u>offender</u> is requested by the <u>group</u> upon a finding of <u>guilt</u>. In the therapeutic style, however, the standard becomes one of <u>normality</u> and the deviant is seen as a <u>victim</u> of mental illness who <u>needs help</u>. Ideally, the <u>deviant</u> persons themselves, though victims of mental illness, seek help on their own behalf.

The penal and compensatory styles are accusatory, that is, they involve winners and losers. "For both, it is all or nothing--punishment or nothing, payment or nothing. By contrast, therapeutic and conciliatory control are remedial styles, methods of social repair and maintenance, assistance for people in trouble" (Black, 1976, p. 4). The idea here is that styles of social control specifically can also be fit into Black's model. For example, when we define breach of contract differently from bad check writing, we are using a compensatory form of legal social control for the former and a penal form of legal social control for the latter.

The problem of mental illness (see Unit 8) can also be looked at through this model of the styles of social control. In one sense the treatment of mental illness follows the therapeutic style, that is, the standard is that of normality, the problem is defined as a need, and the deviant is seen as a victim. However, the solution--while called 'help' may often come closer to 'punishment'. Also, in the therapeutic style, the deviant him/herself initiates the process of seeking help. But in mental illness often the 'help' is forced upon the deviant by society (the group). Thus, elements of both penal and therapeutic styles of social control are evident in the treatment of mental illness. [Keep this in mind when you reach Unit 8 which contains a full discussion of psychiatric social control.]

Legal Social Control

We have now established that law is only one of a variety of means of social control and that styles of social control generally are useful for thinking about styles of legal social control specifically. That is, we can identify within the law elements of a penal style (criminal law), a compensatory style (contract and tort law), a therapeutic style (voluntary commitment to mental institutions), and a conciliatory style (mediation and collective bargaining).

The next question is, how important is legal social control compared to other forms of social control? And what is the relationship between legal and non-legal social control mechanisms. On the one hand it could be argued that "Legal institutions are an important cog in the machinery of social control" (Friedman, 1977, p. 11). Many rules of conduct are announced by and enforced by legal decision makers. While not all norms are legal norms, certainly many of the important rules of proper behavior are promulgated and enforced by legal institutions (e.g., rules against killing, stealing, destroying property). Yet alongside of legal norms are many family, school, or employment norms which may support or come into conflict with legal norms. And in the end, it could be argued we depend less on legal norms than on these other non-legal norms for an orderly, understandable social life. In assessing the value of contract law, for example, Philip Selznick notes, "The law of contracts facilitates and protects concerted activity, but the bonds of organization rest far more on practical and informal reciprocity and interdependence than they do on the availability of formal sanctions. Society is still held together by self-help and not by the intervention of legal agencies" (Selznick, 1963, p. 79).

The relationship between law and other social control is explored in a recent book by Donald Black (The Behavior of Law. New York: Academic Press, 1976), whose ideas on scientific sociology of law were discussed in Unit 2. Black, in this recent publication, tries to make a general statement of the relationship between law and social control which is applicable to all legal systems. His proposition is: "Law varies inversely with other social control" (Black, 1976, p. 107). This means that the role of legal social control increases as the role of non-legal social control decreases, and, conversely, the role of legal social control decreases as the role of non-legal social control increases.

This simple proposition is rich in meaning and application. For example, it suggests that when social control of the family, church, neighborhood, and work place decreases, legal social control increases. This seems to accurately describe America's current reliance on legal social control, a topic explored in detail in Unit 7. Black suggests also that the tendency to treat juvenile lawbreakers more leniently than adult law-breakers can be explained by the fact that juveniles are subject to more non-legal social control than adults (Black, 1976, p. 7). He also believes that his simple proposition explains why ". . .a policeman is more likely to arrest an offender who is subject to no other authority. . ." and that ". . .a citizen is more likely to call the police if he has no one else to help him" (Black 1976, p. 7).

Black argues that all forms of social control vary in relation to other forms. For instance, he says that, "The treatment of mental illness varies inversely with other social control" (Black, 1976, p. 7). As was the case with law, the treatment of mental illness increases as other social control decreases and vice versa. Hence,

> In modern society, for instance, psychiatric care varies inversely with family control. Thus, someone who lives alone is more likely than someone in a family to seek the help of a psychiatrist. Others, including the psychiatrist, are also more likely to define him as mentally ill. He is more likely to be hospitalized, to stay longer, and, if released, to be rehospitalized. And the weaker the social control in a family, the more likely are its members to be defined and treated as mentally ill. But one member may be subject to more family control than another, and so he would have more immunity. A child, for example, can do almost anything without being called crazy, and he is less likely to find himself in a mental hospital. The same applies to someone subject to more social control in other settings, such as among his friends or workmates. In this sense, mental illness varies with its setting. And the less social control of other kinds that is available, the worse it is. (Black, 1976, p. 119)

Conclusion

Social control must be achieved in all societies by some means. Often law is a central and visible means of social control. However, we must recognize that law alone is unlikely to succeed in establishing social order. Family, school, employment, and other sources of control are essential. Alvin Toffler's ideas which you read in Unit 2 seem to reflect the same basic point of view, namely, that we do not need more law in America, but we do need more order. While the styles of control may vary

as indicated in Black's typology, the need to find an appropriate style of
control and the inability of law to provide all necessary control remain
important issues for citizens and social scientists alike.

1. What is social control according to this mini-lecture?

2. What are Black's bases for distinguishing among styles of social control?

3. Using the chart identify how each of the four styles of social control would answer each of the five questions upon which the typology is based. (These five questions should be your answer to the preceding study question)

4. Describe style(s) of social control that applies to the treatment of mental illness.

5. What does Black believe the relationship to be between law and other forms of social control?

6. What does Black believe the relationship to be among other forms of social control?

1. In Mini-Lecture #1 the term "social control" refers to the normative dimension of social existence. Law is a major component of social control, but not the only means of achieving social control. Law here is viewed as 'governmental social control' in order to distinguish it from other non-governmental social control.

2. The typology of social control distinguishes styles of social control based upon how the following questions are answered:

    a. How is the normative standard defined?

    b. How is the problem defined?

    c. Who initiates the action when the standard is violated?

    d. How is the deviant identified?

    e. What solution is seen as appropriate?

3. Sample of how to read the chart:

    As to the first question, "How is the normative standard defined," the penal style defines the standard as a prohibition which must not be disobeyed. The compensatory style simply sees the standard as an obligation, not a prohibition. The therapeutic style sees the standard as a matter of normality and the conciliatory style sees the standard in terms of harmony. The act of killing, for example, might be seen as a violation of a prohibition against such behavior, a breach of an obligation not to kill, a deviation from normality, or a threat to harmony. Each style of social control then proceeds to respond to the remaining questions in a manner consistent with the definition of the standard.

    Note that this typology refers to all types of social control, legal or non-legal. Law can take the form of any of these styles; it is not restricted to a single style.

4. Basically, mental illness illustrates the therapeutic model because the deviant is seen as violating standards of normal behavior and therefore needs help. He/she is a victim of mental illness. However, help often is undistinguishable from the penal solution, punishment, and the initiation of actions against the deviant often comes from the group as in the penal model.

5. Black argues that an inverse relationship exists between law and other forms of social control. He believes that "the role of legal social control increases as the role of non-legal social control decreases and conversely the role of legal social control decreases as the role of non-legal social control increases". Thus, as religious and familial controls weaken, we expect to see the strengthening of legal controls.

6. Black believes that all forms of social control vary in relation to one another in different ways. The example given in the mini-lecture related the treatment of mental illness (one form of social control) to family (another form of social control). The result was that the stronger the family control, the less the likelihood that mental illness will be used to control people.

Mini-Lecture #2

THE THEORY OF DETERRENCE

In Mini-Lecture #1 you learned that law is only one form of social control and that penal law is only one style of legal social control. In this mini-lecture the use of penal law in an effort to control behavior is examined in more detail. The emphasis will be upon the theory of deterrence which is a major justification for the use of the penal style of legal social control. Since "Belief in the deterrent efficacy of penal sanctions is as old as the criminal law itself" (Zimring and Hawkins, 1973, p. 1), it is difficult to stand back and analyze the problem of deterrence. It seems so intuitively obvious that people will refrain from those behaviors which are punished. Nonetheless, it is important to try to think clearly about the issue of deterrence and what follows is designed to help you to do just that.

Definitions

Certain concepts and terms need to be clarified before exploring the theory of deterrence. Franklin F. Zimring and Gordon J. Hawkins' book, Deterrence: The Legal Threat in Crime Control (Chicago: University of Chicago Press, 1973) provides some useful distinctions and will be relied upon for much of what follows. When the legislature prohibits certain conduct (robbery) and directs that a certain prison sentence (5-10 years) be imposed on violators, the following elements are present:

> A legal threat is an attempt by a governmental authority to reduce certain behavior (the threatened behavior) by promising to cause violators to suffer imprisonment or other punishment (the threatened consequences). Those to whom the threat is directed constitute the audience of the threat. (Zimring and Hawkins, 1973, pp. 70-71)

The effects of the legal threat may be varied. The audience may change their behavior in response to the legal threat by not further engaging in the threatened behavior, by changing their style or frequency of engaging in the threatened behavior, or by engaging in the threatened behavior for the first time! Zimring and Hawkins (1973) refer to these audience responses as the channeling effect of the legal threat, "the totality of all changes in the behavior of the audience attributable to existence of a threat" (p. 71). In other words, a legal threat may have many effects ranging from causing members of the audience to NOT do what they would have done, to causing members of the audience to NOW DO what they had not previously done!

Deterrence, therefore, refers only to instances in which people "who would have committed the behavior refrain from doing so" (Zimring and Hawkins, 1973, p. 71) in response to the legal threat. One further complication must be handled. It is possible that while some people may have been deterred, more may have been caused (for whatever reason) to engage in the threatened behavior. The term, net deterrent effect, is used to describe "the total number of threatened behaviors it prevents less those it creates" (Zimring and Hawkins, 1973, p. 71). Therefore, it is quite possible that a particular legal threat deters, but does not have a net deterrent effect because more violations are created than prevented! Lest this strike you as nitpicking, consider (just consider!) the following argument: "Capital punishment is a deterrent, but has no net deterrent effect." The argument might be that indeed some people who, in the absence of capital punishment, would have committed murder do not do so. However, the particular threatened consequences, i.e., capital punishment, communicates to potential murderers that their contemplated act of murder is deemed by society to be an extraordinarily important act--so important, in fact, as to warrant the death sentence. Since the potential killer wants to be important to society, he/she decides to do that which society apparently feels is very important and, thus, guarantee him/herself immortality! The symbolic social statement which the death penalty makes to the audience, therefore, creates more murders than it deters. You need not accept the example to understand the importance of distinguishing the "question of whether deterrent effects are operative . . . from the policy question [of] whether a particular penalty should be employed" (Zimring and Hawkins, 1973, FN. 2, p. 71).

The Process of Deterrence

The question next arises, how do legal threats produce deterrence or net deterrent effects upon the audience. One answer is that people

248

simply avoid behavior likely to result in the unpleasant consequences expressed in the legal threat. This "simple deterrence" notion, of course, assumes that criminal behavior is engaged in only following a rational weighing of the benefits to be gained and the potential costs. This may be true in some cases, but not all.

Another possibility might be that the legal threat communicates to the audience that the threatened behavior is morally wrong. The audience, therefore, refrains from the threatened behavior not out of fear of the threatened consequences, but because the behavior is wrong (or it presumably would not be the subject of a legal threat).

Still another possible model for the deterrence process might be that the legal threat initially produces a fear of the consequences (simple deterrence) and the proper behavior later becomes habitual. For example, in Pennsylvania it is no longer a threatened behavior to turn right at a red light. Yet many drivers still refrain from this previously threatened behavior out of habit.

The Audience

Another dimension to the problem involves whether all members of the audience are equally deterrable and, if not, what factors are involved in distinguishing more from less deterrable types. Psychologists who study threats in general offer many possible approaches. Some say that threats create "an emotional barrier" (Zimring and Hawkins, 1973, p. 93) to the threatened behavior. While certainly a possibility in some cases, this reaction is not universal. In fact, rather than raising a psychological barrier to engaging in the conduct, a threat may make the conduct more desirable. The 'forbidden fruit' theory suggests that "people who felt that the behavior was desirable in the absence of threat may come to consider it even more desirable. . . .Those who originally were neutral about the desirability of a threatened behavior may come to ascribe it some positive value. . ." (Zimring and Hawkins, 1973, p. 95). Thus, the same legal threat may produce contradictory psychological reactions in various members of the audience.

Other personality theories suggest that there are present-oriented and future-oriented types of people. Those with an eye only on the present are less deterrable since they do not consider future consequences of present acts. Still others suggest that there are optimists who underestimate the chance of getting caught and pessimists who overestimate the risks. Obviously, the pessimists would be more responsive to legal threats since they would assume "If only one person gets caught, it will probably be me!"

In addition to personality traits, some have argued that attitudes toward authority are key elements in deterrability. For example, some authoritarian types of people are highly responsive to and obedient to authority. They would be easily deterred. Others are hostile to authority and rebellious, and, therefore, are not easily deterred.

Measuring Deterrent Effects

The difficulties involved in measuring the deterrent effect and net deterrent effect of legal threats are enormous. Two errors of interpretation often made by officials charged with the task of controlling crime are illustrated in the following short stories which are adapted from Zimring and Hawkins. (See Zimring and Hawkins, 1973, pp. 24-32 for further discussion of these errors.)

A. Aunt Jane's Cold Remedy

To cure the common cold, Aunt Jane recommends a "mixture of whiskey, sugar, and hot water." She claims that this treatment will cure all colds within 10 days. Those who take the home cure are almost always cured within the prescribed time and conclude, therefore, that Aunt Jane's remedy works. The problem, of course, is that there is no way to know if these colds would have been cured in 10 days without any treatment at all!

Applied to the crime control problem, this story of invalid inference is replayed yearly by legislators and police. Legal threats are made and new crime control measures are taken following growth in crime rates. When the crime rates decline the inference is invalidly made that the measures taken caused the decline. But just as with the true believers in Aunt Jane's Cold Remedy, the officials fail frequently to check if the abnormally high crime would have dropped back to normal levels in the absence of the new weapons, new patrol systems, new prison, or new types of punishment.

Even if this comparison is made, the officials with a vested interest in demonstrating an ability to deter crime will likely argue

that in the absence of their 'crime remedies' the rates would have gone
<u>even higher</u>. Thus, it becomes logically impossible to invalidate a claim
that the remedy works.

B. Tiger Prevention

The following dialogue takes place in New York City as a policeman encounters a man "snapping his fingers and moaning loudly. . ." (Zimring
and Hawkins, 1973, p. 28).

The Policeman: What are you doing?

The Man: Keeping tigers away.

The Policeman: Why that' crazy. There isn't a wild tiger
within five thousand miles of New York City.

The Man: Well, then, I must have a pretty effective technique.

Quite obviously the man has failed to consider the possibility that factors
other than his finger snapping and moaning account for the lack of tigers
in New York!

Yet this error is made constantly in discussions of what measures
deter criminals. When tough penalties are believed to be the sole factor
preventing skyrocketing crime rates, the advocates of such penalties insist that the penalties deter crime. If we never lower the penalty or
eliminate it, we cannot come to this conslusion validly. To "present
high penalties combined with low crime rates as proof of deterrence [is]
patently absurd" (Zimring and Hawkins, 1973, p. 29).

C. The Warden's Survey

After interviewing convicted murders on the issue of whether capital
punishment deters, the Warden concludes that this legal threat does not work.

Here the error is that the Warden failed to ask the non-murderers
if capital punishment deters them; those murderers that the Warden did
ask were obviously not deterred! Additionally, of course, they would be
unlikely to say anything which would support the continued existence of
captial punishment since they had a clear stake in the results!

The error of studying possible deterrent effects among special groups of people--offenders, poor people, etc.--and making general statements about deterrence on this basis is frequently made. Failure to examine deterrence among law-abiding citizens will produce invalid inferences. Concluding their discussion of these stories, Zimring and Hawkins (1973) state,

> Our tiger preventers and our wardens make contradictory assumptions about the relation between those criminals in jail and the potential crime problem. The tiger prevention advocate assumes that large numbers of law-abiding citizens are held in check by the threat of penalties; indeed, that only severe penalties can perform this job. The warden seems to assume that, when he interviews prisoners, he is talking to the totality of the potential crime problem, or at least to a representative sample. Consequently, because these assumptions are unsupported, both the 'proof' and 'disproof' of deterrence must fail. (p. 32)

Conclusion

This mini-lecture has examined the theoretical dimensions of the problem of deterrence. The critical concepts have been defined. Alternative models of how the deterrence process works have been presented. The issue of who is deterrable has been explored. Some of the errors made in the ongoing debate about deterrence have been illustrated. An examination of the empirical studies on both sides of this issue cannot be adequately covered in this introductory course. But the conceptual and theoretical ideas presented should enable you in future courses to more effectively read and evaluate these studies.

MINI-LECTURE #2 QUESTIONS

1. Define the following terms:

    a. legal threat

    b. threatened behavior

    c. threatened consequence

    d. audience

    e. channeling effect

    f. deterrence

    g. net deterrent effect

2. How can there be a deterrent effect but no net deterrent effect?

3. What is simple deterrence?

4. What is the moral education model of deterrence?

5. Why might legal threats deter some and induce others to violate the law?

6. What types of people do psychologists claim are more and less deterrable?

7. What are the three errors illustrated in the three stories?

   a. Aunt Jane's Cold Remedy

   b. Tiger Prevention

   c. The Warden's Survey

DISCUSSION OF MINI-LECTURE #2 QUESTIONS

1. a. A legal threat is a promise by a legitimate state authority to punish those who engage in acts prohibited by law.

   b. The threatened behavior is the illegal act which the legal threat is designed to reduce.

   c. The threatened consequence is the punishment which the state promises to inflict upon violators.

   d. The audience is the group of people to which the legal threat is addressed.

   e. The channeling effect refers to all of the responses of the audience to the legal threat.

   f. Deterrence refers to those cases in which a person responds to the legal threat by <u>not</u> committing the act which he would have committed in the absence of the legal threat.

   g. Net deterrent effect refers to the difference between the number of threatened behaviors prevented minus the number of threatened behaviors actually created by the legal threat.

2. If more people are stimulated to engage in certain prohibited behavior than to refrain from doing so, then <u>some</u> people may, in fact, be deterred while overall there is no net deterrent effect.

3. Simple deterrence is the model of the deterrence process which assumes that potential violators weigh the costs of non-compliance against the benefits of non-compliance and choose to minimize the costs. Therefore, if the threatened consequence is sufficiently severe people will be deterred. (See "Economics and Law" in Unit 2 for a discussion of this point of view.)

4. The moral education model suggests that by virtue of prohibiting certain conduct and attaching threats of unpleasant consequences, the law teaches us that such conduct is wrong.

5. Psychologists argue that for some people a threat creates an emotional barrier to engaging in prohibited conduct, while for others it makes the conduct more attractive. (See "Psychology and Law" in Unit 2 for further discussion of the psychologist's view of law.)

6.

More Deterrable	Less Deterrable
Future-oriented persons	Present-oriented persons
Pessimists	Optimists
Authoritarians	Anti-authoritarians

7. a. Aunt Jane's Cold Remedy illustrates the error of failing to acquire data which might permit an analyst to compare the effects of a particular legal threat or crime control measure with the expected results in the absence of these measures.

    b. Tiger Prevention illustrates the error of associating the existence of legal threats and the absence of crime in a <u>causal</u> fashion without an examination of alternative causal factors.

    c. The Warden's Survey illustrates the error of generalizing to an entire population on the basis of a highly biased sample.

UNIT SUMMARY

Because law is almost always viewed as providing a social control mechanism, this unit focused upon the concepts of social control generally and deterrence specifically. You saw that the concept of social control itself involved society's definition of and response to deviant behavior. The question of how people are influenced to abide by society's rules is the question of social control.

The styles for achieving this influence on behavior were explored through Black's typology and the relationship among various types of social control was probed through Black's hypotheses.

Because a penal style of legal social control--the criminal law--is widely believed to be an effective means of social control, the question of deterrence was discussed in this unit on social control. The deterrence concept was narrowed and refined through Zimring's and Hawkins' analysis of the problem, and some of the difficulties in past efforts to measure deterrence were illustrated through the three short stories.

REFERENCES

Black, D. The behavior of law. New York: Academic Press, 1976.

Davis, F. J., et al. Law as a type of social control. In F. J. Davis (Ed.), Society and the Law. New York: The Free Press, 1962.

Selznick, P. Legal institutions and social control. Vanderbilt Law Review, 1963, 17, 79-90.

Zimring, E., & Hawkins, G. J. Deterrence: the legal threat in crime control. Chicago: University of Chicago Press, 1973.

UNIT 6

Law As An Instrument Of Social Change

Throughout the course, the relationship between law and society has been described in two ways: law has been seen as a social product, and law has been seen as a social force. In Unit 2, for example, you read about the systems model and the stimulus-response model, both of which emphasized this dual nature of the law and society relationship. In Unit 3 you saw how various social theorists described law as a reflection of the social order; in Unit 5 you saw how law can be used with varying degrees of success to bring about a degree of social control and conformity to social norms. In this unit, law is examined as a means for achieving social change. Unlike the unit on social control, which focused primarily on deterring undesirable behavior, here we will look at law's ability to effect broader social change. Consistent with the conclusion of Unit 5, you will see that law can achieve limited success in generating social change.

Because of the significant role played by the U.S. Supreme Court we will look primarily at its ability to produce social change. This is not to say that congressional enactments or lower court rulings cannot bring about change; it merely reflects a judgment that the Supreme Court's role has been central to the relationship between law and social change.

261

Objectives

After you have completed this unit, you should be able to:

1. Define the following concepts:

   a. aftermath
   b. compliance
   c. impact
   d. "trickle down" theory

2. Describe at least two variables affecting the general impact of course decisions and purpose a hypothesis describing the nature and extend of the impact of each.

3. Explain why the impact of the Supreme Court is limited and what may be done to increase the Court's impact.

Overview

Unit 6 provides you with an introduction to the role of law--especially Supreme Court generated law--in _producing_ social change. Schur demonstrates in the selection from the text that law is limited in its ability to produce change. He also refers to the ongoing debate over the legal enforcement of various moral positions. His theme seems to be to emphasize the limited role of law in social change, a theme that is further developed in Unit 7.

Mini-Lecture #1, "Legal Impact: Theory and Research," is another attempt to provide you with a brief look at a complicated new field of study: legal impact. In this mini-lecture, you are asked to think with some precision about the conceptual approaches to the study of law and social change. In addition, this mini-lecture provides you with a glimpse of the theoretical propositions and empirical studies in the literature.

262

Study Task Checklist

☐   1. A.   Read Mini-Lecture #1, "Legal Impact: Theory and Research."

☐   1. B.   Answer the Study Questions and compare your answers with the Discussion of them.

☐   2. A.   Study Reading #2, "Toward and Beyond A Theory of Supreme Course Impact," by James P. Levine and Theodore L. Becker.

☐   2. B.   Answer the Study Questions and compare your answers with the Discussion of them.

Mini-Lecture #1

LEGAL IMPACT: THEORY AND RESEARCH

In this mini-lecture we will examine some of the theoretical aspects of the study of legal impact and then look at some examples of impact studies. Initially, however, it is useful to clarify more precisely what is meant by 'impact', and some related concepts.

If we are to effectively study the role of law in achieving social change, it is imperative that we define the concepts that we wish to use in our study. A number of concepts with slightly different meanings have been used by those who examine law and social change problems. First, some writers talk about the aftermath of a Supreme Court decision. This refers basically to the events which come in the wake of a decision. Such a notion might be of primary interest to historians interested in the flow of events or lawyers interested in the evolution of constitutional doctrine. However, what occurs after a court decision may or may not be connected causally to that decision. We must be cautious not to conclude that all events which follow a court decision are attributable to that decision.

Another commonly used concept is compliance, a far more precise term than aftermath. Where aftermath refers simply to what follows a court decision, compliance refers specifically to the extent to which people obey a decision. The mere fact that people behave in accordance with a court decision is not evidence of compliance. They may have behaved that way all along or they may behave that way for other reasons. In order to say that there has been compliance we must be able to show that people were aware of the court's decision, that they intended to obey it, and that their behavior conformed with the decision (Wasby, 1970, p. 24). The difficulty with the compliance concept is that it may cause us to overlook certain types of issues. For example, the narrow focus on compliance misses other possible responses to court decisions. If Congress, for example, attempts to alter the court's size, composition, or jurisdiction following an unpopular decision, this is not easily fit into the compliance concept. As Becker and Feeley put it, "The point is that these legislative

(or executive) challenges to the court can exist independent of the degree
to which the particular decision is complied with by administrators, lower
court judges, citizens, etc." (1973, p. 212). In addition, for example,
if the court's decision is complied with reluctantly by the citizens,
the resulting loss of affection for the court may be highly significant,
yet the exclusive concentration on compliance or non-compliance would
not allow us to see this attitudinal result.

Because aftermath includes too much and compliance includes too
little, a number of scholars have been using the term, impact. Becker
and Feeley (1973) define impact as "all policy-related consequences of
a decision" (p. 213). Friedman (1975) writes that impact "means behavior
causally linked to a rule or command, regardless of what the rule-maker
had in mind" (p. 48). The point is that impact focuses on all of the
behavioral responses directly or indirectly caused by a court decision.
Thus, it excludes that part of the aftermath not causally tied to the
decision, and it includes effects of a decision beyond compliance or
non-compliance. Impact and compliance are each useful concepts depending
upon the purposes of the particular study involved.

Variables Affecting Impact

A number of factors affect the nature and extent of the general
impact of court decisions including the specific compliance with decisions.
Below are summarized some of those factors identified by Wasby (1970) as
well as examples of hypotheses which are related to each.

A. Characteristics of the Cases

Wasby indicates that certain aspects of the Court decisions themselves may be related to their impact: for example, the degree of clarity
of the opinion, the vote of the court, i.e., unanimous v. split decisions,
the number of separate dissenting and concurring opinions. He (Wasby,
1970) hypothesizes that "compliance will be more immediate when courts
provide clear guidelines than when they do not" (p. 249), that "ambiguity
in Supreme Court rulings decreases compliance" (p. 250), and that "the
greater the technicality of the language of a decision, the smaller the
impact" (p. 250).

B. Communication of Court Decisions

Because compliance with a decision is dependent upon knowledge of the decision, the process by which citizens and officials learn about court decisions is important. The way in which the press treats a decision and the degree to which relevant officials distribute information about the decision affects its impact. Wasby (1970) hypothesizes that "The greater the number of channels through which decisions are reported, the greater the impact" (p. 252), "Reporting of immediate negative reaction tends to increase non-compliance" (p. 252), and "Information about the specifics of how to comply with a decision will bring greater impact than a general discussion of it" (p. 252).

C. Follow-Up

Because court decisions are not self-executing, it is important that efforts be made to follow-up court decisions if they are to have great impact. Such follow-up may take the form of subsequent cases, administrative pressure, or law enforcement. Wasby (1970) hypothesizes that "The more persistent the 'enforcers' are, the greater the compliance" (p. 258), "compliance is more likely when some reviewing body is available to those complaining of non-compliance" (p. 259), and "compliance with a ruling of the Supreme Court will be more likely when there are frequent follow-up cases than when there are not" (p. 259).

While there are other factors which affect impact and compliance and additional hypotheses about how these factors are related to the various responses to decisions of the Supreme Court, these are three of the most important factors to look at in assessing the impact of a court decision.

Example of Impact Studies

A number of specific efforts have been made to test hypotheses growing out of the impact and compliance notions. Becker and Feeley (1973) collected a number of such studies and categorized them in terms of those focusing on the impact of the Supreme Court rulings on the President and Congress, on lower courts, on state and local governments, and on public understanding of the law.

One interesting effort included there was the attempt to assess the impact of the Miranda decision in Washington, D.C. (Medalie et al, 1968). The Miranda decision requires that warnings of constitutional rights be given to suspects by police prior to custodial interrogations. The court assumed that the warnings would be given and honored, that the defendents would understand them, and that exercising the rights would serve to protect defendant's from unconstitutional abuses. This particular impact study involved interviews with defendants in Washington, D.C. in an effort to test the court's assumptions.

The study revealed that an astonishingly high percentage (40%) of defendants gave statements to police despite their right to remain silent and an astonishingly small percentage (7%) of defendants requested a lawyer despite the presence of volunteer attorneys in the precinct station house (Medalie et al. in Becker and Feeley, 1973, p. 142).

The interviews with defendants suggested that many did not understand the right to remain silent or the right to counsel. Their efforts to explain these rights to interviewers clearly indicated that they failed to understand: the right to remain silent, said one, meant, "I should have the right to say something so they can use it in evidence in court" (Medalie, p. 147); the right to counsel meant, to one, "The police had some lawyer of their own who was working with them" (Medalie, 146). Furthermore, even those who understood the warnings frequently failed to exercise them due to fear that the 'system' would punish them for wasting time. Tougher sentences from judges and more charges from police were apparently enough to deter the exercise of rights. The point is that the Supreme Court may have achieved compliance from police, but had a limited impact on guaranteeing the actual availability of these rights to all defendants.

Conclusion

The question of whether law can produce social change is often looked at in terms of impact and compliance. In this mini-lecture we have looked at the concepts involved in studying this problem, seen examples of hypotheses which might be tested, and looked at an example of an impact study. The specific impact of law on American society is explored further in the materials in Unit 7.

MINI-LECTURE #1 QUESTIONS

1. Distinguish among the concepts of aftermath, compliance, and impact.

2. What types of factors might affect impact and in what ways?

3. What does the Medalie et al. study suggest about Court impact?

1. Aftermath refers to events which follow a Court decision, regardless of causality. Compliance refers to intentional obedience to a decision. Impact refers to all responses, which are traceable to a court decision. Compliance and impact, therefore, refer to different aspects of the problem of assessing the consequences of a court decision. Compliance is different from impact in that the former requires an <u>intent</u> <u>to</u> <u>obey</u>, while the latter does not. That is, there can be many impacts of a Court decision which involve neither <u>intentional</u> responses nor <u>obedience</u>. The impact of a decision in a discrimination case may extend to affecting results of a Presidential election. This, of course, has nothing to do with compliance. Aftermath, is different from both compliance and impact in that it makes no effort to connect the decision to subsequent events.

2. A variety of factors, including the clarity of the opinion, the degree of unanimity in the vote, the guidelines in the opinion, the technicality of language, the process of communication of the decision, the number of subsequent cases, the attitude of enforcement agencies, and the availability of an enforcing body all affect the degree of impact. [In the mini-lecture there are a number of hypotheses suggesting how these factors might affect impact.]

3. Basically the findings of this study indicate the limited ability of the Supreme Court to bring about change. Although achieving formal compliance by the police, <u>Medalie</u> et al. suggest that the impact of <u>Miranda</u> in terms of its apparent goals (the changed awareness by the public of its rights) was scarcely noticeable. Therefore, while <u>compliance</u> was achieved, little substantive change in the defendant's exercise of rights (the protection of which the law sought to secure) was actually noted.

"Toward and Beyond a Theory of Supreme Court Impact" by James P. Levine and Theodore L. Becker is reprinted from AMERICAN BEHAVIORAL SCIENTIST Vol. 13, No. 4 (March/April 1970) pp. 561-573 by permission of the Publisher, Sage Publications, Inc.

JAMES P. LEVINE
AND THEODORE L. BECKER

Toward and Beyond a Theory of Supreme Court Impact

The purpose of this paper is to explain why the Supreme Court has had limited effects on American society, to suggest some means by which the Court's influence can be increased, and to raise some questions about the proper role of social science in this endeavor.

REASONS FOR SUPREME COURT INEFFICACY

Lower Court Autonomy

It is often presumed that the hierarchical organization of the American judiciary centralizes much lawmaking authority within appellate courts and that trial courts generally defer to the Supreme Court in deciding cases of constitutional law. The operation of this role constraint on lower courts is illustrated by the Indiana Supreme Court's reaction to Henry Miller's *Tropic of Cancer*, which was involved in a local obscenity case. After expressing distaste for the book, the Indiana court deferred to the authority of the superordinate court and reversed the conviction.

> Regardless of our personal opinion on this matter both as to the law and the facts, we are bound as judges of this Court, under the oath we took, to follow the Constitution of the United States, as interpreted by the Supreme Court of the United States, and that Court, in our opinion has determined the issue in this case.[1]

1. Cuffel v. State, 215 N.E. 2d 36 (Indiana, 1966).

of most decisions. The Court is often either ambiguous or divided on policy matters, which gives lower courts encouragement to go their own way. Because compromise and negotiations are frequently necessary to obtain the support of most of the Justices (or even a bare majority) behind one opinion (Murphy, 1964: ch. 3), the resulting document is often beset with confusion providing lower courts with few guidelines to decide run-of-the-mill cases. If the Justices persevere and hold out for clearly written principles, the result is often a very split Court and the continuing possibility, of which lower courts are aware, that small changes of personnel will alter the balance on the Court and change its direction. There seems to be an inverse relation between the *clarity of holdings* and the *size of the Court majority*, so Justices must often choose between two routes to ineffectiveness. Chief Justice Earl Warren obtained unanimity in Brown v. Board of Education, but the price may have been the now infamously vague "all deliberate speed" mandate. On the other hand, when Warren in 1966 did spell out precise rules for police interrogations in Miranda v. Arizona,[5] only five Justices subscribed to his majority opinion and four Justices dissented. The Court, like others, may not be able to have its cake and eat it, too.

Even when a united Court is committed to some specific policy, the physical burden of handling a constantly increasing number of appeals often prevents them from periodically reinforcing this commitment and supervising implementation. The Court, for example, terminated its approval of the usage of the due process clause of the Fourteenth Amendment to invalidate economic legislation as early as the 1930s, but Paulsen (1950) has shown that lower courts continued to declare statutes unconstitutional on that basis for many years. Given its limited resources of time and manpower, the Court is simply unable to do much spotchecking of the lower courts except in issue areas of the highest priority.

Finally, linear trends are not characteristic of Supreme Court policy-making. The voting equality cases are atypical, what with the Court from 1962 to 1967 declaring 31 out of 32 instances of alleged malapportionment unconstitutional. Usually the Court exhibits occasional fluctuation or vacillation as it has done in the right to privacy cases. Such equivocation is probably seized upon by lower

5. 384 U.S. 436 (1966).

However, the "trickle-down" theory is at best a very rough first approximation of reality. First of all, there is no solid evidence showing that most trial judges actually feel obliged to follow Supreme Court rulings if they are opposed to them. And unless the duty to comply is internalized, there are few means available to appellate courts to keep lower courts in line, since only a very small proportion of cases are ever appealed. Because the threat of reversal is fairly hollow, the trial judges can act independently with impunity.

Indeed, there are some data which suggest that lower courts frequently apply standards decidedly at variance with those articulated by the Supreme Court. For example, in Betts v. Brady,[2] (since overruled by Gideon v. Wainwright[3]), the Court ruled that defendants in noncapital cases were entitled to state-appointed counsel if special circumstances were present making it impossible for the defendant to represent himself adequately. However, in only 11 out of 139 state appellate cases concerning this issue were special circumstances found (Lewis, 1964: 151). In 1961, the Pennsylvania Supreme Court actually denied a plea for legal aid from an eighteen-year-old boy with an IQ of 59, equivalent to a mental age of nine.[4] Since Betts v. Brady was a landmark case, this smacks of outright defiance of the Supreme Court.

Many institutional features of the judicial system provide ample opportunity for inferior judges to legitimately ignore, modify, or evade high-level policy formulations (see Murphy, 1959). First, lower courts have the authority to make crucial findings of fact which can only be partially controlled by appellate courts. Second, since the fact constellations of any one case are never *exact* replicas of those of other cases, lower courts can often distinguish away alleged precedents ordained on high. Third, the verbiage of Supreme Court language can be manipulated, with favorable sentences elevated to the status of a "holding" which is binding and unfavorable words dismissed as "mere dicta." Fourth, state courts can often insulate themselves from Supreme Court review by grounding their decisions in state law. Thus, judges who want to be obstructive have adequate tools at their disposal.

Another impediment to Supreme Court efficacy is the very nature

2. 316 U.S. 455 (1942).
3. 372 U.S. 335 (1963).
4. Commonwealth ex rel. Simon v. Maroney, 405 Pa. 562 (1961).

courts who oppose the general directions being taken and used to retard policy changes at the trial court level.

Elite Unresponsiveness

Of more concern than lower court compliance with the Supreme Court is the conduct of presumably affected people who never get into the court at all. The real test of the Court's potency are the changes voluntarily initiated by those elites, public and private, whose activities are similar to those declared illegitimate by the Court. Due to the inertia which propels many organizations, there is a natural tendency to carry on established routines and disregard Court holdings that rock the boat. This is especially so where the Court strikes at central practices of the institution and where policy changes are perceived by those in control as being dysfunctional to primary objectives.

Thus, those who operate the criminal courts, which are usually oriented toward conviction (Blumberg, 1967), react negatively to court decisions extending defendants' rights, which would have the effect of turning a fairly efficient bureaucratic process into a time-consuming and nonproductive adversary system. Similarly, officials in the Selective Service System are unlikely to respond positively to judicial restrictions on draft board procedures which would curtail the rapid mobilization of military manpower. Indicative of this is General Hershey's recent disavowal of a federal court declaratory judgment ruling that it was illegal to speed up inductions of draft protestors.

Because no general announcements of policy are communicated to affected parties, it is quite frequent that authorities remain totally unaware of new responsibilities required of them and new norms governing their behavior. Barth found that district attorneys in Wisconsin are very ill-informed about current obscenity rulings (Barth, 1968), and Rabin's (1967) interviews with Selective Service personnel showed that they were oblivious to United States v. Seeger[6] which broadened the legitimate bases for conscientious objection. In a similar vein, Krislov (1968: 194) has pointed out that police train-

6. 380 U.S. 163 (1965).

ing conferences pay virtually no attention whatsoever to development in civil liberties law.

There is frequently a high personal utility to willful noncompliance. Sometimes it is simply good politics to defy Court decisions, as the fortunes of George Wallace and Lester Maddox have dramatically demonstrated. In other cases the payoffs are even greater, as when the policeman in high crime districts obtains greater physical security by shortcutting the requirements of due process in enforcing the law. Muir's (1962: ch. 4) study of educators' reactions to the school prayer decisions points out a less tangible benefit resulting from resistance to the Court: the maintenance of social relationships and the approval of associates. In short, elites often see it in their own self-interest to turn their backs on the Court.

Since the judiciary really lacks the sanctions to coerce compliance, elites often see few risks ensuing from disobedience. Positive programs involving the allocation of considerable economic resources are often required to implement Court doctrines, and judicial enforcement machinery is largely limited to negative instruments such as injunctions and acquittals. Both the cost of litigations and the prerequisites of court utilization (e.g., establishing standing, showing a real case and controversy, actually violating a law) minimize the force of judicial controls. Moreover, the decentralized and uncoordinated nature of many institutions regulated by Supreme Court decisions (such as school boards, police departments, and welfare agencies) magnify the scope of the enforcement problem. The attorneys general of the states supposedly have the authority to spur compliance, but Krislov (1959) and others have shown that they also often have political disincentives to act vigorously. To offend local norms and opinion can be political suicide.

The beneficiaries of Supreme Court policies are often either ill-equipped or unwilling to pressure elites to comply: It is often insular minorities who are supported by the Court, and they lack the resources—the funds, personnel, organization, and information—to mount a cause at the local level. The poor are hardly in a position to push for their constitutional rights to equal governmental treatment.

Also, the cost of pushing compliance usually outweighs the limited satisfaction of having one's interest vindicated. Parents may be irritated by Bible-reading in their children's classrooms, and public employees may be troubled by compulsory loyalty oaths, but the intensity of their grievances is insufficient to motivate them to act. For criminal defendants, the price of insisting on the right to appointed counsel may very well be harsher treatment by the court and stiffer sentences. It is normal for persons to try to maximize their utilities, and fighting for constitutional rights is often just not worthwhile.

Consequently, the deck is rather stacked against widespread voluntary implementation of Supreme Court policies. Institutions such as Congress, with its control over the public fisc, and the executive, with its massive bureaucracy, are in a far better position to promote social change on more than a token basis. For example, it was not until the United States Commissioner of Education started a systematic campaign to enforce the Federal Aid to Education Act of 1965, which prohibited funding of segregated schools, that any serious progress was made toward desegregation of schools in the deep South. Without political action in other quarters, the hands of the Supreme Court are likely to be tied and the status quo ante will probably remain.

Public Unawareness

Although the Supreme Court has the inherent capacity to mold its decisions into powerful political symbols, the empirical evidence on symbolic effects of decisions is still meager. Hyman Sheatsley (1964) analyzed survey data on changes in attitudes toward desegregation from 1942 to 1964 and concluded that the Brown decision had radically accelerated the shift towards acceptance of desegregation. More recently Dolbeare (1969: 185–187) found that the "halo effect" caused by the Supreme Court's virtuous image caused people to applaud the Court's banning of public school prayers, even though they had previously approved of schoolhouse religion. Since political leaders do respond to public moods and sentiments, these kinds of consequences can be important in the formation of public policy. However, there is a missing link in the above line of argument: the communication processes between the Court and the public. Judicial symbols must be widely diffused to be effective, and the findings of survey research are beginning to unfold massive public ignorance

of Supreme Court decisions (Dolbeare, 1967). News coverage of the Court is generally sketchy and frequently either misunderstood or distorted, with major decisions often relegated to back pages or summarized in a couple of column inches (for all but assiduous and devoted readers of the *New York Times*. See Newland, 1964). If the Court is to be a catalyst of major social change, it must reach beyond the legal community (which remains largely untouched anyway) and into the general community.

INCREASING THE SUPREME COURT'S IMPACT

To increase the Court's impact, some traditional practices should be abandoned as quickly as possible while new approaches and procedures are adopted and applied—with imagination, flexibility, and boldness. Since the social isolation treasured by most of the Justices mutes the Court's voice in national politics, we urge, as a start, that the Court give up this haughty posture and begin making serious attempts to relate to the American public.

Some innovations might necessitate legislative action, but others could be instituted by the Court itself, thereby obviating resort to the booby-trapped trail through the legislative obstacle course called Congress. Let us take a candid look at how the Court clues us all in on what it has decided in camera. Its "streamlined" method is rooted in practices developed under Forefather John Jay, as modified by that other great modernist, Forefather John Marshall, as well as by other radical proceduralists. Of course these jurisprudential giants of yesteryear were acquainted, to a degree, with the political system as it existed in their heyday. But need we emphasize that the times, they have a-changed? In today's world, the medium is the message, and the medium that the Court chooses to pass its word is drab, dreary, and humdrum. Verbatim reading of opinions by the Justices to handfuls of court observers and the doling out of advance sheets to lawyers and libraries are that medium. Small wonder that so few get the message!

We are certain that a multitude of arguments, mostly mired in tradition, can be mustered to applaud this musty arrangement. However, if we may be so brash, as political scientists currently interested in a more effective Court, we would suggest a vast array of changes in the props of the setting on opinion day. For one thing, there is surely no reasons, in this, the age of McLuhan, to categorically exclude television from the court chambers. In our era of mass communications, it is almost anachronistic that the Court has shunned the tube for as long as it has. We are well aware, of course, that if the Justices were to perform before the cameras as they now do in the flesh, there is little doubt that their Nielsen ratings would set record lows. Justice Black's ponderous performance on a recent network television interview does nothing to dispel this suspicion.

But can there be any question about the fact that one reason the Court receives so little popular support for important decisions is that the public simply does not comprehend what the Court has said and why the Justices believe their view to be proper? Since television networks donate free time to the President to express his views in news conferences and through prepared speeches, it would seem that they could be convinced (or forced by law) to open their facilities once a month to the Court for a professionally designed program describing and dramatizing what it is that the Court has decided and spelling out the justifications for its policies.

True, this might be nudging the judiciary into the realm of theatrics. But so what? And true, this might compel the Court to employ a staff that would include television or movie directors, actors, and technicians, in order to produce short vignettes about what the Court finds offensive in the actions of some officials and what the scope of its rulings really are. In doing this, the Court will be assuming one of its basic responsibilities; it will be taking a direct hand in creating an illuminating presentation that could truly educate the public on constitutional politics. Years ago, Eugene Rostow (1952: 203) characterized the Justices as "teachers in a vital national seminar" about fundamental political principles, but it is a sad fact that few Americans are enrolled in the course. The Court has ignored its pedagogical functions and has passed the buck to woefully inadequate sources of information, such as harried newspaper reporters, copy editors, and headline writers pressured by deadlines into frequently misinterpreting and malinterpreting.

It is sometimes written that the Presidency became the political power into which it has evolved as the President became aware of the role of mass media in gaining grassroots support. FDR's fireside

chats were a significant device that aided President Roosevelt in consolidating the coalition so essential to his continuation in office through four elections. Several Presidents since have managed to use television, in particular, to their own political advantage so as to maximize the chances for getting favored policies accepted by large segments of the citizenry. The Court's refusal to admit this to itself and its continued abhorrence of this most significant of media may well undermine its remaining vestiges of influence. One can hardly understand or respect even the most eloquent of orators if he speaks only into a paper bag. Only the orator hears a resonance of the beautiful rhetoric; others hear muffled sounds.

Aside from recognizing this failing, there are changes in staffing that the Justices should consider. After all, it is rather absurd to pretend that the only help the Court needs is that of its law clerks and its secretarial and administrative staffs. Neither these people nor the Justices themselves qualify as experts in political analysis or in the arts of public relations and political pressure. How long must we wait until the common knowledge among us that the Court is a political institution is translated into meaningful reforms in how the Court acts in the political system?

For instance, it is well known that the Court frequently runs into stiff opposition from Congress. There have been many studies that detail the hatred and defiance among members of the Senate and the House of Representatives that the Court has triggered by some of its most recent decisions (see, for example, Beaney and Beiser, 1964; Nagel, 1965). But what is worse still is that the Court is frequently misunderstood by even its staunchest supporters who, on the basis of the idle conjecture and often amateurish speculation, bear the onerous burden of communicating accurately to their legislative colleagues the precise holding of the Court and the political and legal reasons behind the Court's decision. What possible benefit can be gained in allowing this fumbling and groping to continue? Whom are we kidding? Whom is the Court fooling? Surely the Congress is not (comprised of), a naive clique of legal positivists who believe en masse that the Court finds the law à la Lord Coke. They recognize that a host of extra legal factors influence the Court's decision as well as we do. Why, then, don't we do for the Court that which we have done for administrative agencies (like the Pentagon) and

Transposed to studies of the Supreme Court, the problem presents itself thusly: we must be alert constantly to future changes in our political system and its processes and consciously determine the point at which we should withdraw scientific support of governmental policies once we believe them to be inimical to political values that we cherish. To fail to see this as a problem would be immoral and irresponsible.

It is easy for many of us who consider ourselves to be a shade of liberal (or even a tint of conservative) to rail at the mosaic of non-compliance with Supreme Court decisions. After all, the Supreme Court is the duly constituted final arbiter of a wide variety of federal and constitutional questions and issues. When it speaks, its words are the *supreme law* of the land. And law must be obeyed. Therefore, as scientists, we can plunge in without any reluctance and treat search into what conditions foster (or undermine) compliance with the malady of defiance. Right? Wrong.

That was the error of the nuclear physicists who trotted gallantly out in quest of the secret of the atomic bomb. But, as many of them discovered later, and as many other scientists who have been employed by the American military-industrial complex have learned more recently, they were utilized to achieve ends that they came to consider evil, unjust and wrong. At some earlier point, they may have had a bargaining position that might have allowed them, as citizens—with power (scientific knowledge)—to influence processes and policies. But they were dazzled by a golden ideological haze that convinced them that American power could only be used for good. Only at a point too far removed, and after the fact, did they come to their normative senses. We must begin to think about this problem now, in all areas of the study of government and politics, and that would certainly include our potential use to the Supreme Court as political scientists and as political advisors.

We do not wish to belabour this point, but there is a thick and durable smog of nonsense that cloaks the actual functioning of the Supreme Court of the United States. The basic function of the Court is surely not the one we find so consistently uttered by much of the political-legal community in this day and age. For liberals, all too often, the Court is pictured as some eternal fortress, of sorts, against encroachments on the democratic process and on individual liberties. To one degree or another, the Court is seen by prominent

furnish the Court with a group of political scientists, lobbyists, and public relations men to plead its case before Congress? These men could also assist the Court in moulding and writing opinions that would hold down potential irritation levels of Congress (and the President) thus enhancing the chances of maximum compliance.

As to the political scientists on an expanded Supreme Court staff, their role would be far more than simply figuring out political ploys and tactics on the Hill. Indeed, the time has come (if not gone) when the Court must officially recognize the need for developing a large store of data on success and failure in implementing its announced law at all levels of government. It would seem to be the proper place, in our scheme of things, to sponsor these studies through the Court itself. As the first section of this paper shows clearly enough, political scientists are already deeply committed to a search into what conditions foster (or undermine) compliance with Supreme Court decisions. As this area of study grows, and as theory begins to take shape, it would seem the height of folly for the Court to dwell in ignorance of the findings as well as of expert advice from political scientists interested in a more effective Supreme Court.

WITHDRAWING SCIENTIFIC SUPPORT

This leads us into the final point we wish to make in this paper. It is a difficult one, and one that plunges us deeply into thorny dilemmas about the appropriate role of empirical scientists assisting those who hold the reins of power.

We have been reminded of late of the naivete of many nuclear physicists, in the early and mid-forties, concerning the uses to which their knowledge and expertise would be put by our government. This blindness has been dramatized by a play entitled *In The Matter of J. Robert Oppenheimer* (presented at New York City Lincoln Center's Vivian Beaumont Theatre during the 1968–1969 season). According to the testimony given at Oppenheimer's security hearing, many of these scientists refused to believe that the bomb would actually be used against the Japanese people. This belief was firm enough to resist change despite the fact that the military had several of these very same scientists (including Oppenheimer) working on problems of heat and blast effects on a variety of Japanese cities!

experts as being an important factor in expanding our freedoms and in developing legal guidelines for expanding our democratic base. And, of course, in a legal sense, and to some degree of political reality, it has had this function of late on the American scene. Our point is that this is more an accident of history and a result of particular personnel than it is an inherent function of the Supreme Court.[7]

Who in their right minds could believe that the United States Supreme Court, or any other high court for that matter, is anything other than an *undemocratic* institution? Despite rationales to the contrary we have no serious structural democratic checks by the populace directly as they exist in Australia and Japan. Of course our Court's judges, as an enlightened and benevolent aristocracy, have had strong democratic and liberal ideals and thus have made decisions that are *pro-*democratic and *anti-*police state. But, and this is critical, there is no guarantee that such a status-quo-oriented, elite-staffed institution will continue to decide as it has in the last decade or so. We must remember that the same Court produced the Dred Scott Decision.[8]

Suppose, for example, President Nixon and his successor—say, a President Agnew—get another twelve years in the White House. Suppose they manage to select an overwhelming number of highly reactionary justices. Suppose the court of Chief Justice Warren Earl Burger reverses precedents (with some relish) and tries to implement a personal policy preference of *seriously* curtailing the protections of the Fifth Amendment. Suppose, even, that the Supreme Court becomes more police-state oriented than many high police administrators and that the latter, contrary to the Court's mandates, devise ingenious plans for evasion, avoidance, and defiance? Thus we might find career bureaucrats trying to sabotage what some people fear as being imminent on the horizon, that is, a drastic "turn to the right." What then for those among us who would be working out a theory on the impact of the Supreme Court? Should we continue to work it out? Should we continue to advise on how the Court can be most effective? The problem that we must ponder is again to set forth

7. For the fullest argument along these lines, see Becker (1969: ch. 5). A more cursory treatment of this point can be found in Becker (1967).
8. Dred Scott v. Sanford, 19 Howard (U.S.) 393 (1857).

specific criteria by which changes in our system and its process and policies should force us to withdraw scientific support, *as a profession!*

This should be debated in our classrooms, in our literature, and at our conventions—local and national. It would be tragic for social scientists to ignore this issue much the same as it was overlooked by the nuclear physicists in the forties and the entire scientific community in the fifties and sixties. After all, we have their lesson to learn from and we are, or should be, *political* scientists.

CONCLUSION

In an age of almost incomprehensibly rapid changes, institutions which fail to keep pace are bound for oblivion. Miller's (1968: ch. 6) ominous predictions about the coming "desuetude" of the Supreme Court may prove to be correct unless the Court adjusts its strategies and tactics. Theodore Roosevelt is alleged to have urged nations seeking world power to speak softly and carry a big stick. To which we add, those who lack big sticks, like the United States Supreme Court, had better learn to yell loudly, plead fervidly, and act shrewdly. The Court's strength is in its symbols; it should make the best of them.

Lest we conclude on a self-righteous and self-assured note, it must be admitted that we of the academy will take *some* of the blame for the tragically wide gulf between the ideals of constitutional doctrine and the reality of political life. Having criticized the Supreme Court for blindly staggering in the dark and cloistering itself inside the marble palace, we must also point a guilty finger at the discipline of political science for failing to light the way and for taking refuge in the ivory tower. Both our research and our teaching have only very recently been directed to the empirical study of institutional practices and their social consequences, which is one area where we *ourselves* can aspire to make a political impact.

Finally, now that increasing attempts are being made to devise more refined theory and collect better data on the impact of the Supreme Court, let us not make the grievous error of being indifferent to the real danger of having our knowledge used for malevolent purposes. If and when the day should come that the Supreme Court becomes repressive, inhumane, and unjust in its policy-making, we may have a political obligation to confound their efforts by quashing our inquiries and withdrawing our counsel. It is not too early to ponder these disturbing possibilities and perplexing dilemmas; 1984 is only fifteen years away.

REFERENCES

BARTH, T. (1968) "Perception and acceptance of Supreme Court decisions at the state and local level." J. of Public Law 17: 308-350.

BEANEY, W. M. and E. N. BEISER (1964) "Prayer and politics: the impact of Engel and Schempp on the political process." J. of Public Law 13: 475-503. (Reprinted on pp. 24-38 of this book.)

BECKER, T. L. (1969) Comparative Judicial Politics. Chicago: Rand-McNally.

——— (1967) "Judicial structure and its political functioning in society." J. of Politics 29: 302-331.

BLUMBERG, A. (1967) Criminal Justice. Chicago: Quadrangle.

DOLBEARE, K. (1969) "The Supreme Court and the states: from abstract doctrine to local behavioral conformity," in T. Becker (ed.) The Impact of Supreme Court Decisions. New York: Oxford Univ. Press.

——— (1967) "The public views the Supreme Court," pp. 194-212 in H. Jacob (ed.) Law, Politics, and the Federal Courts. Boston: Little, Brown.

HYMAN, H. and P. SHEATSLEY (1964) "Attitudes toward desegregation." Scientific Amer. 211: 16-23.

KRISLOV, S. (1968) The Supreme Court and Political Freedom. New York: Free Press.

——— (1959) "Constituency versus constitutionalism: the desegregation issue and the tensions and aspirations of Southern attorneys general." Midwest J. of Pol. Sci. 3: 75-92.

LEWIS, A. (1954) Gideon's Trumpet. New York: Vantage.

MILLER, A. (1968) The Supreme Court and American Capitalism. New York: Free Press.

MUIR, W. (1962) Prayer in the Public Schools. Chicago: Univ. of Chicago Press.

MURPHY, W. (1964) Elements of Judicial Strategy. Chicago: Univ. of Chicago Press.

——— (1959) "Lower court checks on Supreme Court power." Amer. Pol. Sci. Rev. 53 (December): 1017-1031.

NAGEL, S. (1965) "Court-curbing periods in American history." Vanderbilt Law Rev. 18 (June): 925-944.

NEWLAND, C. (1964) "Press coverage of the United States supreme court." Western Pol. Q. 17 (March): 15-36.

PAULSEN, M. (1950) "The persistence of substantive due process in the states." Minnesota Law Rev. 34 (January): 91-118.

RABIN, R. (1967) "Do you believe in a supreme being—the administration of the conscientious objector exemption." Wisconsin Law Rev.: 642-684.

ROSTOW, E. (1952) "The democratic character of judicial review." Harvard Law Rev. 66 (December).

1. What are the three goals of the Levine and Becker article?

2. What is the "trickle-down" theory and why is it seen as an inaccurate description of the role of the Supreme Court?

3. What aspects of the judicial system make lower court autonomy possible?

4. How does elite unresponsiveness limit the impace of the Supreme Court?

5. How does public unawareness limit the impact of the Supreme Court?

6. What recommendations are made to increase the Supreme Court's impact?

7. What is the responsibility of social scientists attempting to find ways to increase the impact of the Supreme Court?

DISCUSSION OF READING #2 QUESTIONS

1. a. To explain the limited impact of U.S. Supreme Court decisions.

    b. To explore ways to increase the court's influence.

    c. To discuss the role of social science in increasing the court's influence.

2. The "trickle-down" theory is the belief that the formal hierarchical structure of American courts reflect the actual operation of the courts. In other words, the Supreme Court's decisions are assumed to "trickle-down" through the lower courts who, presumably, defer to these decisions of the high court. Levine and Becker claim that lower courts frequently circumvent decisions of the Supreme Court.

3. Levine and Becker maintain that lower court autonomy is encouraged by:

    a. the right of the trial courts to establish the facts of a case;

    b. the fact that no two cases are ever identical, i.e., the lower court can always avoid the Supreme Court's rulings by finding that a particular case <u>differs</u> from the case decided by the Supreme Court;

    c. lower courts can interpret some parts of Supreme Court opinions as the "holding" of the case (the binding portion of the opinion) and some parts as "dicta" (the unnecessary and non-binding portion of the opinion);

    d. state courts can choose to base their decisions on state law, thereby often precluding higher court review;

    e. Supreme Court opinions, being the product of negotiation among the Justices, are often unclear and, therefore, give lower courts a wide latitude; and

    f. the Supreme Court's inability to review <u>all</u> lower court decisions.

4. Because the court cannot order all individuals to comply with its rulings, voluntary compliance is necessary if the court is to achieve its purpose. However, due to a lack of information, the existence of political incentive to disobey and the lack of sanctions, voluntary compliance is frequently not forthcoming. Levine and Becker (1970) conclude, "Institutions such as Congress, with its control over the public fisc, and the executive, with its massive bureaucracy, are in a far better position to promote social change on more than a token basis"

5. While pointing to evidence that the Supreme Court can and does change public attitudes, Levine and Becker note that too often the public is either unaware or misinformed about court decisions. Thus, while

281

potential for attitude change is great, the lack of public awareness of Court decisions limits the Court's ability to change attitudes.

6. Levine and Becker's suggestions for increasing the Court's impace include:

    a. televising Supreme Court proceedings in which justices explain their opinions and outline what changes they are requiring in our behavior;

    b. providing the Court with lobbyists, political scientists, and public relations experts to help build public and political support for Court decisions;

    c. doing research on what factors promote and inhibit compliance so that the Court will have greater knowledge of the likely effect of its decisions.

7. Levine and Becker maintain that social scientists ought not to work to increase the impace of the Court without evaluating what the Court seeks to do. They reject the notion of social scientists not being responsible for the misuse of their work. Rather, social scientists must make value judgments about the content of Court decisions and contribute to increasing the impact of the Court only so long as moral and proper decisions are handed down. When that ceases to occur, the social scientist must withdraw from efforts to increase impact.

UNIT SUMMARY

The impact of the Supreme Court upon society has been described and explained to an extent. The ability of lower courts to avoid the dictates of the Supreme Court, the lack of willingness on the part of many officials to obey the Court, and the lack of awareness on the part of the public greatly limit the role of the Court in achieving social change. Impact theory was explored in an effort to identify some of the factors which affect the Court's ability to bring about change, and hypotheses and examples were presented to illustrate the nature of legal impact analysis. While only looking at a slice of the total role of law in bringing about social change, legal impact theory was offered as a fruitful conceptual approach to the more general problem of studying law as an instrument of social change.

REFERENCES

Becker, T.L., & Feeley, M.M. The impact of Supreme Court decisions (2nd ed.). New York: Oxford University Press, 1973.

Friedman, L. The legal system: a social science perspective. New York: Russell Sage Foundation, 1975.

Levine, J.P., & Becker, T.L. Toward and beyond a theory of Supreme Court impact. American Behavioral Scientist, 1970, 13 (4), 561-573.

Medalie, R.J., et al. Custodial police interrogation in our national capital: the attempt to implement Miranda. Michigan Law Review, 1968, 66, 1347-1422.

Schur, E.M. Law and society. New York: Random House, 1968.

Wasby, S. The impact of the United States Supreme Court. Homewood: Illinois, Dorsey Press, 1970.

Beaney, W.J., & Beiser, E.N. Prayer and politics: the impact of Engle and Schempp on the political process. Journal of Public Law, 1964, 13, 475-503.

Berkowitz, L., & Walker, N. Laws and moral judgments. Sociometry, December, 1967, pp. 410-422.

Birkby, H. The Supreme Court and the Bible belt: Tennessee reactions to the Schempp' decision. Midwest Journal of Political Science, 1966, 10, 304-319.

Brady, D. & Kemp, K. Supreme Court abortion decisions and social change. Social Science Quarterly, 1976.

Bullock, S., III, & Rodgers, R., Jr. Coercion to compliance: Southern School officials and school desegragation guidelines. (Mimeographed paper.)

Campbell, T., & Ross, H. The Connecticut crackdown on speeding: time series data in quasi-experimental analysis. Law and Society Review, 1968, 3, 33-53.

Crain, R.L., et al. The politics of school desegregation. New York: Doubleday, 1969.

Gates, R.L. The making of massive resistance: Virginia's politics of public school desegregation. 1954-1956. Chapel Hill: University of North Carolina Press, 1962.

Grossman, J.B., & Grossman, M.H. (Eds.) Law and change in modern America. Pacific Palisades, CA: Goodyear, 1970.

Hanson, R.A., & Crew, R.E., Jr. Policy impact of reapportionment. Law and Society Review, 1973, 8, 69-93.

Ingraham, B.L. Impact of Argersinger (Argersinger v. Hamlin, 92 Sup. Ct. 2006)-one year later. Law and Society Review, 1974, 8, 164-169.

Johnson, R.M. Compliance and Supreme Court decision-making. Wisconsin Law Review, Winter 1967, 170-185.

Koeppen, S.R. Children and compliance: a comparative analysis of socialization studies. Law and Society Review, 1970, 4, 545-564.

Krislov, S., et al. Compliance and the law: a multi-disciplinary approach. Beverly Hills: Sage Publications, 1972.

Muir, W.K., Jr. Prayer in the public schools: law and attitude change. Chicago: University of Chicago Press, 1967.

Muir, W.K., Jr. The impact of Supreme Court decisions on moral attitudes. Journal of Legal Education, 1971, 23, 89-105.

Petrick, M.J. The Supreme Court and authority acceptance. <u>Western Political Quarterly</u>, 1968, <u>21</u>, 5-15.

Rodgers, H.R., Jr. Censorship campaigns in 18 cities: an impact analysis. <u>American Politics Quarterly</u>, 1974, <u>2</u>, 371-392.

Rodgers, H.R., Jr. Law as an instrument of public policy. <u>American Journal of Political Science</u>, 1973, <u>17</u>, 638-647.

Sanders, P.H. The Warren Court and the lower Federal courts. In J. Schmidhauser (Ed.), <u>Constitutional law in the political process</u>. Chicago: Rand McNally, 1963.

Wasby, S.L. <u>The impact of the United States Supreme Court: some perspectives</u>. Homewood, Ill.: Dorsey Press, 1970.

Wasby, S.L. The Supreme Court's impact: some problems of conceptualization and measurement. <u>Law and Society Review</u>, 1970, <u>5</u>, 41-60.

Wasby, S.L. The United States Supreme Court's impact: broadening our focus. <u>Notre Dame Lawyer</u>, 1974, <u>49</u>, 1023-1036.

The <u>Yale Law Journal</u> Editors. Interrogation in New Haven: impact of Miranda. <u>Yale Law Journal</u>, 1967, <u>76</u>, 1519-1648.

UNIT 7

Law In Contemporary American Society

Rationale

As noted in the Course Introduction and reflected in the Course Goals, I want you to become familiar with some of the ideas, theories, and concepts which a variety of scholars have used to organize their thoughts about the general relationship of law and legal institutions to other aspects of society. You have read in Units 1 and 2 about the law from the vantage points of philosophers, sociologists, anthropologists, and political scientists. In Units 3-6 you have seen how law is related to social organization and how law performs the tasks of resolving disputes, providing social control mechanisms, and contributing to social change. It was necessary to examine such questions in order to begin to understand one of the most important concepts in this course; that is, that law is a social institution, rather than a set of rules.

In this unit, I would also like you to become more familiar with the role played by law in American society. Toward this end, you will read in this unit a description of American 'legal culture', i.e., ". . .the network of values and attitudes relating to law, which determine when and why and where people turn to law and government or turn away" (Friedman, 1977, p. 34). The way in which a society will utilize its legal system to resolve disputes, achieve social control, and induce social change will be largely the result of the type of legal culture found in that society. You will also read about the way our legal culture manifests itself in our reliance on legal institutions, legal solutions, and legal symbols. You will then examine a number of contemporary criticisms of this American reliance on law, in general, and on the Supreme Court, in particular. Finally, you will see that despite the general high level of support for the legal system and the unusual willingness of Americans to defer to judicial determinations of major questions of public policy, the majority of Americans rarely seek or receive legal assistance.

Historically, Americans have always tended to be highly supportive of their legal institutions. As early as 1835 Alexis de Toqueville observed that, "Scarcely any political question arises in the United States that is not resolved, sooner or later, into a judicial question" (de Toqueville, 1944, p. 280). The willingness of Americans to allow a non-elected body such as the U.S. Supreme Court to interpret the constitution so as to invalidate acts of the elected Congress and President (judicial review) testifies to our abiding faith in law and legal institutions. The ability of the Supreme Court to prevail over former President Richard Nixon on the issue of the scope of 'executive privilege' is also evidence of our faith in the wisdom of the Supreme Court. America's respect for the Supreme Court is seen repeatedly in the surveys which show that the job of Supreme Court Justice heads the list of prestigious jobs.

The Constitituion itself reflects an undying faith in law. In trying to set up a new government, the first task undertaken by the founding fathers was to set up the 'rules' in the form of a written constitution. Yet it should be obvious to you that 'rules' and 'constitutions' are written on pieces of paper which, themselves, are incapable of producing humane and democratic societies. It is rather the belief in such rules and constitutions which moves men to create and maintain such societies. We need only look at the parade of constitutions which are born and die annually in other parts of the world to see that the legal culture, rather than the legal documents, accounts for our success. Note by contrast that Great Britain has also succeeded in maintaining a democratic society for hundreds of years despite the lack of a written constitution. The point should be clear--legal culture merits our attention.

The list goes on and on. It suggests that Americans have from the very beginning shown a peculiar fondness for law and legal institutions. In Unit 7 then, you will first look at a summary of the studies of American legal culture. Next you will examine a series of arguments which generally conclude that we Americans have relied too heavily on law, that we expect too much from legal institutions, and that these legal institutions are incapable of meeting our expanding demands and expectations.

Objectives

After you have completed this unit, you should be able to:

1. Define the following concepts;

    a. legal culture
    b. legal mobilization
    c. judicial review
    d. post-industrial society
    e. fragmentation/destandardization
    f. ephermeralization/impermanence
    g. the myth of rights
    h. the politics of rights
    i. judicial incapacities
    j. guardian ethic

2. State at least three general propositions about American legal culture.

3. Summarize arguments for and against judicial review.

4. Describe Toffler's view of the future of law in American society.

5. Describe Sheppard's view of the future of law in post-revolutionary American society.

6. State the political limitations on litigation as a means of achieving social change.

7. State the inherent limitations on judicial decision making.

8. Distinguish between the empirical and normative limits of law.

9. State three characteristics of the Burger Court which Glazer takes to be evidence of a permanent change in the court's role.

10. State three reasons why Glazer believes the court will remain permanently activist.

11. Analyze cases illustrating the reliance on the courts to resolve difficult social issues using the ideas and concepts developed in the Mini-Lectures and Readings for this unit.

Overview

This unit provides you with a number of points of view on the role of law in current American life and some speculations about the future role of law in American life. There are three Mini-Lectures and three other Readings which draw your attention to American attitudes toward law, American reliance on law, the future of law, the limits of law, and the growing role of courts as policymaking institutions. Needless to say, this unit is highly selective in its presentation of the role of law in contemporary American society. It is intended to alert you to vital questions, not to exhaust the range of questions and answers on so large a topic.

Mini-Lecture #1, "American Legal Culture," summarizes a number of empirical studies designed to explore the knowledge, attitudes, and satisfaction levels of Americans about legal institutions. The key concepts of legal culture and legal mobilization are discussed in order to show you that factors other than the content of law play important parts in determining the relative effectiveness and potency of legal institutions in society. The ability of law, in other words, to perform social control functions, to resolve disputes, and to be an agent for change and stability is dependent upon legal culture and the style of legal mobilization.

"The American Reliance on Law," Mini-Lecture #2, focuses more specifically on the litigation explosion, i.e., the propensity of Americans to react to a variety of problems with a single thought, "I'll sue the S.O.B." This short essay attempts, after citing some curious examples, to explain why Americans have turned to the law to provide answers and draws attention to the unique role of the Supreme Court in determining the constitutionality of legislative enactments.

Alvin Toffler, author of Future Shock, presents his view of "The Future of Law and Order," in an article of the same title. He is highly critical of the American reliance on law and argues that other institutions will ultimately have to produce social order. He suggests that the "jungle-like overgrowth" of law will strangle us and that law must begin to play less and less of a role if it is to retain its utility for American society.

In a contrasting projection of the future of law in American society, law professor Annamay Sheppard then argues that there will be a crucial need for law and lawyers even after the hypothetical revolution which she outlines. Her blend of socialist idealism and lawyerlike pragmatism stands in contrast to Toffler's apparent disdain for law.

Mini-Lecture #3, "The Politics of Rights and the Limits of Law," offers a political analysis of the limited utility of litigation in achieving social change, a critical analysis of built-in limitations in the judicial process, and a discussion of some general empirical and ethical limits of law. This lecture presents reasons why the previously described American dependence on law must be critically re-examined.

Throughout the unit there are really three types of reliance on law being discussed:

a. Reliance on law in the sense of passing laws (rules) to regulate a complex society.

b. Reliance on law in the sense of individuals filing suits to resolve their personal problems.

c. Reliance on law in the sense of allowing courts to make decisions which in fact constitute broad legislation having an enormous impact on American society.

Toffler's criticisms and Sheppard's comments most directly relate to the reliance on law in the first sense. The discussion of legal culture and legal mobilization discuss aspects of the reliance on law in the second sense. And Mini-Lecture #3 addresses the reliance on law in the third sense.

Finally, Nathan Glazer's article, "Towards An Imperial Judiciary," provides a fuller discussion of reliance on law in this third sense. Applying Arthur Schlesinger's 'Imperial Presidency' notion to the judiciary, Glazer develops the argument that permanent and disturbing changes have produced excessive reliance on the 'imperial judiciary'.

With the aid of these readings you are called upon not only to consider the separate implications of each reading but also to consider your own views on law in contemporary American society, particularly as they are affected by the unit readings. In the final task you are asked to integrate the various points of view expressed in the unit and formulate your own opinion about the role of law in contemporary American society based upon the case described at the end.

Study Task Checklist

☐ 1. A. Read Mini-Lecture #1, "American Legal Culture."

☐ 1. B. Answer the Study Questions and compare your answers with the Discussion of them.

☐ 2. A. Read Mini-Lecture #2, "The American Reliance on Law."

☐ 2. B. Answer the Study Questions and compare your answers to them with the Discussion of them.

☐ 3. A. Study Reading #1, "The Future of Law and Order" by Alvin Toffler.

☐ 3. B. Answer the Study Questions and compare your answers with the Discussion of them.

☐ 4. A. Study Reading #2, "Post-Revolutionary Law and Society" by Annamay T. Sheppard.

☐ 4. B. Answer the Study Questions and compare your answers with the discussion of them.

☐ 5. A. Read Mini-Lecture #3, "The Politics of Rights and the Limits of Law."

☐ 5. B. Answer the Study Questions and compare your answers with the Discussion of them.

☐ 6. A. Study Reading #3, "Towards an Imperial Judiciary" by Nathan Glazer.

☐ 6. B. Answer the Study Questions and compare your answers with the discussion of them.

☐ 7. A. Answer the Unit Study Questions.

☐ 7. B. Compare your answer with the Sample Answer, identifying and examining any differences.

Mini-Lecture #1

AMERICAN LEGAL CULTURE

As indicated in the Rationale, the idea of legal culture involves the knowledge, values, attitudes, and beliefs which people hold about the law, legal institutions, and legal decision makers, such as lawyers, judges, and police. The willingness of people to use the law (legal mobilization), the expectations which people have about the capacity of law to solve problems, the willingness of people to opt for legal or non-legal solutions, and the degree to which people will comply with legal decisions are all closely tied to the legal culture. The process by which people develop these law-related attitudes is called legal socialization. In this mini-lecture we will review some of the basic findings concerning American legal culture and the legal socialization of Americans and briefly explore the consequences for the structure of legal mobilization.

In recent years, a growing number of scholars have undertaken survey research in order to gather information about American attitudes and beliefs about law and law-related phenomena. While keeping in mind that asking people questions is not the only way (or necessarily the best way) to determine what they believe, let's examine some of the major generalizations which emerge from these empirical studies of attitudes toward a) the law generally, b) courts, c) civil liberties, d) lawyers, and e) police. We will not concern ourselves here with methodological problems such as sampling and research design, but rather we will attempt to get a general idea of what these studies collectively suggest to us. Professor Austin Sarat (1977, pp. 427-488) recently did a comprehensive review of the empirical literature on American legal culture. The brief discussion which follows draws heavily from Sarat's excellent essay.

A. Knowledge, Beliefs, and Attitudes About Law

    1. Knowledge of the content of the law is quite low among most Americans. (Albrecht, 1974)

Probably because of lack of personal experience with the law and lack of education about the law, Americans are not generally very well informed about the content of law or the nature of their legal rights. In fact, many

Americans, most notably among the lower social and economic classes, do not readily recognize that they even have a legal problem. There is little or no time devoted to legal education in secondary schools or in undergraduate curricula. Only in professional law education does a student really have an opportunity to learn about the law. While there is a growing trend toward undergraduate legal education, the overwhelming majority of American students are never exposed to law except on television.

This television exposure might account for a second general finding concerning American knowledge of the law.

2. Americans tend to know more about the criminal law than any other type of law. Yet even that knowledge is typically inaccurate or incomplete. (Albrecht, 1974; Michigan Law Review, 1973)

Recent years have witnessed a large number of police shows on prime time television. Kojak, Police Woman, Columbo, Baretta, and The Streets of San Francisco are thought by many observers to profoundly affect American attitudes toward violence and crime by providing potential offenders with excellent ideas and by underplaying the actual pain and horror of violence. However, one recent study offers a positive effect of such programming. In examining the viewing habits of children and their knowledge of certain aspects of criminal procedure, the researchers conclude that the heavy television watchers are more likely than the occasional watchers to be aware of constitutional guarantees against self-incrimination and unreasonable searches, and the right to counsel. Thus, it might be argued that television police shows help to teach American children about the Constitution of the United States.

Another study of police shows (Arons and Katsh, 1977) was less encouraging. A team of lawyers taped and studied all of the police shows broadcast between the Fall of 1974 and the Spring of 1976 in order to find out what information was being communicated to the public concerning police and the law. Assuming that television depictions of the police have some effect on our attitudes toward police and the law, they reasoned, it is critical that we know exactly what information is being passed on to the public. In a detailed analysis of one randomly selected week of programs, the lawyers identified 21 clear constitutional violations, 7 ommissions of constitutional rights, and 15 instances of police harassment or brutality. The most common violations included interrogations of suspects in the absence of Miranda warnings and illegal searches of suspects and their homes. Therefore, the knowledge acquired about the law is likely to be highly distorted, inaccurate, and insensitive to constitutional protections.

3. Individuals with higher levels of education and income know more than those with lower levels about criminal law, but not about consumer law. (Michigan Law Review, 1973)

This is an interesting finding because we would have imagined that those with more education and higher incomes would naturally know much more about the law. However, it appears in at least one study, that dissatisfied consumers, whatever their background, are unlikely to know what the law offers them in terms of redressing the wrong which has been done to them. Despite this finding, however, most scholars agree that lower class social and economic individuals are generally less knowledgeable about the law.

4. Individuals with criminal records are more knowledgeable about sentences for particular crimes than those with no prior records.

This is fascinating because, on the face of it, it would appear that tough sentences do not deter crime since only those who have violated the law are likely to be aware of them! However, it is possible that their knowledge of sentences is acquired after they have been arrested, and, therefore, we must treat this finding with much caution. The same study, by the way, found that those people with the least specific information on the current length of sentences for particular crimes were the most likely to argue that stiffer sentences would be the best solution to the crime problem.

5. The more individuals know about the law and the legal system, the less likely they are to be satisfied with its performance.

This proposition indicates that law is more likely to be highly respected and the performance of the legal system more positively evaluated when knowledge of law is restricted to legal symbols, legal ritual, and legal myth. In other words, so long as we continue to hold idealized images of the justice system and the impartiality of the law and judges, and the belief that our rights will always be protected by the law, we will continue to be highly supportive of the law. However, when our knowledge becomes specific, concrete, and grounded more in experience than symbolism, our evaluation of the law begins to change. Thus, if we have been processed by the criminal justice system, sued in the civil courts, or served as witnesses or jurors, we are less likely to be favorably impressed by the law and its institutions.

6. <u>A majority of low income Americans see the law as an enemy, or an arm of the oppressors, rather than as a means for protecting or asserting their rights.</u>

Most likely, low income Americans have only had negative experiences with the law--either as criminal defendents, defendents in actions to collect debts, or victims of eviction hearings. Consequently, they do not perceive the law as a tool which can be used for their benefit, but rather as an instrument used by others against them.

7. <u>For young children, ages 5-12, law is seen as a source of control. Compliance is justified on the basis of fear of punishment. Older children, ages 13-18, see the law more as an instrument to be used to achieve social goals. They are more likely to see compliance or non-compliance as an issue to be decided following a review of the content of law and the morality of its application in particular circumstances.</u> (Tapp and Kohlberg, 1971; Tapp and Levine, 1974)

This general finding suggests that there is a developmental pattern involved in legal socialization. Younger children see the law and reasons for complying with it quite differently from older children. The repeated similar findings for many children in a variety of cultrual settings lends some credence to this notion. It also implies that it is possible to use the education system to raise the level of legal development of children, i.e., to foster development of more mature and sophisticated reasoning about the nature of law.

B. <u>Attitudes Towards Civil Liberties</u>

1. <u>Only one-third of American adults believe that people should be allowed to make speeches against God or publish books attacking the American political system.</u> (Wilson, 1975)

2. <u>Support for civil liberties of atheists and communists is higher today than it was in the 1950's. Where only 27% of American adults supported freedom of speech for Communists in 1954, 58% do so today.</u> (Erskine and Siepel, 1975)

3. <u>Americans are generally supportive of civil liberties when they are presented in general and abstract terms; they are less supportive when such abstractions are applied to specific instances.</u> (Prothro and Grigg, 1960)

4. <u>Support for civil liberties is higher among better educated and more politically active Americans.</u> (Stouffer, 1955)

The general conclusions of efforts to study American attitudes toward civil liberties suggest that we are not deeply committed to the maintenance of civil liberties for those with whom we disagree. Support for general references to 'free speech' or 'free press' is widespread; support for particular individuals' rights to such speech or press is less widespread. It appears also that those who are politically active and most likely to affect policy outcomes are also the most committed to civil liberties. While there are a variety of criticisms made of these findings, the uniform conclusions of many researchers suggest that these disheartening conclusions cannot be easily dismissed.

C. Attitudes Toward The Supreme Court and Lower Courts

1. Knowledge of the content of Supreme Court decisions is quite low. (Dolbeare, 1967)

Most Americans are unable to name more than one or two decisions made by the high court, and fewer still are able to accurately discuss their content or their consequences. Only the most controversial cases reach the consciousness of most Americans. For example, Brown v. Board of Education, Miranda v. Arizona, and perhaps Bakke v. University of California at Davis are known to many Americans because of their controversial and divisive consequences.

2. A majority of Americans believe that the Supreme Court does a good job.

Even knowledge of decisions with which they disagree seems not to undermine the faith of Americans in the Supreme Court. No one, for example, seriously doubts that the interpretation of the constitution is a proper job for the Supreme Court, though such power of judicial review is not expressly provided for in the Constitution itself.

3. The support for the Supreme Court is a function of powerful myths and symbols associated with the Court and the Constitution. (Casey, 1974)

The myths and symbols (described in Unit 2) rather than the content of decisions of the Court or the content of Constitutional provisions account for the widespread support for the Court. Those in government and out of government enjoy the ". . .sense of continuity and propriety [the constitution] radiates. . .They seek assurance that new actions are consistent with it." (Dolbeare and Edelman, 1977 p. 235) The ambiguity of the Constitutional language itself tends to neatly accomodate to a wide range of policy choices, thus enabling the court to claim that the Constitution either requires or prohibits that which the Court seeks to do.

Convincing evidence of the relative power of symbols over content can be seen in a study done recently in which the Declaration of Independence was presented as a petition to passersby on a street corner in a major American city. Few recognized its radical arguments and few were willing to sign their names to so disruptive and anarchistic a set of principles. It seems that Americans are not highly supportive of civil liberties or of basic principles of American democratic life.

4. <u>Attitudes toward lower courts are generally favorable, but knowledge of their role is very low. Additionally, experience in a lawsuit tends to erode this support--whether one is the 'winner' or the 'loser'.</u> (Walker et al, 1972)

As was the case with the Supreme Court, support for the lower courts seems to be related to myths and symbols about courts. Participation in the actual courtroom process increases dissatisfaction with the process. That both sides of a legal battle seem to feel the same way suggests that it is not simply a matter of being unhappy with the results. Rather, it is a result of disillusionment which grows out of the operation of the legal system itself.

D. <u>Attitudes Towards Lawyers</u>

1. <u>While there is widespread suspicion of lawyers and a lack of faith in their willingness to serve rich and poor clients equally, they are accorded high social status in our society.</u> (Curran and Spalding, 1974)

Lawyers hold a peculiar position in our culture. They are, at the same time, objects of ridicule and recipients of our trust. We frequently criticize them for their reliance on incomprehensible language, their un-willingness to provide legal services to the poor, their excessive fees, and their use of technicalities. Yet, at the same time, we continue to elect them to political office at all levels of government and in all regions of the country. The dual belief that lawyers cannot be trusted and that they ought to be entrusted with political power is testimony to the dominant role played by law in American culture. Detesting them, we nonetheless basically believe that social, economic, and moral problems can best be handled by selecting more lawyers to enact, administer, and adjudicate more laws, based upon legal reasoning and legal solutions.

    2. <u>Prior experience with lawyers is likely to lower one's evaluation of them.</u> (Missouri Bar, 1963)

As with the courts, it appears that the more that is known about lawyers from first hand experience, the less positive is a person's evaluation of lawyers.

E. <u>Attitudes Toward the Police</u>

    1. <u>Young children typically view the police as helpful, powerful, and benevolent.</u> (Easton and Dennis, 1969)

    2. <u>Along with awareness of the President of the United States, awareness of the police constitutes the earliest content of legal consciousness.</u> (Hess and Torney, 1967)

    3. <u>Adolescent children develop more negative attitudes toward the police.</u> (Bouma, 1969)

    4. <u>Black children share with white children the early supportive attitudes toward the police, but evidence a more steep and more rapid erosion of that view by adolescence.</u> (Greenberg, 1970)

Summary of Legal Culture

The importance of the content of legal culture in determining if and how people will use the legal system is a central factor in understanding the operation of the law in American society. Individuals' attitudes toward the police may influence the degree of cooperation they give the police or their willingness to call for police services. Similarly, people's attitudes toward lawyers will be reflected in their willingness to seek legal help. The public's belief in the legitimacy of the courts may be the critical factor in accepting their decisions as binding. The ultimate extension or contraction of civil liberties will depend heavily upon the degree to which Americans believe in them and are willing to provide them. The existence of written guarantees means little in the absence of a supportive legal culture; the availability of elaborate legal procedures are of no value if they are not used. The next section of this mini-lecture explores the way in which American legal culture has helped to mold the process through which cases come to the attention of the legal system--the process of legal mobilization.

Legal Mobilization

Legal culture can produce different types of legal mobilization processes. Legal mobilization refers to the way in which and whether the legal system acquires cases. Basically, cases can either be initiated by individuals or by the state. When the legal system relies primarily on the decisions of individuals to initiate legal action, it is described as a reactive mobilization process. Where the state is the major source of cases, it is called a proactive mobilization process.

The American legal culture has produced basically a reactive mobilization process in which the legal system is principally dependent upon individuals for initiating cases.* Unless private individuals assert that someone has breached a contract with them, deprived them of their property, or done harm to them in some other fashion, the legal system will have no contribution to make to the solution of their problems. There are no government officials who will file suit on their behalf alleging that their new stereos don't work, the landlord has refused to fix the steps, or the mail order house never shipped the Christmas presents. Even in the area of criminal law, where one would suppose that the proactive mobilization process would be operating, America has developed a basically reactive criminal law mobilization process. While the state has the formal role of initiating criminal proceedings, in fact most criminal charges arise out of complaints made by private individuals to the police. Furthermore, where the complaining party decides not to testify against the offender (as often happens when the police are called by a child or wife who has been beaten by a parent or husband) the criminal process is usually stopped at that point.

Donald Black (1973) claims that these two types of mobilization processes are based on different assumptions about the legal system. The reactive mobilization model rests on an entreprenurial model of law in which everyone is assumed to be well informed, rational, and willing to pursue his or her own best interests. This legal market model is analogous to the market model in economics. In this model, attorneys are not allowed to actively

_____

*Note, however, that there are elements of proactive mobilization such as grand jury investigations or justice department investigations. However, even these might be initiated following external individual or group pressures.

persuade private individuals to mobilize the law; individuals must have standing, i.e., they must have personally suffered harm for which they are entitled to a legal remedy, and courts must wait patiently for actual controversies to develop before they may issue rulings. Such a model is consistent with American political and economic values, but probably results in many people never receiving the legal benefits to which they are technically entitled. Also, it probably means that those individuals with more knowledge, higher incomes, and more status are more likely to benefit from the law.

The proactive mobilization process, on the other hand, rests on a social-welfare model of law where ". . .the legal good of the citizenry [is] defined by government administrators" (Black, 1973, p. 138). In a sense, this type of system imposes law, rather than simply providing the opportunity to utilize law. The proactive model is likely to be more dominant where there is greater tension between the ruler and the ruled.

As Black notes about the mobilization processes, whether reactive or proactive,

> In theory the law is available to all. In fact,
> the availability of law is in every legal system
> greater for the citizenry of higher social status,
> while the imposition of law tends to be reserved
> for those on the bottom. Thus, the mobilization
> of law, like every legal process, reflects and
> perpetuates systems of social stratification. In
> contemporary Western [American] society, the
> availability of law is nevertheless greater for
> the mass of citizens then in any previous historical
> period, and the trend is toward ever-greater avail-
> ability. And yet it appears that the scope and
> depth of legal imposition is also greater than ever
> before . (Black, 1973, p. 141)

As you read in Unit 1, American law grows out of a natural law tradition which itself has divine origins. While the connection of law with religion has disappeared for the most part, the deep faith usually associated with religious phenomena has remained as part of America's attitude toward law. As political scientist Herbert Jacob notes,

> Twentieth-century American law possesses none of the outward
> characteristics of the divine; it is entirely a secular
> creation. Yet it continues to benefit from popular respect
> for the sacred. People are taught to respect law alone among
> the institutions of government, simply because it is law. One
> may speak disparagingly about presidents, congressmen, and
> generals; indeed, the quadrennial presidential election campaign
> encourages harsh rhetoric against such authorities. One may

insult the president at the White House and only be condemned as a boor, but disrespect for the lowliest judge in the court-room will bring a jail sentence. Respect for the law is urged by many people--even if one disagrees with it and seeks to change it--as a necessary barrier to anarchy. (Jacob, 1978, p. 9)

Summary

In this mini-lecture you have been introduced to the concepts of legal culture and legal mobilization and have read a summary of some empirical efforts to determine the particular content of American legal culture.

In light of the discussion in this unit's rationale which argues that Americans have historically been highly supportive of legal institutions for solving major policy problems, the findings reported in this mini-lecture appear somewhat contradictory. For example, we see from the various studies that Americans are generally poorly informed about the details of law and legal procedures, yet they seem willing to trust that the Supreme Court will make proper decisions concerning the _real_ meaning of the constitution. They voice distrust of lawyers and dissatisfaction with the legal system, but continue to litigate their disputes with increasing frequency. They voice support for constitutional abstractions but hesitate to extend civil liberties to groups who pose threats to core American values. Poorer Americans rarely use courts and perceive the law to be the weapon of the upper classes, rather than a tool available to all. Nonetheless, there is widespread support for the Supreme Court and widespread agreement on the high status generally ac-corded to lawyers and judges.

How can one interpret these seemingly inconsistent findings? Perhaps they are not as inconsistent as it appears at first glance. It is possible for example, to be unable to recite detailed information about court decisions, statutes, and legal procedures, and yet hold the law in high regard. In fact, one might argue that, if Americans believe deeply enough in the general value of legal process and legal solutions, then there is no need for them to acquire knowledge of the details of legal proceedings. The mere fact that the 'LAW' has been the basis for a particular decision may preclude the need for them to delve more deeply except, perhaps, where a personal interest is affected.

The general distrust of lawyers expressed by many Americans and especially by lower income Americans may discourage them from using the courts, but not necessarily the more prosperous, middle and upper income

Americans. In other words, the high level of litigation in America (which
is described in the next mini-lecture) may be primarily the result of middle
and upper income groups bringing lawsuits rather than lower income groups.
Americans of middle and upper incomes could simultaneously distrust and
recognize the value of retaining lawyers, while poorer Americans fail to
recognize the value of hiring lawyers or believe that to do so for them would
be futile. (The basis for such perceptions of class and racial bias are
explored in Units 4 and 5.)

The support for constitutional rights but the relative lack of support
for specific extensions of such rights to unpopular groups poses a more complex
problem. There seems to be no way to reconcile this contradiction in American
legal culture. However, note that there is a significant difference between
announcing one's unwillingness to extend rights to unpopular groups and taking
action designed to deprive them of such rights. Furthermore, to argue that
the various studies demonstrate an unwillingness to extend rights to unpopular
groups requires one to believe that particular constitutional provisions compel
us to permit certain types of 'protected conduct'. To illustrate what I am
getting at, simply think about the recent claim by Nazi's that they have a
constitutional right to parade in a predominantly Jewish area in celebration of
Hitler's birthday. Isn't it possible to voice general support for the constitutional value of 'free speech' but to disagree on whether such a right
covers the Nazi march? If so, then the alleged inconsistencies in American
legal culture may be less than the researchers maintain is the case.

Finally, remember that the complex set of attitudes, beliefs, and
values which people hold about law (legal culture) largely determine the
type of legal mobilization processes which will be found in a particular
legal system. The American legal mobilization process is primarily reactive
in nature; that is, lawyers, trial courts, and appelate courts must wait for
cases to be brought to them.

The constellation of attitudes making up America's legal culture is
supportive of the reactive model of legal mobilization. The deep American
faith in law expresses itself in the penetration of law into American life;
the skepticism of law, particularly among those of the lower strata of society,
expresses itself by the fact that these Americans do not utilize the law to
its fullest potential. Nonetheless, the combination of widespread general
faith in law and partial distrust of specific laws, lawyers, judges, and
processes is consistent with the reactive mobilization model and helps to
account for its existence in American law.

1. What is legal culture?

2. Why is legal culture seen as an important element in understanding the role of law in American society and particularly the process of legal mobilization?

3. Briefly summarize the empirical findings concerning American legal culture with reference to:

      a.   Law generally

      b.   Civil liberties

      c.   Courts

      d.   Lawyers

      e.   Police

1. Basically, legal culture refers to ideas, attitudes, and expectations about law, legal institutions, and legal decision makers. As a concept, it can be distinguished from legal substance, i.e. the actual content of the laws, and legal structure, i.e. the organizational dimensions of courts, police departments, and appellate jurisdictions.

    The role of legal culture can be clarified in a simple illustration. Suppose that two neighbors who share a common driveway between their homes disagree over who owns the driveway. They both maintain that their property extends across the entire driveway. One neighbor blocks the driveway claiming that the other has no right to use it. There are various ways in which our two neighbors might proceed.

    > One family could give way to the other. They could ask a friend or a priest to settle the matter. They could agree to toss a coin. They could go to court. The incident could turn into a blood feud. Obviously, there are many reasons why they might want to choose any of these alternatives. Take the court alternative: a lawsuit would cost money. Structure matters too. Are courts easy to approach? Are they conveniently located? How long will a lawsuit take? The two sides might also consider substance: they consult a lawyer and find out that their chance of winning is large (or small) because of the state of the law. Each may also be affected by aspects of legal culture: is going to court a thing that people do (or do not do)? What would their other neighbors think about the lawsuit? Could they expect to get justice in court? Do they consider judges corrupt or stupid, or honest and impartial? Would they feel uncomfortable in court, embarassed or exposed? What do they know about law, lawyers, and courts? What has been their prior experiences with law? All these and other attitudes, values, and opinions make up the cultural element.
    >
    > Social forces do not 'make' law directly. First, they pass through the screen of legal culture. This is the vital screen of ideologies, beliefs, values, and opinions that takes interests and desires and determines their fate: whether to be turned onto the legal system in the form of demands, or to be shunted off onto another track, or to dribble off into oblivion". (Friedman, 1977, p. 7)

2. The decision to use law or to rely on alternative social mechanisms, such as family, religion, or community, is a function of the type of legal culture in society. The propensity to define problems as 'legal' as opposed to 'political' or 'moral' is the result of legal culture. In American society, many major problems come to be defined as legal in character. As you will read in Mini-Lecture #2, "The American Reliance On Law," Americans are highly litigious, i.e., quick to invoke the legal process, and unusually willing to refer almost any public or social issue to the courts for resolution.

Another concept which is important in understanding the critical contribution of legal culture is 'legal mobilization', or the "process by which a legal system acquires its cases" (Black, 1973, p. 126). In America, where the dominant legal mobilization process is reactive and requires individual citizens to initiate legal proceedings, if cases are not brought to the attention of the legal system by members of the public then whatever it offers in terms of achieving social control, dispute settlement, or social change cannot be brought to bear upon actual cases. As Black States, "Mobilization is the link between the law and the people served or controlled by the law" (Black, 1973, p. 126). Legal culture is a major determinant of legal mobilization.

3. a. Americans have little knowledge about law and tend to become less pleased with the legal system as they become more familiar with it.

    b. Americans are not deeply committed to civil rights and civil liberties for those whom they fear and dislike. While paying lip service to general statements of civil liberties, Americans stop short of applying these general statements in concrete situations.

    c. The U.S. Supreme Court is the repository of powerful myths and symbols which result in widespread support for the Court despite little knowledge of its actual decisions.

    d. Lawyers are viewed with great suspicion by most Americans, and yet lawyers are given major political positions all over the country. As with the legal system generally, prior contact seems to reduce respect.

    e. Young children acquire highly supportive attitudes toward the police, but these attitudes are sharply modified during adolescence, particularly among members of minority groups who come to see the police as the coercive arm of the oppressors.

Mini-Lecture #2

THE AMERICAN RELIANCE ON LAW

In the previous mini-lecture some of the conclusions of empirical studies of American attitudes towards, beliefs about, and knowledge of law were summarized. Despite the low level of information about law and despite the suspicious attitudes of many toward the law, Americans in recent years have continued to turn to the legal system for solutions to an ever-expanding range of personal and social problems. More specifically, Americans have been turning to the courts, rather than legislatures for solutions. Insofar as the American legal culture accords great prestige to judges and particularly U.S. Supreme Court Justices, it makes sense to find Americans bringing their problems to court.

To illustrate this American tendency to invade the courthouse, we need only look at some of the questions before courts in the 1970s. A case was recently brought in federal court by some disgruntled football fans who believed that the officials in a St. Louis Cardinal v. Washington Redskin game had erroneously ruled that an endzone pass which had been caught, then dropped, had been held long enough to constitute a touchdown! The fact that the thought of court action even entered the minds of the fans reveals a type of reliance on law which is not present in most societies. In another sports case, a professional hockey player was arrested after injuring another player with his hockey stick during a regulation game. His trial resulted in a hung jury. But the idea that the criminal justice system might take an increased interest in sports violence further supports the notion that law is reaching deeper and deeper into American life.

In the highly publicized Karen Ann Quinlan case, the courts were asked to decide whether elaborate life support machines could be turned off at the request of the parents of a girl whose brain cells had apparently been totally destroyed. In many other cultures, such a question would more likely be resolved by religious leaders and families.

A remarkable constitutional case grew out of the refusal of a kindergarten teacher in Lansdale, Pennsylvania to promote one of the children to first grade. Claiming that the boy was not ready for first grade, the teacher ordered him retained in kindergarten for a second year. The boy's mother refused to send him to kindergarten the second year and was charged with aiding his truancy! That case was dismissed following a finding that kindergarten is not compulsory, and, therefore, the mother's actions in keeping the boy home did not add up to aiding a truant! However, on behalf of her son, she brought a suit alleging that her son's constitutional rights had been violated. Specifically, she claimed that the school's failure to provide reasons for the retention constituted a violation of 'due process', and the fact that other children were promoted while one was retained constituted a violation of 'equal protection'. Incredible as it may sound, a federal court agreed that there were constitutional requirements for promotion to first grade which the school had failed to meet. Other similar school-related cases have recently been finding their way to the courts. The Supreme Court has said that prior to a suspension students are entitled to at least a hearing in which they are told why they are to be suspended and allowed to give their side of the story. The Court also has held that paddling does not violate the constitutional ban on cruel and unusual punishment. Lower courts have been asked to decide if a community college is liable where a teacher performs ineffectively in the classroom. It will not be unusual in the future for teachers to be sued by students if their grading policies are seen as arbitrary or their examinations seen as unfair.

Before discussing this phenomenon further, one more example is in order. A book recently published by lawyer Paul B. Ashley, entitled Oh Promise Me, But Put It In Writing, argues that prospective marriage partners, roommates in college, and all other cohabitants ought to prepare contracts in which they spell out in detail the responsibilities and obligations of all parties! To contemplate the "no smoking clause," the "who takes out the garbage clause," and the "distribution of time to be spent with each set of in-laws clause" stretches our legalism to its outer limits. Without even discussing the obvious benefits to the legal profession, such a proposal again highlights America's love affair with law. To attempt to reduce intimate human relationships to enforceable binding agreements reflects almost a magical faith in an already overburdened institution: law.

The American reliance on law has resulted in increasing caseloads in both state and federal courts. Between 1970 and 1975 the cases pending before a U.S. District Court judge at any given time rose from 285 to 355. Between 1960 and 1970 the number of civil suits in the federal courts has doubled. Between 1960 and 1975, the volume of civil suits has doubled in Los Angeles and tripled in the State of Massachusetts. The number of lawyers has grown from 250,000 in 1957 to 425,000 in 1977.

The reasons for the growing American reliance on law and particularly on the judicial branch of government are varied. First, America has a strong natural law tradition which orients us toward the notion of 'rights'. The American revolution was launched after King George III violated the 'rights' of the colonists. The Declaration of Independence talks about "inalienable rights"; the constitution embodies a series of guarantees in the Bill of Rights; and President Carter is widely praised for his concern for 'human rights'.

Second, the traditional legal institution--the legislature--has proven itself unwilling or unable to meet the growing demands made upon it by Americans. Enacting a law is a slow and uncertain path to achieve one's goals. Asserting a right before a court often yields speedier results. In addition, legislators, being more directly politically accountable than judges, often are quite content to allow difficult questions to be settled in court. After all, judges either never or rarely must face the voters.

A related reason for the growing American penchant for litigation is the obvious success of the civil rights movement in pursuing that strategy during the 1950s and 1960s. Brown v. Board of Education did much more than declare that "separate but equal" schools for blacks and whites violated the Constitution. It symbolically communicated to Mexicans, women, homosexuals, students, prisoners, welfare recipients, aliens, Indians and others that successful challenges to oppressive practices could be mounted and that such challenges could be more rapidly brought in the courts than in the legislatures. Combined with the activist orientation of the Justices sitting on the Warren Court and the lessening of some technical barriers to entering the federal courts, the litigation explosion and the expanding claims of 'rights' by previously silent segments of society was given great impetus.

310

The consequences of American reliance on law, and specifically on the courts, ought to be briefly examined. The Supreme Court since <u>Marbury v. Madison</u> has had the power of judicial review, i.e., to declare unconstitutional any legislative acts or official action taken on the basis of legislative authority which are contrary to provisions of the constitution. It is our belief in and reliance on law which ultimately accounts for our willingness to allow as few as five or six Supreme Court Justices to undo what elected legislators have seen fit to do. Why, one might ask, would a democratic people allow so undemocratic an institution as the Supreme Court to acquire so much power?

Political scientist Robert Dahl offers a dialogue between a critic and a defender of the power of judicial review (1972, p. 193). First, the critic argues that <u>whether judicial review is desirable or undesirable, it clearly is not democratic</u>. To permit non-elected lifetime appointees to prevail over elected representatives in debates over what the constitution 'really' means is profoundly undemocratic. The response to this criticism is that American democracy is a <u>limited</u> democracy and judicial review provides a mechanism for sustaining limited government.

The critic then replies that <u>the limited nature of American democracy will be preserved only so long as the voters desire it</u>. Therefore, judicial review is unnecessary if the voters desire to maintain limited governments, and it is useless if the voters should decide to favor a different brand of government, or, put another way, the court cannot save us from ourselves if we are determined to act in a self-destructive manner. The response made to this argument is that in the long run perhaps the Supreme Court cannot save us from ourselves, but in the short run it very well might do just that.

Another argument against judicial review and excessive reliance on judicial solutions generally is that <u>such a decision making system reduces our capacity for self-government</u> (Cox, 1976, p. 117). Once an issue has been defined as legal in nature, the number of people actually involved in deciding that issue is drastically reduced in size and scope. In fact, lawyers, judges and litigants are the principal people left to resolve what may be a broad social or political question. The <u>Bakke</u> case, which forms the subject of Unit 10, is a good example.

In deciding whether a particular statute or official action is constitutional or unconstitutional the Supreme Court ideally simply looks at the statute in question, looks at the relevant provision of the Constitution and proclaims either a match or a mis-match. As Dahl suggests (1972, pp. 200-201), the court faces a difficult dilemma. It is required by the nature of the issues it faces to apply non-legal criteria, that is, to make policy choices or political decisions. For the court to decide the questions posed by white claims of 'reverse discrimination' it must go beyond the technical language of the constitution and the statutes and consider various social and political consequences. Yet the legitimacy of the court's decisions-- in fact its very ability to continue to authoritatively make decisions-- rests on a popular belief that exclusively legal criteria are employed in making judicial decisions. Thus, the paradox: if the court is accepted as political, it ceases to be seen as legitimate; but if it actually relies exclusively on legal criteria, it will be unable to reach decisions on key questions which are brought to it. Dahl indicates that the solution is to maintain the myth of the latter and the reality of the former.

If the Supreme Court, in other words, is ever perceived by the mass of Americans to be merely making political choices rather than applying constitutional and statutory law, it will lose its authority. The following questions then emerge: Does the tremendous activism of the Supreme Court in recent years and the increasing American reliance on law undermine the legitimacy of the Court? Will overdependence on the law result in the weakening of law? Archibald Cox, responding to these kinds of questions, describes the basis of the court's legitimacy this way: "The court's legitimacy rests largely upon the realization that the major influence in a decision is not personal fiat, but principles which bind the judge as well as the litigants and which apply uniformly to all men not only today, but yesterday and tomorrow" (Cox, 1976, p. 109). Professor Cox, by emphasizing enduring principles as the basis for the court's legitimacy, lends added weight to the argument that perceived politicization of the court will undermine its authority.

1. What do the unusual cases described in the mini-lecture illustrate about the role of law in American society?

2. How do you think that the operation of the legal process might be affected by the litigation explosion described in the mini-lecture?

3. Why do Americans so readily define problems in terms of rights, duties, and law?

4. On what grounds has judicial review, a manifestation of American reliance on law, been criticized and defended?

5. What is the actual source of the authority of the Supreme Court to invalidate legislative and official acts?

6. How do the demands made on the court work to undermine its legitimacy?

DISCUSSION OF MINI-LECTURE #2 QUESTIONS

1. The basic point which is illustrated by the cases is that Americans define a wide variety of problems and disagreements as legal in nature. The American legal culture is highly supportive of the judiciary, and, therefore, it is not surprising to find people quickly resorting to lawsuits when they feel they have been wronged or unfairly treated. Where other societies rely more heavily, for example, on religious solutions to problems, Americans turn more readily to the legal system.

2. The litigation explosion has resulted in heavier caseloads, particularly of civil cases. The corresponding growth in criminal prosecutions has probably led to greater pressure for plea bargaining in order to reduce the caseload.

3. Several possible reasons are suggested in the mini-Lecture. First, the natural law tradition which is at the core of American law makes us receptive to the idea that there exist certain 'rights' and that individuals can and should assert those rights when they have been violated. Second, it is suggested that American legislative institutions, which traditionally have been the primary law-making bodies, have proven to be less viable than courts for the achievement of many legal objectives. Third, the civil rights movement's early successful use of the judicial, rather than legislative, process pointed the way for subsequent groups' efforts. Fourth, the activist Warren Court indicated its willingness to aggressively move to legitimize the rights claims of many minority Americans.

4. The basic criticisms have been:

    a. Judicial review is undemocratic.

    b. Judical review cannot maintain restrained government if the voters do not want such a government.

    c. Judicial review cannot save us from ourselves.

    d. Judicial review reduces our capacity for self-government.

    The defenders argue:

    a. Judicial review is completely consistent with the American concept of limited government.

    b. Judicial review can save us from ourselves by permitting a non-elected elite to prevent a misguided political majority from destroying the government.

    c. Judicial review is logical because the Supreme Court, being an adjudicatory body, is in the best position to determine whether or not particular legislative and official acts are contrary to the Constitution.

5. The Supreme Court's authority to invalidate the actions of other branches and levels of government derives ultimately from the public's belief that legal, not political, criteria are followed in determining the constitutionality of particular acts.

6. The suggestion is made that the more policy issues we attempt to resolve through the judical system the greater the likelihood that the Court will become viewed as a policymaking, rather than a judicial, institution. If that perception does become widely held, the Supreme Court's legitimacy is likely to be undermined.

Alvin Toffler

The Future of Law & Order

NO SOCIAL PROBLEM has received more public attention in the last decade than the breakdown of law and order. A society of the future without law and order would be a very unpleasant place—even more unpleasant than our urban centres are today. Yet I do not think we can understand the present breakdown unless we examine the possibility that we are moving into a wholly new phase in the history of law. We may be passing beyond the "Golden Age" of law to a new way of life in which law will play a different and sharply reduced role.

What I have to say about the relationship of laws to life in a period of social revolution is more in the nature of notes and ruminations than a set of fixed or finished ideas. And it is seen, of course, from the point of view of an amateur Law-and-Order watcher, not a professional. Yet, in the face of a future that is likely to differ radically from the present, we are all, of necessity, amateurs. No one, no matter how professional, can speak with certainty about the shape of the newly-emerging order and the laws that will be needed in it.

In this context, no symbol of the American future seems more chilling in its significance than the shooting of Governor George Wallace. Mr Wallace may be demagogic in his promises and mistaken or hypocritical in his analysis of what is wrong, but he is clearly right when he says that law and order are breaking down in the United States; and he has the wounds to prove it. It is difficult to argue with a headline that says, as a recent one from the *New York Post* did: BOMB PENTAGON. Or about the fact that you can buy heroin openly on many a street corner in New York City. Or the fact the airplanes are hijacked with unnerving frequency. Or that a third of America is afraid to walk alone in the streets at night. Or that there are 90 million American guns in private hands. Or that some of the most prominent "Law-and-Order" politicians have themselves apparently broken the laws against wiretapping and common burglary.

Not so many years ago, the National Commission on the Causes and Prevention of Violence prophesied that, unless corrective action was taken quickly, the US ghettos would become "places of terror, perhaps entirely uncontrolled during the night-time hours." It went on to predict that schools, playgrounds, apartment houses, libraries, and other structures would need day-time police, and that armed guards would have to "ride shotgun" on our means of transportation, our buses and trains. Anyone who lives in a major US city, or who has been frisked on the way into a jet, knows that we have already fulfilled many of these nightmarish predictions.

Recently my wife received a call from a friend of ours, a young woman employed as a researcher by one of our leading magazines. She wept as she told of the daylight murder of a young man who had been her friend, and of the knifing of another—both within the same week. The fact that she and her friends happened to be black was incidental, as casualties on both sides of the colour line show.

ALL THIS DRAWS ATTENTION to criminal law. Yet that is only the most dramatically troubled part of our legal system. In both criminal *and* civil law, the judicial system is cracking under unprecedented strain. In the US Federal Courts, 8,600 civil cases have been jammed up for three years or more. And last year 96,000 additional cases were filed. State and local courts were so overloaded that in New York (where there is a backlog of 10,000 felony cases) a judge ruled recently that, except in homicide cases, any suspect not brought to trial within six months would be automatically freed.

ALL THE HEADLINES about shootings and muggings and all the statistics about the judicial log-jam fade into insignificance, however, when they are compared with a single situation at a recent meeting of the Harlem Research Council. Faced with a climbing rate of crime, America is often said to be "a lawless nation." Nothing, it seems to me, could be further from the truth. We

Reprinted with the permission of Encounter, LTD, (July, 1973), pp. 13-23.

probably have more law per square inch than any nation in the world. In fact, if there is anything that distinguishes our situation, it is an overgrowth of law and regulation to the point of such choking complexity that the society cannot carry out some of its most needed and basic functions.

At the Harlem Research Council I listened to a discussion of the need for Day-Care Centres, so that black mothers on welfare could be freed to get jobs. Now everyone from the President down is in favour of this 100-percent-American idea that people on welfare ought to work. And yet the number of Day-Care Centres is negligible.

At that meeting, an executive of the American Telephone & Telegraph Corporation, who happened to be present because the company is interested in Day-Care Centres for its AT&T employees, reported that present regulations were so constricting that it required the approval of 11 different city and state agencies to operate a fully legal Day-Care Centre. The result, he said, is the emergence of a new phenomenon—"underground" Day-Care Centres, illegal, unlicensed. In short, it was necessary to break the law to carry out even so simple and desirable a function. I find this far more upsetting than the usual accounts of crime and judicial overload. For when law stands in the way of simple, innocuous, widely approved social change, something is ominously out of control. When ordinary people must break the law to accomplish purposes the society itself regards as admirable, it is hard to insist at the same time that they should "respect law and order."

And so we have a paradoxical picture. Many laws are ignored with impunity; police are ineffective and corrupt in many places; courts are overloaded; jails are Attica-like; and a monstrous excess of laws actually stands in the way of even simple and obviously needed change.

Simultaneously, however, we find that laws are non-existent with respect to a whole range of problems that either now do, or soon will, confront the society with profound ethical and political problems. We had enough laws to obstruct the creation of Day-Care Centres in Harlem; but we have no laws to control the application of such biological breakthroughs as "cloning" which may make it possible, before long, in effect, to create genetic carbon copies of ourselves. We have no laws to regulate some of the new "birth technologies" that may make motherhood obsolete and make it possible to raise embryos outside the body of the woman. There are no laws to control

or regulate the initiation of possibly irreversible processes in biology and in ecology. There are no laws to deal with problems like "information-overload" in the society. We have inadequate laws to control the unfair externalisation of costs by large corporations. We have inadequate laws for dealing with the high-powered communication technologies now being developed.

One could continue to list scores of areas of technological and social change, some of them with enormous implications, that are, for all intents and purposes, ignored by the law. For law-makers tend to be backward-looking instead of anticipatory, and when they do look ahead it is ordinarily for only a short distance. This mismatch between the problems rapidly emerging from the society and the existing patchwork of laws, intensifies the crisis. It means that much of our legal system is essentially obsolete.

I DO NOT THINK we can begin to deal with this crisis until we recognise its scope. And to do this we must first look outside the United States. It is highly significant, yet often forgotten by Americans, that they are not the only country whose legal system is now caught up in traumatic change. In France, in Canada, in Germany, in Italy, in England, we see similar signs of a sea change, a fundamental shift in the way law is regarded. England, too, staid and traditional, is having its bombings as well, and not only in Northern Ireland. Instead of the messages signed by The Weathermen (or "The Weather People," as they now prefer to be known) the notes are signed by "The Angry Brigade". It is perhaps symptomatic of shifting British attitudes toward law and authority, in general' that eleven-year-olds recently demonstrated in the streets against caning in the schools, evidently still an educational practice.

In Germany, on the same day that a bomb went off in Washington's Pentagon, another went off at the Hamburg headquarters of the Springer publishing empire, injuring some 15 people. And a recent survey there indicated that even in that nation, whose citizens are reputed to be "sheep-like" in their obedience to law and the state, fully 34% of the population think that a law should not be obeyed if it is unjust. Perhaps the rest of the world should cheer any sign that the German people are beginning to question authority; but the breakdown of law and order is usually bad news for any democracy. And when the breakdown becomes sufficiently serious, ordinary people, "good decent folk", begin to search desperately for some politician—on a white horse, or in a wheelchair—who, they hope, can put things back together again.

It may encourage certain American politicians of the "law and order" stripe to know that in Italy, where the legal *and* political systems have both been shaken badly in recent months, 73% of the voters in a recent poll indicated a willingness to give up full political powers temporarily to a "strong man" with this proviso: "So long as he was just and democratic." However, only 6.3% could suggest who this man might be, and nearly 53% said he did not exist or they did not know if he existed. One wonders what a similar survey would reveal about the American political psyche.

Since something like a legal crisis is occurring in many countries simultaneously, with all of them anxiously appointing Commissions or Study Panels to search for reform measures, it would seem that certain common pressures are at work, and that it is a mistake to conceive of the present crisis in the USA as an isolated phenomenon. This suggests that some of our most cherished American explanations of the problem are either childish or trivial.

To BELIEVE THAT law is breaking down in the United States because the Supreme Court for a short span of time went "soft on crime" is to duck the issue. Did all the supreme courts in all these other nations suddenly and at the same time decide to coddle criminals? It seems unlikely. Did parents in all these countries simultaneously adopt Doctor Spock as their guide to permissive child-rearing? To think that law has broken down because we've all suddenly simultaneously "gone soft" is superficial, if not, indeed, silly. Even if it were true, the question would remain, *Why?* As for the other side, there are those who say the laws are breaking down because they are "too repressive." But are the laws of today more repressive than, say, those of 20 years ago? And if not, why is the legal crisis upon us now, rather than in 1953? The laws, indeed, may be repressive, but repressive laws do not necessarily make a legal crisis.

IF WE ARE TO DEAL with a legal crisis, it seems to me we are going to have to probe more deeply. What is happening is deeper than

most of our judges and lawyers, our presidents and our presidential candidates, suspect. For what is happening is not merely the breakdown of law, but, more important, the breakdown of the underlying order upon which law is based.

Today in all the high-technology nations, from Japan and Sweden to Germany and the United States, we are living through what could be called the general crisis of industrial society. Regardless of its political forms, regardless of the peculiar cultural and historical features that make it different in each country, the industrial system is dying. And until we understand this salient fact, we cannot comprehend what is happening to our law and order. Thus the crack-up of our legal systems is only part of a much larger revolution, the shift to a super-industrial society.

When I say that the industrial system is dying, I am referring to a particular kind of social system that has specific and well-known characteristics. It is a society based on mass production in factories using mechanical, pre-automated machinery. It is a society with bureaucratic, top-down organisational forms in its businesses, schools and government. It is a society based on an essentially materialist value system.[1] Industrial society is a society in which most workers do routine and repetitive work and fill standardised roles. It is a society in which men and women are drenched in standardised ideas distributed from the top down *via* the mass media. It is a society with a relatively simple class structure; and so on.

This is the kind of society that most of us were born into, and this is the kind of society that our legal system serves. But we are now passing through the first stage of a vast trans-national upheaval, a bursting wave of revolutionary change from which a new-style society is already beginning to emerge. This new super-industrial order will be radically different from the industrial order. It will have different technologies, different family institutions, different values, different conceptions of time, space and beauty—and it will have to have totally different legal arrangements as well.

Nobody can blueprint in detail the characteristics of this emergent civilisation. But we can, by looking squarely at what is happening today, describe some of the basic forces powering this revolution. Two basic processes, it seems to me are under way, and they are keys to the breakdown of order. One is fragmentation and the second ephemeralisation. Let me first examine fragmentation.

---

[1] This is true on both the Capitalist side of the world and the Communist side. Industrial societies essentially take for granted that economic gain is the appropriate goal of public and private activity.

CONVENTIONAL SOCIAL SCIENCE has told us for a century or more that technology standardises people, that it makes us "all alike." We have all heard or uttered the complaint that industrial society and technology create human robots. This may have been true at one time, but one of the fundamental changes in our lives, I believe, is a turnabout in the kinds of technology we deal with and in the consequences of the new technology. For today a new technology is rapidly proliferating which multiplies the choices available to us and thereby enhances rather than suppresses the differences among us.

I can illustrate this in a number of ways. The simplest, though most trivial, way, is to look at the material culture around us, the goods, the products, the consumer packages. It used to be that one drove up to a gas station and the man said "Do you want regular or premium?" But now, if one drives up to a SUNOCO station, he asks whether you want 190, 200, 210, 220, 230, etc., or 2-, 3-, 4- or 5-star. And this is not a purely American phenomenon. The London *Times*, for example, carries an advertisement in which British Petroleum announces: "Now you don't have to buy the wrong octane for your car." It shows a long-haired young man, a clergyman, a bowler-hatted elderly gentleman, a matronly lady, and a chic young *Cosmopolitan* girl, each with a placard on which a different octane is represented. In this way, SUNOCO here and B.P. there have begun to multiply the options of the consumer. (I don't know whether the options are real—whether the gasoline under all those numbers is really different. It may be that 210, 220 and 239 are all the same.) But, as a consumer, my once simple decision is beclouded by options. What's happening here, however, is part of a larger scheme of things. Thus the same process is occurring with respect to all kinds of products. It is true of cigarettes, of automobiles, of telephones.

I can remember when there was a single standard black handset, one type of telephone, in the US The slogan of the telephone company then was "Universal Service." Its goal was to put the same phone in every home. Starting in the early 1950s we began to move toward the pink "Princess" phone and all different sizes, colours, and models, so that today, instead of a single basic telephone, there are no fewer than 1500 varieties of models, sizes, styles and specialised telephones available for special purposes: underwater phones, explosion-proof phones, phones for the hard-of-hearing, etc.

Nor is it only telephones, cars, and cigarettes. It is true of diapers and dog food. Another ad that illustrates it beautifully is from the *New York Times*. It shows drawings of fully 44 different kinds of eyeglass frames. It says, "If you can't find the frame you want at Meyrowitz, you'd better have your eyes checked." If we have to go through this much trouble to buy eyeglass frames, it may be we ought better have our heads checked. Be that as it may, at the simplest level, what we are doing is providing a multiplicity of options, and our choices are becoming more and more complex.

Certainly, it may well be that these are largely trivial choices, and that most of us burn up a great deal of energy making trivial choices, while some of the truly important choices are not available to us. We don't have a smog-free automobile—that's a choice I would like to have, but don't.

Nevertheless, trivial or not, our choices are multiplying, and this, quite apart from other psychological and social consequences, brings with it an enormous proliferation of certain kinds of law. For example, the US Patent Office in 1969 faced an avalanche of 32,600 applications for registered brand-names. Product proliferation has vastly increased, and the problems involved in simply registering the brand and fighting off competitors who want to use similar names have become extremely intense. The more kinds of products and styles and models there are, the more defects are possible, the more types of lawsuits, the more contracts, the more paperwork, and the more regulatory rulings. The 1500 different types of telephones, for example, require enormous amounts of legal work and rule-making from the Federal Communications Commission and from each of the 50 State Public Utility Agencies.

THIS ENORMOUS EXTENSION of material goods is based in part on a generation of increasing consumer affluence. We can *afford* to be different. But more important, I think, is something happening deep down in the technological innards of the society. This is perhaps best symbolised by a computer-based laser gun just introduced into the clothing industry. Before industrialism and mass production arrived on the scene, if a man wanted a piece of clothing made, he went to a tailor or a seamstress, or his wife sewed it. In any case, it was done on a handcraft basis, to his individual measure. All sewing was essentially custom tailoring. Then came the industrial revolution when we discovered that it was more efficient, in some ways, to produce identical clothes on a mass production basis. Under this system, the worker placed layer upon layer upon layer of cloth, one on top of the other; he next laid a pattern on top; then, with an electric cutting knife, he cut around the edges of the pattern and produced multiple, identical cut-outs of the cloth. These were then subjected to identical processing and came out identical in size, shape, colour, and so forth.

The new laser machine operates on a radically different principle, however, and it exemplifies a great deal of the new technology now coming in. This machine does not cut 10 or 50 or 100 or even 500 shirts or jackets at a time. It cuts one at a time. But it cuts it faster and cheaper than the mass production methods employed until now. Indeed, the president of GENESCO, the largest manufacturer of apparel in the US says, "The laser machines can be programmed to fill an order for one garment economically." What that suggests is that some day even standard sizes may disappear. It may be possible to read one's measurements into a telephone, or to go into a store and be measured or photographed and have the machine produce exactly one garment cut to one's personal, individualised dimensions.

This is, in effect, custom tailoring or handcraft on a high technology basis. It is virtually a dialectical return—a reinstatement of a system of production that flourished before the Industrial Revolution but is now based on the most advanced, sophisticated technology. It is not a return, however, to handcraft, but an advance to "headcraft." And it symbolises a monumental change not only because it requires, reflects, or creates de-standardised production, but because such a production system needs de-standardised *workers*. Such a system no longer requires tens of thousands of workers all doing the same routine and repetitive tasks day in and day out. It needs people who can use their heads, who can manipulate symbols, who possess a certain amount of creativity, and who can deal with first-time or unusual problems. And so, in our material culture, in that whole complex of technology-products-hardware-goods-consumption, we are shifting from a standardised to a de-standardised culture.

THE SAME IS increasingly true in education. It seems to me there is an enormous—and overdue—push for individualisation of instruction.

Just as we individualise the production of a shirt, we are now trying to individualise education. We have struggles over community control. In New York, Blacks have said: "Look, you White people have tried to run the schools for a long time and you've pumped out a standard White-oriented message to all children and you've utilised the same educational methods for all. It hasn't worked for our kids very well. We want the right to be different. We want the right to run our own schools, in our own way, and to give our kids a de-standardised education. . . ." Recently the US Supreme Court approved the right of the Amish religious sect to keep their children out of the common public school system, thus approving their right to be different. We experiment with "voucher plans" likely to break up the standardised big-city school systems. So here, too, we see a movement toward fragmentation or diversification rather than consolidation, cohesiveness, and uniformity.

In the media the same tendencies are obvious. We have recently witnessed the death of major magazines with large circulations—magazines like *Life* and *Look* and the *Saturday Evening Post*. Some said this symbolised "the end of print." Not at all. What has happened is a population explosion of mini-magazines, magazines that carry multiple specialised messages to small groups, instead of a single message to 10 or 20 million people at the same time. Media-carried messages are now being segmented with special messages going to special groups. Thus we have a proliferation of special-interest publications which zero in on the most refined interests. *The Graphic Antiquarian*, for example, is for collectors of photographical memorabilia, early historical cameras, and the like. We now have hundreds, indeed thousands, of such special-interest publications, and that, too, reflects a de-standardisation of the media and our informational environment.

Even in television the same process is occurring. Television is not the most advanced communications technology, which is the way it usually conceives of itself. It is, in fact, a primitive technology. It is only as we move into the second generation and third generation of video technology, with the introduction of cable television and video cassettes, that we begin to get a new communication system radically different from the old one, and once again following the same change pattern.

The old system is known as broadcasting, and the very word "broadcasting," means transmission of a message from one point to many points. ABC, CBS, and NBC, through their rather centralised control over our communications system, send identical messages at the same hour to tens of millions of Americans, so that everyone sees the Johnny Carson Show at the same time, perhaps with an hour or two delay. A standardised message is carried to tens of millions of people, exactly as though a standardised product were being manufactured for them. The importance of cable and cassette is that these break that system down. They increase to an almost unlimited number the available channels. This means that everybody, or every group, can have his, her or their own views, messages, and values reflected and amplified through the media.

We used to bemoan the monopoly of the press. The number of daily newspapers declined for many years, although I believe it has now stabilised. But now we have been witnessing the birth of an increasing number of "underground" papers, specialised papers, papers critical of the press itself. And so, all across the board, the new technologies, whether engaged in manufacturing clothing or manufacturing automobiles or manufacturing messages, permit and even, one might say, encourage a move from standardisation to de-standardisation, which is perhaps another word for fragmentation.

The same is even true of language. Lexicographers are surprised in surveying the United States just how much regional difference still prevails. There is a growing loss of a common vocabulary and, again, it is not limited to the United States. In Canada, the French-Canadians fight for the right to speak French, and in France, as we can read in *Le Monde*, the Alsatians are fighting for the right to speak Alsatian. As one headline puts it: "It's *chic* to speak Alsatian" these days.

A^{ND SO}, instead of nations coming together, coalescing, they are, it appears to me, becoming more different. Significantly, this is true not only at the level of material culture and ideational culture, but also of the social structure. This explains why we have seen the process of ethnicisation taking place in our country. It explains why the French-Canadians are fighting, not only for their language, but for their right to lead their own kind of lives and to be treated

fairly. It is why Canada talks about developing a "mosaic culture." It is why Blacks say "Black is beautiful." It is why Poles call for Polish power, and the Italians create an Anti-Defamation League.

We are becoming what some Japanese sociologists call a "multi-channel" society. More and more sub-cultures are springing up from the soil of the larger society; and this special differentiation has profound psychological effects on individuals. Here, for example, are the words of a young man living in a Commune, and explaining why.

"Isn't this separatism every place you look. How about between the races? Or this new woman power issue. . . . I never felt it like this last time, total coming apart. And I felt, I really felt. For the first time that chasing my tail off into the hinterlands was not just an escape. But it was more like a positive action, finding a place with kindred souls to come together. . . . They're trying to stop that splintering off of everything and come together."[2]

Psychologist Herbert Gerjuoy at the State University of New York in Albany puts it another way. He is describing our options, indeed our "over-choice" in personality styles:

"A century ago, when somebody was growing up, he usually dealt with many fewer people than somebody does today. He spent the larger portions of his time with members of his family, because he did not spend as many years at school. . . . Also, the school was usually much smaller, and there were fewer different teachers. Many students knew only one or two different teachers for their entire school career. Similarly, there were fewer different ministers, doctors, storekeepers, etc., to get to know. A very important additional difference . . . was that 100 years ago there was no television or radio in the home to give the child a chance to meet many different kinds of strangers from many different walks of life and even from different countries. A century ago, very few people ever saw a foreign city. Now almost everyone has, at least on television.

"The results of all of this is that 100 years ago people had only a small number of different people to imitate or model themselves after. Their choices were even more limited by the fact that the people they could model themselves after were themselves all of limited experience."

What has happened, then, is a material and cultural fragmentation that penetrates deep into our psyche, as well as into the social structure, causing, in the end, enormous political fragmentation as well. Thus, I believe, we are, in fact, coming apart politically.

Once again we must step outside the United States to see that the process is not just local. Some French-Canadians, for example, if I may refer to them once again, are fighting for "the liberation of Quebec." Friends of mine who are relatively responsible officials in the Canadian

---

² Quoted in Roy Ald's excellent book, *The Youth Communes* (Tower Publications. New York. 1970).

Government say that it is not far-fetched to believe that within five or ten years Quebec will either be an independent nation, or at least have achieved some different status with respect to the federal government of Canada. In Northern Ireland, in Brittany, in many different countries, we see secessionist pressures building up. Even New York City is now talking about "seceding" from the "colonial power" exercised in Albany, and with good reason. A former member of the British Cabinet with whom I talked not long ago suggested that after a British entry into the Common Market, it would not surprise him to see the Scots, the Northern Irish, and the Welsh demanding their own representatives in Brussels, rather than simply accepting English representation. Everywhere there are centrifugal political forces at work.

A JAPANESE POLITICAL SCIENTIST has recently described America in words that are exact and acute and, therefore, absolutely terrifying. According to Professor Yonosuke Nagai of the Tokyo Institute of Technology, America is in the midst of a crisis that originates in these centrifugal forces. They are, he says,

> pulling American institutions apart, throwing the pieces outward from the center.... The United States is becoming a divided nation, a nation without a unified general will. Blacks, Southerners, students, women, policemen, Italian, Irish, and Jewish immigrants—even the WASPs, whose position is declining—all seek outlets for long-accumulated complaints and dissatisfactions. And all have come to share a delusion of persecution, a belief that the rights that they should enjoy are being taken away from them by others.
> What has happened is that substantial and structural problems have so shaken American society and politics that the institutions have lost their ability to restore themselves. Highly advanced technological innovation and automation have disrupted the system structures of population, capital and information in American society. In the process, the balance of the eco-system of society has been so severely damaged it probably cannot be restored.

I think Professor Nagai is right, except that it is not solely an American phenomenon. It is, to one degree or another, happening in many of the high technology nations. And all of this must, of course, have the deepest implications for the future of law.

THE SOCIAL ORDER has exploded, has been torn apart, propelled in many different and even contradictory directions by strange new technological and psychological forces. This fragmentation radically increases the number of conflicts to be resolved by the judiciary, so that Warren Burger, Chief Justice of the US Supreme Court, refers to a "litigation explosion." Simultaneously, the fragmentation encourages the addition of new laws, layer upon layer of choking legal restrictions, prohibitions and constraints. It is as though we hope that through the multiplication of law we could somehow hold the whole tottering structure together.

LAW IS AFFECTED, however, by another force in the super-industrial revolution, and this is the phenomenon for which I have used the word "ephemerálisation," the phenomenon of transience or temporariness or impermanence. It is the special character of the super-industrial revolution that it happens fast. The so-called neolithic revolution (as it was described by V. Gordon Childe) stretched over millennia and the industrial revolution took centuries; but the super-industrial revolution will be compressed into decades.

This, too, creates very special problems for law because most of our legal and constitutional arrangements are based on the unspoken assumption of permanence. They are based on the tempo, the steady rhythm, of an earlier, more slowly moving civilisation. Today the accelerated forces of change create exactly the opposite condition. The rhythm of change is unsteady, irregular, volatile, hard to predict. And, instead of relationships lasting a long time, they grow more temporary with every fleeting day.

We are shifting (to give only one example) to a system based on extremely short-lived organisational relationships. We are moving from the old bureaucratic structures, which were built to last forever, to new types of organisations called task forces, or ad hoc protest groups, or temporary projects, or problem-solving teams, and so on—each brought together for short periods of time and then dismantled. This system I have termed "ad hocracy," and it contrasts strongly with the old bureaucratic, pyramidal permanence that we used to have. The legal system does not know how to contend with this form of guerrilla organisation, whether in business, education, politics, or elsewhere.

Similarly, we are shifting toward more temporary interpersonal relationships. When I grew up, a best friend was somebody who stayed with one during all of one's childhood and adolescence.

That is no longer true for a great many young people today. Because of geographical, occupational, and social mobility, they are learning that even best friends are temporary. Fathers are transferred to the North or the West or the Southeast and best friends are sequentially ripped out of the lives of young people.

The statistic that might be regarded as the most severe challenge to law in the whole society is not the number of crimes but the fact that some 40 million Americans change their place of residence in any twelve-month period. That is an incredible uprooting procedure. I don't know any society that could deal with that kind of fluidity and mobility.

The law, then, designed for permanence and for a much less diversified social system, finds it difficult to come to grips with the new high speed society, the transient, ephemeral problems, the issues and crises that fire off quickly and then are often forgotten two weeks later, but were nevertheless important at the moment.

THE MORE RAPID the rate of change in technology, in family life, in religion, in education, in sexual behaviour, in fashion and in life-style, the greater the freedom of the individual. He is no longer necessarily locked in the painful old patterns. But he also finds it harder and harder to know what will happen next, to predict the consequences of his own behaviour and the reaction of other people or institutions to him. And when this happens, the social order begins to break down—not merely the law. The law is more easily replaceable. What breaks down is the underlying social regularity or pattern. For the glue that holds societies together internally is, precisely, predictability, a complex set of expectations that are met with sufficient regularity to give people a sense that things work, that the social structure can protect and serve them.

The anthropologist of law, E. A. Hoebel, put it simply. He said that people living together must be able to predict what the others will do.

> If each were actually liable to pop off along any one of all the different lines of behaviour human beings are potentially capable of, the result would be chaotic, indeed. Any organisation of complex activities and social life would be quite impossible .... Continued frustration of individual expectancies would soon reduce all men to neurotics and psychotics.[3]

---

[3] E. A. Hoebel, *The Law of Primitive Man* (Harvard University Press. 1967).

In primitive societies there is a built-in natural order. The sun rises and sets. Agriculture is routine, life is routine. The social system is relatively undifferentiated and uncluttered. People conduct transactions on a face-to-face basis with people they have known all their lives. Knowing one another, they know what to expect of one another. They know the consequences of stepping out of line, and the law in such societies is only minimally required.

It is when life becomes increasingly "non-routine," when novelties intrude, when surprises and astonishments are perpetual accompaniments to daily life, when complexity grows to the point that most interactions are no longer face-to-face with people we have known since childhood, that law becomes essential.

The law, above all, is a mechanism for clarifying and *predicting* the reactions of other people to certain classes of behaviour. This is why it bolsters the social order. Law can be seen as a tool used to build the needed predictability into the society. It helps predict what will happen when we violate a contract, what will happen if we steal an automobile or forge a cheque or slander a competitor or smuggle contraband.

US Supreme Court Justice Benjamin Cardozo, in a classic statement, defined a law as a rule of conduct "so established as to justify a prediction ... that it will be enforced by the courts." His distinguished colleague Oliver Wendell Holmes defined law as "prophecies of what the courts will do."

It is in this sense that most lawyers, whether they think of themselves in this way or not, are paid professional futurists. Much of their work consists of forecasting, or predicting, for a client what consequences will flow from contemplated action. Will the contract hold up in court? Will the Justice Department let the merger go unchallenged? Will the Inland Revenue Service upset the corporate structure? And so on. Sometimes lawyers even have to put their own money where their predictions are, as when they render an "opinion of counsel," which, in effect, guarantees the client against a faulty forecast. Even as simple a thing as a contract is a pledge made about some future action to be taken, a prediction of what will happen sometime in the future.

When the rate of change is accelerated and the super-industrial revolution bursts upon us, it becomes more and more difficult to make accurate predictions. Thus, the increasing speed of change and the ephemerality associated with it creates a profound paradox for our legal systems.

IF THE LAW IS PERMANENT or fixed, then the society cannot change very easily; and if the system becomes too rigid, the pressures are liable to build such a head of steam that they simply explode in violence, until the legal system cracks and new, "permanent" laws are written to take the place of the old ones. If, on the other hand, laws are not fixed and permanent, if they are flexible and subject to change, if they, too, are seen as temporary, ephemeral, they permit legitimate change to take place. They permit the system to adapt to the fast on-rushing future. But they do not provide much predictability. The businessman finds it hard to plan if he knows that the tax law will be changed at year end. A young girl finds it hard to know how to behave if the abortion law passed by the New York Legislature of 1971 is repealed in 1972 or shortly thereafter. A young man cannot plan his education if the draft law changes every month or two.

And so there is an inherent paradox, and the super-industrial revolution challenges the law at many points. As the society fragments, more and more groups spring up to effectuate an ever wider variety of goals and value systems and conflicts. This demands that the law find ways of managing and resolving the inevitable conflicts among them. But, as the society also grows more temporary, even these sub-groups become more temporary. They come and go, with the teddy-boys followed by the hippies followed by the skin-heads, each, in turn, passing into oblivion or transmuting into something new. Can laws be written, enacted and repealed fast enough to keep up with all of this accelerating social turnover, not to mention the turnover of technology and business forms? In my view they cannot.

To put it simply, when the society fragments or differentiates, more laws are required to help hold the pieces in equilibrium. Beyond a point, however, this leads to a jungle-like overgrowth of law. Concurrently, when the society changes rapidly, melting into successive forms or stages at high speed, laws must be changed to reflect the new circumstances. But the more frequently they are revised, the less predictive they become and the less valuable.

This is why, although the reform of present judicial procedure may be important, although it is necessary to fight for certain appropriate changes in law, and to clear away the dead wood through decriminalisation, from a long range point of view, if that is all we do, it is a losing struggle. The law in this case is dead. I simply do not believe that we can hold the society together with law, and I believe that every time we try to do it by simply adding laws, we choke ourselves to death.

THE ANSWER TO THE CRISIS, therefore, lies not in the law, but in the reconstitution of social order. We are at the end of 10,000 years of legal history. Before the "neolithic revolution" (*i.e.* the invention of agriculture and the settlement of cities) law existed. Primitive societies had well-developed legal systems; but they played a distinctly subordinate role in the life of the society. It is only with the coming of complex, urbanised societies that law grew, at least in the West, to a dominant position in our lives. With the super-industrial revolution our goal must be for law once again to assume a subordinate role.

This does not mean that we should stop trying to improve the legal system by making the courts function more smoothly, clearing the judicial log-jam, or rewriting the law books.

We shall have to explore new technology—computers, cable systems, picture-phones, and the like—that could make it possible to assemble a jury instantaneously through random processes or to represent specific sub-publics. (We could guarantee, for example, that when a Harlem Black goes on trial, he or she faces a jury consisting of randomly represented Blacks or on which some predetermined fraction of the randomly selected group is black.) But while we are busy employing "futuristic" approaches, we ought also to take some lessons from primitive societies in which much of the legal machinery was or still is *ad hoc.*

Among the Ifugao tribesmen of Luzon there are careful rules about who gets the children and the property in the case of a divorce. To eliminate dispute, each party chooses a referee. These "*monhangdad*" are not professional divorce-lawyers and are part of no formal court, but decide any differences and receive a small fee for their service. They, in effect, constitute a temporary court and then dissolve it when the case is over. Among the Yurok Indians (according to the anthropologist A. L. Kroeber) a plaintiff would, in effect, hire two representatives from a community other than his own. (They could not be relatives.) In turn, the defendant would do likewise. These intermediaries or "crossers" would go back and forth, listening to each party's evidence and arguments about the justice and legality of his case, and render a decision for damages. Court was then not adjourned but dismantled.

We are not about to return to Rousseauian innocence, and no simple analogy is intended; but the idea that many problems might be resolved outside the formal legal system, or that not all courts need to be permanent, ought to be systematically explored in our search for solutions. The choice of temporary, non-professional or para-professional legal aid has, obviously, not been adequately pursued.

Similarly, we shall have to bring the laws that do exist into some semblance of timeliness. This means that despite what I have said about the burgeoning overgrowth of law, we need an agenda of "future laws" or laws needed to make sure we experience a future.

LAW IS A RESPONSE to what might be termed predictable deviation from social norms. Usually a law is written only when sufficient deviation has occurred to warrant the prediction that further deviation will occur. This occurs after the fact. We need now to think in terms of *anticipatory law*. Rather than waiting for some bizarre disaster to occur, for example, before we turn legislative attention to it, we need to attempt, as best we can, to anticipate those problems that will or ought to be legally regulated. Thus we need to take steps now—not five or ten years from now—to regulate experimentation with the biological process, referred to earlier, called "cloning." It is possible for a group of intelligent lawyers, legislators, and laymen, perhaps with some help from professional futurists, to prepare a tentative agenda to identify some of the social and technological problems that are likely to burst upon us in the decade or two immediately ahead. A Commission on Anticipatory Law ought to be a part of the legal-legislative system at all levels of government.

We are caught in a rapidly accelerating treadmill, and it is clear we cannot simply get off it by calling a moratorium on new laws. If this is so, however, we must also accelerate the rate at which we discard obsolete law. To save shelf space, some libraries eliminate books for which they have had no call in some fixed period of time, say, ten years. Perhaps we need to apply a similar pruning principle to law, automatically striking any law that has not been tested or called into service within some reasonable period of time, say 15 or 20 years. Whether we adopt an automatic procedure of this kind or not, it is evident that we shall have to make wider use of decriminalisation and codification, seen not as once-in-a-lifetime emergency measures, but as a continuing process.

We shall, moreover, have to shift the entire character of the punishment system in society. Today our systems typically punish in one of two ways: time or money, sometimes permitting one to be converted into the other; it is jail or fine. This extremely narrow and unimaginative approach to social sanction has two consequences. First, the courts miss many opportunities for encouraging rehabilitation through empathy, and for education of the public. And second, the man with the money suffers less than the man without because he can afford his fine more easily. Both these consequences further reduce social support for the law.

There is, however, another class of sanction available to us that I call "experiential." They do not put the guilty person in prison or, except coincidentally, deprive him of money. They make him undergo certain experiences. We do a little of this today, but so little that when a judge sentences a youth to clean a wall on which he has written graffiti, it warrants a feature item in the daily newspaper. Judges also occasionally send convicted persons to psychiatric treatment or drug rehabilitation programme or to school. But we make very little use of experiential sanctions.

In the future, I believe, we will make far greater use of them, recognising their profound educational and rehabilitative value. Here are some examples of how this might be done: while some of them are trivial, they illustrate a process that might be applied to more serious matter as well. Thus, instead of hitting a parking violator with a succession of, by and large, useless fines, a judge could, under an experiential system do the following. Sentence him to a day of street cleaning, during which he must remove the garbage from under the illegally parked cars. Or perhaps park a city truck in the offender's driveway for a week. Or impound his car not for an hour or two, but for a month or two, so that the sentence forces experiential changes in the offender's life. Today we impound for the wrong reasons and for the wrong time periods.

A vandal who has ripped a seat on the bus or subway might be sentenced to a day or two in a seat factory, or at painting and maintenance work at the depot. Offenders who ripped the telephone book out of the public booth might be given a week of cleaning the urine smell out of those phone booths. A shoplifter who has taken clothing from a store might have her own clothes impounded for a week or a month, and so forth. One could, it seems to me, be far more imaginative in the kinds of things we do.

In a more serious case, the executive of a corporation found guilty of selling dangerously defective automobiles might be sentenced to thirty days as mechanic's helper repairing them, or operating a tow truck, or serving as attendant in a hospital where victims of defect-related accidents were stitched up, preferably as an attendant in their rooms. Or perhaps such an offender might personally indemnify the victim's children so the victim can send his children to college. And so on. Indeed, if confinement is to be the method, why confinement to a prison where crime and sodomy tend to be the curriculum: why not confinement to his own home? Or to some community agency to serve without pay for a fixed period?

Obviously, there are many practical problems connected with this approach. Yet such experiential sanctions accord more fully with the essentially post-materialist value system which is beginning to emerge in our society.

EVEN MORE IMPORTANT, we need a much deeper vision. Whatever we do must be seen as a step, carefully thought out, toward the redesign of the whole social system. The changes we make should not be haphazard. We need to create them, to pattern them, in such a way that they help us recreate a sane social order.

Until we tackle seriously the task of restructuring our society, its family system, its economic and technological institutions, and above all its political machinery, we shall be forced to live in a society that is out of control. Until we begin to recreate an order based, in part, on much smaller and more decentralised units, our society will continue to run out of control. Until we experiment and develop self-policing mechanisms, so that sub-groups in the society (whether they are Chicanos, or Blacks, or homosexuals, or surfers) are left free to develop their own values, while taking responsibility for the policing of their own members—until this is the case, our society will run out of control.

The notion of self-policing communities is, in itself, not totally foreign to us. In the United States most police functions are reserved to local, as distinct from national, authorities. Yet the communities served by these local authorities are often so large, and so diverse, that the result is an attempt to impose uniform control over radically non-uniform populations. Moreover, because of our agricultural heritage, the American units are typically geographical.

We have also experimented with certain minimal forms of self-policing in non-geographical units—various industries and professions, for example. These non-geographical or functional units seldom carry much enforcement authority, although one could easily see how they might. By making an entire profession or industry or some sub-group of it collectively responsible, to some degree, for the behaviour of individual practitioners or companies, it is possible for the larger society to exert pressure on the group which, in turn, therefore, polices its members.

What we do not have anywhere is a significant example of a non-geographical self-policing unit that is sub-cultural rather than functional. For example, we nowhere expect or assume that hippies, or surfers, or homosexuals, or Hungarian/Asian immigrants will, as a group, maintain order among themselves at the risk of order being imposed by the society at large.

In the decade ahead I believe we shall have to experiment with a wide variety of self-policing mechanisms at geographical, functional, and sub-cultural levels. By focusing our attention on this problem, we begin to attack the central crisis facing us, and we move towards an ultimate reduction in the relative importance of law *per se*. We need to remember something that the anthropologists have only learned in the past century: that while man can live, and often does, without law, he cannot live without order.

THIS, THEN, is the deeper challenge. We need to replace law with a degree of order. We can no longer allow runaway changes in technology, in land development, in resource exploitation, in bio-science, and transportation, to destroy order without creating fresh order to take its place. Until we begin to choose our future, rather than letting it overwhelm us, we shall be forced to live in a society that is choking us with too much law in the wrong place, at the wrong time, for the wrong purposes, while depriving us of the essential ingredients of civilised life, a sense of personal safety and social order.

1. In Toffler's view, what is the current role of law in American society?

2. What does Toffler mean when he asserts that industrial society is being replaced by post-industrial society?

3. What are the two processes at work in post-industrial society?

4. What are the implications of this new type of 'order' for the law?

5. What solutions does Toffler envision for dealing with the problems of post-industrial society?

1. Toffler recognizes that there is a breakdown of order in American Society in terms of air highjacking, political assassinations, and violent crime, but he argues that, nonetheless, we have "more law per square inch than any nation in the world." He claims that we have too much law in the sense that legal regulations must be complied with at every turn and that in fact this compliance is often impossible. This situation brings about the need to break laws in order to carry out simple functions deemed socially necessary. His example of the 'underground', unlicensed Day Care Center emerging to avoid the burdensome requirements for a licensed center illustrates the point.

   In addition, however, new problems arise rapidly for which few or no regulatory laws are available. The current controversy over human 'cloning', i.e., the Technique of producing a genetically identical duplicate of an organism, definitions of death, and computerized information banks are all issues for which only tentative legal answers are available.

2. The industrial society which emerged out of the industrial revolution was characterized by mechanical mass production, bureaucratic structure, and standard or fixed roles. People were bombarded with standardized products from the factories and standardized ideas from the media. In contrast, the post-industrial society has "different technologies, different family institutions, different values, different conceptions of time, space and beauty--and it will have to have totally different 'legal arrangements as well" (Toffler, 1973, p. 15).

3. a. Fragmentation or de-standardization refers to the multiplication of options made available to us by new technology. Whereas the old mass production technology tended to limit and standardize our choices, the newer technologies produce almost an endless array of choices for us to make in daily life. His examples are worth noting.

    In politics: We no longer compete with one another to demonstrate how 'American' we are. In fact, ethnic, religious, racial, and regional pride are emerging among all groups.

    In education: At the time Toffler wrote this article, pressures continued to mount for individualized instruction in grade schools and self-designed majors in colleges. New departments in universities compete with traditional disciplines and new interdisciplinary programs appear annually.

    In filling your gas tank: Where once we faced only the choice of high-test or regular, we now have three to five possible gasolines to choose from, not to mention full-service versus gas only and self-serve versus attendant-served!

    b. Ephemeralization or Impermanency refers to a special quality of post-industrial society, namely, that it changes very rapidly. The stability and quasi-permanent nature of the industrial society has given way to an impermanence in which the generation gap has been reduced to a year or two! Students in college in 1968 and in 1978 experienced totally different realities. Again, note his examples.

    In organization: Bureaucracy is replaced by 'ad-hocracy' in which teams and commissions are created and dissolved to address specific problems.

In personal relationships: With 40 million Americans annually shifting their residences, the idea of growing up in one house and raising one's own family there has been forgotten. More likely, a return to one's birthplace will reveal a shiny new McDonald's rainbow or a six-lane expressway. Friendships become transient as people become transient, and rootlessness becomes the American way of life.

4. As to fragmentation or de-standardization, Toffler argues that the increase in the number and variety of products available results in more types of lawsuits, more contracts, more lawyers, more administrative rulings, and more paper. De-standardization has resulted in disorder. Where the 'proper role' of woman and man, black and white, worker and boss, teacher and student, policeman and citizen were once clear and unchallenged, today there are every-increasing conflicts about the 'natural order' or 'the way things are supposed to be'. As a result, there are redoubled efforts to restore order through new laws and increased numbers of people mobilizing the law to declare their rights against those who deny them their new roles.

   In terms of ephemeralization or impermanence, Toffler argues that law, by its nature, is well-suited to a permanent social order, but ill suited to the new social situation. Law relies on precedent, on past definitions and decisions. But as society lurches forward, changing its position on major issues every five years, law becomes impaired, or, worse, useless. Law's value depends upon its ability to help us predict what others will do. Thus, Toffler sees a paradox: if law is too resistant to change, it will ultimately be violently overthrown, but, if law is too responsive to a rapidly changing society, it loses its ability to guide us by predicting what others will do.

   In his words, "when society fragments. . .more laws are required to help hold the pieces in equilibrium. . .however, this leads to a jungle-like overgrowth of law. When society changes rapidly, laws must be changed to reflect the new circumstances. But the more frequently they are revised, the less predictive they become and the less valuable" (p. 21).

5. For Toffler, the problems of post-industrial society are less problems of law than of social order. Thus, what we need is not more law, but more order in our social relations. In primitive society, he notes, law played a subordinate role due to the greater stability of the underlying social order. During the industrial age, law become more central. In the future, law will have to once again become less central in our lives. Toffler advocates a variety of imaginative ways for dealing with policing, punishing, and adjudicating disputes. He concludes that if we are to void total disorder, we must work more to create a new type of order and less to create new types of law.

POST-REVOLUTIONARY LAW AND SOCIETY

Annamay T. Sheppard

Panel Discussion--Meeting of American Legal Studies Association--Rutgers Law School, Newark

March, 17, 1978

When I was first asked to participate in a panel discussion about post-revolutionary law and society I was confident that the invitation would shortly be followed by some description of the revolution to the post of which my thoughts were to be directed. It occurred to me, for example, that it would be useful to know where the revolution took place. (Until the posters went up I wasn't even sure that the United States was a candidate.) I was also curious about who made the revolution and how; about the preconditions to which it responded; and about the objectives that the revolutionaries had in mind. Finally, it seemed that there was some utility in knowing how post was post.

Since all of these would affect my projections, I inquired of your president. He suggested that any reasonable revolution would do, and that I might describe life and law on the first day of any reasonable new society. At that juncture I was tempted, like Mel Brooks' 2000 year old man when he was asked his opinion of Sir Arthur Conant Doyle, to say, "Both good" and let it go at that. But here was an opportunity which is seldom available to lawyers: I could create the facts--and when you create the facts, your outcome analysis can be made to sound eminently reasonable.

So these are the facts I created:

First: The revolution took place in the United States.

Second: The preconditions to revolution were economic breakdown, characterized by widespread, long-term unemployment; deterioration of vital services and life supports; and severe, protracted political repression in answer to protest. (I pass here the chance to explore the reasons why these conditions come about, since my assignment is to discuss the new society rather than the old one.)

Reprinted with the permission of Rutgers University School of Law, Newark, N.J.

Third: The revolutionaries were industrial and agricultural workers joined by members of what we now sometimes call the welfare class; by the lower echelons of the military; and by some intellectuals.

Fourth: The opponents of the revolution were members of the controlling economic establishment; sizable portions of middle and upper management of the economic establishment; petty entrepeneurs; government officials; police; upper echelons of the military; the legal profession in all of its branches; the upper echelons of organized religion; the mass media; and most intellectuals. Their intra-revolutionary responses varied from active resistance to surly passivity.

Fifth: The revolution was a violent upheaval in response to neo-fascist repression of protest and the inaccessibility of political avenues for peaceful change.

Sixth: The central objectives of the revolution were seizure and collective ownership of the means of production and the restoration of personal liberty.

That is my scenario. What role for the law in the reconstitution of society under these new ground rules? To answer that question it is necessary first to try to get a handle on the nature of the law as we now know it. Much of its present substance, installed and adjusted over a long period of time, is a codification of the ground rules of the system which, in our hypothetical, has aged, failed and been forcibly overthrown. A major portion of the law of the old system would be dysfunctional in the new setting. For example, immediate and sweeping change would be required in the law governing private property rights and relationships; the law governing taxation; the law governing the creation and maintenance of business organizations; the law governing employment relations; the law governing public entitlements of every kind; the law governing mass communications, to mention far less than all.

It seems likely, too, that the new society would look sympathetically upon proposals for altering the remedial aspects of tort law and both the substance and punitive aspects of the criminal law.

In addition to dismantling the old law, our day-one revolutionary forces would have an immediate and pressing need to create a whole new body of substantive rules to govern the newly collectivized society.

To whom might those revolutionary forces look for that new substance? Bear in mind the facts which I have created. Most of the lawyers were opponents of this revolution. Most of them (with some notable exceptions recorded in the files of the now defunct FBI) were the hired guns of the old system in which they served as legislators, judges, advocates, administrators and executives for the benefit of the now-deposed ownership class. In the eyes of the revolutionary forces they might well seem a bad lot. Moreover, for purposes of creating an entire new economic order, their skills would be substantively deficient. Economists, scientists, planners would be more likely change agents than lawyers; and it is probable that these are the experts to whom the new society would turn for a restructuring of the substance of the law governing economic relations. Is it curtains, then, for the lawyers and the old instruments of law? I think not. At the very least, lawyers would be needed for the statutory and regulatory articulation of post-revolutionary law. The molding of language to social goals is no small skill, and it is lawyers who have that skill.

Moreover, the very size and complexity of society would require the maintenance of legal machinery. Think of the myriad tasks that would be required in the post revolutionary period:

1. The restoration of public order;

2. The implementation of rules of personal behavior;

3. The creation and maintenance of systems of dispute resolution between individuals;

4. The retooling of an educational establishment;

5. The creation of new mechanisms for the development of the arts and culture;

6. The restructuring of systems for delivery of child care, medical care, housing, old age benefits and a plethora of other services;

7. The development of extremely complex systems for regulating the economy;

8. The creation of mechanisms for harmonizing the competing claims of economic and political sub-groups in the society;

9. The development of instruments for participation, by 200 million people, in the economic, social and political life of the new system.

All of these undertakings require a machinery which can derive and implement transferable legal principles.

Could pre-revolutionary legal systems meet these needs? I postulate that, in substantial measure, they could.

Law, as we now use the term, is a function of legislatures, administrative tribunals, executive branches of government, and courts. All of these are both creators and implementors of the law within the limits of the power of each. All are at least theoretically bound by constitutional limitations. Each, at least theoretically, checks the other. Each is a massive system, with multiple sub-systems of internal control. The worm in this legal machinery, I suggest, is not so much the machine but who uses it and for whose benefit and ends. Certainly some quite elaborate law-creating machinery, whether this one or its clone or analogue, will still be required in newborn socialism. But my far-from-complete laundry list of the law-related tasks of the new society suggests yet another and absolutely basic undertaking for which the law must be responsible. For this post-revolutionary society, bent as it may be on the creation of a just order, will inevitably spawn its own contradictions.

Focus for a moment on the opponents of the revolution, whom I have described as ranged along a line from active hostility to passive unhappiness. Are the political and participatory rights of these groups to be suspended until the revolution is 'secure'? If so, by what process and against what standards will these 'anti's' be sorted, labelled and judged? For how long will they be immobilized? And what will be the consequences, for a society with participatory goals, of the suspension of rights in the name of proletarian security? What effect, for example, on art, culture, education, economic development, public order? What effect on participatory instruments?

The stewardship of the new society will require a vast new managerial class--those economists, planners and scientists to whom I have already referred as the post revolutionary legislators. History teaches that, if not on day-one, then certainly by day-three of the revolution, the goals of the revolution will be endangered unless the revolutionaries have some viable machinery for controlling these controllers. For in every organized society there is a built-in tension between the long-range objectives of the societal apparati and the felt and competing needs of individuals and sub-groups in the society. This tension can be constructively contained only when there are rights and powers reserved to the people which are beyond the control of the managers of social apparati. Here I obviously have in mind rights of franchise; of privacy; of expression; of protest; indeed, of revolution. In short, those risky rights to lever the system which are essential to its sound development.

The proper and natural vehicle for the protection of these rights is a legal system which is independent of the other functions of government and which is committed not to the managerial apparti but to the people.

Here, I think, reenter the lawyers--bringing with them some of the useful tools of the old system in the hands of new actors. Such tools might well include notions of checks and balances as they appear in both our constitutional and adjudicative systems.

To be sure, these new lawyers will be cut from a different cloth than their contemporary counterparts. They will come from a different place and serve a different clientele, and it is hardly likely that they will receive contingent fees for their services! But lawyers they will be, responsible for the theoretical and practical development of useful legal principles for the implementation of the participatory rights of the people. In short they will be the servants of the revolution and the adversaries of the new establishment, trained and equipped to do combat with the developing rigidities of that establishment. If they are absent, I hypothesize that the resolution will fail.

Here ends my analysis. After all, I was only responsible for day-one of socialist America. Perhaps next year someone else will be assigned the task of creating the facts about how socialism fared and then analyzing, within manageable time limits, by what science, magic and luck, socialist humanity was born and the state withered away.

1. What conditions led to the 'second American Revolution'?

2. Which groups were united for the purpose of revolution?

3. Which groups opposed the revolution?

4. What were the central objectives of the revolution?

5. What immediate needs did the new society have on the day after the revolution?

6. Why would restoration of a legal system be desirable?

7. Why would lawyers re-emerge?

1. Annamay Sheppard, a law professor, sees an American society plagued by unemployment, political unrest and repression, and general economic breakdown which provide the pre-conditions for revolution.

2. Basically, she conjures up the image of a revolt led by the poor, the military rank and file, a few intellectuals, and a coalition of industrial and farm workers.

3. The economic elites, government officials, the police, the military elite, the majority of the intellectual establishment and the legal profession opposed the revolution and sought to preserve the existing social, political, and economic system.

4. The revolutionaries sought to socialize or collectivize the ownership of the means of production--factories, industries, etc.---and to restore the personal freedoms lost during the reactionary defense of the defunct American system.

5. Despite the idealism of the revolutionaries, the day after the revolution would bring concrete problems which demand immediate attention. Among them would be problems of restoring and maintaining social order, writing rules to control personal conduct, creating means to resolve disputes, designing mechanisms for resolving competing claims of groups in society, etc. The needs of this new system have an uncanny resemblance to social control, dispute settlement and social change--the very core of law's role in our society today.

6. Professor Sheppard believes that the legal system is the "proper and natural vehicle" to protect the rights of individuals, to control the new revolutionary government, and to balance individuals' short-range and the government's long-range objectives.

7. The skills of the lawyer in using language to further the social goals of the revolutionary government, in designing rules and regulations, in resolving disputes, in developing legal principles, and in serving the revolution in countless other ways would make the lawyer once again a central participant in American society the day after the revolution.

COMMENT: This creative effort by Professor Sheppard is most interesting because it reveals both a deep concern about the direction in which current American society is headed and an abiding faith in law, the legal profession, and the legal system to play a key role in bringing about a 'post-revolutionaty' better society. It is a fascinating mixture of radical vision and traditional trust in law. As she puts it, "The worm in this legal machinery, I suggest, is not so much in the machine but who uses it and for whose benefit and ends." In other words, with law, lawyers, and the legal process in the hands of a new and, hopefully, better regime, it will be possible to produce the just society. Unlike Toffler, whose vision of the new society includes a decreased role for law, Sheppard's vision suggests an increased role for law, albeit for revolutionary purposes!

THE POLITICS OF RIGHTS AND THE LIMITS OF LAW

Up to this point in this unit we have looked at the content of American legal culture, its manifestation in a heavy reliance upon law and legal institutions, one futurist's notions about the role of law in the newly developing American social order, and one law professor's vision of the future role of law. In this mini-lecture we will look at several arguments concerning the inability of the legal paradigm to produce satisfactory solutions to all of our public policy problems. We will look at the following three points of view:

A. Litigation is seriously limited as a means of achieving public policy changes because the political struggle which follows a court decision can render that decision meaningless.

B. The same attributes to the adjudication process which make it useful in resolving some private disputes may render it ill-suited to resolving major public policy questions.

C. There are both empirical and ethical limits on the capacity of law to contribute to society's need for social control, dispute settlement, and social change.

A. The Politics of Rights

In his recent book, The Politics of Rights, Stuart Scheingold (1974) attacks what he calls the "myth of rights" and advocates its replacement by the "politics of rights." His central thesis is that judicial declarations which grant or recognize rights will only lead to the actual realization of those rights where a successful political fight is waged following the judicial announcement.

'Rights', in the natural law tradition of American law, are permanent and universal. All human beings are entitled to them by virtue of being human beings. The obvious difficulties associated with identifying the content of our natural rights and the suspicion that claims of natural rights are typically political, social, or economic claims in disguise have led to serious skepticism about this entire concept of 'rights'.

A more empirical notion of 'rights' is offered by Professors Jay Sigler and Joel Fineberg who argue that a 'right' is nothing more than a 'valid claim', that is, " a claim which is recognized and accepted by authoritative decision makers (courts, legislatures, governors). . ." (Sigler, 1975, p. 5) Thus, 'rights' grow out of 'claims' made by people who seek authoritative statements of the validity of their claims.

But Scheingold maintains that these ideas of 'rights' as 'natural rights', or 'rights' as 'valid claims' have seduced us into believing that there is a "direct linking of litigation, rights, and remedies with social change" (Scheingold, p. 5). This is the essence of the "myth of rights." As illustrated below, the myth of rights suggests that to achieve change, one need only assert a claim of right and receive judicial support. It will follow that the right will be realized and society will respond and move into conformity.

LITIGATION——▶ DECLARATION OF RIGHTS——▶ REALIZATION OF RIGHTS——▶ SOCIAL CHANGE

Nothing could be further from the truth. In the alternative perspective, the "politics of rights," the declaration of rights by the courts is seen as only the beginning of a political battle to reform social practices. In the politics of rights, as illustrated below, the declaration of rights is seen basically as a tool, a political resource, or that which can be used in the struggle to achieve change. There are many types of such political resources--money, knowledge, votes, organization--and the judicial declaration of rights is added to the arsenal and may help those who benefit from it to achieve their goals. Further, the declaration of rights may serve as a formal statement or a goal of governmental policy. But a goal is not synonymous with its achievement. Declarations of rights in the politics of rights, can also provide a collective identity and assist in the mobilization of the affected groups to fight for the rights recognized by the courts.

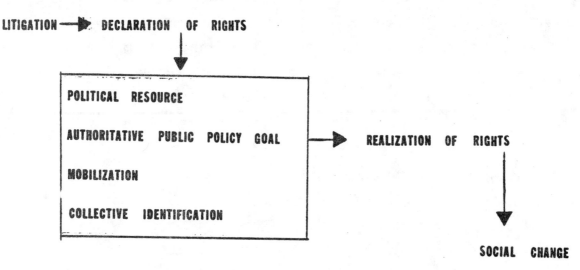

LITIGATION ➔ DECLARATION OF RIGHTS

POLITICAL RESOURCE

AUTHORITATIVE PUBLIC POLICY GOAL

MOBILIZATION

COLLECTIVE IDENTIFICATION

➔ REALIZATION OF RIGHTS

SOCIAL CHANGE

In the politics of rights, then, the declaration of rights is nothing but a contingent result whose value varies dramatically with the strength of political support and opposition for its implementation. The point is that the traditional belief (the myth of rights) leads us to erroneously expect that social change will follow from successful litigation. It is not that litigation is useless; rather, it is that litigation is limited as a means to achieve social change. Such a perspective is consistent with the findings reported in Unit 6 concerning the impact of decisions of the U.S. Supreme Court. One need only look back to the political battle which followed (and continues) the declaration in Brown v. Board of Education that racially separate schools were inherently unequal or ahead to the political battle which inevitably will follow the Bakke decision (Unit 10) to see the value of Scheingold's analysis of the politics of rights.

B. The Limits of Adjudication

An interesting argument has recently been made (Horowitz, 1977) to the effect that the process of adjudication itself is poorly suited to making general social policy. Basically, Horowitz argues that the function of making social policy has been superimposed upon the courts, whose structure and process are designed to decide individual cases, not to write broad public policy. He identifies a number of these 'judicial incapacities'. First, he argues that judicial decision makers--judges and lawyers--are generalists rather than experts. Courts rely on specialized information provided to them by expert witnesses who are hired by the litigants to present a somewhat distorted version of the specialized information. The lawyers structure their arguments to be persuasive to generalist judges, not specialized experts. The practice of rotating judges from civil to criminal divisions virtually guarantees that the judges will be frequently ill-informed on the subject matter before them. Note the difference between the courts on one hand, and Congress and the Executive on the other. The committee system of the Congress and the expectation that each individual member will carve out a policy area of specialization enables the Congress as a whole to master extraordinarily complicated subjects. Similarly, the executive branch possesses enormous special expertise by virtue of its career civil servants who spend their lives dealing with particular policy areas. Compared to the judges--who are increasingly asked to make public policy--the Congress and the Executive branch are better-equipped to make public policy.

Next, Horowitz maintains that the process of adjudication itself makes the courts peculiarly unfit to make public policy. The focus of an adjudication is on the issue of legal rights: "Does the plaintiff have a right or not?" Such a focus, says Horowitz, restricts the examination of alternatives and costs. Judges must answer that question; they cannot, in most cases, deal with an alternative question. They may be able to choose among remedies after they decide the answer, but, even there, they are far more limited than the legislature or the executive. More importantly, in theory at least, once the judges decide that the plaintiff _does_ have the right which he or she has asserted, the costs--financial, social or political--of granting that right cannot be considered. The legislature, on the other hand, can examine a wider range of alternatives and weigh their costs against their benefits and against competitive needs.

Third, Horowitz argues that adjudication is, by its very nature, disjointed and piecemeal. Forced to decide only the cases which are brought to it, the courts invariably produce unclear guidelines when they attempt to make public policy. By viewing as isolated and discrete a case which represents a policy problem of wide proportions, the courts are unable to adequately deal with the consequences and implications of their decisions. This passive posture of waiting for cases to be brought led philosopher Lon Fuller to comment that, "Courts are like defective clocks; they have to be shaken to set them going" (Fuller, 1964, p. 52).

In addition, Horowitz points out that the cases which ultimately reach the courts are likely to be <u>unrepresentative</u> of the problems in the particular policy area involved because lawyers are more prone to bring extreme cases to court since they are more easily won. Thus, the court may decide a major question of public policy on the facts of an <u>atypical</u> case, thus producing confusion and perhaps hostility.

Legal fact finding is different from other efforts at fact finding in that it is limited by various rules of evidence. The 'hearsay' rule, for example, often excludes research reports and articles from court examination. Finally, Horowitz suggests that the courts are not well equipped to review the implementation of policy. Unlike the Congressional committees and sub-committees who oversee policy implementation, the courts typically have no such mechanism and simply must await further cases. Where the courts do try to oversee implementation, as they did in the Boston School desegre-gation case, the judge became so involved that he was spending an inordinate amount of time on details of implementation. On one day, for example, the judge was involved in deciding the type and number of tennis balls to be purchased for the tennis program at South High School!

The argument here is that we rely on courts to make public policy when the structure and process of court decision making is not designed to do that.

There are some additional issues concerning this argument about which you should be thinking. First, it may be the case that arguments which favor Congress over the courts as the better means of public policymaking are merely disguised policy preferences. It is far more convincing, for example, to argue the relative advantages of Congressional over court policymaking than to say that the courts are wrong on abortion, reverse discrimination, busing, and the rights of criminal defendants. In other words, are people more likely to talk about 'judicial incapacities' when they <u>like</u> the decisions of the court or when they <u>dislike</u> them? Are they more likely to extol the virtues of Congressional policy making when they approve or dis-approve of the <u>content</u> of that policy?

Second, suppose Congress, the more politically sensitive branch of government, fails to act. Should courts sit by passively in the face of injustices? Often it is easier for courts to take actions which are politically volatile precisely because they are insulated from voter reprisals.

Finally, Americans continue to be receptive to natural rights types of arguments. Thus, if a person has a right, he or she has it despite Congressional reluctance to legislate it or executive willingness to implement it. It is, therefore, deeply imbedded in our legal culture, that rights must be recognized and courts must step in where other institutions fear to tread in order to protect those rights.

C. The Limits of Law

Beyond the limitations suggested by the politics of rights and the judicial incapacities, there are additional empirical and ethical limits to the capacity of law to contribute to the need for social control, dispute settlement, and social change. Empirical limits "are determined by law's capability in fulfilling its functions." Ethical limits "are determined by normative judgments indicating law's appropriate reach" (Danielski, in Pennock and Chapman, 1974, p. 8). In other words, there are two separate, though related questions involved here. The first is concerned with what it is _possible_ for law to accomplish, and the second is concerned with what it is _proper_ for law to attempt.

There are two broad senses in which we think about the empirical limits of law (Greenwalt, in Pennock and Chapman, 1974, pp. 76-87). First, laws have _limited effectiveness_ in achieving the goals which lawmakers (legislators or judges) have in mind in announcing them. Our discussion of the problems of deterrence (Unit 5) made clear that the goal of lawmakers in establishing threats of punishment for certain acts was to prevent people from engaging in certain conduct which they otherwise would have done. Certainly, the law is limited in its ability to achieve this goal. Laws prohibiting the sale of alcoholic beverages, gambling, prostitution and many other forms of behavior simply have not resulted in the disappearance of these behaviors. These examples deal with the problems associated with _obedience_ to law. The refusal of people to obey the law constitutes a limit on its effectiveness.

A related problem in the area of legal ineffectiveness arises when the law _is obeyed_, but, nonetheless, fails to accomplish the goals for which it was enacted. If we prohibit the killing of deer in order to protect the species, but find that strict obedience by hunters leads to overpopulation, starvation, and extinction for deer, then legal effectiveness has been impaired, and another limit of law has been reached.

A second general sense of the empirical limits of law revolves around the issue of practicality. In other words, it is often the case that it is simply impractical to employ the law to achieve certain ends. The cost of enforcement--both financial and in terms of sacrificing other values--may limit the law's utility. For example, in the area of social control, we could enforce laws governing sexual conduct only at great financial cost and at the expense of highly valued privacy. We could use more sensitive mechanisms for dispute settlement, perhaps, only at great cost and at the expense of the principle of generality which is at the core of our jurisprudence. Furthermore, if we were willing to expend the resources needed to enforce certain laws, we might create hostility or disrespect for the law and, thus, undermine law's ability to achieve other valued objectives.

Law may also be limited by its very nature. Since laws are rules stated in general terms which are to be applied to categories of persons, rather than to individuals, they often will yield unjust, but consistent results. Because it is important for laws to be clear and predictable, it is likely that they will be limited in their ability to be sensitive to the moral subtleties of particular cases. How often are litigants in small claims courts or landlord-tenant disputes told by the judge or board of arbitrators, "You are, perhaps, morally justified in your claims, but legally you cannot prevail." This is not suggested as a criticism of law, but rather as an intrinsic, if unfortunate, limit to law. As one philosopher states the problem, "The regularity of law, as contrasted with the infinite variety of life, defies justice. . . yet the alternative to regularity, discretion, provides constant opportunity and invitation to arbitrariness, which brings us back to the original source of the demand for law" (Pennock, in Pennock and Chapman, 1974, p. 6).

Turning to the normative limits of law, we are faced with the issue of whether or not law ought to be involved. Regardless of questions of possible effectiveness, the use of law to regulate behavior might be objected to on other grounds. It is not enough, in other words, to argue that it would work to justify an argument that we should do it! While this is not the place to go into an extended discussion of various libertarian positions on this point, suffice it to say that there are some spheres of conduct, generally private acts which do not harm others, into which law ought never to intrude.

This enormously complex problem is made more difficult because the empirical and normative limits of law are inextricably linked to one another. In other words, it might be argued that law should not (normative) be used to do what it cannot (empirical) do, or that law should not (normative) be employed where the practical costs (empirical) are too high (normative). While not attempting to probe more deeply into these problems, you should now be familiar with some of the complex issues involved in the limits of law.

1. What conception of 'rights' underlies the 'myth of rights'?

2. What is the 'myth of rights'?

3. How does the idea of the 'politics or rights' differ from the 'myth of rights'?

4. What are 'judical incapacities'?

5. How do these 'judicial incapacities' limit the adjudicatory process as a useful means for resolving broad policy questions?

6. What is the difference between an empirical and a normative limit of law?

7. Briefly distinguish the effectiveness limit from the practical limit of law.

8. How do empirical and normative limits of law relate to each other?

DISCUSSION OF MINI-LECTURE #3 QUESTIONS

1. The concept of rights is a cloudy one. People claim that they 'possess' 'rights', yet you have never seen a 'right'. In natural law thinking, we, as human beings, all possess a minimum number of such rights. Even legal positivists maintain that we possess these rights--not by virtue of being human beings, but by virtue of the creation of such rights by legitimate agents of the political state. The less metaphysical notion of rights as valid claims contributes equally to the 'myth of rights'.

2. The 'myth of rights' refers to the attractive view that a direct link exists between the judicial announcement that a person possesses a particular right and the realization of that right by the person. This is followed, almost automatically, by societal acceptance of the judicial pronouncement and societal change to guarantee the right in the future.

3. The politics of rights adopts a political perspective in which the declaration of rights signifies not a realization of those rights by an individual nor a general recognition of those rights by society. Rather, the announcement is interpreted as one of many political tools which may be more or less skillfully used in the ensuing struggle for the realization of the rights by individuals and the recognition of rights by society. While litigation producing declarations of rights is not dismissed as a means of achieving political or social justice, the politics of rights perspective highlights the contingent or conditional quality of legal rights.

4. The term 'judicial incapacities' refers to the built-in weaknesses of courts and judges as public policymaking institutions and decision makers. The idea is that while well-equipped to perform certain tasks, such as resolving concrete disputes over who owns a parcel of land, they are ill-equipped to perform others involving fundamental public policy questions affecting millions of Americans in all sectors of society.

5. The central points explored in the Mini-Lecture are:

   a. The propensity of judges to be generalists rather than specialists hinders them in deciding broad public policy issues.

   b. The legal paradigm's attention to legal rights narrows the focus of inquiry, thus excluding considerations of cost, alternatives, and competing solutions.

   c. The disjointed movement of courts as they decide the cases brought before them is not appropriate to the task of broad policymaking because the emphasis is on the consequences to the litigants, not to the implications for entire segments of society or for society generally.

      In sum, the position taken is one which asserts a lack of fit between structures of courts and functions increasingly performed by them.

The nagging problem of separating theoretical arguments about proper and effective functioning of courts from arguments over the content of court decisions is raised for your consideration.

6. Empirical limits of law pertain to the problems of law's <u>ability</u> to achieve its purposes. Normative limits pertain to the <u>desirability</u> of law's achieving particular goals.

7. Law is ineffective when it is disobeyed, or when it is obeyed, but produces results contrary to those intended. Law is also limited by practical costs of its enforcement--either in terms of money, other values, or reduced respect for the law generally.

8. The relationship between empirical and normative limits is complex. Whether law <u>will</u> be obeyed (empirical) is partly a function of whether people believe that it <u>should</u> be obeyed (normative); whether law <u>should</u> be employed (normative) is partly a function of whether it <u>will</u> be enforced (empirical); whether law <u>will</u> be enforced (empirical) is partly a function of whether the costs of enforcement <u>should</u> be incurred (normative). Thus, the empirical and the normative limits are inextricably tied to one another. While it is useful to isolate them for purposes of analysis, it is impossible to treat them as entirely independent of one another.

Reprinted with permission of National Affairs, Inc., The Public Interest, Volume 41, Fall 1975, pp. 104-113.

Reading #3

Towards an imperial judiciary?

NATHAN GLAZER

... The justices wear black gowns, being not merely the only public officers, but the only non-ecclesiastical persons of any kind whatever within the bounds of the United States who use any official dress.
—The American Commonwealth

A NON-LAWYER who considers the remarkable role of courts in the interpretation of the Constitution and the laws in the United States finds himself in a never-never land—one in which questions he never dreamed of raising are discussed at incredible length, while questions that would appear to be the first to come to mind are hardly ever raised. This is particularly the case when the concern of the non-professional observer is with social policy rather than with constitutional law as such.

Thus, fine distinctions in the use of evidence in criminal cases are debated at length, and used as a basic test in judging whether a court or individual justices are liberal or conservative; whereas one sees little discussion of why judges may hold up hundreds of millions of dollars in federal payments to states and cities to force them to make numerous civil service appointments, or why judges may require a state or city to provide extensive and specifically defined social services. The original *Brown* decision on school desegregation was properly debated at length by our leading constitutional authorities. But what are arguably the most disruptive decisions ever made by the courts—the requirement that children be bused to distant schools—have excited much less professional interest than popular interest.

One reason for this disparity is that judges and lawyers are trained to see continuity in the development of constitutional law. However far-reaching the actions the courts take, the lawyers who propose such actions and the judges who rule on them are committed by the logic of legal reasoning to insist that they are only unveiling a rule that existed all along in the recesses of the Constitution or the bowels of legislation: Nothing new has been added, they say, even though great consequences follow from their decisions. Political scientists who study the courts are somewhat freer to see truly original developments in the constitutional law, but they generally do not go beyond interpreting these developments as part of a cycle. If the court changes, to them it changes within a well-understood pattern, in which periods of activism symmetrically contrast with periods of quietism: At some point the Supreme Court, exercising its power to interpret the Constitution and the laws and to overrule the interpretations of legislatures and executives,[1] goes too far—thus, we have the *Dred Scott* decision, or the decisions overruling the actions of the New Deal in the mid-1930's. An explosion then results: as a result of the *Dred Scott* decision, a war; as a result of the anti-New Deal decisions, the court-packing plan. To the political scientist, the court follows not only its own logic but the logic of public opinion. Since it is without the independent power to enforce its decrees, the Court then withdraws. Its withdrawal is assisted ultimately by the appointment power of the President, who is in closer touch with public opinion. A period of quietism thus succeeds a period of activism. This is a reasonable description of the pattern of judicial interpretation, supported by history and by American constitutional arrangements, and this is as far as one of our best-known analysts of the Supreme Court, Robert McCloskey, went.

There is, however, another perspective on judicial interpretation, one which is generally identified with outraged legislators, Presidents, governors, and people: The Court has gone too far, they say,

[1] In this article, I do not plan to go into the question of the sources of this power, whether given in the Constitution, or seized by Chief Justice Marshall, or properly or improperly established—it is there, and it is permanent,

From Warren to Burger

These are sweeping assertions, yet the course of the law since 1969 supports them. For in 1969 something was supposed to happen, and didn't. In his first term, President Nixon, who opposed the Warren Court's activism, succeeded in making four appointments, and the period of activism that had begun with the *Brown* decision of 1954 was supposed to come to an end, as the Warren Court was replaced by the Burger Court. Instead, there have been more far-reaching decisions—if estimated by the impact on people and their everyday lives—since 1969 than in 1954-1968, even with four Nixon-appointed Justices. In 1971 the *Swann* decision for the first time legitimated massive busing of children to overcome segregation in a large city; in 1974 the *Keyes* decision for the first time legitimated such massive busing in a Northern city, and in addition legitimated standards of proof for *de jure* segregation that were so loose that it guaranteed that *de jure* segregation could be found everywhere (which meant that the Court's narrow 5-4 decision in *Milliken*—which overturned lower court requirements for the merger of Detroit and its suburbs in order to create, through busing, schools with smaller proportions of black children—could very likely be circumvented by demonstrating that the suburbs, too, were engaged in *de jure* segregation). In 1971 the Court legitimated federal government guidelines for the use of tests in employment that required strict standards of "job-relatedness" if, on the basis of such tests, differing proportions of certain ethnic and racial groups were given employment. This decision has, in effect, declared illegal most efforts by employers, public and private, to hire more qualified employees. Since apparently all tests select differing proportions of one group or another, and few tests can be shown to be job-related by the strict standards of the guidelines, most employee hiring on the basis of tests now can be labeled discriminatory and employers may be required, either by lower court orders or by Department of Justice consent decrees, to hire by racial and ethnic quotas—a practice which is specifically forbidden by the Civil Rights Act of 1964 and (one would think) unconstitutional because of its denial of the "equal protection of the laws." In 1973, the Burger Court ruled in *Roe* and *Doe* that just about all state laws on abortion were unconstitutional and decreed that state laws must treat each third of the pregnancy period according to different standards. In 1975 it spread the awesome limitations of "due process" to the public schools, which now could not restrict the constitutional rights of students by suspending or expelling them without at least something resembling a criminal trial. In 1975 it agreed, in the first of a series of important cases on the rights of mental patients, that harmless persons could not be detained involuntarily in mental hospitals.

The list could be extended. It is true that the Court stayed its hand in other cases that could have had enormous consequences: In particular, it refused to accept the argument that states must ensure that financial support of schools be unaffected by differences in community wealth, and it did not allow a challenge by inner-city residents to suburban zoning ordinances. But in both areas state courts are active, and it is hard to see what is to prevent them from decreeing for their states (as the courts of New Jersey already have) the revolution in equalization of school financing and zoning that the Supreme Court has refused to decree for the nation.

What was most striking is that all of these cases—and many others extending the reach of government, whether it wished it or not, into the lives of people, and of the courts over the actions of legislatures and communities—were made despite the rapid appointment of four Justices by President Nixon. The Nixon Justices either supported the majority in 9-0 decisions (e.g., *Swann*), or split (thus only one of the four dissented from the majority in *Doe* and *Roe*), and the return of the quietistic phase of the cycle will not satisfy us, for the Court is engaged in a damaging and unconstitutional revolution that even the cyclical return of a period of quietism cannot curb. The lawyers who must operate within the assumption of continuity are inclined to dismiss such outrage, and the legal commentators who look at the long stretch of history are sure that quietism will replace activism—as it has before—and that the courts will retire from the front pages of the newspapers. Yet in 1975, all the evidence suggests that this third perspective is really the correct one: The courts truly have changed their role in American life. American courts, the most powerful in the world—they were that already when Tocqueville wrote and when Bryce wrote—are now far more powerful than ever before; public opinion—which Tocqueville, Bryce, and other analysts thought would control the courts as well as so much else in American life—is weaker. The legislatures and the executive now moderate their outbursts, for apparently outbursts will do no good. And courts, through interpretation of the Constitution and the laws, now reach into the lives of the people, against the will of the people, deeper than they ever have in American history.

and only rarely (in *Goss*, on due process for students) voted as a bloc against the majority of five who had served on the Warren Court.

Supreme Court analysts and reporters very often tell a different story from this, because in judging the Court, they tend to focus on the endless details of what is or is not allowed in criminal law—the use of confessions, searches, and the like. Emphasizing the criminal law, they apparently see a retreat where another observer might see a modicum of common sense. But I believe all agree that the Burger Court has been surprisingly like the Warren Court; and this raises the question of why the expected turn has not yet taken place—seven years after Nixon was elected, and after four of his appointees were on the court.

The end of a conservative judiciary?

Three characteristics of the Burger Court, and of the Warren Court, have excited less interest than they might have, and would suggest that we must at least consider the possibility that there has been a permanent change in the character of the courts and their role in the commonwealth, rather than simply a somewhat extended activist cycle.

First, the activist cycles of the past have always been characterized by conservative Courts, acting to restrict liberal Congresses, Presidents, or state governments—the Marshall Court, the Taney Court, and the Taft-Hughes Courts. This made sense: The Court, after all, was designed by the Founders to be a conservative institution, a check on popularly elected legislatures and an elected (even if not at the beginning *popularly* elected) President. The Court was appointed, and it held tenure for life. It was, as Alexander Bickel wrote, paraphrasing Hamilton in the 78th *Federalist* paper, "the least dangerous branch." To quote Hamilton: "Whoever attentively considers the different departments of power must perceive, that, in a government in which they are separated from each other, the judiciary, from the nature of its functions, will always be the least dangerous to the political rights of the Constitution; because it will be least in capacity to annoy or injure them. The Executive not only dispenses the honors, but holds the sword of the community; the legislature not only commands the purse, but prescribes the rules by which the duties and rights of every citizen are to be regulated." (As we shall see, however, the legislature no longer controls the purse, if the Court rules otherwise, nor prescribes the rules govern-

ing duties and rights—though the sword is still in the hands of the Executive.)

But something extraordinary has happened when a liberal Court confronts a conservative executive and legislature, as the Warren Court did after the election of President Eisenhower: The *natural* expectations, the order of history, have been reversed. It is even more extraordinary when, after 15 years of appointments to the Supreme Court and the subordinate courts by conservative Presidents (against seven years by liberal Presidents), this strange posture still persists.

A second extraordinary feature of the post-1954 activism is a corollary in part of the first: In the past the role of activist courts was to *restrict* the executive and legislature in what they could do. The distinctive characteristic of more recent activist courts has been to *extend* the role of what the government could do, even when the government did not want to do it. The *Swann* and *Keyes* decisions meant that government *must* move children around to distant schools against the will of their parents. The *Griggs* decision meant that government *must* monitor the race and ethnicity of job applicants and test-takers. The cases concerning the rights of mental patients and prisoners, which are for the most part still in the lower courts, say that government *must* provide treatment and rehabilitation whether it knows how or not. Federal Judge Weinstein's ruling in a New York school desegregation case seems to say that government *must* racially balance communities. And so on.

An interesting example of this unwilled extension of governmental action is that of the Environmental Protection Agency (EPA). It did not wish to issue rules preserving pure air in areas without pollution or imposing drastic transportation controls. To the EPA, this did not seem to be what Congress intended; but under court order, it was required to do both. Similarly, the Department of Health, Education, and Welfare (HEW) apparently did not want to move against the Negro colleges of the South, now no longer segregated under law but still with predominantly black enrollments, nor was this in the interests of those colleges, or their students, or indeed anyone else—but Federal judges required HEW to do so.

In these, as in other cases, government is required to do what the Congress did not order it to do and may well oppose, what the executive does not feel it wise to do, and most important what it does not know how to do. How *does* one create that permanently racially balanced community that Judge Weinstein wants so that the schools may be permanently racially balanced? How does one create that good community in Boston public housing that Judge Garrity wants so that vandalism repair costs may be brought down to what the authority can afford? How does one rehabilitate prisoners? Or treat mental patients? Like Canute, the Judges decree the sea must not advance, and weary administrators—hectored by enthusiastic, if ignorant, lawyers for public advocacy centers—must go through the motions to show the courts they are trying.

Reconsidering the cyclical theory

A third feature of the new activism which is also extraordinary: The Court's actions now seem to arouse fewer angry reactions from the people and the legislatures. The power of the Court has been exercised so often and so successfully over the last 20 years, and the ability to restrict or control it by either new legislation, constitutional amendment, or new appointments has met with such uniform failure, that the Court, and the subordinate courts, are now seen as forces of nature, difficult to predict and impossible to control. Thus, one may contrast the outburst over the school prayer decisions of 1962-3 with the relative quietude of response to the abortion decisions of 1973. Or, contrast the effort to adopt a constitutional amendment to control the sweep of reapportionment decisions in 1964-66 with the general view in Congress today that any effort to control the Court on busing by means of a constitutional amendment has no chance of succeeding.

This is, of course, not necessarily witness to the strength of the Court as such: What it reflects, in addition, is the agreement of large sectors of opinion—even if it is still minority opinion—with the Court's actions. But this opinion in favor of the Court is shaped by the reserves of strength the Court possesses: the positive opinion of the Court in the dominant mass media—the national television news shows, the national news magazines, and the most influential newspapers; and the bias in its favor among the informed electorate generally, and among significant groups of opinion-leaders. The Court is further the beneficiary of two accidents of political history (or at least they may be accidents): Because he was running against Barry Goldwater, Lyndon Johnson had an overwhelming victory in 1964, and helped bring into office so many liberal Congressmen that the powerful effort to limit the Court on reapportionment was blunted. And because of the Watergate scandal, so many liberal Congressmen were returned to Congress in 1974 that the natural life of the activist cycle in the Court's history was extended at least two years, and perhaps longer. Thus this Congress will not start any amendment process to limit the Court on busing. (It is understood that liberal Congressmen today, as against our previous history, support the power of the Court. If new appointments bring about the expected conservative switch, that position may change.)

The key point, however, is that the major limitation on the Court's power—public opinion, expressing itself through the Presidency and the Congress—has not come into effect to limit this Court. Outrage at its actions was stronger 12 or 13 years ago than it is today, though the intrusive reach of the Court's actions into the daily life of citizens has become much stronger. Ironically, the President who once wanted to impeach Justice Douglas may well find that the Justice who has served longest on the Supreme Court may survive his own Presidential term.

What I am suggesting is that we must reconsider the theory that activist cycles are succeeded by quiescent ones. This belief was based on the view that public opinion in the end controls the Court, which has the power of neither purse nor sword, and that the Court is thus pretty much where the Founders and Chief Justice Marshall established it, as one of the three coequal branches of government, with great moral authority but little else. In contrast, it appears that the controls on Court power have become obsolescent and that the role of the Court—and courts generally—has changed significantly, such that the most powerful Court and Judiciary in the world have become even more powerful, raising questions of some gravity for the Commonwealth. Of course, any long-range view shortly may be made irrelevant by current events. Two more conservative appointments, one might think, and the Court will revert, only eight years later than one might have expected, to its quietistic phase, and President and Congress will resume their positions of dominance. But there are a number of other factors, which must at least be considered, which would argue that the matter is more serious.

The factors affecting the Court's power transcend, I believe, the question of the individual outlooks and philosophies of the present Justices or their potential successors. It is true that in an institution in which individuality is so dominant that 5-4 decisions on vital matters affecting the nation are common—with no apparent influence that can be exerted on the minority to change its vote so that the nation may accept these decisions with better grace—the character of individual Justices is not a matter to be taken lightly. However, there are three factors that argue that the activist phase of the present Court will not easily be reversed, and two of them are quite new.

The new Constitutional logic

The first factor is well-known and broadly discussed in the constitutional law literature: The Court must work out the logic of positions once taken, and it cannot easily withdraw from the implications of these positions. Thus, if "standing" to sue has been radically expanded so that many interests and individuals who in the past had no access to constitutional adjudication of their claims now have such access, a systemic change has occurred, and it is not possible to revert to an earlier, more restrictive view of "standing."

Whether one calls it a constitutional revolution or not—and such excellent analysts as Philip Kurland argue that there was substantial continuity by the Warren Court with past rulings—the power to enter litigation has been greatly expanded in recent years, and new rulings have been laid down on substantive issues which ensure that a great deal of new litigation will ensue to establish their bounds. Archibald Cox, writing from the perspective of his service as Solicitor General under Presidents Kennedy and Johnson—long before some of the most radical decisions were made, in the post-1971 Court—made this revealing summary of the situation in 1967:

The Warren Court has been quick to slough off the restraints its predecessors erected for deciding whether and when the Court will adjudicate constitutional issues. The precepts of wise constitutional adjudication that were taught law students in the 1930's counseled postponement and avoidance . . . interference with the work of a coordinate branch of the federal government or a sovereign state was thought justifiable only in cases of absolute necessity. The party attacking the statute had to show its unconstitutionality applied to him. . . . The plaintiff must demonstrate his standing by showing that he was injured. . . . Equity would not enjoin the enforcement of an allegedly unconstitutional statute where the unconstitutionality could be raised as a defense in a criminal prosecution, except in the most exceptional conditions. The constitutional battles of the 1930's were often fought on these procedural grounds. Those seeking to sustain new governmental activities . . . could rest satisfied with blocking judicial intervention. . . .

Today, the attitude is changed, and the rules of judicial self-restraint that looked to the avoidance of constitutional rulings have been eroded in opinions strongly suggesting that the present Court feels it has a responsibility to make its influence felt in support or check of other branches of government, or in innovation, even though not coerced by the necessities of litigation.

There is still some life in the old restraints, as we may see in the zoning case, where the Court in a 5-4 decision did not accept that inner-city residents in general were damaged by suburban zoning practices. But a Court cannot radically and totally ignore precedent, particularly when it has created expectations. It is still a court of law. And so, the logic of decisions once taken must be worked out. If due process is now something that must be taken into account not only by the legislatures and executives, but by schools and colleges and businesses, the logic of that position must be worked out. A line undoubtedly will be set at some point, but where that will be is uncertain.

Of course, it must be understood, it is not only the Court that expands the area of litigation through new rulings. Just as the executive is required by the Court to institute procedures and rulings and rights it would prefer not to (as in the case of the EPA), the establishment of new ground for legal action is also the result of legislative and executive action, and the courts must enforce these new laws. Thus the reach of due process is extended not only by the courts—though I believe they have played the largest roles—but by legislatures. The Colorado legislature has recently required due process in all cases of dismissal or non-renewal of appointment in many of the state's colleges—an act which has been described as instituting "instant tenure." Due process is even more significantly extended by executive action implementing legislation, as in the recent HEW guidelines implementing non-discrimination by sex in federally-supported education activities. As is known, these guidelines ban single-sex physical education classes (with certain exceptions), and require each school to set up grievance procedures for complaints of discrimination on grounds of sex. Many Congressmen thought this went beyond the legislation Congress had passed, but in 1975 there was a different Congress from that which passed the Higher Education Act in 1972—perhaps an aberrant Congress as a result of Watergate—and this Congress, it seems, will not intervene. In any case, once the elaborate process of legislation has worked its course, it is hard for Congress, owing to its clumsy and complex procedures, to control implementation of legislation by the executive, and it is impossible for Congress to control the interpretation by the judiciary of that implementation.

However, even if due process expands as a result not only of the actions of courts but also of legislatures and executives, it does so on the basis of the teaching of the Court, a teaching almost universally applauded by those who are considered qualified to judge. If

the circuit courts, the state courts. They are also taught by the Supreme Court. As the right to sue expands, as the meaning of due process and equal protection is broadened, more and more kinds of actions in the courts to expand the reach of social policy become possible.

Most cases, of course, never reach the Supreme Court. The law is then established under the lower courts and an egregious and unchallenged intrusiveness of the courts spreads under the general protection given by some larger decisions. Conceivably, the Supreme Court itself might find objectionable the actions of some lower court judge to implement its decisions. The Court, for example, might object to a lottery, decreed for school assignments by a Charlotte judge, which ties students to schools on the basis of race, regardless of their changes in residence; or to the banning of anti-busing meetings by a Denver judge; or to the ethnic quotas decreed for the selective secondary schools in Boston by a Boston judge; or to the same judge's wholesale recasting of the educational programs of the Boston school department and his requirement that contracts for unwanted advice be given by the financially burdened Boston schools to the colleges and universities in the Boston area, because the judge and his appointed experts thought that such advice might help the process of desegregation through busing. We could give many other examples of action that might or might not fall under the general guidelines set by the Supreme Court in key decisions. But even in the United States, litigation has its limits. Many of these issues will never come to the Supreme Court—or an overburdened Court may refuse to deal with them when they do, and lower court decisions will stand as the law.

We might envisage this first factor—working out the logic of positions already taken—as a kind of indigestion, in which a boa constrictor, having swallowed a goat, must allow it to go through its entire length to be absorbed. So must these new expansions in "standing," due process, equal protection, and the like work their way through the entire system. They are far from having done so.

The Court is committed to an activist posture, with great impact on various areas of life, by the expansion of the reach of the legal principles on the basis of which it operates. Some assert, and in some angry dissents Justices themselves charge, that no legal logic guides the Court—that it is simply legislating its views on difficult problems. If the Court truly has cut loose from legal principles, one may envisage either that it may continue in an activist posture steadily, or that, with the appointment of new conservative judges,

the Court expands due process in every sphere, and teaches that this is the teaching of the Constitution, then it is no surprise if legislatures and executives follow that teaching in good measure on their own.

Broadening the reach of legal principles

The logic of the wider expansion of "standing" and of due process and of equal treatment of the laws, we may be sure, has not yet been worked out: There is a good deal more to come. "More to come" means a continued and powerfully intrusive role for the courts that they cannot avoid. We have gone so far in just a few years that cautions uttered just a few years ago now seem archaic. Thus, eight years ago, Archibald Cox wrote with some discomfort on the expansion of the doctrine that private action came under constitutional protection if it involved a "state interest":

How could a court rule that discrimination at lunch counters violated the 14th Amendment without going on to rule that the amendment is also violated by discrimination in employment, in admitting pupils to private colleges, and in the sale and rental of housing? It would immeasurably advance the cause of human justice to have on the statute books open housing laws, fair employment practices acts, and the like; but it would be amazing to find that all the hard legislative fights were unnecessary and the will of the people is irrelevant because the legal requirements were long ago written into the 14th Amendment. . . .

Perhaps the consequence [of the expansion of the notion of state interest] should not frighten us . . . but I wonder whether we should not pay a heavy price in terms of the loss to the richness, variety, and the initiative of our present pluralistic society. . . .

Consider the effect upon educational institutions. Though few will defend racial discrimination, one can fairly ask whether Notre Dame should be barred from preferring Roman Catholics or Baylor from giving preference to Baptists. . . . Should [every school's or college's] admission practices and perhaps its examinations be subject to judicial scrutiny for due process of law?

Clearly all this, in large measure, has come to pass. A recent decision of the respected Second Circuit has decreed that actions by foundations also require due process—after all, foundations are set up under state law, are granted tax exemption, are regulated by legislation, etc. And so every disappointed grant-seeker will have access to a due process whose full dimensions will have to be determined by other courts and other cases.

The working out of the logic of a position is not only the work of the Supreme Court. It is also the work of the lower federal courts,

it will simply feel free to abandon the ground staked out by its predecessors and reverse precedents wholesale.

When government expands

But a second factor that sustains the permanent activism of the court is the enormous increase in the reach of government itself. When government expands, it could seem reasonable that the Court must extend its reach also. It must consider issues of equity and due process and equal protection in all the varied areas of education, health care, housing, and access to government services of all types. It must consider the varied impact of new subsidies, and controls and restrictions based on safety or environmental considerations. It is true that as government expands it sets up quasi-judicial bodies to adjudicate difficult decisions, but there is one major route of appeal in our system from these multifarious quasi-judicial bodies, and that is to the federal courts, and only one final appeal, to the Supreme Court. The expanded reach of government also means that new bases for decision-making by courts must be taken into account, that the "facts" on the basis of which lower courts rule become more and more complex. One murky realm opened up by this new complexity is the use of social science data—or perhaps some might say its misuse—as one side or another believes that the research findings of the moment support its position. To quote Archibald Cox again:

findings is not established for long, social science may "require" new laws when the findings which support old laws are overturned. For instance, social scientists now think they may well be able to make a case for deterrence, and the fragmentary findings that supported some part of the decisions on school desegregation steadily have become weaker.

The expanded reach of government not only explains a more activist Court; in the minds of many analysts, it also justifies it. Perhaps it does. But one reason it does is that courts are dissatisfied with how legislatures and executives run their respective spheres, and while they do not egregiously reach out to express their dissatisfaction—courts, after all, must wait for cases to come to them—when the cases do come to them, they stretch their hands out very far indeed to make corrections. Consider issues raised in some recent cases: inadequate medical treatment for prisoners; welfare to applicants delayed beyond some reasonable time; public housing poorly maintained and in poor repair; mental patients not receiving treatment. The courts and their defenders say that if the legislature and executive are incapable of action in these and similar cases, then the courts must act.

Modern psychology has raised doubts concerning freedom of the will that raise skepticism of the very notion of crime. Sociologists have cast doubt upon the efficacy of punishment and deterrence in the face of the social, economic, and psychological causes of criminal conduct. When an issue is nicely balanced between the interests of the public and the claims of individual liberty, the substitution of such doubts for once-accepted verities may be enough to tip the scales against the prosecution.

If this is true in criminal procedure, may not similar forces be partly responsible for the turmoil in other areas of constitutional law? . . . While the social scientists [are] changing our understanding of man . . . judges will inevitably be stimulated to reexamine the law's own presuppositions. One wonders, indeed, whether the gulf between the Supreme Court and the Congress is not partly a reflection of the closer kinship the justices have with the intellectual community.

However, as this passage will suggest to the 1975 reader, social science may provide successively new bases for new laws: Since the pattern of development in the social sciences is such that a set of

Going to the root of problems

There is much justice here. Ward Elliott, who has sharply criticized the activist role of the Court in the reapportionment cases in The Rise of Guardian Democracy, agrees that in some states there was extreme malapportionment, about which something should have been done by someone. Increasingly, however, the courts have gone beyond the wrong presented to them to sweepingly reorganize a complex service of government so that the wrong can be dealt with—in the Court's mind, at least—at its root. Thus, a judge might decree, "Let this prisoner receive adequate medical care"—or, as he did instead, go to experts to provide a complete program of medical services for prisons on the basis of what professionals asserted was necessary, a program which the state insisted it could not afford. A court could require that welfare recipients receive more rapid treatment, but what a federal judge in Massachusetts did was to suspend all federal government welfare reimbursements to the state until the state hired 255 more social workers.[2] If public hous-

[2] The Boston Globe reported (February 28, 1975) that the Legislature voted, under constraint to prevent the cutoff of federal welfare funds, to appropriate the funds to hire the social workers.

ing was demonstrated to be in poor repair, the judge could have said, "Fix it." But in this case, he enjoined the expenditure of other state funds for new housing, requiring that they be used for massive rehabilitation of old housing, appointed a master to determine the best way to repair and keep the house in repair, and suggested that the Boston Housing Authority didn't know how to create the kind of good community in which vandalism would not take place.[3] Similarly, judges are now determining with the aid of psychiatric experts what a proper system of psychiatric care in a mental hospital should be.

The justification in these and many other cases is that the legislature and executive won't act. This justification will not hold water. The legislature and executive have far more resources than the courts to determine how best to act. If they don't, it is because no one knows how to, or there is not enough money to cover everything, or because the people simply don't want it. These strike me as valid considerations in a democracy, but they are not considered valid considerations when issues of social policy come up as court cases for judgment. For example, no desegregation decision that I know of has been stayed by the fact that there is not enough money or that other school and educational services will suffer, perfectly valid considerations for legislatures, executives, and administrators —but the kind of consideration that no judge considers worthy of notice.

Having decided that the other two branches won't act, judges decide to act on their own, and increasingly are intrigued by the opportunity to go to the root of the problem. Unfortunately in many of these areas of social policy there is no clear knowledge of what the root of the problems is, though an expert can always be found who will oblige a judge with an appropriate program. A public health specialist will oblige the judge with a program for medical care that follows the standards of his professional association, standards that hardly any public body may be able to afford to meet or is interested to meet. And so with a psychiatrist, social work specialist, or school specialist. Clearly, if the judge has decided that the services in question are inadequate, or that they violate the constitution, or the laws, or the health code, or equal treatment, or whatever, he will find some expert who agrees with him.

Thus, the reach of government, already grossly expanded beyond its capacity to perform, is further expanded by the courts. Many elected officials now believe that government cannot deliver what has been promised in certain areas, either because of limited resources or knowledge; but it will be an interesting question whether the courts will now allow government to withdraw from these areas. Efforts to restrict welfare expenditure in those states where it has become a huge burden have been fought tooth and nail in the courts, and one may be sure that every other effort to withdraw from the provision of service will also be fought, by the professional advocacy centers now established to protect the rights of various groups of citizens and recipients of government benefits, and by the beneficiaries themselves. Much will depend on the temper of the courts, and on the guidance the Supreme Court gives.

The new litigation

Finally, there is a third factor which suggests that a highly activist and intrusive judiciary is now a permanent part of the American Commonwealth: The courts will not be allowed to withdraw from the broadened positions they have seized, or have been forced to move into, because of the creation of new and powerful interests, chief among them the public advocacy law centers. It can hardly be an accident that the failure of the expected conservative cycle to succeed the activist cycle of 1954-68 occurred at the same time that many new centers were established for the promotion of social change through litigation. At the beginning of the 1960's there apparently existed only one such center—the NAACP Legal Defense Fund. Under the Economic Opportunity Act, many poverty law centers were created. Many other centers, receiving government or foundation aid, were established in almost every field of social policy—welfare, education, housing, health, environment—and for almost every group of potential clients—Mexican-Americans, Puerto Ricans, Indians, prisoners, mental health patients, etc. Law for the pro-

United States District Judge Frank H. Freedman ordered the cutoff of Federal welfare funds—about $550 million a year. . . . But he said he would stay his order if the $1.2 million is approved this week. . . . He . . . threatened a new cutoff of funds if the state does not hire an additional 90 social workers before June 30. . . . The order for 90 more social workers, in addition to the 255, will force the Dukakis administration to file another deficiency budget. . . . Freedman also ordered that all new positions be carried over into the next fiscal year. In addition, he said that state must make permanent the 154 social worker job slots that are now covered under the federally-paid Comprehensive Employment Training Act (CETA).

[3] The Supreme Judicial Court of Massachusetts overruled the enjoining of state housing funds; what is interesting is that the lower court judge thought that he had the power to require state bond issues designed for one purpose to be used for another.

motion of social change became enormously popular with law students, and many sought posts in the new centers.

Of course, this revolutionary change in the landscape of the practice of law itself reflected broader changes: a rising critical attitude toward government, a widespread belief among many sectors of the population in the unfairness and unjustness of an adversary posture and denunciatory rhetoric—which all complemented nicely the standard practices of litigation. Law—for the purpose of the correction of presumed evils, for changing government practices, for overruling legislatures, executives, and administrators, for the purpose indeed of replacing democratic procedures with the authoritarian decisions of judges—became enormously popular. The number of law students rose rapidly, in response to new opportunities for litigation, and also serving as insurance of expanded litigation, owing to the increasing number of lawyers.

It is not easy to disentangle the complex web of elements that has created the powerful and permanent interests engaged in constitutional litigation to expand the scope and power of government; that these interests have been created, and have replaced those powerful business interests of the 1930's and 1940's that engaged in constitutional litigation to *restrict* the power of government, is not to be denied. In the social policy decisions of the courts, one sees many such interests at work: professional organizations, unions, clients, and recipients of benefits. Owing to changes in constitutional law, these interests now have greater access to the courts, concerning more grievances, than ever before. Public advocacy law firms may represent their interests, without the need for plaintiffs themselves to provide for their own legal fees. There is much in this situation which makes possible the separation of constitutional cases from any given client or interest. There are cases where the plaintiff seems to have disappeared—for example, the continuing effort to force the Southern states to eliminate the identifiably black character of their formerly segregated black colleges. But the cases lead a life of their own, with lawyers to argue them, with ghostly plaintiffs who never appear and, for all one knows, may not exist. Lawyers strive for objectives in the service of ideologies that cannot be realized through the legislative and executive functions of government but may be through the agency of authoritarian courts.

In all this there is much of the "guardian ethic" that Ward Elliott has characterized and criticized in his study of reapportionment. At first it was believed that a strict reapportionment of electoral districts on the basis of one man to one vote would shift some power to the cities or to the minorities who lived in them. Quite early it became clear it would not—at best it would help the conservative suburbs. In the event it turned out that it had almost no consequence at all. An ideological exercise was nevertheless carried out by those who thought they knew better, or who simply wanted to clean up the messiness of history and the past, unfortunately at the cost of stripping away the last shred of pretense that states had some degree of sovereignty, and by losing great stores of respect for the neutrality and objectivity of the courts. Other cases show the same insistence on uniformity that Elliott characterizes as part of the "guardian ethic": Thus, no one must pray or read the Bible in any school, even when there is no one to object.

But if the "guardian ethic" often became dissociated from any concrete interest, one must recognize that these concrete interests do exist. One must also recognize that they were encouraged to come into being and to grow by the explosion of publicly supported litigation for the establishment of new rights. People unaware of grievances—women, or prisoners, or welfare recipients, or Mexican-Americans—were educated to feel them by those who seemed to divine what those grievances should be, and even if they were insufficiently concerned to act on them, lawyers were readily available, paid for by government or foundations, to take up their interests. Moral fervor and outrage, properly aroused by great inequalities in American life—in particular, the legal and extra-legal subordination of Negroes—were transferred in the course of the 1960's to practices that most citizens did not think iniquitous or outrageous or improper at all.

Of course, people will disagree where iniquity ends and when moral outrage is unjustified. Some will be satisfied when the right to vote is guaranteed, others only when literacy laws are suspended, others only when literacy laws are translated into any language a voter may know, and voters form a perfect statistical cross section, by race and ethnicity and age, of the population. Some will be satisfied when discrimination is outlawed, others only when quotas by ethnicity and sex are set for every job. Some will be satisfied when prisoners and mental patients are not abused, others only when the procedures that they think will lead to rehabilitation or cure are imposed by the courts. The law, generally made by judges but with the assistance also of legislatures and administrators, has moved insensibly from the first of each of these alternatives, which is as far as anyone wanted to go 10 years ago, to the second.

In 1954 the Court abandoned prudence and for 15 years firmly and unanimously insisted that the segregation and degradation of the Negro must end. It succeeded, and eventually the legislative and executive branches came to its side and the heritage of unequal laws and unequal treatment was eliminated. That was indeed a heroic period in the history of the court. But even heroes may overreach themselves. It is now time for the Court to act with the prudence that must in a free society be the more regular accompaniment of its actions.

We may debate whether we have a better society or commonwealth or a worse one as a result. I believe we have a considerably worse one, because a free people feels itself increasingly under the arbitrary rule of unreachable authorities, and that cannot be good for the future of the state. Even the guardians of the "guardian ethic"—the better educated, the establishment, the opinion-makers—are now doubtful of many of the rulings they urged when, unable to institute them through the elected representatives of the people, they made law through recourse to the courts. But in the meantime the great fund of respect and trust by the people for governmental institutions has been drawn down; the courts, trying to create a better society, have increasingly lost the respect and trust of the people—which in the end is what sustained and must sustain the remarkable institution of a supreme judiciary in American life. Even in 1965, McCloskey could write, "Judicial realism' has eroded the traditional mystique that often lent authority in other days. . . ." That trust is considerably further eroded 10 years later. "To construe the law," Bryce wrote of the Supreme Court, "that is, to elucidate the will of the people as supreme lawgiver, is the beginning and end of their duty." Bryce then adds in a footnote:

'Suppose, however,' someone may say 'that the court should go beyond its duty and import its own views of what ought to be the law into its decision as to what is the law. This would be an exercise of judicial will.' Doubtless, it would, but it would be a breach of duty, would expose the court to the distrust of the people, and might, if repeated or persisted in a serious matter, provoke resistance to the law as laid down by the court.

We have seen efforts at resistance: All have failed, and there is little enough now. Some may see this as the triumph of law instituting justice; I suspect it is rather the apathy of cynical and baffled people, incapable of seeing what actions may release them from the toils of the intrusive courts.

A final quotation from Bryce:

In America the Constitution is at all times very hard to change: much more then must political issues turn on its interpretation. And if this be so, must not the interpreting court be led to assume a control over the executive and legislative branches of government, since it has the power of declaring their acts illegal?

There is ground for these criticisms. The evil they point to has occurred and may recur. But it occurs very rarely, and may be averted by the same prudence which the courts have hitherto generally shown.

1. What are the three perspectives on the role of the courts which Glazer has identified?

2. How does the performance of the Supreme Court since the addition of the Nixon appointees (Burger, Blackmun, Powell, and Rehnquist) support Glazer's perspective?

3. What are the three characteristics of the Burger Court which Glazer takes as evidence of a permanent change in the role of the Supreme Court?

4. What three reasons are offered to explain why the Supreme Court, in Glazer's opinion, will remain permanently activist?

5. What does Glazer mean by the 'guardian ethic'?

DISCUSSION OF READING #3 QUESTIONS

1. Glazer claims that lawyers and judges tend to see court decisions as flowing logically from the Constitution or statutes. Therefore, since the courts are only 'unveiling a rule that existed all along' there is no cause for concern over the fact that courts seem to be penetrating ever more deeply into the policymaking process. Political scientists, on the other hand, tend to see the court's role as part of a never-ending shifting back and forth between periods of relative activism and relative passivity dependent upon changes in public opinion and the political climate. The third perspective, which is Glazer's view, suggests that American courts have taken on a new role, one of permanent activism. Neither public opinion, nor the legislature or the executive can effectively restrain what might be termed a 'runaway' court. Today, Glazer argues, the courts "reach into the lives of the people, against the will of the people, deeper than they ever have in American history."

2. Despite the expectation that the four Nixon appointments to the Court would reverse the activist trend set under the leadership of Chief Justice Earl Warren, a number of major activist decisions have been handed down. The Swann decision upholding busing in certain circumstances, the Griggs decision which required that employment tests which resulted in the exclusion of minorities had to be clearly 'job-related' in order to stand, the abortion decision, and many others were made by the Burger Court which everyone said would not take so active a role in policymaking. Rarely have the Nixon appointees voted as a bloc in opposition to the justices who had been part of the Warren Court surge of judicial activism.

3. a. Unlike previous periods of Court activism in which conservative Courts voted to restrain liberal Congresses and Presidents, during the Eisenhower years, 1952-1960, we saw a liberal Court opposing a conservative President. This opposition continues even after a conservative President (Nixon) tried to remake the Court in his own political image.

   b. Unlike previous periods of Court activism in which Courts sought to prevent the other branches of government from taking action, the Warren and Burger Courts have sought to extend the role of other branches of government even when they did not desire to act.

   c. Unlike previous periods of Court activism during which there were frequent public outcries and Congressional or Presidential efforts to curb the Court's power, there are relatively few serious efforts today. Glazer concludes, ". . .it appears that the role of the Court--and courts generally--has changed significantly, such that the most powerful Court and Judiciary in the world have become even more powerful, raising questions of some gravity for the Commonwealth."

4. a. Legal reasoning dictates that positions once taken must generally be followed in future cases. Therefore, as the logic of recent Court decisions unfolds, more and more will be brought under the judicial umbrella. As Glazer vividly puts it, "We might envisage this first factor--working out the logic of positions already taken-- as a kind of indigestion, in which a boa constrictor, having swallowed a goat, must allow it to go through its entire length to be absorbed.

So must these expansions in 'standing', due process, equal protection, and the like work their way through the entire system. They are far from having done so."

b. The growth in the role of government leads to a corresponding growth in the role of the judiciary. The more that government undertakes, the more charges of unfairness there will be. The more rules which government promulgates, the more interpretations will be required.

c. Litigants will not permit the intrusive courts to back away from their expanded position. The new legal consciousness of everyone from Mexicans and Puerto-Ricans to homosexuals, singles, mental patients, and consumers will produce a never-ending parade of cases which courts will be unable to ignore.

5. Glazer suggests that a type of paternalistic attitude has emerged in which the Court 'takes care of' us whether we need it or not. What began with the civil rights movement has spread to completely different areas of American life. The idea that sensitive liberals and activist attorneys had an obligation to bring injustice to the attention of the Courts who, in turn, had an obligation to correct these injustices constitutes the 'guardian ethic'. While not denying the tremendous contribution made by courts to the civil rights movement, Glazer suggests that, "moral fervor and outrage. . .were transferred in the course of the 1960's to practices that most citizens did <u>not</u> think iniquitous, outrageous, or improper at all."

A final thought on Glazer's article: Go back and re-read the very last sentence. If it is his argument that there are permanent changes in the Court's role which are the result of powerful forces, don't you think it strange that he implies that the solution can be found by the Court simply acting with prudence?!

UNIT STUDY QUESTIONS

To help you to draw together the ideas expressed in the Unit and to begin to formulate your own opinions on the questions raised by the various authors, complete the exercises below. After you have written your answers, read the sample answers that have been prepared for you. They will serve as a model for assessing your own responses as well as a summary of some of the central arguments of the unit.

Facts

Law and Society student, Seymour Tasks, filed suit in federal court claiming that his instructor's examination violated the "due process" clause of the constitution because it asked questions about material which the student had no notice he would be expected to know. The Pennsylvania Supreme Court decision is expected this month.

Question 1

Based upon the materials in Unit 7, what do you think this case illustrates about the role of law in American society?

American legal culture tends to be highly supportive of legal institutions and legal solutions to problems. It is not surprising, therefore, to find a dissatisfied External studies Student defining his poor performance as a consequence of the deprivation of his constitutional rights. Furthermore, the American propensity toward natural law or natural rights approaches makes it likely that the student will find this approach quite reasonable. After all, if the instructor was in error then the student has a right to have his low grade altered. The case also is further evidence of the growing American reliance on law for solving all types of disputes.

Toffler might view this case as further evidence of the decline of social order. The law ultimately cannot successfully hold together the educational order if the teacher-student relationship is re-defined as an adversary relationship to be judged according to legal rights and duties. Other means will have to be developed (see Unit 4, for example) to solve these types of disputes.

Facts

A white male, aged 29, seeks admission to the University of Pittsburgh Medical School. He is refused admission and he sues the University alleging that the special admissions program for minority students resulted in race discrimination against him. He claims that the reservation of places in the freshman class for minority students only constitutes discrimination against whites on the basis of race. After the Pennsylvania Supreme Court held that the University program was discriminatory, the University appealed to the United States Supreme Court which will issue a ruling next week.

Question 2

Drawing upon the mini-lectures and readings by Toffler, Glazer, and Sheppard, discuss the following:

a. Is the Supreme Court able to handle this problem effectively?

and

b. What is the long run implication of the Supreme Court deciding cases like this?

NOTE: DO NOT concern yourself with what the court might say. This is a separate issue to be addressed in Unit 9.

I.   The Supreme Court is asked in this case to make a dramatic
public policy decision which will have ramifications for racial
policies in America for decades to come. While such reliance on
Courts is common in America, it is not desirable. As pointed out in
'The American Reliance on Law,' this is a problem which might be
better defined as political, social, or economic rather than strictly
legal. Furthermore, to allow an unrepresentative, unelected body of
9 persons to make so wrenching a social choice is undemocratic. The
'imperical judiciary' continues to dominate our political life beyond
acceptable limits.

       Toffler would argue that the Court cannot produce social order
anyway by issuing dramatic decisions. In fact, the decision in this
case--whicever way it goes--will result in _more_ government regulation,
more guidelines, _more_ racial tension, _less_ order and _less_ justice.

       The idea of the 'politics of rights' suggests that the Court
will be unsuccessful--at least in the short run--in achieving its goals--
whatever they turn out to be. Political pressures from civil rights
groups will continue to mount if the 'affirmative action' plan of the
University is struck. Conversely white groups will subvert the implementation of further such special preference plans if this one is
upheld.

       Additionally, the Court is intrinsically not well equipped to
adjudicate a broad social dispute of this sort. By focusing exclusively
(and necessarily) upon Pitt and the rejected medical student, the Court
will fail to examine many alternatives and fail to consider many consequences. Pitt's program probably is quite different from many others
which will be affected by the decision. Finally, it is most likely
impractical to either order the end to or foster further development of
such programs. Politics, not law, must dictate the extent to which
affirmative action programs can be expanded or restricted.

       Sheppard might conclude that the court must make this critical
decision because the rights of Americans must be protected in order
to avoid revolution. But on this issue, a large portion of Americans
are likely to feel that their rights have been ignored whatever happens!

       Yet despite alleged limitations on law and despite suggestions
that law cannot re-create social order, perhaps America's basic inclination
toward natural law and human rights should prevail. After all, if
legislators refuse to deal with sensitive issues and individual rights
have been violated, then the Supreme Court must and should read the
constitution and decide which rights must prevail under its language.

       Courts cannot, it is true, solve all human dilemmas. But they
are prefereable to bloodshed, political turmoil, and politcally popular
but morally wrong solutions.

REFERENCES

Albrecht, S. Cognitive barriers to equal justice before the law. Un-
    published manuscript, 1974.

Arons, S., & Katsh, E. How t.v. cops flout the law. Saturday Review,
    March 19, 1977, pp. 11-18.

Bouma, D. Kids and cops. Grand Rapids: Erdmans, 1969.

Black, D. The mobilization of law. Journal of Legal Studies, January 1973,
    pp. 125-149.

Casey, G. The Supreme Court and myth. Law and Society Review, 1974, 8,
    385-

Cox, A. The role of the Supreme Court in American government. New York:
    Oxford, 1976.

Curran, B., & Spalding, F. The legal needs of the public. Chicago: American
    Bar Association, 1974.

Dahl, R. Democracy in the United States. Chicago: Rand McNally, 1972.

Dolbeare, K. The public views the Supreme Court. In H. Jacob, (Ed.), Law,
    Politics and the Federal courts. Boston: Little Brown, 1967.

Dolbeare, K., & Edelman, M. American Politics. Lexington: D.C. Heath, 1977.

Easton, D., & Dennis, J. Children in the political system. New York: McGraw
    Hill, 1969.

Fineberg, J. The nature and value of rights. The Journal of Value Inquiry,
    1970, 4, 252-253.

Friedman, L. Law and society. Englewood Cliffs: Prentice Hall, 1977.

Glazer, N. Towards an imperial judiciary? The Public Interest, 1975, 41,
    104-123.

Greenberg, E. Orientations of black and white children to political authority.
    Social Science Quarterly, 1970, 51, 562-

Hess, R., & Torney, J. The development of political attitudes in children.
    Chicago: Aldine, 1967.

Horowitz, D. The courts and social policy. Washington: Brookings Institution,
    197.

Jacob, H. Justice in America (3rd ed.). Boston: Little, Brown, and
    Company, 1978

Kessel, J. Public perceptions of the Supreme Court. Midwest Journal of
    Political Science, 1966, 10, 167-

The Michigan Law Review Editors. Legal knowledge of Michigan citizens. _Michigan Law Review_, 1463.

A motivational study of public attitudes and law office management. St. Louis: Missouri Bar, 1963.

Pennock, R., & Chapman, J. _The limits of law_. New York: Lieber Atherton, 1974.

Prothro, J., & Grigg, C. Fundamental principles of democracy. _Journal of Politics_, 1960, _22_, 276-

Sarat, A. Studying the American legal culture: an assessment of survey evidence. _Law and Society review_, Winter 1977, pp. 427-488.

Scheingold, S. _The politics of rights_. New Haven: Yale University Press, 1974.

Sheppard, A. T. _Post revolutionary law and society_. Presentation to American Legal Studies Association Annual Meeting, March 1978.

Sigler, J. _American rights policies_. Homeword: Dorsey Press, 1975.

Stouffer, S. _Communism, conformity, and civil liberties_. New York: Doubleday, 1955.

Tapp, J., & Kohlberg, L. Developing senses of law and legal justice. _Journal of Social Issues_, 1971, _27_, 65-

Tapp, J., & Levine, F. Persuasion to virtue. _Law and Society Review_, 1970, _4_, 565-

Tocqueville, A. de. _Democracy in America_. New York: Kropf, 1944.

Toffler, A. The future of law and order. _Encounter_, July 1973, pp. 13-23.

Walker, Darlene, et al, Contact and support: an empirical assessment of public attitudes toward the police and courts, _North Carolina Law Review_, 1972, _51_, 43-

Wilson, W. C. Belief in freedom of speech and press. _Journal of Social Issues_, 1975, _31_, 69-

UNIT 8

Law And Psychiatry

Rationale

In Units 1 and 2 you learned that one of the major functions of law
is to provide institutions and procedures for resolving disputes and achieving
a degree of social control. You also examined the legal culture in the United
States and the American tendency to rely on the courts to provide answers to
an ever expanding array of political, social, economic, moral, and interpersonal questions and conflicts. Glazer's notion of the "imperial judiciary",
Toffler's discussion of the inability of law to produce a stable social order
in post-industrial America, Horowitz's analysis of the inherent weaknesses
of courts which he terms "judicial incapacity", and Scheingold's formulation
of the "politics of rights" all point toward one conclusion: that the faith
that Americans have in law and their willingness to allow the legal system
to decide virtually all major public policy controversies are not matched
by any corresponding ability of the legal system to fulfill these expectations.

Having identified the social control function of law, however, we can
easily forget that there are many other institutions and systems which provide
mechanisms of social control. The concepts of mental 'health' and mental
'illness' as employed by psychiatrists can be powerful mechanisms of social
control--though we tend not to think of them in that fashion. Psychiatric
conclusions, for example, which result in a lifetime spent in a mental institution differ little, if at all, from legal conclusions which result in a
lifetime spent in prison. Thus, the practice of psychiatry can be considered

a means of achieving social control--more similar to the criminal justice system in its impact on people than it is to the traditional practice of medicine. The point is that by emphasizing the social control function of law, we tend to assume that <u>most</u> social control is effected through the legal system. In this unit you will study the social control function of psychiatry and try to decide if psychiatry is properly involved in such matters or if it is being used to bypass and usurp the proper job of the legal system.

As is evident from a review of the literature in this area, the main argument for moving away from the legal model to the psychiatric model for dealing with those people who are presumed to be 'sick' is that such people are in need of 'treatment,' 'care,' and 'help' which are best provided by experts and administrators who are not hamstrung by the technicalities of traditional adjudicatory mechanisms. In other words, if a person 'needs treatment,' then to waste a great deal of time talking about his or her 'rights' and the proper legal procedures serves merely to delay the rendering of such badly needed 'treatment.' The use of psychiatry versus the use of legality to achieve social control represents the ". . .revision of traditional mechanisms in the direction of a nonadversary and expert-administered process" (Schur, 1968, p. 198).

Before agreeing too quickly with the arguments of Units 1 and 2 concerning the limits of the legal system, the idea that law <u>cannot</u> meet all of our needs, and the view that we <u>rely excessively</u> on the law, you should read the materials in this unit with great care. In this discussion of law and psychiatry you will see that the underlying theme is that the idea of mental 'illness' as 'diagnosed' by doctors is utilized to <u>avoid</u> the law and the legal system. Whereas the argument of earlier units has been that we use law <u>too much</u>, the argument of this unit is that <u>we do not use law enough</u>.

Objectives

After you have completed all of tasks in this unit you should be able to do the following:

1. Define the following concepts:

    a. mental illness--in Szasz' view

    b. mental illness--in Schoenfeld's view

374

c. literalization of metaphor

d. medical model

e. right to treatment

f. insanity defense

g. incompetency to stand trial

h. involuntary hospitalization or involuntary commitment

i. problems in living.

2. State and explain Szasz' ideas on mental illness and the law.

3. State three criticisms of Szasz' ideas and then state how Szasz would refute each.

4. Describe the Rosenhan study and how it realtes to Szasz' and Schoenfeld's views of mental illness.

5. Describe the implications of Rosenhan's study for determining the appropriate role of law versus psychiatry in achieving and maintaining social control (i.e. should we use psychiatry to bypass the legal system?).

6. Describe the role played by psychiatrists in court.

7. Apply Szasz' perspective in an analysis of a given psychiatric legal situation.

8. Describe how psychiatry is used as a means of social control.

Overview

In this unit you will be studying the relationship between law and psychiatry. Some writers see the problem as one arising out of the tension between the need for legality and the need for expert decision making. On the one hand, we wish to guarantee the integrity of the legal process by requiring that all formal and procedural technicalities be adhered to before people are deprived of their freedom and placed in mental institutions. But on the other hand, the desire to 'help' and to provide services to 'sick' people requires that we bypass the legal technicalities in order to place these 'sick' people as rapidly as possible under the care of psychiatrists and other experts. If a psychiatrist has already determined that a person suffers from paranoid schizophrenia, it makes little sense to allow that person's attorney to delay his or her receiving that care by raising technical objections to hearsay evidence, constitutional guarantees of one sort and another, and so on. Thomas Szasz, the psychiatrist whose ideas will dominate our discussion of this problem disagrees. Szasz argues that the psychiatrist, in fact, is <u>not</u> as expert on such matters at all. Therefore, the tension which many see between the need for legality and the need for expertise disappears; if there are no experts, there is no tension! This line of thinking will become clear to you as you read through the materials about Szasz, answer the Study Guide questions, and read my discussions. Before exploring these issues, I have provided you with a mini-lecture describing the current role played by psychiatrists in court.

Thomas Szasz is a psychiatrist who maintains that there is no such thing as mental 'illness.' The use of the term 'illness,' according to Szasz, represents what he calls the literalization of a metaphor. Reading #2, "Psychiatry and Crime: The Contribution of Thomas Szasz," is an attempt to summarize the enormous volume of books, essays, and articles written by Dr. Szasz in his ongoing battle with institutional psychiatry. After exploring Szasz's contention that institutional psychiatry hides behind the mask of medicine while it controls human behavior and deprives its victims of their freedom, the paper discusses the implications of such a view for particular legal problems, such as the insanity defense, incompentency to stand trial, civil commitment, the right to treatment, and victimless crimes. I think that Szasz' views may shock you, and I know that they will intrigue you. As you will readily detect in Reading #2, the authors are highly sympathetic to these views. You, of course, need not be persuaded in the least and should have no reservations about writing critical (or even hostile) comments in the margins!

Readings #3 and #4 offer you an exchange of views on Szasz' theories. First you will read a critique of Szasz written by C.G. Schoenfeld, a prominent attorney and the Book Review Editor of <u>The Journal of Psychiatry and Law.</u> You will see in his analysis some of the arguments which are commonly made against Szasz; other arguments are presented in Reading #2. Juxtaposed to Schoenfeld in Reading #4 is a point by point refutation of these arguments. I hope that reading these two articles will enable you to make some judgment on your own as to the relative merits of the two positions. The final required article, Reading #5, is a fascinating account of an experiment which purports to test the ability of psychiatrists in state mental hospitals to distinguish 'sick' persons from 'well' persons. Rosenhan's study will stimulate your thinking, I hope, about the nature of mental 'illness' and the role of psychiatry in social control. If you wish, you might then read the satiric optional reading, Reading #6, to see how Szasz can be distorted for humorous ends!

In reading the materials in this unit, try to identify precisely what arguments are being made and the precise nature of the disagreements between Szasz and his many critics. Do they really address the same questions or are they frequently talking past one another? Bear in mind that the overall question for you revolves around the proper role of psychiatry and of law. If Szasz is correct and mental 'illness' is only a myth, then psychiatrists would have no basis for undertaking the awesome responsibility of deciding who and under what circumstances a person ought to be deprived of his or her liberty by being incarcerated in a state institution. On the other hand, if Szasz is wrong, then physicians, rather than lawyers and judges, ought to have the flexibility to treat their patients however they see fit.

Study Task Checklist

☐ 1. A. Read Mini-Lecture #1, "Psychiatrists in Court."

☐ 1. B. Answer the Study Questions and compare your answers with the Discussion of them.

☐ 2. A. Study Reading #1, "Law, Language, and Forensic Psychiatry," by Lee S. Weinberg and Richard E. Vatz.

☐ 2. B. Answer the Study Questions and compare your answers with the Discussion of them.

☐ 3. A. Study Reading #2, "A Analysis of the Views of Thomas S. Szasz" by C. G. Schoenfeld.

☐ 3. B. Answer the Study Questions and compare your answers with the Discussion of them.

☐ 4. A. Study Reading #3, "Szasz and the Law: An Alternate View" by Lee S. Weinberg and Richard E. Vatz.

☐ 4. B. Answer the Study Questions and compare your answers with the Discussion of them.

☐ 5. A. Study Reading #4, "On Being Sane in Insane Places" by D. L. Rosenhan.

☐ 6.   At this point you may enjoy reading the Optional Reading, "A Szaszian View of Death, or the Myth of Death" by Richard E. Vatz and Lee S. Weinberg.

☐ 7.   Complete the Unit Assignment.

Mini-Lecture #1

PSYCHIATRISTS IN COURT

Before you begin the rest of the readings it is important that you understand something about the role played by psychiatrists in legal proceedings, the central types of legal proceedings with which we will be concerned, and the relevant substantive law.

Psychiatrists are asked to testify in court for several reasons. Sometimes the psychiatrist is asked to testify about a 'diagnosis', 'treatment', or 'prognosis' for his or her own 'patient'. At other times the psychiatrist is asked by either the state, the court, or an individual defendant to provide expert opinion on the mental condition of the defendant either at the time of an alleged offense or at the time of trial. At still other times the psychiatrist is asked to testify with respect to standards of psychiatric practice or to express an opinion on a relevant issue in the case. Such expert witnesses are paid a fee as compensation for time spent in preparing and presenting their opinons. It is generally easy to find expert testimony on both sides of most questions.

In all of these situations the psychiatrist merely provides the court with so-called "expert" knowledge. The judge or jury is never required to follow the advice of the experts. The psychiatric expert witness has no power to order any particular result. In fact, however, courts typically rely quite heavily--if not completely--on psychiatric testimony. The reason for this dependence is that judges and juries usually believe that psychiatrists are uniquely qualified to make decisions about the lives of people who are 'mentally ill'. Given this reliance on psychiatric expertise, the legal system tends to informally relinquish its decision making power while formally retaining complete control.

Psychiatrists are involved in many types of legal proceedings. They are often asked to give opinions on whether or not an individual was 'of sound mind' when executing a will or signing a contract. They may be asked to given an opinion on the extent of psychological harm suffered by a party to a personal injury case. They may become involved in child abuse or child custody cases in terms of assessments of the mental condition of the parents or the mental consequences for the child. In fact, psychiatrists are found testifying in almost every type of case that comes before our courts.

In this unit, however, you will read primarily about incompetency to stand trial, the insanity defense, and the involuntary civil commitment. In the hearing to determine competency to stand trial the issue revolves around the criminal defendant's mental state at the time of his or her trial. Basic notions of fairness which dictate against trying an individual who is not present in the courtroom are said also to dictate against trying a person suffering from a mental 'illness'. The test of whether or not people are sufficiently mentally impaired involve their capacity to understand the nature of the charges against them and their capacity to help their lawyers prepare proper defenses. If found incompetent to stand trial, the defendant is given time to regain his or her competency, at which time the trial is begun. The role of the psychiatrist at a competency hearing is to give an opinion on the defendant's present mental condition. Again, while the court retains full authority over this matter, the opinion of the psychiatrist is going to probably determine the result.

The second area about which you will read a great deal is the insanity defense in a criminal trial. The insanity defense involves the question of criminal responsibility and, therefore, focuses on the mental state of the accused at the time he or she allegedly committed the crime. The standard or test of insanity varies from jurisdiction to jurisdiction.

The three most common tests of insanity are the M'Naghten Rule, the Durham Rule, and the Model Penal Code Rule. The M'Naghten Rule emerged out of the 1843 trial in Britain of Daniel M'Naghten who was charged with the murder of Edward Drummond, Sir Robert Peel's secretary. Following his acquittal by reason of insanity and his subsequent incarceration in a mental institution, the British House of Lords announced that a finding of insanity required that ". . .it must be clearly proved that, at the time of committing the act, the party accused was laboring under such a defect of reason, from disease of the mind, as not to know the nature and quality of the act he was doing or, if he did know it, that he did not know what he was doing was wrong." The psychiatrist, then, can testify as to whether a person, at the time of the offense, was mentally disabled and whether the criminal act resulted from that mental disability.

The 1954 Durham Rule states that ". . .an accused is not criminally responsible if his unlawful act was the product of a mental disease or defect." The Durham Rule was an effort to 'liberalize' the M'Naghten Rule by making it somewhat easier to successfully plead the insanity defense. The psychiatrist under the Durham Rule need not be concerned with whether or not the accused knew what he or she was doing or whether or not he knew that it was wrong; the psychiatrist is free to testify on the mental condition of the accused in 'medical' terms which are familiar to him or her.

The third test is the American Law Institute's Model Penal Code test which states that ". . .a person is not responsible for criminal conduct if at the time of such conduct as a result of mental disease or defect he lacks substantial capacity either to appreciate the criminality [wrongfulness] of his conduct or to conform his conduct to the requirements of law."

Each of these tests of insanity and the subtle variations of them in different states provide the legal framework within which psychiatrists operate in the courtroom. It is not my purpose here to devote a great deal of time to an analysis of the various legal criteria for successfully pleading insanity or the various evidentiary problems involved in the plea. I only wish to familiarize you with the relationship between psychiatrists and these two types of criminal proceedings so that you can understand the significance of the materials which follow.

Finally, you will see reference made in this unit to the involuntary commitment hearing, a civil action in which people who have violated no law are sent to 'hospitals' and confined there against their will. Here the psychiatrist will typically be employed to give an opinion on whether a person is likely to be harmful to himself or herself or to others. Once again, the psychiatrist is presumed to possess expert medical knowledge which will enable him or her to make such a prediction.

In all of these legal settings, remember that the psychiatrist is formally only offering his or her medical opinion. It is this medical claim of expertise which comes under heavy attack in the readings which follow.

1. Of what importance is the testimony of expert witnesses in court?

2. On what types of issues are psychiatrists typically asked to give an expert opinion?

3. What are the key differences between the issue of incompetency to stand trial and the insanity defense?

4. What are the three major legal tests for insanity?

1. The testimony of the expert witness is important because judges and juries tend to believe that the 'expert' is better qualified than they are to make the right decision. However, technically, the expert's opinion is purely to advise and inform the judge and jury who have no obligation to take his/her advice or rely on his/her information.

2. Psychiatrists testify on issues of mental capacity to write a will or contract, psychological effects on children of various family law decisions, competency to stand trial, and insanity of criminal defendents. The point is that psychiatrists are now presumed capable of testifying in a wide range--if not unlimited range--of legal issues.

3. The incompetency to stand trial issue concerns the defendant's mental state at the time of trial; the insanity plea relates to his/her mental state at the time of the crime. The test for incompetency relates to the defendant's ability to understand and cooperate enough to receive a fair trial; the insanity tests relate to whether he/she ought to be held legally responsible for a criminal act which he/she committed.

4. The major tests of insanity in use today are the M'Naghten Rule, the Durham Rule, and the Model Penal Code Rule.

Law, Language, and Forensic Psychiatry*

*Lee S. Weinberg***
*Richard E. Vatz****

INTRODUCTION

As therapeutic models and psychiatric explanations of criminal behavior increasingly dominate both theoretical and applied criminology, the "heretical" challenges posed by Dr. Thomas Szasz[1] take on new significance. Too frequently, the growing awareness of the potential implications of Dr. Szasz' views of criminology, law, and the operation of the criminal justice system manifests itself in attacks which either misconstrue or misrepresent Szasz' rich theoretical framework.

In this article, we seek to explicate the theoretical perspective of Thomas Szasz, identify common misconceptions held by his critics, and examine the implications of his views for five ethical/legal issues in the operation of the criminal justice system: 1) the plea of "not guilty by reason of insanity," 2) the newly announced right of the mentally ill to treatment, 3) the finding of incompetency to stand trial, 4) the involuntary civil commitment process, and 5) the concept of victimless crimes. The scope of Szasz' theory and its implications for our philosophies and institutions of criminal justice can hardly be overstated. Furthermore, it is our view that reforms consistent with Szasz' theoretical perspective would produce a more effective, more just, more respected, and more humane system of criminal justice.

THE MYTH OF MENTAL ILLNESS

The underlying theme woven into each of Szasz' books[2] and arti-

---

* Prepared for the Academy of Criminal Justice Sciences annual meeting in New Orleans, March 9-11, 1978.

** Professor, University of Pittsburgh, J.D., Ph.D.

*** Professor, Towson State University, Ph.D.

1. Thomas S. Szasz is Professor of Psychiatry at the State University of New York Upstate Medical Center.

2. For an index of Szasz's major works, see Vatz & Melia, *Bibliographic Essay*, Q. J. SPEECH (1977). Particular reference is made to T. SZASZ, THE MYTH OF MENTAL ILLNESS (1961).

cles is that mental "illness" is a myth. Szasz argues that use of the medical model is a pretense by which psychiatrists claim to understand behavior which we find strange or frightening. In fact, the medical model primarily serves to accredit or discredit certain behaviors. A somewhat extended discussion of Szasz' views is necessary for worthwhile debate on their implications for the criminal justice system.

Szasz maintains that mental "illness" is not illness at all; rather, "illness" is used metaphorically to refer disapprovingly to socially disvalued behaviors. The problem in the metaphoric use of the term "illness" is that we have erroneously taken it literally when used in conjunction with the term "mental." "Illness" metaphors in other contexts, indeed most metaphors, are seen for what they are. For example, a headline in a recent New York Times article concerning a prolific author states, "For Edna O'Brien, Writing is a Kind of Illness,"[3] but no one would believe that medical help was needed. Yet, while "mental illness" is similarly nonmedical, we immediately summon physicians to "treat" this behavior which we do not like or understand. As Szasz states: "[N]ot only is there not a shred of evidence to support [the idea that mental illness is akin to physiological disease], but, on the contrary, all the evidence is the other way, and supports the view that what people now call mental illnesses are, for the most part, communications expressing unacceptable ideas, often framed in an unusual idiom."[4]

The literalization of the "illness" metaphor allows the medical community to intrude upon the lives of those deemed to be "ill." It was generally accepted that David Berkowitz, the "Son of Sam" killer must have been "sick" to have killed innocent teenagers in an apparently random fashion. Thus, having been defined as "ill," he was immediately "examined" by doctors and "diagnosed." In effect, there is a compounded literalization of metaphor as the mentally "ill" are "diagnosed" and "treated" instead of punished.

Psychiatrists erroneously assume, argues Szasz, that behavior, thought, and beliefs are chemically or neurologically caused. Yet it has not, and probably cannot, be demonstrated that there is a one-to-one correspondence between particular neurological or chemical occurrences and particular beliefs. While not maintaining that be-

---

3. N.Y. Times, Oct. 11, 1977, at 42.
4. T. SZASZ, IDEOLOGY AND INSANITY 19 (1970) [hereinafter cited as IDEOLOGY].

havior takes place in a chemical vacuum, Szasz argues that any behavior may or may not be accompanied by particular chemical events, and that no particular chemical events have ever been associated with particular behaviors.

Additionally, Szasz distinguishes disease or illness from mental "illness" through the recognition of the differing role played by symptoms in each. For example, if a person has pains in his chest, the symptoms may point to the presence of coronary heart disease. However, in mental "illness," the "symptom" points to nothing. In fact the symptom *is* the disease. Only in the case of mental "illness" is a symptom taken as sufficient evidence for the conclusion that illness is present.[5]

ETHICS AND MEDICINE

Two areas of ethical concern arise from the use of the medical model in dealing with deviant social behavior. First is the problem of the ethical defensibility of psychiatrists pretending, through the clever use of language, to be something which they are not. As Szasz suggests, psychiatry has managed to clothe itself in "the logic, the imagery, and the rhetoric of science, and especially medicine."[6] This deception, whether conscious or unconscious, results in unrequested "therapeutic" interventions and serious deprivations of liberty. Second, and of far more concern, is the covert ethical judgment inherent in each psychiatric "diagnosis" of mental "illness." According to Szasz, to say that an individual is mentally "ill" entails a covert judgment about either reality or ethics. For example, David Berkowitz' claim that he was directed by "Sam" to commit murder justifies a finding of mental "illness" *only* if we do not believe that he did receive such instructions,[7] and if we deny the possibility of his strategic lying. Thus, a disagreement about "reality" is a necessary component of this "diagnosis," unlike a diagnosis of lung cancer or kidney failure. Similarly, in a recent Pennsylvania case, *Commonwealth v. Thomas*,[8] a man who threw his two month daughter down a flight of concrete steps, picked her up and threw

---

5. For a discussion of the role of symptoms, see T. SZASZ, LAW, LIBERTY, AND PSYCHIATRY 12-14 (1963) [hereinafter cited as LAW, LIBERTY AND PSYCHIATRY].

6. *See* IDEOLOGY, *supra* note 4, at 4.

7. Note, for example, that evangelist Billy Graham's assertions that he has spoken to God have *not* resulted in medical interventions.

8. No. 76-06031 (C.P. Allegheny County, Pa. April 26, 1977).

her down the steps again was acquitted by reason of insanity. Rather than convicting this defendant, we absolve him of legal responsibility by attributing his acts to schizophrenia, a mental "illness". In other words, certain acts which are peculiarly offensive and incomprehensible to most observers are translated into "medical" diagnoses. In effect, under the guise of medicine, we permit psychiatrists to prevail over "patients" in debates about reality and ethics.

RESPONSIBILITY AND AUTONOMY

Thomas Szasz challenges the conventional notion that certain people should not be held responsible for their conduct when it results from mental "illness"; for Szasz, such "illnesses" are nothing but linguistic devices. The "ill" person, in other words, is the one whose definitions of reality and himself are not accepted.[9] Furthermore, Szasz places primary emphasis on human autonomy—the right of every individual to define for himself who he is and what is in his best interests. Following John Stuart Mill, Szasz believes that a person's definition of his own best interests *is* his own best interest.

Having summarized the basic theoretical position of Dr. Szasz, we attempt to further elaborate on his thinking by identifying several errors commonly made by his critics.

MENTAL HEALTH AND MENTAL ILLNESS

A frequent criticism of Szasz focuses on the alleged contrasting conditions of mental health and mental illness. It is assumed that mental "health," like physical health, is a definable and valued condition to be achieved. Szasz is asked to demonstrate that people whom psychiatrists "diagnose" as mentally "ill" are, in fact, normal or "healthy." Such a request[10] entirely misses the point. As we have argued elsewhere:

Szasz does not maintain that such people are "normal"; indeed, he would find the question meaningless and irrelevant

---

9. Szasz writes: "The poet persuades many to see the world as he does; the lover, one; the lunatic, none." T. SZASZ, HERESIES 37 (1976).

10. *See* Schoenfeld, *An Analysis of the Views of Thomas S. Szasz*, 4 J. L. & PSYCH. 245 (1976).

. . . . If a man machine-gunned infants in a maternity ward, Szasz would surely not say that it is "normal." He would say, however, that you will not shed light on this behavior by discussing it in medical terminology.[11]

DRUGS, THERAPIES, AND ETHICS

A second major misunderstanding arises out of Szasz' position on various "treatments" to which "patients" are required to submit with or without their consent. While critics such as Richard H. Guilluly[12] and Dr. Jonas Rappoport[13] and journalists such as Howard K. Smith[14] continue to question whether drugs or shock "treatments" are effective, it is argued that drugs do great good and that patients later will express their gratitude for having been subjected to them. Szasz does not maintain that drugs will not relieve depression or otherwise alter moods and perceptions. However, the fact that drugs provide relief from depression does not demonstrate to Szasz that depression was caused by a chemical deficiency. Szasz suggests that more revealing than the relationship between drug therapy and patient is the drug therapy and psychiatrist relationship. He states, "[W]hatever might be the effects of modern psycho-pharmacologicals on so called mentally ill patients, their effects on the psychiatrists who use them are clear, and unquestionably 'beneficial': they have restored to the psychiatrist what he had been in grave danger of losing—namely his medical identity."[15]

Contrary to the misrepresentations often made concerning Szasz' supposed opposition[16] to the use of drugs, Szasz strongly *supports* the rights of adults to ingest any chemicals or drugs for therapeutic purposes. What he opposes is the *forced* ingestion of chemicals by physicians. The point at issue is not the advisability of drug usage, rather it is the question of who is to decide who may ingest what. Szasz argues that in a free society the individual has the right to decide whether he or she wants "treatment."

---

11. Weinberg & Vatz, *Szasz and the Law: An Alternative View*, 4 J. L. & PSYCH. 551, 552-53 (1977).

12. *See* Guilluly, *For the Sake of the Patients*, in The Baltimore Sun, Sept. 12, 1977, at 18, col. 2 [hereinafter cited as Guilluly].

13. Comment and Controversy, WBAL, Baltimore, January 15, 1977 [hereinafter cited as Comment].

14. Madness and Medicine, ABC-TV Documentary, April 26, 1977.

15. IDEOLOGY, *supra* note 4, at 22.

16. *See generally* Guilluly, *supra* note 12.

Perhaps the most ironic misrepresentation is the consistent effort to depict Szasz as a "radical" psychiatrist. In fact, his views have profoundly "conservative" implications. His general argument that man has the right to define himself and his own best interests without the interference of others, and his specific arguments upholding the right to commit suicide and advocating the abolition of the insanity plea and the elimination of forensic psychiatry would place him comfortably in the school of social thought currently known as "conservatism."

Finally, Szasz is commonly criticized for offering no alternatives to the system of institutional psychiatry which he claims is essentially fraudulent and destructive of human dignity and autonomy. Szasz says that many people indeed are depressed, unhappy, despondent, and even self-destructive. Clearly, he believes, such individuals are experienceing "problems in living." Such problems, Szasz argues, are typically diffuse and general but are made to appear to be specific and discrete *only* as a consequence of the psychiatric categories used to describe them. Psychiatrists, by virtue of their *medical* training, do *not* acquire any special insights into the ethical, moral, and social problems faced by men; therefore, they should not be empowered to forcibly inject drugs into others, nor deprive them of their freedom under the guise of rendering treatment. Whether it is rational to take one's own life and what society should do about mass murderers and political assassins are not medical matters. Thus, Szasz offers no alternatives because institutional psychiatry should simply not exist.

We turn our attention next to Szasz' contributions to several key ethical/legal controversies currently facing the criminal justice system.

ETHICAL ISSUES IN CRIMINAL JUSTICE

The major thrust of Szasz' efforts, as we have argued, is to identify the inappropriateness of the use of medical terms, concepts, and personnel to deal with "problems in living." His underlying theme is that the definitive human struggle is between the definer and the defined, with the victor being he who controls language. He argues that

> the struggle for definition is veritably the struggle for life itself
> . . . . In ordinary life, the struggle is not for guns, but for words;

whoever first defines the situation is the victor; his adversary the victim . . . . In short, he who first seizes the word imposes reality on the other; he who defines thus dominates and lives; and he who is defined is subjugated and may be killed.[17]

The prefatory comments are crucial to understanding the relevance of Szasz to ethical issues in criminal justice. Only after we appreciate the power of linguistic definition can we see why "medical" problems such as acquittal by reason of insanity, issues of mental competency to stand trial, rights to medical "treatment," involuntary civil commitments, and victimless crimes are not matters of *medicine* but of *ethics, morality,* and *politics*. The kinds of issues which we address in this paper are not issues upon which medically trained people have any peculiar competence. Szasz' central contribution is, therefore, to "de-medicalize" these issues and to bring debate upon them back into the realm of ethics, morality, and politics. Neither the "effectiveness" of alternative treatment, nor the "accuracy" of competing psychiatric "diagnoses" are at stake. Rather, the issue is the desirability of our society evolving into an oppressive therapeutic state where individual freedom will be subjugated to collectivist values.

The Insanity Plea and the Insanity Verdict

Since the case of Daniel M'Naghten[18] in 1843, juries have been permitted to find defendants not guilty by reason of insanity. While courts have struggled to define a proper test or standard to determine if the defendant was mentally "ill," or, more properly, "insane" at the time he committed the criminal act, Szasz would argue that the courts have failed to discuss the real issue. Since "all tests of criminal responsibility rest on the premise that people 'have' conditions called 'mental diseases,' which 'cause' them to commit criminal acts,"[19] the validity of these tests necessarily depends on the existence of mental "illness." Szasz disputes the very existence of such "illness." Thus, asking a psychiatrist to give a *medical* opinion on whether the defendant knew right from wrong or knew the nature or quality of his act or whether the act was the product

---

17. T. Szasz, The Second Sin 24-25 (1973).
18. Daniel M'Naghten's Case, 8 Eng. Rep. 718 (1843).
19. Ideology, *supra* note 4, at 100.

of the defendant's mental disease or defect presents an *ethical* question masquerading as a *medical* question.

Typically, a defendant found "not guilty by reason of insanity" is sent for an indefinite period to a "hospital" for the criminally insane to be "treated." Such "treatment" raised the threat of life imprisonment in the "hospital" and was preferable only to the death penalty; thus, defendants traditionally raised the insanity defense only if the death penalty was the alternative. Today, the availability of the death penalty is much more limited, and a decrease in insanity pleas would be expected. However, some courts have become more sensitive to the legal implications of the successful invocation of the insanity defense, and we are, therefore, likely to see an increasing number of defendants raising the insanity defense. For example, the Court of Appeals for the District of Columbia held in 1968 that a defendant acquitted by reason of insanity was entitled to a new finding of fact as to his "present insanity."[20] "Hence persons found not guilty by reason of insanity must be given a judicial hearing [before commitment in a mental institution] with procedures substantially similar to those in civil commitment proceedings . . . . The trial determined only that there was a reasonable doubt as the defendant's sanity in the past; present commitment is predicated on a finding of present insanity."[21]

In the Pennsylvania case, *Commonwealth v. Thomas*, the confusion that may result from approaching this ethics problem as a medical question becomes apparent. Pennsylvania, in line with *Bolton v. Harris*,[22] has a Mental Health Act under which the defendant could *not* be committed to a "hospital" following his acquittal without a showing that he was insane at the time he was to be committed. However, doctors agreed that the defendant's "mental illness" was "treatable" with "medication"—so long as he took his pills he was considered sane! To avoid releasing this defendant, the judge sent him to jail (not a hospital) for a parole violation based on a prior offense on which he *also* was found not guilty by reason of insanity.

A recent New York case further illustrates the consequences of confusing ethics and medicine. A man who stabbed his wife sixty times with a kitchen knife, then taped his baby's mouth shut and

---

20. *See* Bolton v. Harris, 395 F.2d 642 (D.C. Cir. 1968).
21. *Id.* at 650-51.
22. 395 F.2d 642 (D.C. Cir. 1968).

strangled him with an electric cord was found not guilty by reason of insanity. Following one year of "treatment" in a maximum security "hospital," his *doctors* declared that he was no longer dangerous. He was transferred to a nonsecure "hospital" where he was permitted to leave at will. This defendant subsequently walked away from the institution and has not yet been found.

Clearly, to permit continued deceptive employment of the medical model to make difficult moral judgments is more than a matter of linguistics, as many of Szasz' critics insist. Szasz argues that psychiatrists cannot detect the presence or absence of criminal responsibility with a medical examination and diagnosis. Rather, the decision to hold a person criminally responsible for his unlawful conduct is solely an *ethical* one to be made by those people chosen by society to perform this awesome task — the jury. Medicine is entirely irrelevant; forensic psychiatrists are therefore equally irrelevant.

Since the insanity defense results either in extensive involuntary "hospitalization" or increasingly, in *no* punishment at all, Szasz advocates the abolition of the insanity defense. He argues:

> Either we regard offenders as sane, and punish them; or we regard them as insane, and, though excusing them for crime officially, punish them by treating them as beings who are less than human. It seems to me that there is a more promising alternative. Let us not consider mental illness an excusing condition. By treating offenders as responsible human beings, we offer them the only chance, as I see it, to remain human.[23]

RIGHT TO TREATMENT

The Supreme Court's landmark decision in *O'Connor v. Donaldson*[24] provides clear evidence that Szasz' views have not yet penetrated the judicial system. In *Donaldson*, the Court held that Kenneth Donaldson, who spent fifteen years in a mental institution, had to be released because he was not dangerous, he was capable of living outside the institution, and he had received no "treatment" during the entire period of his confinement. The Court refused to decide whether a person confined because he *was* dangerous had a similar right to be either "treated" or released and whether a non-

---

23. LAW, LIBERTY, AND PSYCHIATRY, *supra* note 5, at 137.
24. 422 U.S. 563 (1975).

dangerous "patient" such as Donaldson might be confined if "treatment" *were* made available.

From Szasz' point of view, the entire debate over the right to unrequested, but by the Supreme Court's decision necessary, "treatment" further obscures the real issue. If mental "illness" is a myth, then unrequested "treatment" of "patients" in "hospitals" becomes assault and battery on prisoners. After *Donaldson*, Szasz maintained that, "The crucial question thus remains unanswered: on what grounds, if any, may an individual be deprived of liberty by being incarcerated in a mental hospital."[25] Upon his release, Donaldson argued, "Mainly, my disease was that I refused to admit that I was ill. From what I've seen and heard, that is the worst disease you can have — refusing to admit that you have a disease."[26] Donaldson, in effect served a fifteen year "prison" term. His chief offense — refusing to allow others to define his failures as a husband, father, and working man as a matter of mental "illness."

While the Supreme Court has not yet decided whether a patient has the right to refuse "treatment," a few lower courts have said that absent the "patient's" consent, "treatment" can result in unconstitutional cruel and unusual punishment. In *Mackey v. Procumier*,[27] a prison inmate agreed to go to a mental "hospital" to undergo electroconvulsive therapy. He alleged that despite his protests, the doctors instead administered the drug anectine to him as part of a program of "aversive therapy." The drug, which creates the sensation of suffocation or drowning, was injected when his behavior was deemed inappropriate. The court held that proof of such allegations might constitute cruel and unusual punishment. In another case, the Court of Appeals for the Eighth Circuit held that the unrequested administering of apomorphine, a drug which causes vomiting, to misbehaving mental patients was cruel and unusual punishment.[28] The notion of a right to refuse "treatment" still begs the question posed by the theories of Thomas Szasz; there can be no "treatment" if there is no "illness." Nevertheless, it is encouraging to see courts reasoning through these cases under the framework provided by the cruel and unusual *punishment* clause. The courts,

---

25. Szasz, *On Involuntary Psychiatry*, in N.Y. Times, October 15, 1975, at 46, col. 4.

26. Time, July 7, 1975, at 44.

27. 477 F.2d 877 (9th Cir. 1973).

28. Knecht v. Gillman, 488 F.2d 1136, (8th Cir. 1973). The Iowa facility involved here considered swearing to be a sufficient misbehavior to warrant the injection of apomorphine.

perhaps, are beginning to perceive the real nature of the issue.

Szasz summarizes his attitude toward the "right to treatment" as follows: "The idea of a 'right' to mental treatment is both naive and dangerous. It is naive because it accepts the problem of the publicly hospitalized mental patient as medical rather then educational, economic, religious, and social. It is dangerous because the remedy creates another problem: compulsory medical treatment."[29] Psychiatrists insist on the use of the medical model for understanding behavior; on the other hand, they are not willing to accord mental "patients" the same right that medical patients now have — the right to refuse treatment. Even when a "treatment" is less offensive, it still, as Murray Edelman suggests, "superimposes a political relationship upon a medical one."[30] Thus, "mental" patients do not hold dances, they have dance therapy. If they play volleyball, that is recreation therapy. If they engage in group discussion, that is group therapy. Even reading is 'bibliotherapy' . . . ."[31]

In sum, the legal debate over the "right to treatment" fails, for the most part, to reach the critical ethical, moral, and political dimensions of the problem. For "treatment" is erroneously defined as "helping," while in fact it functions to permit some people (psychiatrists) to limit the freedom and autonomy of other people (patients). As Edelman states,

> Because the helping professions define other people's statuses (and their own), the special terms they employ to categorize clients and justify restrictions of their physical movements and of their moral and intellectual influence are especially revealing of the political functions language performs and of the multiple realities it helps to create.[32]

It is not possible to "treat" behavior which is not symptomatic of disease; to to do is merely to use language to make it easier for "men considered mentally healthy to degrade and mistreat men considered mentally sick."[33]

---

29. Law, Liberty, and Psychiatry, *supra* note 5, at 215.

30. Edelman, *The Political Language of the Helping Professions*, 4 Pol. and Soc'y 297 (1974).

31. *Id.*

32. *Id.* at 296.

33. Ideology, *supra* note 4, at 217.

As we have indicated above, Szasz argues that allowing doctors to answer ethical/legal questions of sanity *as if* they were medical ones is both deceptive and dangerous. The role of doctors in determining whether a criminal defendant is "competent" to stand trial may be even more dangerous than their role in presenting the insanity defense; there have been far more involuntary mental commitments resulting from the finding of incompetency than from the finding of insanity. A recent survey by the Joint Information Service of the American Psychiatric Association indicates that "of all admissions to mental hospitals of mentally ill offenders, 52 percent result from determinations of incompetency to stand trial, and only 4 percent from findings of not guilty by reason of insanity."[34]

A recent article by prominent forensic psychiatrists Herbert E. Thomas and John H. Hess maintains: "Certainly most doctors would agree that their proper function in hearings to determine competency consists of a scientific evaluation of the patient and an accurate and useful presentation of the scientific conclusions to the court."[35] These psychiatrists then complain that too often the psychiatrist in the competency hearing "not only evaluates the defendant's psychological status, but judges his behavior, estimates its social and ethical significance, and decides on a fitting consequence, be it commitment or trial."[36] Hess and Thomas fail to understand that what they condone and what they condemn are identical. The "proper" "scientific" judgments which they support are, in fact, nothing more than the normative judgments which they oppose.

The justification for following a doctor's medical opinion that a defendant is not competent to stand trial is, predictably, that such a finding benefits the defendant. Yet the question of whether or not his competency will be evaluated does not lie exclusively in his hands. If the defendant does not argue his incompetency, the prosecution may request or the court may, at its own discretion, require that a defendant be "examined" before trial to assess his competency. If the defendant refuses to undergo the court-ordered "examination," he may be punished for contempt. Szasz argues: "If

---

34. Hess, Pearsall, Slichter & Thomas, *Competency to Stand Trial,* in READINGS IN LAW AND PSYCHIATRY 616 (Allen, Ferster, Rubin eds. 1975).

35. *Id.* at 621.

36. *Id.*

the pretrial psychiatric examination is really for the defendant's benefit, why should he be punished for refusing it? If, on the other hand, it is not for his benefit, then it must be for the benefit of either the judge or the prosecution."[37] The Supreme Court has said that not only *may* a judge raise the issue of competency *sua sponte*, but that he *must* do so where there is evidence suggesting that the defendant may not be competent, even though the defendant has waived the defense of incompetency by failing to request a psychiatric examination and hearing.[38] As the Court stated, "it is contradictory to argue that a defendant may be incompetent, and yet knowingly or intelligently 'waive' his right to have the court determine his capacity to stand trial."[39]

Historically, the finding of incompetency to stand trial resulted in automatic and indefinite confinement in a mental "hospital." Since the mental "hospitals" often failed to "treat" or even "reexamine" many of their "patients," the unlucky person who, "for his own benefit," was found incompetent to stand trial might have spent the remainder of his life in a "hospital"; if convicted, he might have been eligible for parole after five years in prison. Again, the confusion is primarily caused by the mistake of allowing the medical model to be employed to handle ethical or legal matters. Paradoxically, as the legal rights of the "mentally ill" are increasingly recognized, the ethics as medicine error is compounded. In the 1972 decision of *Jackson v. Indiana*,[40] the Supreme Court ruled that a defendant committed to a "hospital" after being found incompetent to stand trial may only be detained as a "patient" for a reasonable time to see if he is likely to regain his competency. If he becomes competent, he must be released and then tried if the state wishes; if he appears unlikely to regain competency, he must either be released or committed under the civil commitment procedure. However, as state laws governing civil commitments are rewritten to afford greater rights to those being involuntarily committed, the results become less rational. For example, although a defendant is found incompetent to stand trial, he might *not* fall within the ever-narrowing categories of people who can be civilly committed. Or, he may be incompetent to stand trial but "treatable" with

---

37. LAW, LIBERTY, AND PSYCHIATRY, *supra* note 5, at 164.
38. Pate v. Robinson, 383 U.S. 375, 385 (1966).
39. *Id.* at 384.
40. 406 U.S. 715 (1972).

"medication" readily available on an "outpatient" basis. In either case, it is likely that greater numbers of serious offenders will avoid the entire criminal justice system.

Szasz' theoretical model mandates the elimination of the incompetency finding. The test of legal competency is the capacity of the defendant to understand the nature of the charges against him and to assist his lawyer in preparing a proper defense. Szasz would agree that on *ethical* grounds a defendant ought not be tried in absentia; he would also agree that if a doctor can testify that a defendant is unconscious due to a brain tumor, then we can decide on *ethical* grounds that the defendant is incompetent and should not be tried. However, where no medical condition exists — and that, of course, is his basic thesis — there is *no* justification for asking *doctors* whether the defendant "understands" the charges and is "capable" of assisting in his defense. Such questions are normative, not medical, and should be decided on ethical grounds, not medical grounds.

INVOLUNTARY CIVIL COMMITMENT

Szasz unambiguously states: "I am unqualifiedly opposed to involuntary mental hospitalization and treatment. To me, it's like slavery; the problem is not how to improve it, but how to abolish it."[41] Involuntary hospitalization is legal in form, but medical in fact. Again, inordinate and unjustified power is granted to doctors to make difficult decisions of morality. One intensive study of civil commitment hearings reports that, although taking place in a legal setting, "the decisions are treated almost exclusively as medical decisions."[42]

A recent symposium on the new Pennsylvania Mental Health Procedures Act[43] reported the preliminary findings of a similar study in progress in Allegheny County. Those committed, generally unable to secure their own psychiatrists, are often quiet and nondangerous when they appear at the commitment hearing due to the drugs which they have been given during the short emergency treatment and confinement prior to the hearing. One Mental Health

---

41. Szasz, *A Psychiatrist Views Mental Health Legislation*, 9 WASHBURN L. REV. 224, 234 (1970) [hereinafter cited as *Psychiatrist*].

42. Fein & Miller, *Legal Process and Adjudication in Mental Incompetency Proceedings*, SOCIAL PROBLEMS, Summer, 1972, at 63.

43. PA. STAT. ANN. tit. 50, §§ 7101-7503 (Purdon Supp. 1978-1979).

Review officer, the judge in such hearing, concluded that he therefore had to rely on the medical testimony of the state psychiatrist because the quiet condition of the respondent was generally misleading. Thus, if a respondent is angry and rebellious, it is probably assumed that he *is* dangerous; if he is not angry and rebellious, it is attributed to his sedated condition and discounted in favor of psychiatric "diagnosis."

A brief examination of the new Pennsylvania commitment process further demonstrates the conceptual quagmire and the continued role of psychiatrists as social control agents rather than medical agents. The 1976 legislation was required by the judicial invalidation of the prior law for its unconstitutionally vague standard.[44] Along with many other states, Pennsylvania now requires a finding of severe mental disability which results in a person posing a "clear and present danger of harm to others or to himself" for involuntary civil commitment.[45] Thus, "dangerousness" becomes the primary grounds for involuntary commitment and psychiatrists have become the experts who establish the presence of mental disabilities resulting in "dangerousness." Szasz writes: "Drunken drivers are dangerous both to themselves and to others. They injure and kill many more people than, for example, persons with paranoid delusions of persecution. Yet, people labeled paranoid are readily committable, while drunken drivers are not."[46] While some psychiatrists[47] admit they are unable to predict long-term "dangerousness," they maintain they are able to predict short-term "dangerousness" and that, at a minimum, they can identify which individuals have "mental illnesses" which will respond to "treatment." Refusing to recognize that "mental illnesses" are wholly rhetorical phenomena, both courts and psychiatrists continue to make ethical decisions in the name of medicine.

Szasz recognizes society's right to enact a criminal code which punishes people who harm other people. Szasz plainly states his view that "if someone is suspected of lawbreaking, he should be accused, tried, and, if convicted, sentenced. If the sentence calls for loss of liberty, he should be confined in an institution that's penal,

---

44. *See Note, Standards for Involuntary Civil Commitment in Pennsylvania*, 38 U. PITT. L. REV. 535 (1977).

45. PA. STAT. ANN. tit. 50, § 7301(a) (Purdon Supp. 1978-1979).

46. LAW, LIBERTY, AND PSYCHIATRY, *supra* note 5, at 46.

47. *See* note 13 and accompanying text *supra.*

not medical, in character . . . . If jails are bad, and of course many are, they should be improved. Placing lawbreakers, or suspected lawbreakers, in mental hospitals against their will is not a proper substitute for prison reform."[48] Predicitons of future dangerousness are regularly made in probation and parole decisions. Such decisions, while difficult, are not medical.

On the other hand, Szasz rejects the notion that harm to oneself constitutes a legitimate basis for incarceration in a mental institution. The right to do what one wants with one's body is absolute. Whether or not it is deemed "rational" to act in a self-destructive fashion, or even to commit suicide, is an ethical, moral, and religious question to which psychiatrists have no better answers than anyone else. This is the final ethical issue to be examined in light of the views of Thomas Szasz.

CRIMES WITHOUT VICTIMS

For Szasz, the category of offenses loosely labelled "crimes without victims" should be called "victims without crimes." The punishing of homosexuality offers an intriguing illustration of the continuing misuse of both criminal law and medicine. On the one hand, the American Psychiatric Association, in 1973, altered its Diagnostic and Statistical Manual to declare that homosexuality is no longer an "illness." Homosexuality is now viewed as "one form of sexual behavior and, like other forms of sexual behavior which are not by themselves psychiatric disorders, is not listed in this nomenclature of mental disorders, *i.e.*, the diagnostic category entitled "sexual orientation disturbance."[49] Such an action supports Szasz' contention that mental "illness" is a myth — medical illnesses cannot be voted out of existence.

On the other hand, efforts to use the criminal law to punish consenting adults for deviant sexual practices have often been met successfully with the argument that it is unconstitutional to punish someone for having a "condition" or an "illness." This very argument provided the rationale for the Supreme Court decision in *Robinson v. California*[50] which invalidated a California statute mak-

---

48. *Psychiatrist, supra* note 41, at 237.

49. AMERICAN PSYCHIATRIC ASSOCIATION DIAGNOSTIC AND STATISTICAL MANUAL 44 (6th ed. 1973).

50. 370 U.S. 660 (1962).

ing it a criminal offense to be "addicted" to narcotics. The Court reasoned: "It is unlikely that any State at this moment in history would attempt to make it a criminal offense for a person to be mentally ill . . . ."[51] Mental illness and addiction, then, are seen as medical conditions to which the criminal law may not be constitutionally applied.

Thus, for Szasz, whether one chooses to engage in homosexual behavior or to take drugs is neither a matter of medicine, nor a matter of criminal law; it is a matter of personal choice and personal morality. In addition, Szasz rejects the concept of drug "additction" itself. He maintains that "while addiction is ostensibly a medical and pharmacological problem, actually it is a moral and political problem."[52] He rejects the position that "drug addiction is a disease, 'like any other,' which has now reached 'epidemic' proportions, and whose 'medical' containment justifies the limitless expenditures of tax monies and the corresponding aggrandizement and enrichment of noble medical warriors against this 'plague'."[53] The fact that it is possible to kill oneself by abusive injection of drugs does not justify their prohibition. The fact that people *will not* stop taking drugs does not demonstrate their *inability* to stop — only their *unwillingness*. The increased tolerance which can be biologically *learned* can be biologically *forgotten*.

SUMMARY AND CONCLUSIONS

We have sought in this article to present a summary of the ideas contained in the prolific works of Thomas Szasz, and to explore their implications for a series of issues confronting the criminal justice system. As is evident, the adoption of Szasz' perspective would result in a rethinking of the role of medicine in the criminal justice system, the role of the criminal law and the civil law in reducing human freedom, and, ultimately, in the definition of what it means to be free. While not frequently discussed in criminal justice literature to date, Thomas Szasz poses an intellectual challenge which will, sooner or later, have to be met by scholars in our field, as well as in the other social sciences, law, and medicine. While

---

51. *Id.* at 666.
52. Szasz, *The Ethics of Addiction*, in THE RHETORIC OF No. 195 (2d ed. 1974).
53. *Id.* at 188.

having only initiated the discussion of the views of Thomas Szasz among students of the criminal justice system, it is our hope that further analysis will be stimulated by our efforts.

1. What are the five legal issues for which Szasz' views have vast implications?

2. What is the unique meaning of 'symptom' in the context of mental 'illness'?

3. a. What is the medical model.

    b. Why does Szasz argue that it represents a literalization of metaphor?

4. If administering drugs to those who are deemed to be mentally 'ill' relieves their 'illnesses', how can Szasz argue that they were not 'sick'?

5. a. What does Szasz believe ought to be done about the insanity defense?

    b. Why does Szasz take this position?

6. What happens to people who have been acquitted by reason of insanity?

7. a. What is the 'right to treatment'?

    b. Why does Szasz call it 'naive' and 'dangerous?'

8. a. What is meant by incompetency to stand trial?

    b. What does Szasz believe ought to be done about it?

9. a. What is involuntary hospitalization or involuntary civil commitment?

    b. On what grounds may involuntary committments be legally obtained in Pennsylvania?

10. What is Szasz' view of involuntary hospitalization?

11. What does Szasz think about the prediction of dangerousness criterion as grounds for involuntary commitment?

12. Why does Szasz say that 'victimless crimes' ought to be called 'victims without crimes'?

13. How does Szasz say that society should deal with individuals who commit terrible and incomprehensible acts of violence?

1. The implications of Szasz' views for five areas of the legal system are discussed: the plea of "not guilty by reason of insanity," the finding of incompetency to stand trial, the newly announced right to treatment, the involuntary civil commitment process, and the concept of 'victimless crimes'.

2. Szasz argues that only in the case of mental 'illness' is the symptom--strange or frightening behavior--sufficient to conclude that an illness is present. In the case of all other illnesses, the symptom--pain, bleeding, etc.--is only an indication of illness. If the doctor looks further and finds none, he/she will conclude that despite the symptoms, the patient is not sick. This does not occur in the case of mental 'illness'.

3. a. For Szasz, the medical model is the belief that we can understand unusual behavior in terms of notions of disease and cure. Once we have identified the 'cause' of strange behavior to be a disease or an 'illness', we naturally turn to physicians to 'treat' the 'patients' who suffer from these 'illnesses'. That is what is meant by the 'medical model'.

    b. Szasz, however, maintains that the use of such a model for dealing with strange or undesirable behavior represents the literalization of a metaphor. In other words, in calling someone 'sick' we are only using the word 'sick' as a metaphor. However, we have taken ourselves literally and gone on to adopt the medical model as a result.

4. The fact that the drugs had desirable results does not logically demonstrate that the prior 'illness' was caused by some biochemical imbalance or deficiency. If you were unhappy and ingested certain drugs right now you would begin to feel quite happy! However, that would not prove that your present lack of happiness was caused by the physiological need for such drugs.

5. a. He believes that it should be abolished.

    b. He believes that the issue of criminal responsibility is a legal/ social/ethical one. Society can, through its legal institutions, define and re-define its notion of responsibility, but DOCTORS have no special competency in this area. The issue of who is to be held responsible ought to be a legal one made without reference to or reliance upon the totally uninformed opinions of physicians. If behavior is not medically produced, then doctors have no useful knowledge to offer to courts.

6. Such people are either found to be presently sane and, therefore, released or they are found to be presently insane and sent to 'hospitals' against their wishes for 'treatment' or until they again become 'well.'

7. a. The right to treatment, as discussed in <u>O'Connor v. Donaldson</u>, requires that a non-dangerous patient in a mental institution who is capable of living outside of the institution must either receive treatment or be released.

b. Szasz says that this is naive because it defines the problem in
       terms of the medical model and that it is dangerous because it
       leads to the problem of forced or unrequested "treatment" being
       imposed upon 'patients'.

8. a. Incompetency to stand trial involves the capacity of the defendant
       to understand the nature of the charges against him/her and to
       assist his/her lawyer in preparing a proper defense. It is the
       defendant's 'sanity' at the time of trial which is at issue, rather
       than his/her 'sanity' at the time he/she allegedly committed the
       act. (That, of course, is the insanity defense.)

   b. Szasz again argues that medical experts are entirely irrelevant
       to determining the legal matter of whether or not to try a
       particular defendant. Normative matters such as these are in
       the province of law, politics, or ethics, but not medicine.

9. a. When persons who have broken no law are forced against their will
       to be placed in a mental institution, they are said to have been in-
       voluntarily committed.

   b. Under the new Pennsylvania law the prediction of dangerousness
       to oneself or to others is the main ground for involuntary commit-
       ment.

10. He opposes such deprivation of liberty in all circumstances.

11. Szasz believes that many other people, such as drunk drivers, are in-
    finitely more dangerous than paranoid schizophrenics, and he sees no
    reason to make it possible to commit the latter but not the former.
    Clearly, he would say, it is not the degree of danger posed which is
    really the ground for commitments, but rather the desire of some people
    to exercise power over other people for any number of reasons.

12. The use of the criminal law to punish people for engaging in self
    destructive or offensive behavior ought to be viewed as 'criminal'.
    Thus, to prohibit gambling, prostitution, and drug use is to create
    'victims' where there are no 'crimes'.

13. He says, in essence, that people who commit such acts ought to be charged
    with violations of the criminal laws, tried, and, if convicted, sent to
    prison. He says that to discuss such heinous acts in medical terms does
    absolutely nothing to help use understand them; it does, however, serve
    justify the use of doctors and drugs. In addition, to treat a defendant
    as not being responsible for his acts is to dehumanize him.

Reprinted with the permission of Federal Legal Publications, Inc., 95 Morton Street New York, NY 10014 Journal of Psychiatry and the Law, Summer, 1976, pp. 245-263.

Reading #2

An analysis of the views of Thomas S. Szasz

BY C. G. SCHOENFELD, ESQ.

Szasz' thesis that there is no such thing as mental illness, that psychiatrists are persecutors, oppressors, and torturers, and that the so-called mentally ill should be treated like everybody else is analyzed in detail. The analysis reveals that Szasz fails to support his views with appropriate evidence, ignores crucial evidence contrary to these views, makes egregious mistakes of logic, engages in various forms of "word magic," and commits blatant factual and legal errors.

Dr. Thomas S. Szasz is by far the most prodigious, and surely the best known, writer today on the relationship between psychiatry and the law. That he is also extraordinarily articulate, intelligent and persuasive, learned, and a brilliant stylist besides, cannot be denied. Yet, unfortunately, his gifts appear to be matched by his faults; indeed, so much so, that some of the most eminent and respected writers on psychiatry and the law have denounced him as an intemperate and untrustworthy propagandist who "has a demagogue's flair for personal abuse"[1] and who "all too often misrepresents facts."[2] In the words of one such student of psychiatry and the law, Szasz "has lost all regard for the intellectual honesty and integrity of his own scholarship."[3]

My purpose here is not to engage in name-calling or in polemics, however. Rather it is to examine in detail the basic thesis that Szasz has advanced in a series of articles and books during the past 15 years. This thesis is that: There is no such thing as mental illness (no such thing as neurosis, psychosis, insanity, "madness," and so on). To the extent that conditions now labeled mental illness may actually exist, they are really

"problems in living" (ethical, social, legal, political, and other problems). Hence, psychiatrists who diagnose and treat what they regard as mental illnesses are really persecutors, oppressors, and torturers, who sometimes even create the conditions they are supposed to cure; persons now labeled mentally ill should not be sent involuntarily to so-called mental institutions; if they commit crimes, they should be prosecuted and punished like everyone else.

There is no such thing as mental illness (no such thing as neurosis, psychosis, insanity, "madness," and so on).

To support his thesis that there is no such thing as mental illness—no such thing as neurosis or psychosis—Szasz fails to offer for what one would suppose to be the "best evidence" of his viewpoint: clinical evidence. That is, he fails to offer to his readers detailed descriptions, case histories, and the like of a representative cross section of persons whom psychiatrists usually judge to be neurotic or psychotic, but whom he has interviewed or examined as a psychiatrist, and whom he has demonstrated to be completely normal. Persons who are terrified of heights, or of entering small enclosures, or of leaving their home; others who feel compelled, usually in the privacy of their bedroom or bathroom, to perform certain bizarre rituals; still others who steal things they neither need, use, sell, nor really want; so-called fetishists who literally worship certain articles of clothing or parts of the body; masochists who have an overwhelming need to be "disciplined" by being cursed, whipped, and even urinated and defecated upon; exhibitionists who cannot resist exposing their genitals in public, and particularly in front of small children. It is clinical evidence (detailed investigative reports, case histories, etc.) showing that a representative sample of such putative neurotics are completely healthy that Szasz, perhaps understandably, fails to offer to his readers. Persons in a so-called catatonic stupor who are apparently oblivious of the world around them; others who are convinced that they are being relentlessly persecuted by unidentified enemies out to poison or otherwise destroy them; still others who believe that they are God's emissaries or angels—or even God himself—and that, as such, they have the power to destroy the world; so-called depressives who may lacerate and maim themselves, and for whom suicide may seem to be the obvious "solution" to all their problems; patients who are actively hallucinating and who may be wildly manic and assaultive—it is detailed reports of interviews and examinations conducted with a representative cross section of these putative psychotics which reveal that—mirabile dictu—they are as mentally healthy as you or I, that Szasz fails to offer to his readers.

Instead of providing such evidence, Szasz relies upon arguments concerning the words "mental illness" to prove that there is no such thing as neurosis, psychosis, insanity, "madness," and so on. In brief, he contends that there cannot be an illness unless physical signs or symptoms of it exist. And since (in his view) there are no physical signs or symptoms of the so-called mental illnesses, it follows that neurosis, psychosis, insanity, "madness," and the like do not exist.[4]

Unfortunately for Szasz' argument, physical signs or symptoms of mental illness frequently do exist. For example, electroencephalograms have shown that the brain wave patterns of many persons whom psychiatrists regard as seriously mentally ill are often highly erratic and abnormal.[5] Further, a whole range of physical signs or symptoms ranging from facial tics and allergic reactions to serious gastric and pulmonary disorders have been shown to reflect the presence of mental disorders. Indeed, the whole area of psychosomatic medicine is concerned with the very close relationship that has been shown to exist between neurosis and psychosis and physical or bodily disorders. In fact, it may be contended that the very strange behavior of many neurotics and psychotics is itself "physical" evidence of mental illness.

But even if all this were not so, Szasz' argument in effect assumes, rather than proves, that there is no such thing as mental illness. That is, he assumes that there cannot be an illness unless physical signs or symptoms of it exist. And having also made the assumption, discussed above, that there are no signs or symptoms of mental illness, he inevitably concludes that neurosis, psychosis, insanity, "madness," and the like do not exist. As a logician might put it, Szasz' argument "begs the question."

Admittedly—and as Szasz emphasizes when he discusses the word "illness"—when there is a physical illness, physical signs or symptoms of it usually appear. But it hardly follows that, as Szasz assumes, physical signs or symptoms are needed to prove the existence of mental illness. Indeed, an analysis of the definitions of the word "illness" offered in the unabridged edition of the Merriam Webster and other leading dictionaries soon reveals that Szasz's belief that physical signs or symptoms constitute a defining characteristic of the term is clearly idiosyncratic and amounts to an attempt to create a private definition of it.[6]

But even if Szasz's definition of the word "illness" were shared by today's lexigraphers, Szasz's argument would still be unsound, since it attempts to do what is philosophically and epistemologically impossible: to define something out of existence. As philosophers and logicians have pointed out to generations of students: 'When you have stated the defining characteristics of X, you have proved nothing one way or the other about whether an X exists. . . . When you are able to define a word in terms of characteristics A, B, and C, you have still not shown that there exists anything in the universe that has characteristics A, B, and C. You cannot legislate centaurs into existence by defining a word, any more than you can legislate black swans out of existence by redefining the word 'swan.' From defining X, you can draw no conclusions whatever about whether there are any X's in the world; that is not a matter for definition but for scientific investigation.'[7] In short, to determine whether or not mental illness (or anything else) exists, empirical evidence is needed. Szasz' attempt to define mental illness in terms of physical signs or symptoms—coupled with his assumption that there are no such signs or

obligations, a third may be in the midst of getting a divorce, a fourth may find it impossible to pass the courses he is taking at school, a fifth may have been arrested for murder, rape or whatever—all of them may be said to have "problems in living." Yet it is *also* true—and far more meaningful and helpful—to say that the first man has a health problem, the second an economic problem, the third a marital problem, the fourth a learning problem, and the fifth a legal problem. Not only does the phrase "problems in living" fail to prove helpful when someone attempts to understand or to resolve the problems so described, but its very vagueness and generality—its essential meaninglessness—imposes its own confusion.

Possibly in an attempt to help to overcome this objection, Szasz sometimes tries to be more specific concerning the meaning of "problems in living" by stating that what he is really talking about are ethical, social, legal, political, and other problems. Unfortunately, however, Szasz *assumes*—rather than *proves*—that what psychiatrists now term mental illness may be some other problem. One looks in vain for evidence (detailed investigative reports, case histories, and the like) demonstrating that a representative sample of the persons whom psychiatrists now regard as neurotic or psychotic are really suffering from the effects of ethical, social, legal, political, and other problems. Moreover, Szasz seems unable to accept the possibility that the conditions psychiatrists label neuroses or psychoses may reflect not only ethical, social, legal, political, or other "problems in living," *but mental illness as well*. As David P. Ausubel has put it: "There is no valid reason why a particular symptom cannot both reflect a problem in living *and* constitute a manifestation of disease."[10] Or as another analyst of Szasz' writings has noted, there seems to be a strange quirk in Szasz' reasoning which repeatedly leads him to the conclusion that 'phenomenon A belongs either to class (category) X or to class (category) Y, but never to both."[11]

What may be the most telling objection to Szasz' assertion that the conditions psychiatrists label neuroses and psychoses are not mental illnesses, but are instead "problems in living," is that

symptoms and that therefore there is no such thing as mental illness—is an outrageously highhanded attempt to do what is philosophically and epistemologically impossible; to define mental illness out of existence.

To try to determine at this point why as well-educated and philosophically sophisticated a person as Szasz would attempt to define mental illness out of existence would be to delay unduly consideration of the second element of Szasz' basic thesis detailed at the beginning of this paper. Still it ought to be noted that by seeking to define mental illness out of existence. Szasz may be revealing the presence and influence of a belief that words can actually create or destroy—a possibility that finds considerable support in numerous statements by Szasz . overestimating greatly the power of words, such as: "In ordinary life, the struggle is not for guns but for words: whoever first defines the situation is the victor; his adversary, the victim."; "In the animal kingdom, the rule is, eat or be eaten; in the human kingdom, define or be defined."[8] In any event, to believe that words can be used to create or destroy is to believe in *word magic*: something which, as psychoanalysts have learned, is typical at the age of two or so, but which becomes increasingly unusual thereafter.[9]

To the extent that conditions now labeled mental illness may actually exist, they are really "problems in living" (ethical. social, legal, political, and other problems).

Aware, perhaps, that the conditions psychiatrists label mental illness may reveal that "something" is amiss, Szasz asserts that insofar as these conditions actually exist (a matter upon which he is vague and equivocal at times), they are really "problems in living."

Unfortunately, the phrase "problems in living" is so very vague and general that it can be used to describe practically every problem a person may have. One man may have contracted a disease, another may be unable to meet his financial

this assertion fails to take into account the huge amount of evidence that has accumulated (particularly during the past hundred years or so) which certainly seems to reveal that these conditions are indeed mental illnesses. For example, there is a veritable mountain of evidence—including what are literally tens of thousands of highly detailed clinical reports, case histories, and the like—which clearly appear to demonstrate *that neuroses and psychoses frequently emerge as a result of the developmental difficulties occurring in infancy and childhood when the problems that arise can hardly be described as ethical, social, legal, or political.*

Psychiatrists who diagnose and treat what they regard as mental illnesses are really persecutors, oppressors, and torturers, who sometimes even create the conditions they are supposed to cure.

Szasz' charge that psychiatrists who diagnose and treat what they regard as mental illnesses are really persecutors, oppressors, and torturers, who sometimes even create the conditions they are supposed to cure, is so dramatic, idiosyncratic, and extreme, that one would suppose that Szasz would be prepared to back it up with a plethora of irrefutable evidence. Unfortunately, however, one finds that he makes little or no effort to meet this burden of proof. For example, he offers little or no evidence that psychiatrists have either exacerbated or created mental illnesses. And, by the same token, he avoids dealing with the huge amount of evidence that psychiatrists have helped to ameliorate and cure mental illnesses.

Had Szasz been able to adduce convincing evidence that neuroses and psychoses are non-existent, he would have been better able to justify his failure to prove that psychiatrists are persecutors, oppressors and torturers. After all, if neuroses and psychoses do not exist, it may well be justifiable to suggest that psychiatrists who attempt to treat these conditions are, in actuality, persecutors, oppressors, and torturers. As has been

seen, however, Szasz' "word magic" cannot begin to be considered an adequate substitute for the clinical evidence needed to support the contention that there is no such thing as mental illness.

It should be noted here that when Szasz discusses psychiatry and psychiatrists, he sometimes distinguishes between what he terms private or voluntary psychiatry (psychiatric services that a person voluntarily secures for himself) and involuntary or "institutional" psychiatry (psychiatric services that are imposed upon a person alleged to be emotionally ill, most usually in a state mental institution). Szasz utterly condemns institutional psychiatry, often in such statements as: "There are, and can be, no abuses of institutional psychiatry, because institutional psychiatry *is,* itself, an abuse, just as there were, and could be, no abuses of the Inquisition, because the Inquisition *was,* itself, an abuse. Indeed, just because the Inquisition was the characteristic and perhaps inevitable abuse of Christianity, so institutional psychiatry is the characteristic and perhaps inevitable abuse of medicine."[12] Szasz is more equivocal concerning voluntary psychiatry, sometimes lumping it together with institutional psychiatry, but sometimes admitting that it may have limited value as a form of "applied secular ethics."[13]

When discussing both voluntary and involuntary psychiatry, however, Szasz—characteristically—fails to offer what one would suppose to be the "best evidence" of his charges. That is, he fails to interview or to examine a representative cross section of the persons whom private—and especially institutional—psychiatrists have treated, and to show that a large percentage of these patients have been persecuted, oppressed, and tortured. Instead—and, once again, characteristically—he relies on the *repetition of dramatic but unsupported charges* of persecution, oppression, and torture by psychiatrists to "prove" his point.

Examples of this technique of *alleging rather than proving* abound in Szasz' book *The Manufacture of Madness,* in which he presents what he conceives of as "historical evidence" to justify his charge that psychiatrists are persecutors, oppressors, and torturers. For instance, he declares that today's so-called mental patients are the equivalent of or analogous to yesterday's witches and heretics, and that today's psychiatrists are the equivalent of or analogous to yesterday's Inquisitors who persecuted, oppressed, and tortured witches and heretics.[14] Now, it is undoubtedly true that some persons alleged in the past to be witches and heretics were persecuted, oppressed, and tortured by some religious leaders; and it may even be true that some of these alleged witches and heretics were persons whom some psychiatrists today would be likely to regard as mentally ill. By no means does it follow, however—as Szasz certainly implies—that most or all persons alleged in the past to be witches and heretics would be considered mentally ill by most or all of today's psychiatrists. And, in addition, it certainly does not follow; indeed, there is not a scintilla of evidence to show, that, as Szasz asserts, today's psychiatrists are the equivalent of yesterday's Inquisitors.

Even more serious than Szasz' failure to prove the dramatic charges that he makes are the gross errors of fact that mark the historical discussions not only in The Manufacture of Madness, but also in its companion volume The Age of Madness.[15] In the latter volume, for example, Szasz asserts that when Benjamin Rush, the 18th-century physician and so-called father of American psychiatry, advocated the "moral treatment" of insanity, what Rush had in mind was the coercion of the mental patient by means of force and fear. The fact is, however—as can be readily ascertained by consulting the writings of Rush and his contemporaries—that "what really characterized moral treatment was just the opposite: a reduction in the use of force and deception."[16] Indeed, in attempting to illustrate his charge that psychiatrists are, and have always been, persecutors, oppressors, and torturers, Szasz literally turns history on its head when he asserts that the celebrated French physician Philippe Pinel also believed that "the principal method of treatment used by the alienist ought to be coercion of the patient, by means of both force and fraud."[17]

One can only wonder if Szasz himself believes this assertion, since he surely knows that it is this selfsame Philippe Pinel who is justly famous for striking off the chains of the mental patients at the Bicêtre, an act which has always been regarded as a milestone in society's attempts to humanize the treatment of mental patients.

Unfortunately, equally blatant errors of fact tend to characterize attempts by Szasz in such works as Law, Liberty, and Psychiatry[18] and Psychiatric Justice[19] to describe cases culled from the professional literature of both law and psychiatry which he believes support his view that psychiatrists are persecutors, oppressors, and torturers. In Psychiatric Justice, for example, Szasz declares that the Court's decision in the well-known case of Durham v. North Carolina, though ostensibly an attempt to broaden the legal definition of insanity so as to protect seriously mentally-ill defendants from criminal prosecution, was actually an attempt to oppress Negroes like the defendant Monte Durham by maintaining state control over them and thus depriving them—particularly in the South—of the civil rights enjoyed by whites. A reading of the facts in Durham v. North Carolina soon reveals, however, not only that Szasz' interpretation of it is both outrageous and absurd, but also that—alas for Szasz' argument—the defendant Monte Durham was not a Negro, but a Southern white! It is the appearance (and repetition) of such egregious errors of fact in Szasz' writings that seems to have caused eminent psychiatrists and lawyers—Manfred S. Guttmacher and Bernard L. Diamond, for instance—to question Szasz' integrity.[20] To quote from Diamond's review of Law, Liberty, and Psychiatry: "Szasz appears to abandon his sense of professional integrity and to leave behind his clinical skills and experience. He discusses clinical cases and quotes extensively from the professional literature to support his conclusions. I am familiar with the details of certain of these cases, and I know very well the professional articles from which he draws material. I am indignant and outraged by the apparent distortion and falsity of this material."[21]

Persons now labeled mentally ill should not be sent involuntarily to so-called mental institutions; if they commit crimes, they should be prosecuted and punished like everyone else.

As has been seen, Szasz' thesis that there is no such thing as mental illness is, to say the least, dubious. Nevertheless, because the non-existence of mental illness is the premise upon which Szasz bases his conclusion that persons now labeled mentally ill should not be sent involuntarily to so-called mental institutions—as well as his further conclusion that if such persons commit crimes, they should be prosecuted and punished like everyone else—it is perhaps understandable that Szasz offers comparatively little data to support these conclusions. After all, if mental illness is simply a "myth" (a term Szasz stresses in his seminal work *The Myth of Mental Illness*[22]), it is hard to imagine an acceptable reason for labeling people mentally ill, sending them against their wishes to mental institutions, and freeing them from the restraints and penalties normally imposed by the law. Indeed, on this basis it may even be possible to defend Szasz' failure to confront what is surely a veritable mountain of evidence—psychoanalytic and historical particularly[23]—which casts the most serious doubts upon his view that the involuntary commitment of the "insane" to mental institutions ought to be abolished; and that instead, these unfortunates ought to be subjected to the processes and penalties of the criminal law. Also, in line with the foregoing, there is no consideration by Szasz that prison might be just one of those institutions where these various abuses, oppressions, persecutions, and tortures that he seeks to avoid actually take place, and in fact probably to a far greater degree toward disturbed people than is the case in mental institutions. On the other hand, the existence or non-existence of mental illness can hardly be used to justify the incredible number of misconceptions and errors concerning the law—examples of which will now be given—that mark Szasz' discussions of society's treatment of the mentally ill and related matters.

dramatic statement that rule making by administrative agencies is "a system of . . . lawlessness."[24] In making this charge, Szasz seems unaware however, that the power of an administrative agency to make rules may be expressly conferred by statute; that the formulation of these rules is often hedged about with significant restrictions)including the need to hold public hearings, to publish the rules in the *Federal Register* before they become operative, and so on); and that the rules are usually subject to legal challenge in the courts.

Further, Szasz goes on to assert that administrative law "exempts public officials—acting in performance or in purported performance of their official duties—from the jurisdiction of ordinary legal tribunals,"[25] apparently failing to realize that, once administrative remedies are exhausted, many if not most decisions handed down by administrative officials in controversies with private parties are reviewable in the courts.

In addition, Szasz seems to believe that administrative agencies—*as contrasted with the courts*—are inappropriate forums for adjudicating controversies between the public and private individuals. As Szasz sees it, because the persons who work for administrative agencies are public employees, they will inevitably favor the government in controversies between the government and private parties.[26] In so arguing, Szasz seems unaware of the many safeguards (provided by the Administrative Procedure Act, for example) to minimize any progovernment bias that may exist among employees of administrative agencies. Also, he seems unaware that *many administrative agencies exhibit a strong bias not in favor of the public, but rather in favor of the industries they regulate.*[27]And even more to the point here, he appears to forget that *the judges in ordinary courts—like the employees of administrative agencies—are themselves civil servants employed by the public.* Hence, contrary to what Szasz seems to believe, employment by the government in no way distinguishes judges in ordinary courts from judges in administrative agencies—and, therefore, cannot serve as a basis for supposing that the

In *Law, Liberty, and Psychiatry,* for instance, Szasz makes the

414

former are superior to the latter in controversies between the government and private parties.

Szasz' errors and misconceptions concerning the law seem to be particularly blatant thus when he attempts, for example, to provide a theoretical basis for the view that the involuntary commitment of the so-called insane to mental institutions ought to be abolished; and that instead, these persons ought to be treated like everyone else under the law—he contrasts what he describes as the "legal" concept of the state with the "medical" concept of the state. Thus, in a comparatively recent article entitled "Justice In the Therapeutic State" (in which Szasz tends to use such terms as "law," "justice," and the "state" interchangeably), he contends that: "In the legal concept of the State, justice is both an end and a means. When such a State is just, it may be said to have fulfilled its domestic function. It then has no further claim on its citizens, save for defense against external aggression. What people do, whether they are virtuous or sinful, healthy or sick, rich or poor, educated or stupid, is none of the State's business."[28]

Unfortunately—or perhaps fortunately—no such state has ever existed, nor exists at present. What records we have reveal that from the most ancient times to the present, societies have always tried to protect some group interests that are likely to have conflicted with the urges and desires of some of their members. The ancient restrictions upon cannibalism and incest provide obvious cases in point.[29] Indeed, the achievement of a workable balance between individual and group interests is the *sine qua non* of life in society. In any event, however, it is doubtful that even the most ancient times to the present defenders of individual rights and freedoms would deny that societies have the right to try to prevent epidemics, to protect their water supply from pollution and their food supply from depletion and destruction, to require their members (to have the education needed) to understand and obey the laws of society, and so on. Further, implicit in Szasz' description of "the legal concept of the State" is the view that there is only one such concept, and that this is what Szasz is describing. The fact is,

like everyone else—would be to extend this paper far beyond its intended limits. After all, these are matters which hundreds—if not thousands of books and articles touch upon.[33] Nevertheless, a few brief comments concerning Szasz' views seem required here.

To begin with, "all societies we know of have classified some of their members into categories analogous to our term 'mentally ill.'"[34] And, indisputably, the so-called mentally ill present extremely troublesome social problems that "will not vanish by slight of hand or pen."[35]

Szasz states repeatedly that he wants to shield persons who are labeled mentally ill from discrimination and oppression by society. Yet he seems unaware that subjecting these persons to prosecution and punishment under the criminal law, especially if they are unable to control the urges that beset them, or lack the mental clarity or capacity needed to aid their counsel in preparing an adequate defense, may itself be a form of discrimination and oppression. Szasz' stated desire to protect persons accused of being mentally ill also presumably finds reflection in his demand that their involuntary commitment to mental institutions be prohibited. Yet Szasz seems to fail to realize that commitment to a mental institution may offer desperately needed help and protection to persons who are so disorganized and bewildered that they cannot take care of themselves.[36]

In addition, Szasz seems to be unaware that, historically, his "solution" to the problems posed by the presence in society of persons considered to be mentally ill—insisting upon their "freedom" to sleep in doorways and to wander in confusion and bewilderment through the streets, and his demanding that they be prosecuted and punished for the crimes they commit—was tried for centuries and found wanting. Szasz somehow seems to forget that the crimes which he himself alleges the mentally ill were once accused of such as heresy and witchcraft, were once punished in such horrible ways as stoning to death and burning at the stake. And as the investigations of Dorothia

Dix reveal, the "freedom" enjoyed by the mentally ill before the creation of the modern mental institution was the "freedom" to be locked away in an attic, cellar, or outhouse, and the "freedom" to wander lost and neglected through the countryside, without family, friends, sustenance, or hope.[37]

The point is that, as Norman Dain has stressed, "eliminating involuntary commitment will not eliminate the social problems created, especially in a mass society, by the existence of people who cannot function at a certain level or in certain socially prescribed ways."[38] Or as Robert Scharf has so movingly put it: "A person who is in danger because of a lack of insight into his own mental illness is a special case before society and the law. It is unbrotherly and unloving to think that his safety and treatment are less important that his personal freedom, when his ability to choose is hobbled or absent. Only an ideological zealot can contend that a person's life is worth the philosophical purity of having every individual, whatever his state of mind, entirely determine his own fate."[39]

As the discussions in the preceding pages have sought to reveal, Szasz clearly fails to prove the highly questionable thesis analyzed in this paper that he has been advancing in a series of books during the past 15 years. Not only does he fail to support his views with obviously needed evidence as well as ignoring a huge amount of evidence contrary to these views, but he substitutes assumptions, repetitive assertions, and "word magic" for proof, commits elementary and blatant errors of logic, so misinterprets and misrepresents relevant facts and applicable law that colleagues have accused him of having "lost all regard for the intellectual honesty and integrity of his own scholarship."[40]

All of this is, of course, a great pity. Szasz is, by far, today's best known writer on the relationship between psychiatry and the law. His books are widely read and his views are often referred to and quoted. Had he not claimed far more than he could possible prove—had he admitted, for example, that he was

however, that what Szasz considers to be "the legal concept of the State" is but one among many possible concepts of the state; and is no more the lawful or "legal" concept of the state than the Communist, Fascist, or Hottentot concept of the state—or your or my concept of the state.

Another one of Szasz' many mis-statements concerning the law is his declaration that: "The notion common to all diverse concepts of justice is *contract*, the expectation that we shall keep our promises to others and they shall keep theirs to us. . . ."[30] Because Szasz' description of the word "contract" differs markedly from the technical way in which lawyers usually define the term,[31] its employment in this inaccurate manner in an article presumably devoted to describing differences between "legal" and "medical" methodology is likely to confuse and mislead the reader.

But even if this problem did not exist, Szasz' statement would still be unsound, since—as studies by numerous legal scholars reveal—there are many concepts of law and justice (terms which, as has been pointed out, Szasz tends to use interchangeably) that appear to have nothing whatsoever to do with the notion of contract, certainly as Szasz defines it. The ancient view (advocated particularly by the Sophists) that justice is "the interest of the stronger" is such a "noncontractual" concept of justice, as is the view that justice is what God or an earthly sovereign commands—as, indeed, is the belief that justice is synonymous with morality, or synonymous with divine or human reason. In fact, at least six of the 12 basic conceptions of law and justice described by the renowned legal scholar Roscoe Pound have little or northing to do with the concept of contract, either as Szasz employs it or as lawyers usually define it.[32]

To turn now from an examination of Szasz' errors and misconceptions concerning the law to a discussion of the merits of his views that persons now labeled mentally ill should not be sent involuntarily to so-called mental institutions—and that if they commit crimes, they should be prosecuted and punished

416

unable to demonstrate that there was no such thing as mental illness; and that all he could hope to show was that the conditions psychiatrists describe as mental illnesses may *also* reflect ethical, social, legal, political, or other problems—as David P. Ausubel has put it, "since personality disorder and immorality are ... [not] mutually exclusive conditions, the concept of mental illness need not necessarily obscure the issue of moral accountability"[41]—it is doubtful that peers would refer to his books as "pernicious"[42] or describe him as a propagandist and demagogue.[43]

Notes

1. Alan A. Stone, "Psychiatry Kills: A Critical Evaluation of Dr. Thomas Szasz," *Journal of Psychiatry and Law*, I, No. 1 (Spring 1973), pp. 23, 25.

2. *Id.* at 28.

3. Book review by Bernard L. Diamond of Thomas S. Szasz' *Law, Liberty, and Psychiatry*, in *California Law Review*, LII (1964), pp. 899, 905.

4. See *e.g.*, Thomas S. Szasz, *Law, Liberty, and Psychiatry* (New York: Macmillan, 1963), pp. 12-13.

5. See, *e.g.*, D. F. Scott and Martin S. Schwartz, "EEG Features of Depressive and Schizophrenic States," *British Journal Of Psychiatry*, CXXVI (1975), pp. 408-13.

6. *Webster's New International Dictionary of the English Language* (2d ed., unabridged; Springfield, Mass.: G & C. Merriam Co., 1955), p. 1241; see also *The Random House Dictionary of the English Language* (unabridged; New York: Random House, 1973), p. 710.

7. John Hospers, *An Introduction to Philosophical Analysis* (New York: Prentice-Hall 1953), pp. 36-37.

8. Thomas S. Szasz, *The Second Sin* (Anchor Books ed.; Garden City. New York: Doubleday, 1974), pp. 23, 25.

9. See Sandor Ferenczi, "Stages in the Development of the Sense of Reality," in *Sex in Psycho Analysis* (New York: Dover, 1956), pp. 181, 194-96.

10. David P. Ausubel, "Personality Disorder Is Disease," *American Psychologist*, XVI (1961), pp. 69, 72.

11. Stone, *op. cit.*, p. 25.

12. Szasz, *The Second Sin, op. cit.*, pp. 83-84.

13. Thomas S. Szasz, "Medicine and Madness," *Journal of Psychiatry and Law*, III, No. 2 (Summer 1975), pp. 215, 222.

14. Thomas S. Szasz, *The Manufacture of Madness* (Delta Books ed.; New York: Dell Publishing, 1970), pp. xv, xvi, xix-xx, 57.

15. Thomas S. Szasz, *The Age of Madness* (New York: Aronson, 1974).

16. Book review by Norman Dain of Thomas S. Szasz' *The Age of Madness*, in *Journal of Psychiatry and Law*, III, No. 3 (Fall 1975), pp. 381, 382.

17. Szasz, *The Age of Madness, op. cit.*, p. 18.

18. Szasz, *op. cit.*

19. Thomas S. Szasz, *Psychiatric Justice* (New York: Macmillan, 1965).

20. Manfred S. Guttmacher, "Critique of Views of Thomas Szasz on Legal Psychiatry," *Archives of General Psychiatry*, X (1964), pp. 238, 240-45. It may be appropriate to note here that the references to Monte Durham in Szasz' *Psychiatric Justice* have been edited out of both the text and index of the paperback edition of this book (First Collier Books Edition, 1971), without any indication to the reader that this or any other changes have been made in the original edition of the book (except, perhaps, for a footnote on page 269, referring to a newspaper published in 1968).

21. Diamond, *op. cit.*, p. 902.

22. Thomas S. Szasz, *The Myth of Mental Illness* (New York: Hoeber-Harper, 1961).

23. See, *e.g.*, C. G. Schoenfeld, "Psychoanalysis, Criminal Justice Planning and Reform," *Criminal Law Bulletin*, VII, No. 4 (May 1971), pp. 313-27; Dain, *op. cit.*

24. Szasz, *Law, Liberty, and Psychiatry, op. cit.*, p. 216.

25. *Ibid.*

26. *Id.* at 218.

27. This "fact of life" regarding administrative agencies is periodically "rediscovered" by investigative journalists. Thus, in a recent syndicated column, Jack Anderson charges that administrative agencies "have been captured by the industries they are supposed to regulate." (*Staten Island Advance*, October 12, 1975, p. E1.)

28. Thomas S. Szasz, "Justice in the Therapeutic State," in Lynn Irvine, Jr. & Terry Brelje, *Law, Psychiatry and the Mentally Disordered Offender* (Springfield, Ill: Thomas, 1973), II, pp. 18, 26.

29. One relevant work that immediately comes to mind here is Sigmund Freud's anthropological study *Totem and Taboo.*

30. Szasz, "Justice in the Therapeutic State," *op. cit.*, p. 19.

31. See, *e.g.*, the various definitions of "contract" in *Black's Law Dictionary* (3d ed.; St. Paul, Minn.: West Publishing, 1933), pp. 421-25.

32. See Roscoe Pound, *An Introduction to the Philosophy of Law* (rev. ed.; New Haven, Conn.: Yale University Press, 1954), pp. 26-29.

33. See, *e.g.*, the huge number of citations in Herbert Fingarette, *The Meaning of Criminal Insanity* (Berkeley, Calif.: University of California Press, 1972).

34. Dain, *op. cit.*, pp. 384-85.

35. *Id.* at 385.

36. See, *e.g.*, Book review by Robert D. Scharf of Bruce Ennis' *Prisoners of Psychiatry*, in *Journal of Psychiatry and Law*, II, No. 3 (Fall 1974), pp. 361, 366.

37. See Dain, *op. cit.*, p. 383.

38. *Id.* at 384.

39. Scharf. *op. cit.*, p. 368.

40. Diamond, *op. cit.*, p. 905.

41. Ausubel, *op. cit.*, p. 73.

42. Guttmacher, op. cit., p. 244.

43. Stone, *op. cit.*, p. 25.

1. According to Schoenfeld, what is the role of physical evidence in establishing the presence of mental illness?

2. On what 5 grounds does Schoenfeld attack Szasz' theory?

3. What evidence does Schoenfeld claim is needed for Szasz to prove his point that mental illness is a myth?

4. Why does Schoenfeld reject Szasz' contention that what is called mental illness represents only 'problems in living'?

5. Why does Schoenfeld think that Szasz is wrong in saying that lawbreakers ought to go to prison, not to hospitals?

DISCUSSION OF READING #2 QUESTIONS

1. He states that brain wave patterns and other physical or organic evidence indicates that there is a medical state appropriately called mental illness.

2. Schoenfeld claims that Szasz fails to provide proper evidence for his views, that he makes logical, factual, and legal errors, and that he employs 'word magic' to make his argument.

3. Schoenfeld argues that Szasz must provide clinical evidence that those people labelled mentally ill by other psychiatrists are, in fact, perfectly normal and healthy.

4. Schoenfeld argues that the term is too vague and general and, therefore, is meaningless. He says that developmental difficulties occurring in one's infancy and childhood which result in mental illness are well documented and cannot be described as ethical, political, or social problems in living.

5. Schoenfeld says that prisons frequently commit the very abuses and persecutions which Szasz so forcefully opposes and that to follow Szasz' suggestions would probably lead to more human suffering rather than less. To subject people who are not able to control their impulses to a criminal prosecution and imprisonment is itself discriminatory and oppressive. People who lack insight into their own problems pose a special situation for law and society and must be treated differently.

A SPECIAL REPRINT
WINTER 1976

THE JOURNAL OF

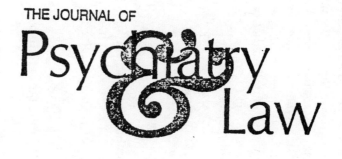

Psychiatry
& Law

SZASZ AND THE LAW: AN ALTERNATIVE VIEW

by Lee S. Weinberg, Esq., Ph.D. and
   Richard E. Vatz, Ph.D.

Reprinted with the permission of Federal Legal Publications
Inc., 95 Morton St. New York, NY 10014, Journal of
Psychiatry and the Law, Winter, 1976, pp. 551-558.

Szasz and the law: an alternative view

BY LEE S. WEINBERG, ESQ., PH.D.
AND RICHARD E. VATZ, PH.D.

In a previous issue C. G. Schoenfeld attempted to disprove Thomas Szasz' theory that mental illness is a "myth" and to dispute Szasz' contention that current views of "mental illness" promote violent subjugation of human freedom in institutional and legal settings. This article argues that typical of many who criticize Dr. Szasz, Mr. Schoenfeld misunderstands and misrepresents Szasz' rich theoretical arguments concerning "mental illness" and the prevalent use in law and institutional psychiatry of medical models for analyzing human behavior. Additionally, the authors urge responsible researchers to further pursue the implications of an accurate understanding of Szasz' arguments for legal theory and practice.

In the Summer 1976 issue of *The Journal of Psychiatry and Law*, Mr. C. G. Schoenfeld offers "An Analysis of the Views of Thomas Szasz." In his article, Mr. Schoenfeld attempts to disprove Dr. Szasz' theses regarding the existence of "mental illness" and to dispute the accuracy of Szasz' description of the attitudes and actions of those who serve institutional psychiatry. In this answer to Mr. Schoenfeld, we will argue that he fails in the former because he simply does not understand Szasz' argument and is only partially successful in the latter which, in any event, is less crucial to an understanding of Szasz' theory. Schoenfeld argues that Szasz ". . . fails to support his views with appropriate evidence, ignores crucial evidence contrary to these views, makes egregious mistakes of logic . . . and commits blatant factual and legal errors."[1] The author has outlined, interestingly enough, the precise areas of weakness which we believe lead *him* astray in his critique of Szasz. In

addition, he claims he will avoid "name calling" and "polemics"[2] while in the same article calls Szasz a variety of names including "ideological zealot,"[3] "propagandist,"[4] and "demagogue."[5]

The major problem in Schoenfeld and in many other critiques of Szasz is a failure to perceive the rich theoretical perspective being offered. Szasz intertwines traditional theories of psychiatry and forensic psychiatry with theories of semiotic behavior. The superficial level of Schoenfeld's critique, however, can be seen in his reliance on dictionary definitions of "illness,"[6] an approach which ignores all anthropological, rhetorical, and meta-linguistic analyses of the way in which language functions to create the reality which we "see." His derisive reference to "word magic"[7] further reveals his inability to grasp Szasz' rhetorical perspective. In asserting that Szasz attempts to achieve the ". . . philosophically and epistemologically impossible . . . [feat of defining] something out of existence,"[8] Schoenfeld has overlooked, for example, the recent action of the American Psychiatric Association in defining the "disease" of homosexuality out of existence.

Additional evidence of Schoenfeld's lack of understanding of Szasz is his failure to address himself directly to the arguments in *The Myth of Mental Illness* which he identifies as Szasz' "seminal work,"[9] but cites only once in his article, and then merely to prove that Szasz indeed said that mental illness was a "myth."[10] In asking for "clinical evidence [of] . . . persons whom psychiatrists usually judge to be neurotic or psychotic, but whom he [Szasz] has interviewed or examined as a psychiatrist, and whom he has demonstrated to be completely normal,"[11] Schoenfeld again misses the entire point of the argument. Szasz does not maintain that such people are "normal"; indeed, he would find the question meaningless and irrelevant. The central point that Szasz makes is simply that such people and their behavior cannot be understood by use of a medical framework or medical language. That is, the medicalization of language is a pretense by which psychiatrists claim they understand behavior but which, in fact, only serves to accredit or discredit it. If a man machine-gunned infants in a maternity ward, Szasz would surely not say that it is "normal." He would say, however, that you will not shed light on this Szasz behavior by discussing it in medical terminology. Szasz would never argue that "they are as healthy as you or I,"[12] a point which Schoenfeld believes must be made to sustain Szasz' position. Again, Schoenfeld misunderstands. Szasz rejects the term "mental health" as well as "mental illness" since he rejects medical metaphors for understanding behavior.

Had Schoenfeld understood the foregoing, he would not have asked for "evidence" that mental illness does not exist. You cannot prove the nonexistence of anything, and in particular, you cannot, of course, prove the nonexistence of a metaphor. This confusion in Schoenfeld accounts for his analogizing Szasz' contention that mental illness is a myth to legislating "black swans out of existence by redefining the word 'swan.'"[13] Szasz says that mental illness (unlike swan) is a metaphor. What sorts of evidence does one proffer to disprove a metaphor? Usually, one does not need any evidence at all since most metaphors are recognized as such. If we say that someone who is ugly is a "dog" we would not call a kennel since we realize that "dog" here is a metaphor. With mental illness, however, Szasz contends that we mistake the metaphor for reality and thereby enfranchise the medical field to deal with aberrant behavior. In essence, Szasz doesn't think that killers are "normal"; he simply doesn't think their problem is medical. You don't prove the inappropriateness of a medical metaphor for understanding unusual behavior by disputing that the behavior is unusual or abnormal. You show it by fully accounting for the behavior in nonmedical ways.

The "... developmental difficulties occurring in infancy and childhood"[14] which Schoenfeld outlines are precisely what Szasz would agree are often involved. What are these problems if they are not "problems in living"? Schoenfeld attacks the "vagueness and generality"[15] of Szasz' notion of "problems in living." However, the term accurately reflects Szasz' position; namely, that such problems are diffuse and general and only appear to be specific and discrete as a consequence of the psychiatric categories used to describe them. Once more, Schoenfeld's criticism stems from a misreading of the Szasz position.

In sum, it is simply not Szasz' position at all that Schoenfeld's list of strange and/or dangerous people are "as mentally healthy as you or I."[16] The whole point is that they are communicating in unconventional idiom or acting in a manner understandable, perhaps, only to them.[17] When Schoenfeld describes "exhibitionists who cannot resist exposing their genitals in public" or others "who are compelled ... to perform bizarre rituals"[18] he begs the question of the person's alleged lack of control of his own behavior. More significantly, however, he misses Szasz' point which is not that such people are normal, but that their behavior cannot be made understandable by reference to a medical model. Szasz prefers the model of game playing, which Schoenfeld would realize if he read or understood The Myth of Mental Illness. As to the rituals, they may be seen as "bizarre" or "uplifting" depending upon who has the power to define what symbolic behavior is legitimate. It is this very point which Schoenfeld mistakenly interprets when he says that Szasz implies "... that most or all persons alleged in the past to be witches and heretics would be considered mentally ill by most or all of today's psychiatrists."[19] In fact, Szasz is merely making the argument that behavior perceived to be strange by those in power at any particular point in history will be discredited by whatever discrediting mechanism is operative at the time.

To prove the existence of mental illness, Schoenfeld uses the same illogic that he attributes to Szasz; in fact, he uses the exact such logical fallacies. He accuses Szasz of begging the question, that is, proving a conclusion by assuming it in the premise. He says Szasz attempts to "... define something out of existence."[20] This assumes that "mental illness" does exist, which is precisely the point in question. This elementary logical error is ubiquitous in Schoenfeld's article, and again results from his lack of understanding of Szasz. Another logical error

the Lord Chief Justice of England to show skepticism of administrative law among the administrators themselves.[24] For someone so upset by Szasz "blatant errors of fact"[25] this is a surprisingly blatant error of fact. Equally disturbing is Schoenfeld's attack on Szasz for "alleging rather than proving"[26] his argument. Schoenfeld, for example, states that Szasz provides no examples of psychiatric persecution. We simply refer him to *Ideology and Insanity*, *Ceremonial Chemistry*, or Szasz' many articles in *The New Republic* and *Psychology Today*, none of which is cited in Schoenfeld's article. Furthermore, Schoenfeld totally ignores his own standard of proving rather than alleging when he tells us that Bernard L. Diamond is "... indignant and outraged by the apparent distortion and falsity..."[27] which Diamond finds in *Law, Liberty, and Psychiatry*. While adequate to demonstrate Diamond's attitude toward Szasz, this is wholly inadequate to demonstrate that Szasz' portrayal of institutional psychiatry is inaccurate.

Schoenfeld's suggestion that Szasz is unaware that "... prison might be just one of those institutions where these various abuses, oppressions, persecutions and tortures that he seeks to avoid actually take place ..."[28] is both inaccurate and irrelevant. Szasz not only agrees with that but has often argued the need for major change in the prison system himself. However, the inadequacy of the prison system has absolutely nothing to do with the validity or invalidity of Szasz' contention concerning mental illness. It only means that society probably will continue to ignore the inhumane treatment of those in prison just as it ignores what occurs in mental institutions. Szasz' question concerns the notion of medical persons dealing with nonmedical problems and justifying it through the clever, if unconscious, use of language; he is not attempting to prove that prisons are more humane than mental institutions.

In an effort to dispute Szasz' argument that many administrators are servants of the state, not the "patients," Schoenfeld raises the well-established fact that clientele groups

is Schoenfeld's argument that those labelled neurotic or psychotic are mentally ill in view of physical signs which are present:

Unfortunately for Szasz' argument, physical signs or symptoms of mental illness frequently *do* exist. For example, electroencephalograms have shown that the brain wave patterns of many persons whom psychiatrists regard as seriously mentally ill are often highly erratic and abnormal. Further, a whole range of physical signs or symptoms ranging from facial tics and allergic reactions to serious gastric and pulmonary disorders have been shown to reflect the presence of mental disorders.[21]

This is to argue *a posteriori*. We rarely look for such disturbances in what we consider normal behavior. In addition, if we found such physical evidence in a person whose behavior was conventional, we would not call it mental illness. Furthermore, when a person is "stricken" with mental illness and we discover certain EEG patterns, we rarely have prior EEG information on that individual. Quite possibly, he had the same EEG patterns when he was considered "mentally healthy." Szasz argues that the unconventional behavior itself is not a sign or symptom of illness, but rather necessary and often sufficient evidence of "mental illness." Certainly, unusual behavior can be seen as "physical evidence"[22] of mental illness only through the use of Schoenfeld's own peculiar type of "word magic." For Szasz, then, the fact that the symptoms of mental illness *are* the disease shows the falsity of the medical model. Moreover, even in cases of brain disease such as brain tumors or Huntington's chorea, the metaphor of mental illness is totally misleading. As Szasz maintains throughout *The Myth of Mental Illness*, even in the small percentage of those people who demonstrate organic brain disease, their *behaviors* cannot be understood through chemical-neurological terms.

Schoenfeld also is faulty in his own use of evidence, a charge he makes against Szasz. For example, he argues that in *Law, Liberty, and Psychiatry*, "Szasz makes the dramatic statement that rule making by administrative agencies is a 'system of lawlessness.'"[23] Szasz, in fact, isn't saying this but is quoting

424

have frequently captured the agencies which supposedly regulate them in the public interest.[29] However, the analogy is a poor one. Quite unlike the groups Schoenfeld sees as being able to influence the administrative agencies which regulate them, mental patients do not have their people sitting as administrative judges, administrators, and staff researchers.

Unfortunately, Mr. Schoenfeld, who is a competent scholar with a solid background in problems of law and psychoanalysis,[30] fails to come to grips with the nature of the Szazian position he seeks to destroy. He relies heavily on "... respected writers on psychiatry and the law ..."[31] rather than trying to comprehend what Szasz is saying. For an author to attack someone who he admits is the "... most prodigious, and surely the best known, writer today on the relationship between psychiatry and the law ..."[32] requires him to be fully conversant with the subject's positions and works. Again, we find Schoenfeld remiss in both his comprehension of Szasz' concepts and his selective research which ignores many of Szasz' major writings. It certainly comes as no surprise to us that psychiatrists, and especially institutional psychiatrists, those most threatened by the implications of Szasz' theory, would vociferously denounce him and defend their continued ability to practice a lucrative, high status trade. Nor does it surprise us that many lawyers who criticize Szasz find it difficult to deal with his broad perspective. We feel that if more people actually understood what Dr. Szasz has said, they would be better equipped to handle his arguments; they are simply too important to be dealt with inaccurately or illogically.

Notes

1. C. G. Schoenfeld, "An Analysis of the Views of Thomas S. Szasz," *The Journal of Psychiatry and Law*, IV (Summer, 1976), 245.

2. *Ibid.*

3. *Ibid.* p. 260.

4. *Ibid.* p. 261.

5. *Ibid.*

6. *Ibid.* p. 248.

7. *Ibid.* p. 249.

8. *Ibid.* p. 248.

9. *Ibid.* p. 255.

10. *Ibid.*

11. *Ibid.* p. 246.

12. *Ibid.* p. 247.

13. *Ibid.* p. 248.

14. *Ibid.* p. 251.

15. *Ibid.* p. 250.

16. *Ibid.* p. 247.

17. See Richard E. Vatz and Trevor Melia, Bibliographic Book Review of Thomas S. Szasz, in *Quarterly Journal of Speech* (forthcoming).

18. Schoenfeld, *op. cit.*, p. 246.

19. *Ibid.*, p. 253.

20. *Ibid.*, p. 248.

21. *Ibid.*, p. 247.

22. *Ibid.*

23. *Ibid.*, p. 256.

24. Thomas S. Szasz, *Law, Liberty, and Psychiatry* (New York: Macmillan, 1963), p. 216.

25. Schoenfeld, *op. cit.*, p. 254.

26. *Ibid.*, p. 252.

27. *Ibid.*, p. 254.

28. *Ibid.*, p. 255.

29. See Theodore J. Lowi, *The End of Liberalism* (New York: W. W. Norton, 1969) for a detailed argument along these lines.

30. See C. G. Schoenfeld, *Psychoanalysis and the Law* (Springfield, Illinois: Charles C. Thomas, 1973).

31. Schoenfeld, *op. cit.*, p. 245.

32. *Ibid.*

1. What arguments do Weinberg and Vatz provide to reject Schoenfeld's claim that Szasz fails to provide the proper type evidence to support his 'myth of mental illness' statement.

2. What defense is raised to Schoenfeld's claim that 'problems in living' is too vague and general a concept to deal with behavioral problems?

3. How do Weinberg and Vatz respond to Schoenfeld's claim that there is
    a great deal of organic evidence of mental illness?

1. Weinberg and Vatz argue that Schoenfeld does not really understand what Szasz is saying. Szasz does not seek to prove that those labelled mentally ill by other psychiatrists are, in fact, perfectly normal or healthy. Rather, he maintains that references to normality or health are appropriate for medical situations and entirely inappropriate for behavioral situations. Sickness, in a medical context, represents the deviation from health, a well defined state; however, 'sickness' in the behavioral context, represents deviation from a social norm. Thus, if the norm changes, behavior which was 'sick' one day may be deemed 'healthy' the next. Needless to say, we cannot do away with real illnesses so easily. For example, homosexuality ceased to be seen as a disease only when attitudes toward such behavior became more liberal. However, changed attitudes toward cancer could never cause us to view cancer victims as healthy.

2. Weinberg and Vatz argue that the very problems which Schoenfeld discusses as developmental problems are covered by Szasz' 'problems in living'. To use specific terms, as psychiatrists are prone to do, is to create the impression of precision and understanding where vagueness and generality are more accurate reflections of our knowledge.

3. They argue that since we only look for physical disturbances in those people deemed to be 'ill,' we have no idea whether such disturbances commonly occur in the rest of the 'normal' population or if such disturbances have always been present in the mentally 'ill' even when they were acting quite normally.

Reading #4

On Being Sane

in

Insane Places

D. L. Rosenhan

If sanity and insanity exist, how shall we know them?

The question is neither capricious nor itself insane. However much we may be personally convinced that we can tell the normal from the abnormal, the evidence is simply not compelling. It is commonplace, for example, to read about murder trials wherein eminent psychiatrists for the defense are con- tradicted by equally eminent psychia- trists for the prosecution on the matter of the defendant's sanity. More gen- erally, there are a great deal of conflict- ing data on the reliability, utility, and meaning of such terms as "sanity," "in- sanity," "mental illness," and "schizo- phrenia" (1). Finally, as early as 1934, Benedict suggested that normality and abnormality are not universal (2).

What is viewed as normal in one cul- ture may be seen as quite aberrant in another. Thus, notions of normality and abnormality may not be quite as accu- rate as people believe they are.

To raise questions regarding normal- ity and abnormality is in no way to question the fact that some behaviors are deviant or odd. Murder is deviant. So, too, are hallucinations. Nor does raising such questions deny the exis- tence of the personal anguish that is often associated with "mental illness." Anxiety and depression exist. Psycho- logical suffering exists. But normality and abnormality, sanity and insanity, and the diagnoses that flow from them

The author is professor of psychology and law at Stanford University, Stanford, California 94305. Portions of these data were presented to collo- quiums of the psychology departments at the University of California at Berkeley and at Santa Barbara; University of Arizona, Tucson; and Harvard University, Cambridge, Massachusetts.

may be less substantive than many believe them to be.

At its heart, the question of whether the sane can be distinguished from the insane (and whether degrees of insanity can be distinguished from each other) is a simple matter: do the salient characteristics that lead to diagnoses reside in the patients themselves or in the environments and contexts in which observers find them? From Bleuler, through Kretchmer, through the formulators of the recently revised *Diagnostic and Statistical Manual* of the American Psychiatric Association, the belief has been strong that patients present symptoms, that those symptoms can be categorized, and, implicitly, that the sane are distinguishable from the insane. More recently, however, this belief has been questioned. Based in part on theoretical and anthropological considerations, but also on philosophical, legal, and therapeutic ones, the view has grown that psychological categorization of mental illness is useless at best and downright harmful, misleading, and pejorative at worst. Psychiatric diagnoses, in this view, are in the minds of the observers and are not valid summaries of characteristics displayed by the observed (3–5).

Gains can be made in deciding which of these is more nearly accurate by getting normal people (that is, people who do not have, and have never suffered, symptoms of serious psychiatric disorders) admitted to psychiatric hospitals and then determining whether they were discovered to be sane and, if so, how. If the sanity of such pseudopatients were always detected, there would be prima facie evidence that a sane individual can be distinguished from the insane context in which he is found. Normality (and presumably abnormality) is distinct enough that it can be recognized wherever it occurs, for it is carried within the person. If, on the other hand, the sanity of the pseudopatients were never discovered, serious difficulties would arise for those who support traditional modes of psychiatric diagnosis. Given that the hospital staff was not incompetent, that the pseudopatient had been behaving as sanely as he had been outside of the hospital, and that it had never been previously suggested that he belonged in a psychiatric hospital, such an unlikely outcome would support the view that psychiatric diagnosis betrays little about the patient but much about the environment in which an observer finds him.

This article describes such an experiment. Eight sane people gained secret admission to 12 different hospitals (6). Their diagnostic experiences constitute the data of the first part of this article; the remainder is devoted to a description of their experiences in psychiatric institutions. Too few psychiatrists and psychologists, even those who have worked in such hospitals, know what the experience is like. They rarely talk about it with former patients, perhaps because they distrust information coming from the previously insane. Those who have worked in psychiatric hospitals are likely to have adapted so thoroughly to the settings that they are insensitive to the impact of that experience. And while there have been occasional reports of researchers who submitted themselves to psychiatric hospitalization (7), these researchers have commonly remained in the hospitals for short periods of time, often with the knowledge of the hospital staff. It is difficult to know the extent to which they were treated like patients or like research colleagues. Nevertheless, their reports about the inside of the psychiatric hospital have been valuable. This article extends those efforts.

Pseudopatients and Their Settings

The eight pseudopatients were a varied group. One was a psychology graduate student in his 20's. The remaining seven were older and "established." Among them were three psychologists, a pediatrician, a psychiatrist, a painter, and a housewife. Three pseudopatients were women, five were men. All of them employed pseudonyms, lest their alleged diagnoses embarrass them later. Those who were in mental health professions alleged another occupation in order to avoid the special attentions that might be accorded by staff, as a matter of courtesy or caution, to ailing colleagues (8). With the exception of myself (I was the first pseudopatient and my presence was known to the hospital administrator and chief psychologist and, so far as I can tell, to them alone), the presence of pseudopatients and the nature of the research program was not known to the hospital staffs (9).

The settings were similarly varied. In order to generalize the findings, admission into a variety of hospitals was sought. The 12 hospitals in the sample were located in five different states on the East and West coasts. Some were

old and shabby, some were quite new. Some were research-oriented, others not. Some had good staff-patient ratios, others were quite understaffed. Only one was a strictly private hospital. All of the others were supported by state or federal funds or, in one instance, by university funds.

After calling the hospital for an appointment, the pseudopatient arrived at the admissions office complaining that he had been hearing voices. Asked what the voices said, he replied that they were often unclear, but as far as he could tell they said "empty," "hollow," and "thud." The voices were unfamiliar and were of the same sex as the pseudopatient. The choice of these symptoms was occasioned by their apparent similarity to existential symptoms. Such symptoms are alleged to arise from painful concerns about the perceived meaninglessness of one's life. It is as if the hallucinating person were saying, "My life is empty and hollow." The choice of these symptoms was also determined by the *absence* of a single report of existential psychoses in the literature.

Beyond alleging the symptoms and falsifying name, vocation, and employment, no further alterations of person, history, or circumstances were made. The significant events of the pseudopatient's life history were presented as they had actually occurred. Relationships with parents and siblings, with spouse and children, with people at work and in school, consistent with the aforementioned exceptions, were described as they were or had been. Frustrations and upsets were described along with joys and satisfactions. These facts are important to remember. If anything, they strongly biased the subsequent results in favor of detecting sanity, since none of their histories or current behaviors were seriously pathological in any way.

Immediately upon admission to the psychiatric ward, the pseudopatient ceased simulating *any* symptoms of abnormality. In some cases, there was a brief period of mild nervousness and anxiety, since none of the pseudopatients really believed that they would be admitted so easily. Indeed, their shared fear was that they would be immediately exposed as frauds and greatly embarrassed. Moreover, many of them had never visited a psychiatric ward; even those who had, nevertheless had some genuine fears about what might happen to them. Their nervousness, then, was quite appropriate to the nov-

430

elty of the hospital setting, and it abated rapidly.

Apart from that short-lived nervousness, the pseudopatient behaved on the ward as he "normally" behaved. The pseudopatient spoke to patients and staff as he might ordinarily. Because there is uncommonly little to do on a psychiatric ward, he attempted to engage others in conversation. When asked by staff how he was feeling, he indicated that he was fine, that he no longer experienced symptoms. He responded to instructions from attendants, to calls for medication (which was not swallowed), and to dining-hall instructions. Beyond such activities as were available to him on the admissions ward, he spent his time writing down his observations about the ward, its patients, and the staff. Initially these notes were written "secretly," but as it soon became clear that no one much cared, they were subsequently written on standard tablets of paper in such public places as the dayroom. No secret was made of these activities.

The pseudopatient, very much as a true psychiatric patient, entered a hospital with no foreknowledge of when he would be discharged. Each was told that he would have to get out by his own devices, essentially by convincing the staff that he was sane. The psychological stresses associated with hospitalization were considerable, and all but one of the pseudopatients desired to be discharged almost immediately after being admitted. They were, therefore, motivated not only to behave sanely, but to be paragons of cooperation. That their behavior was in no way disruptive is confirmed by nursing reports, which have been obtained on most of the patients. These reports uniformly indicate that the patients were "friendly," "cooperative," and "exhibited no abnormal indications."

The Normal Are Not Detectably Sane

Despite their public "show" of sanity, the pseudopatients were never detected. Admitted, except in one case, with a diagnosis of schizophrenia (10), each was discharged with a diagnosis of schizophrenia "in remission." The label "in remission" should in no way be dismissed as a formality, for at no time during any hospitalization had any question been raised about any pseudopatient's simulation. Nor are there any indications in the hospital records that the pseudopatient's status was suspect. Rather, the evidence is strong that, once labeled schizophrenic, the pseudopatient was stuck with that label. If the pseudopatient was to be discharged, he must naturally be "in remission"; but he was not sane, nor, in the institution's view, had he ever been sane.

The uniform failure to recognize sanity cannot be attributed to the quality of the hospitals, for, although there were considerable variations among them, several are considered excellent. Nor can it be alleged that there was simply not enough time to observe the pseudopatients. Length of hospitalization ranged from 7 to 52 days, with an average of 19 days. The pseudopatients were not, in fact, carefully observed, but this failure clearly speaks more to traditions within psychiatric hospitals than to lack of opportunity.

Finally, it cannot be said that the failure to recognize the pseudopatients' sanity was due to the fact that they were not behaving sanely. While there was clearly some tension present in all of them, their daily visitors could detect no serious behavioral consequences—nor, indeed, could other patients. It was quite common for the patients to "detect" the pseudopatients' sanity. During the first three hospitalizations, when accurate counts were kept, 35 of a total of 118 patients on the admissions ward voiced their suspicions, some vigorously. "You're not crazy. You're a journalist, or a professor [referring to the continual note-taking]. You're checking up on the hospital." While most of the patients were reassured by the pseudopatient's insistence that he had been sick before he came in but was fine now, some continued to believe that the pseudopatient was sane throughout his hospitalization (11). The fact that the patients often recognized normality when staff did not raises important questions.

Failure to detect sanity during the course of hospitalization may be due to the fact that physicians operate with a strong bias toward what statisticians call the type 2 error (5). This is to say that physicians are more inclined to call a healthy person sick (a false positive, type 2) than a sick person healthy (a false negative, type 1). The reasons for this are not hard to find: it is clearly more dangerous to misdiagnose illness than health. Better to err on the side of caution, to suspect illness even among the healthy.

But what holds for medicine does not hold equally well for psychiatry. Medical illnesses, while unfortunate, are not commonly pejorative. Psychiatric diagnoses, on the contrary, carry with them personal, legal, and social stigmas (12). It was therefore important to see whether the tendency toward diagnosing the sane insane could be reversed. The following experiment was arranged at a research and teaching hospital whose staff had heard these findings but doubted that such an error could occur in their hospital. The staff was informed that at some time during the following 3 months, one or more pseudopatients would attempt to be admitted into the psychiatric hospital. Each staff member was asked to rate each patient who presented himself at admissions or on the ward according to the likelihood that the patient was a pseudopatient. A 10-point scale was used, with a 1 and 2 reflecting high confidence that the patient was a pseudopatient.

Judgments were obtained on 193 patients who were admitted for psychiatric treatment. All staff who had had sustained contact with or primary responsibility for the patient—attendants, nurses, psychiatrists, physicians, and psychologists—were asked to make judgments. Forty-one patients were alleged, with high confidence, to be pseudopatients by at least one member of the staff. Twenty-three were considered suspect by at least one psychiatrist. Nineteen were suspected by one psychiatrist *and* one other staff member. Actually, no genuine pseudopatient (at least from my group) presented himself during this period.

The experiment is instructive. It indicates that the tendency to designate sane people as insane can be reversed when the stakes (in this case, prestige and diagnostic acumen) are high. But what can be said of the 19 people who were suspected of being "sane" by one psychiatrist and another staff member? Were these people truly "sane," or was it rather the case that in the course of avoiding the type 2 error the staff tended to make more errors of the first sort—calling the crazy "sane"? There is no way of knowing. But one thing is certain: any diagnostic process that lends itself so readily to massive errors of this sort cannot be a very reliable one.

The Stickiness of Psychodiagnostic Labels

Beyond the tendency to call the healthy sick—a tendency that accounts better for diagnostic behavior on admission than it does for such behavior after a lengthy period of exposure—the data speak to the massive role of labeling in psychiatric assessment. Having once been labeled schizophrenic, there is nothing the pseudopatient can do to overcome the tag. The tag profoundly colors others' perceptions of him and his behavior.

From one viewpoint, these data are hardly surprising, for it has long been known that elements are given meaning by the context in which they occur. Gestalt psychology made this point vigorously, and Asch (13) demonstrated that there are "central" personality traits (such as "warm" versus "cold") which are so powerful that they markedly color the meaning of other information in forming an impression of a given personality (14). "Insane," "schizophrenic," "manic-depressive," and "crazy" are probably among the most powerful of such central traits. Once a person is designated abnormal, all of his other behaviors and characteristics are colored by that label. Indeed, that label is so powerful that many of the pseudopatients' normal behaviors were overlooked entirely or profoundly misinterpreted. Some examples may clarify this issue.

Earlier I indicated that there were no changes in the pseudopatient's personal history and current status beyond those of name, employment, and, where necessary, vocation. Otherwise, a veridical description of personal history and circumstances was offered. Those circumstances were not psychotic. How were they made consonant with the diagnosis of psychosis? Or were those diagnoses modified in such a way as to bring them into accord with the circumstances of the pseudopatient's life, as described by him?

As far as I can determine, diagnoses were in no way affected by the relative health of the circumstances of a pseudopatient's life. Rather, the reverse occurred: the perception of his circumstances was shaped entirely by the diagnosis. A clear example of such translation is found in the case of a pseudopatient who had had a close relationship with his mother but was rather remote from his father during his early childhool. During adolescence and beyond, however, his father became a close friend, while his relationship with his mother cooled. His present relationship with his wife was characteristically close and warm. Apart from occasional angry exchanges, friction was minimal. The children had rarely been spanked. Surely there is nothing especially pathological about such a history. Indeed, many readers may see a similar pattern in their own experi-

ences, with no markedly deleterious consequences. Observe, however, how such a history was translated in the psychopathological context, this from the case summary prepared after the patient was discharged.

This white 39-year-old male . . . manifests a long history of considerable ambivalence in close relationships, which begins in early childhood. A warm relationship with his mother cools during his adolescence. A distant relationship to his father is described as. becoming very intense. Affective stability is absent. His attempts to control emotionality with his wife and children are punctuated by angry outbursts and, in the case of the children, spankings. And while he says that he has several good friends, one senses considerable ambivalence embedded in those relationships also. . . .

The facts of the case were unintentionally distorted by the staff to achieve consistency with a popular theory of the dynamics of a schizophrenic reaction (15). Nothing of an ambivalent nature had been described in relations with parents, spouse, or friends. To the extent that ambivalence could be inferred, it was probably not greater than is found in all human relationships. It is true the pseudopatient's relationships with his parents changed over time, but in the ordinary context that would hardly be remarkable—indeed, it might very well be expected. Clearly, the meaning ascribed to his verbalizations (that is, ambivalence, affective instability) was determined by the diagnosis: schizophrenia. An entirely different meaning would have been ascribed if it were known that the man was "normal."

All pseudopatients took extensive notes publicly. Under ordinary circumstances, such behavior would have raised questions in the minds of observers, as, in fact, it did among patients. Indeed, it seemed so certain that the notes would elicit suspicion that elaborate precautions were taken to remove them from the ward each day. But the precautions proved needless. The closest any staff member came to questioning these notes occurred when one pseudopatient asked his physician what kind of medication he was receiving and began to write down the response. "You needn't write it," he was told gently. "If you have trouble remembering, just ask me again."

If no questions were asked of the pseudopatients, how was their writing interpreted? Nursing records for three patients indicate that the writing was seen as an aspect of their pathological behavior. "Patient engages in writing behavior" was the daily nursing com-

ment on one of the pseudopatients who was never questioned about his writing. Given that the patient is in the hospital, he must be psychologically disturbed. And given that he is disturbed, continuous writing must be a behavioral manifestation of that disturbance, perhaps a subset of the compulsive behaviors that are sometimes correlated with schizophrenia.

One tacit characteristic of psychiatric diagnosis is that it locates the sources of aberration within the individual and only rarely within the complex of stimuli that surrounds him. Consequently, behaviors that are stimulated by the environment are commonly misattributed to the patient's disorder. For example, one kindly nurse found a pseudopatient pacing the long hospital corridors. "Nervous, Mr. X?" she asked. "No, bored," he said.

The notes kept by pseudopatients are full of patient behaviors that were misinterpreted by well-intentioned staff. Often enough, a patient would go "berserk" because he had, wittingly or unwittingly, been mistreated by, say, an attendant. A nurse coming upon the scene would rarely inquire even cursorily into the environmental stimuli of the patient's behavior. Rather, she assumed that his upset derived from his pathology, not from his present interactions with other staff members. Occasionally, the staff might assume that the patient's family (especially when they had recently visited) or other patients had stimulated the outburst. But never were the staff found to assume that one of themselves or the structure of the hospital had anything to do with a patient's behavior. One psychiatrist pointed to a group of patients who were sitting outside the cafeteria entrance half an hour before lunchtime. To a group of young residents he indicated that such behavior was characteristic of the oral-acquisitive nature of the syndrome. It seemed not to occur to him that there were very few things to anticipate in a psychiatric hospital besides eating.

A psychiatric label has a life and an influence of its own. Once the impression has been formed that the patient is schizophrenic, the expectation is that he will continue to be schizophrenic. When a sufficient amount of time has passed, during which the patient has done nothing bizarre, he is considered to be in remission and available for discharge. But the label endures beyond discharge, with the unconfirmed expectation that he will behave as a schizophrenic again. Such labels, conferred by mental health professionals, are as influential on the patient as they are on his relatives and friends, and it should not surprise anyone that the diagnosis acts on all of them as a self-fulfilling prophecy. Eventually, the patient himself accepts the diagnosis, with all of its surplus meanings and expectations, and behaves accordingly (5).

The inferences to be made from these matters are quite simple. Much as Zigler and Phillips have demonstrated that there is enormous overlap in the symptoms presented by patients who have been variously diagnosed (16), so there is enormous overlap in the behaviors of the sane and the insane. The sane are not "sane" all of the time. We lose our tempers "for no good reason." We are occasionally depressed or anxious, again for no good reason. And we may find it difficult to get along with one or another person— again for no reason that we can specify. Similarly, the insane are not always insane. Indeed, it was the impression of the pseudopatients while living with them that they were sane for long periods of time—that the bizarre behaviors upon which their diagnoses were allegedly predicated constituted only a small fraction of their total behavior. If it makes no sense to label ourselves permanently depressed on the basis of an occasional depression, then it takes better evidence than is presently available to label all patients insane or schizophrenic on the basis of bizarre behaviors or cognitions. It seems more useful, as Mischel (17) has pointed out, to limit our discussions to *behaviors*, the stimuli that provoke them, and their correlates.

It is not known why powerful impressions of personality traits, such as "crazy" or "insane," arise. Conceivably, when the origins of and stimuli that give rise to a behavior are remote or unknown, or when the behavior strikes us as immutable, trait labels regarding the *behaver* arise. When, on the other hand, the origins and stimuli are known and available, discourse is limited to the behavior itself. Thus, I may hallucinate because I am sleeping, or I may hallucinate because I have ingested a peculiar drug. These are termed sleep-induced hallucinations, or dreams, and drug-induced hallucinations, respectively. But when the stimuli to my hallucinations are unknown, that is called craziness, or schizophrenia—as if that inference were somehow as illuminating as the others.

The Experience of Psychiatric Hospitalization

The term "mental illness" is of recent origin. It was coined by people who were humane in their inclinations and who wanted very much to raise the station of (and the public's sympathies toward) the psychologically disturbed from that of witches and "crazies" to one that was akin to the physically ill. And they were at least partially successful, for the treatment of the mentally ill *has* improved considerably over the years. But while treatment has improved, it is doubtful that people really regard the mentally ill in the same way that they view the physically ill. A broken leg is something one recovers from, but mental illness allegedly endures forever (18). A broken leg does not threaten the observer, but a crazy schizophrenic? There is by now a host of evidence that attitudes toward the mentally ill are characterized by fear, hostility, aloofness, suspicion, and dread (19). The mentally ill are society's lepers.

That such attitudes infect the general population is perhaps not surprising, only upsetting. But that they affect the professionals—attendants, nurses, physicians, psychologists, and social workers—who treat and deal with the mentally ill is more disconcerting, both because such attitudes are self-evidently pernicious and because they are unwitting. Most mental health professionals would insist that they are sympathetic toward the mentally ill, that they are neither avoidant nor hostile. But it is more likely that an exquisite ambivalence characterizes their relations with psychiatric patients, such that their avowed impulses are only part of their entire attitude. Negative attitudes are there too and can easily be detected. Such attitudes should not surprise us. They are the natural offspring of the labels patients wear and the places in which they are found.

Consider the structure of the typical psychiatric hospital. Staff and patients are strictly segregated. Staff have their own living space, including their dining facilities, bathrooms, and assembly places. The glassed quarters that contain the professional staff, which the pseudopatients came to call "the cage," sit out on every dayroom. The staff emerge primarily for caretaking purposes—to give medication, to conduct a therapy or group meeting, to instruct or reprimand a patient. Otherwise, staff

keep to themselves, almost as if the disorder that afflicts their charges is somehow catching.

So much is patient-staff segregation the rule that, for four public hospitals in which an attempt was made to measure the degree to which staff and patients mingle, it was necessary to use "time out of the staff cage" as the operational measure. While it was not the case that all time spent out of the cage was spent mingling with patients (attendants, for example, would occasionally emerge to watch television in the dayroom), it was the only way in which one could gather reliable data on time for measuring.

The average amount of time spent by attendants outside of the cage was 11.3 percent (range, 3 to 52 percent). This figure does not represent only time spent mingling with patients, but also includes time spent on such chores as folding laundry, supervising patients while they shave, directing ward cleanup, and sending patients to off-ward activities. It was the relatively rare attendant who spent time talking with patients or playing games with them. It proved impossible to obtain a "percent mingling time" for nurses, since the amount of time they spent out of the cage was too brief. Rather, we counted instances of emergence from the cage. On the average, daytime nurses emerged from the cage 11.5 times per shift, including instances when they left the ward entirely (range, 4 to 39 times). Late afternoon and night nurses were even less available, emerging on the average 9.4 times per shift (range, 4 to 41 times). Data on early morning nurses, who arrived usually after midnight and departed at 8 a.m., are not available because patients were asleep during most of this period.

Physicians, especially psychiatrists, were even less available. They were rarely seen on the wards. Quite commonly, they would be seen only when they arrived and departed, with the remaining time being spent in their offices or in the cage. On the average, physicians emerged on the ward 6.7 times per day (range, 1 to 17 times). It proved difficult to make an accurate estimate in this regard, since physicians often maintained hours that allowed them to come and go at different times.

The hierarchical organization of the psychiatric hospital has been commented on before (20), but the latent meaning of that kind of organization is worth noting again. Those with the

Table 1. Self-initiated contact by pseudopatients with psychiatrists and nurses and attendants, compared to contact with other groups.

Contact	Psychiatric hospitals		University campus (nonmedical)	University medical center		
				Physicians		
	(1) Psychiatrists	(2) Nurses and attendants	(3) Faculty	(4) "Looking for a psychiatrist"	(5) "Looking for an internist"	(6) No additional comment
Responses						
Moves on, head averted (%)	71	88	0	0	0	0
Makes eye contact (%)	23	10	0	11	0	0
Pauses and chats (%)	2	2	0	11	0	10
Stops and talks (%)	4	0.5	100	78	100	90
Mean number of questions answered (out of 6)	*	*	6	3.8	4.8	4.5
Respondents (No.)	13	47	14	18	15	10
Attempts (No.)	185	1283	14,	18	15	10

* Not applicable.

most power have least to do with patients, and those with the least power are most involved with them. Recall, however, that the acquisition of role-appropriate behaviors occurs mainly through the observation of others, with the most powerful having the most influence. Consequently, it is understandable that attendants not only spend more time with patients than do any other members of the staff—that is required by their station in the hierarchy —but also, insofar as they learn from their superiors' behavior, spend as little time with patients as they can. Attendants are seen mainly in the cage, which is where the models, the action, and the power are.

I turn now to a different set of studies, these dealing with staff response to patient-initiated contact. It has long been known that the amount of time a person spends with you can be an index of your significance to him. If he initiates and maintains eye contact, there is reason to believe that he is considering your requests and needs. If he pauses to chat or actually stops and talks, there is added reason to infer that he is individuating you. In four hospitals, the pseudopatient approached the staff member with a request which took the following form: "Pardon me, Mr. [or Dr. or Mrs.] X, could you tell me when I will be eligible for grounds privileges?" (or " . . . when I will be presented at the staff meeting?" or ". . . when I am likely to be discharged?"). While the content of the question varied according to the appropriateness of the target and the pseudopatient's (apparent) current needs the form was always a courteous and relevant request for information. Care was taken never to approach a particular member of the staff more than once a day, lest the staff member become suspicious or ir-

ritated. In examining these data, remember that the behavior of the pseudopatients was neither bizarre nor disruptive. One could indeed engage in good conversation with them.

The data for these experiments are shown in Table 1, separately for physicians (column 1) and for nurses and attendants (column 2). Minor differences between these four institutions were overwhelmed by the degree to which staff avoided continuing contacts that patients had initiated. By far, their most common response consisted of either a brief response to the question, offered while they were "on the move" and with head averted, or no response at all.

The encounter frequently took the following bizarre form: (pseudopatient) "Pardon me, Dr. X. Could you tell me when I am eligible for grounds privileges?" (physician) "Good morning, Dave. How are you today?" (Moves off without waiting for a response.)

It is instructive to compare these data with data recently obtained at Stanford University. It has been alleged that large and eminent universities are characterized by faculty who are so busy that they have no time for students. For this comparison, a young lady approached individual faculty members who seemed to be walking purposefully to some meeting or teaching engagement and asked them the following six questions.

1) "Pardon me, could you direct me to Encina Hall?" (at the medical school: ". . . to the Clinical Research Center?").

2) "Do you know where Fish Annex is?" (there is no Fish Annex at Stanford).

3) "Do you teach here?"

4) "How does one apply for admission to the college?" (at the medical

school: ". . . to the medical school?").

5) "Is it difficult to get in?"

6) "Is there financial aid?"

Without exception, as can be seen in Table 1 (column 3), all of the questions were answered. No matter how rushed they were, all respondents not only maintained eye contact, but stopped to talk. Indeed, many of the respondents went out of their way to direct or take the questioner to the office she was seeking, to try to locate "Fish Annex," or to discuss with her the possibilities of being admitted to the university.

Similar data, also shown in Table 1 (columns 4, 5, and 6), were obtained in the hospital. Here too, the young lady came prepared with six questions. After the first question, however, she remarked to 18 of her respondents (column 4), "I'm looking for a psychiatrist," and to 15 others (column 5), "I'm looking for an internist." Ten other respondents received no inserted comment (column 6). The general degree of cooperative responses is considerably higher for these university groups than it was for pseudopatients in psychiatric hospitals. Even so, differences are apparent within the medical school setting. Once having indicated that she was looking for a psychiatrist, the degree of cooperation elicited was less than when she sought an internist.

Powerlessness and Depersonalization

Eye contact and verbal contact reflect concern and individuation; their absence, avoidance and depersonalization. The data I have presented do not do justice to the rich daily encounters that grew up around matters of depersonalization and avoidance. I have records of patients who were beaten by staff for the sin of having initiated verbal contact. During my own experience, for example, one patient was beaten in the presence of other patients for having approached an attendant and told him, "I like you." Occasionally, punishment meted out to patients for misdemeanors seemed so excessive that it could not be justified by the most radical interpretations of psychiatric canon. Nevertheless, they appeared to go unquestioned. Tempers were often short. A patient who had not heard a call for medication would be roundly excoriated, and the morning attendants would often wake patients with, "Come on, you m——f——s, out of bed!"

Neither anecdotal nor "hard" data can convey the overwhelming sense of powerlessness which invades the individual as he is continually exposed to the depersonalization of the psychiatric hospital. It hardly matters *which* psychiatric hospital—the excellent public ones and the very plush private hospital were better than the rural and shabby ones in this regard, but, again, the features that psychiatric hospitals had in common overwhelmed by far their apparent differences.

Powerlessness was evident everywhere. The patient is deprived of many of his legal rights by dint of his psychiatric commitment (21). He is shorn of credibility by virtue of his psychiatric label. His freedom of movement is restricted. He cannot initiate contact with the staff, but may only respond to such overtures as they make. Personal privacy is minimal. Patient quarters and possessions can be entered and examined by any staff member, for whatever reason. His personal history and anguish is available to any staff member (often including the "grey lady" and "candy striper" volunteer) who chooses to read his folder, regardless of their therapeutic relationship to him. His personal hygiene and waste evacuation are often monitored. The water closets may have no doors.

At times, depersonalization reached such proportions that pseudopatients had the sense that they were invisible, or at least unworthy of account. Upon being admitted, I and other pseudopatients took the initial physical examinations in a semipublic room, where staff members went about their own business as if we were not there.

On the ward, attendants delivered verbal and occasionally serious physical abuse to patients in the presence of other observing patients, some of whom (the pseudopatients) were writing it all

down. Abusive behavior, on the other hand, terminated quite abruptly when other staff members were known to be coming. Staff are credible witnesses. Patients are not.

A nurse unbuttoned her uniform to adjust her brassiere in the presence of an entire ward of viewing men. One did not have the sense that she was being seductive. Rather, she didn't notice us. A group of staff persons might point to a patient in the dayroom and discuss him animatedly, as if he were not there.

One illuminating instance of depersonalization and invisibility occurred with regard to medications. All told, the pseudopatients were administered nearly 2100 pills, including Elavil, Stelazine, Compazine, and Thorazine, to name but a few. (That such a variety of medications should have been administered to patients presenting identical symptoms is itself worthy of note.) Only two were swallowed. The rest were either pocketed or deposited in the toilet. The pseudopatients were not alone in this. Although I have no precise records on how many patients rejected their medications, the pseudopatients frequently found the medications of other patients in the toilet before they deposited their own. As long as they were cooperative, their behavior and the pseudopatients' own in this matter, as in other important matters, went unnoticed throughout.

Reactions to such depersonalization among pseudopatients were intense. Although they had come to the hospital as participant observers and were fully aware that they did not "belong," they nevertheless found themselves caught up in and fighting the process of depersonalization. Some examples: a graduate student in psychology asked his wife to bring his textbooks to the hospital so he could "catch up on his homework"—this despite the elaborate precautions taken to conceal his professional association. The same student, who had trained for quite some time to get into the hospital, and who had looked forward to the experience, "remembered" some drag races that he had wanted to see on the weekend and insisted that he be discharged by that time. Another pseudopatient attempted a romance with a nurse. Subsequently, he informed the staff that he was applying for admission to graduate school in psychology and was very likely to be admitted, since a graduate professor was one of his regular hospital visitors. The same person began to engage in

psychotherapy with other patients—all of this as a way of becoming a person in an impersonal environment.

The Sources of Depersonalization

What are the origins of depersonalization? I have already mentioned two. First are attitudes held by all of us toward the mentally ill—including those who treat them—attitudes characterized by fear, distrust, and horrible expectations on the one hand, and benevolent intentions on the other. Our ambivalence leads, in this instance as in others, to avoidance.

Second, and not entirely separate, the hierarchical structure of the psychiatric hospital facilitates depersonalization. Those who are at the top have least to do with patients, and their behavior inspires the rest of the staff. Average daily contact with psychiatrists, psychologists, residents, and physicians combined ranged from 3.9 to 25.1 minutes, with an overall mean of 6.8 (six pseudopatients over a total of 129 days of hospitalization). Included in this average are time spent in the admissions interview, ward meetings in the presence of a senior staff member, group and individual psychotherapy contacts, case presentation conferences, and discharge meetings. Clearly, patients do not spend much time in interpersonal contact with doctoral staff. And doctoral staff serve as models for nurses and attendants.

There are probably other sources. Psychiatric installations are presently in serious financial straits. Staff shortages are pervasive, staff time at a premium. Something has to give, and that something is patient contact. Yet, while financial stresses are realities, too much can be made of them. I have the impression that the psychological forces that result in depersonalization are much stronger than the fiscal ones and that the addition of more staff would not correspondingly improve patient care in this regard. The incidence of staff meetings and the enormous amount of record-keeping on patients, for example, have not been as substantially reduced as has patient contact. Priorities exist, even during hard times. Patient contact is not a significant priority in the traditional psychiatric hospital, and fiscal pressures do not account for this. Avoidance and depersonalization may.

Heavy reliance upon psychotropic

medication tacitly contributes to depersonalization by convincing staff that treatment is indeed being conducted and that further patient contact may not be necessary. Even here, however, caution needs to be exercised in understanding the role of psychotropic drugs. If patients were powerful rather than powerless, if they were viewed as interesting individuals rather than diagnostic entities, if they were socially significant rather than social lepers, if their anguish truly and wholly compelled our sympathies and concerns, would we not *seek* contact with them, despite the availability of medications? Perhaps for the pleasure of it all?

The Consequences of Labeling and Depersonalization

Whenever the ratio of what is known to what needs to be known approaches zero, we tend to invent "knowledge" and assume that we understand more than we actually do. We seem unable to acknowledge that we simply don't know. The needs for diagnosis and remediation of behavioral and emotional problems are enormous. But rather than acknowledge that we are just embarking on understanding, we continue to label patients "schizophrenic," "manic-depressive," and "insane," as if in those words we had captured the essence of understanding. The facts of the matter are that we have known for a long time that diagnoses are often not useful or reliable, but we have nevertheless continued to use them. We now know that we cannot distinguish insanity from sanity. It is depressing to consider how that information will be used.

Not merely depressing, but frightening. How many people, one wonders, are sane but not recognized as such in our psychiatric institutions? How many have been needlessly stripped of their privileges of citizenship, from the right to vote and drive to that of handling their own accounts? How many have feigned insanity in order to avoid the criminal consequences of their behavior, and, conversely, how many would rather stand trial than live interminably in a psychiatric hospital—but are wrongly thought to be mentally ill? How many have been stigmatized by well-intentioned, but nevertheless erroneous, diagnoses? On the last point, recall again that a "type 2 error" in psychiatric diagnosis does not have the

same consequences it does in medical diagnosis. A diagnosis of cancer that has been found to be in error is cause for celebration. But psychiatric diagnoses are rarely found to be in error. The label sticks, a mark of inadequacy forever.

Finally, how many patients might be "sane" outside the psychiatric hospital but seem insane in it—not because craziness resides in them, as it were, but because they are responding to a bizarre setting, one that may be unique to institutions which harbor nether people? Goffman (4) calls the process of socialization to such institutions "mortification"—an apt metaphor that includes the processes of depersonalization that have been described here. And while it is impossible to know whether the pseudopatients' responses to these processes are characteristic of all inmates—they were, after all, not real patients—it is difficult to believe that these processes of socialization to a psychiatric hospital provide useful attitudes or habits of response for living in the "real world."

Summary and Conclusions

It is clear that we cannot distinguish the sane from the insane in psychiatric hospitals. The hospital itself imposes a special environment in which the meanings of behavior can easily be misunderstood. The consequences to patients hospitalized in such an environment—the powerlessness, depersonalization, segregation, mortification, and self-labeling—seem undoubtedly counter-therapeutic.

I do not, even now, understand this problem well enough to perceive solutions. But two matters seem to have some promise. The first concerns the proliferation of community mental health facilities, of crisis intervention centers, of the human potential movement, and of behavior therapies that, for all of their own problems, tend to avoid psychiatric labels, to focus on specific problems and behaviors, and to retain the individual in a relatively non-pejorative environment. Clearly, to the extent that we refrain from sending the distressed to insane places, our impressions of them are less likely to be distorted. (The risk of distorted perceptions, it seems to me, is always present, since we are much more sensitive to an individual's behaviors and verbalizations than we are to the subtle con-

textual stimuli that often promote them. At issue here is a matter of magnitude. And, as I have shown, the magnitude of distortion is exceedingly high in the extreme context that is a psychiatric hospital.)

The second matter that might prove promising speaks to the need to increase the sensitivity of mental health workers and researchers to the *Catch 22* position of psychiatric patients. Simply reading materials in this area will be of help to some such workers and researchers. For others, directly experiencing the impact of psychiatric hospitalization will be of enormous use. Clearly, further research into the social psychology of such total institutions will both facilitate treatment and deepen understanding.

I and the other pseudopatients in the psychiatric setting had distinctly negative reactions. We do not pretend to describe the subjective experiences of true patients. Theirs may be different from ours, particularly with the passage of time and the necessary process of adaptation to one's environment. But we can and do speak to the relatively more objective indices of treatment within the hospital. It could be a mistake, and a very unfortunate one, to consider that what happened to us derived from malice or stupidity on the part of the staff. Quite the contrary, our overwhelming impression of them was of people who really cared, who were committed and who were uncommonly intelligent. Where they failed, as they sometimes did painfully, it would be more accurate to attribute those failures to the environment in which they, too, found themselves than to personal callousness. Their perceptions and behavior were controlled by the situation, rather than being motivated by a malicious disposition. In a more benign environment, one that was less attached to global diagnosis, their behaviors and judgments might have been more benign and effective.

References and Notes

1. P. Ash, *J. Abnorm. Soc. Psychol.* **44**, 272 (1949); A. T. Beck, *Amer. J. Psychiat.* **119**, 210 (1962); A. T. Boisen, *Psychiatry* **2**, 233 (1938); N. Kreitman, *J. Ment. Sci.* **107**, 876 (1961); N. Kreitman, P. Sainsbury, J. Morrisey, J. Towers, J. Scrivener, *ibid.*, p. 887; H. O. Schmitt and C. P. Fonda, *J. Abnorm. Soc. Psychol.* **52**, 262 (1956); W. Seeman, *J. Nerv. Ment. Dis.* **118**, 541 (1953). For an analysis of these artifacts and summaries of the disputes, see J. Zubin, *Annu. Rev. Psychol.* **13**, 373 (1967); L. Phillips and J. G. Draguns, *ibid.* **22**, 447 (1971).
2. R. Benedict, *J. Gen. Psychol.* **10**, 59 (1934).
3. See in this regard H. Becker, *Outsiders: Studies in the Sociology of Deviance* (Free Press, New York, 1963); B. M. Braginsky,

D. D. Braginsky, K. Ring, *Methods of Madness: The Mental Hospital as a Last Resort* (Holt, Rinehart & Winston, New York, 1969); G. M. Crocetti and P. V. Lemkau, *Amer. Sociol. Rev.* 30, 577 (1965); E. Goffman, *Behavior in Public Places* (Free Press, New York, 1964); R. D. Laing, *The Divided Self: A Study of Sanity and Madness* (Quadrangle, Chicago, 1960); D. L. Phillips, *Amer. Sociol. Rev.* 28, 963 (1963); T. R. Sarbin, *Psychol. Today* 6, 18 (1972); E. Schur, *Amer. J. Sociol.* 75, 309 (1969); T. Szasz, *Law, Liberty and Psychiatry* (Macmillan, New York, 1963); *The Myth of Mental Illness: Foundations of a Theory of Mental Illness* (Hoeber-Harper, New York, 1963). For a critique of some of these views, see W. R. Gove, *Amer. Sociol. Rev.* 35, 873 (1970).

4. E. Goffman, *Asylums* (Doubleday, Garden City, N.Y., 1961).

5. T. J. Scheff, *Being Mentally Ill: A Sociological Theory* (Aldine, Chicago, 1966).

6. Data from a ninth pseudopatient are not incorporated in this report because, although his sanity went undetected, he falsified aspects of his personal history, including his marital status and parental relationships. His experimental behaviors therefore were not identical to those of the other pseudopatients.

7. A. Barry, *Bellevue Is a State of Mind* (Harcourt Brace Jovanovich, New York, 1971); I. Belknap, *Human Problems of a State Mental Hospital* (McGraw-Hill, New York, 1956); W. Caudill, F. C. Redlich, H. R. Gilmore, E. B. Brody, *Amer. J. Orthopsychiat.* 22, 314 (1952); A. R. Goldman, R. H. Bohr, T. A. Steinberg, *Prof. Psychol.* 1, 427 (1970); unauthored, *Roche Report* 1 (No. 13), 8 (1971).

8. Beyond the personal difficulties that the pseudopatient is likely to experience in the hospital, there are legal and social ones that, combined, require considerable attention before entry. For example, once admitted to a psychiatric institution, it is difficult, if not impossible, to be discharged on short notice,

state law to the contrary notwithstanding. I was not sensitive to these difficulties at the outset of the project, nor to the personal and situational emergencies that can arise, but later a writ of habeas corpus was prepared for each of the entering pseudopatients and an attorney was kept "on call" during every hospitalization. I am grateful to John Kaplan and Robert Bartels for legal advice and assistance in these matters.

9. However distasteful such concealment is, it was a necessary first step to examining these questions. Without concealment, there would have been no way to know how valid these experiences were; nor was there any way of knowing whether whatever detections occurred were a tribute to the diagnostic acumen of the staff or to the hospital's rumor network. Obviously, since my concerns are general ones that cut across individual hospitals and staffs, I have respected their anonymity and have eliminated clues that might lead to their identification.

10. Interestingly, of the 12 admissions, 11 were diagnosed as schizophrenic and one, with the identical symptomatology, as manic-depressive psychosis. This diagnosis has a more favorable prognosis, and it was given by the only private hospital in our sample. On the relations between social class and psychiatric diagnosis, see A. deB. Hollingshead and F. C. Redlich, *Social Class and Mental Illness: A Community Study* (Wiley, New York, 1958).

11. It is possible, of course, that patients have quite broad latitudes in diagnosis and therefore are inclined to call many people sane, even those whose behavior is patently aberrant. However, although we have no hard data on this matter, it was our distinct impression that this was not the case. In many instances, patients not only singled us out for attention, but came to imitate our behaviors and styles.

12. J. Cumming and E. Cumming, *Community Ment. Health* 1, 135 (1965); A. Farina and K. Ring, *J. Abnorm. Psychol.* 70, 47 (1965);

H. E. Freeman and O. G. Simmons, *The Mental Patient Comes Home* (Wiley, New York, 1963); W J. Johannsen, *Ment. Hygiene* 53, 218 (1969); A. S. Linsky, *Soc. Psychiat.* 5, 166 (1970).

13. S. E. Asch, *J. Abnorm. Soc. Psychol.* 41, 258 (1946); *Social Psychology* (Prentice-Hall, New York, 1952).

14. See also L. N. Mensh and J. Wishner, *J. Personality* 16, 188 (1947); J. Wishner, *Psychol. Rev.* 67, 96 (1960); J. S. Bruner and R. Tagiuri, in *Handbook of Social Psychology,* G. Lindzey, Ed. (Addison-Wesley, Cambridge, Mass., 1954), vol. 2, pp. 634–654; J. S. Bruner, D. Shapiro, R. Tagiuri, in *Person Perception and Interpersonal Behavior,* R. Tagiuri and L. Petrullo, Eds. (Stanford Univ. Press, Stanford, Calif., 1958), pp. 277–288.

15. For an example of a similar self-fulfilling prophecy, in this instance dealing with the "central" trait of intelligence, see R. Rosenthal and L. Jacobson, *Pygmalion in the Classroom* (Holt, Rinehart & Winston, New York, 1968).

16. E. Zigler and L. Phillips, *J. Abnorm. Soc. Psychol.* 63, 69 (1961). See also R. K. Freudenberg and J. P. Robertson, *A.M.A. Arch. Neurol. Psychiatr.* 76, 14 (1956).

17. W. Mischel, *Personality and Assessment* (Wiley, New York, 1968).

18. The most recent and unfortunate instance of this tenet is that of Senator Thomas Eagleton.

19. T. R. Sarbin and J. C. Mancuso, *J. Clin. Consult. Psychol.* 35, 159 (1970); T. R. Sarbin, *ibid.* 31, 447 (1967); J. C. Nunnally, Jr., *Popular Conceptions of Mental Health* (Holt, Rinehart & Winston, New York, 1961).

20. A. H. Stanton and M. S. Schwartz, *The Mental Hospital: A Study of Institutional Participation in Psychiatric Illness and Treatment* (Basic, New York, 1954).

21. D. B. Wexler and S. E. Scoville, *Ariz. Law Rev.* 13, 1 (1971).

22. I thank W. Mischel, E. Orne, and M. S. Rosenhan for comments on an earlier draft of this manuscript.

1. How did Rosenhan structure his study?

2. What were the basic findings?

3. Why were the pseudopatients not discovered after they stopped faking the symptoms which got them admitted?

4. Does Rosenhan's study support Szasz' or Schoenfeld's view of mental illness?

1. He sent out a number of pseudopatients to mental institutions to fake the symptoms of mental illness and thereby gain admission to the hospitals. Upon admission, the pseudopatient stopped faking his/her symptoms and behaved thereafter in a normal fashion. Subsequently, in the second phase of the study, Rosenhan told the mental institutions that he was going to repeat the experiment and that they should be aware that pseudopatients would be seeking admission to their hospitals. However, no pseudopatients were sent.

2. The pseudopatients were diagnosed as being mentally ill based on their faked symptoms and admitted. In the second phase of the study, the hospitals claimed to have located a large number of pseudopatients, though none had been sent out by the researcher.

3. Rosenhan says that all behavior of the pseudopatients following their diagnosis was interpreted to support that diagnosis. Thus, it became impossible to appear normal in the eyes of the hospital staff since all acts were interpreted as further evidence of mental illness. While the real patients were able to detect who the pseudopatients were, the hospital staff was not.

4. Quite plainly, Rosenhan has demonstrated the inability of psychiatrists to distinguish the 'sick' from the 'well'. Note that the inability to make this distinction does not demonstrate that there is no such thing as mental illness, as Szasz argues. It is possible that the reasons for the success of Rosenhan's pseudopatients lies in the poor quality of the particular hospitals involved (though he denies it) or from the underdeveloped state of medical knowledge in this area. Thus, while Rosenhan's study probably will please those who agree with Szasz more than those who agree with Schoenfeld, it cannot be said to have proven one right and the other wrong.

In this unit you have learned what psychiatrists are asked to do in a variety of legal settings and why some critics of forensic psychiatry believe that psychiatry is merely social control masquerading as medicine. You have seen how the legal system relies extensively on psychiatric experts to make difficult legal, ethical, and political decisions concerning people's freedom. The very notion of mental illness which gives psychiatric experts their presumed expertise and accounts for their persuasive appeal before judges and juries has been refuted by Szasz, Rosenhan, Vatz, and me and defended by Schoenfeld.

The difficult issues raised in this unit remain unresolved. I hope that you will give serious thought, however, to the question of whether there is any such condition properly called mental 'illness' and to the question of whether psychiatric experts have acquired inordinate power within the legal system to the ultimate detriment of human freedom.

In the end we are faced _not_ with the question of whether society needs some means of influencing its members to behave in conformity with group expectations (social control), but rather with the question of _which_ means of social control best achieves the dual purposes of maintaining social order and protecting human freedom. If Szasz is correct, then psychiatric social control suffers two fatal flaws. First, it is based on the false premise that deviant behavior is a medical phenomenon to be treated by physicians; and second, psychiatric social control is insensitive to human and legal rights. Once legal social control is replaced by psychiatric social control, the role of the state is vastly expanded.

In conclusion, consider the following view expressed by Szasz in his latest book, _The Myth of Psychotherapy_, and think about the ultimate implications of psychiatric versus legal social control.

> Most people now believe that it is a good thing that the state defines for them what is sickness and what is treatment and that the state pays for any treatment they need. Sooner or later, people will realize that what this means is that the state may, and will, define as treatment that which the rulers want to do to the people; and that the state may, and will, tax the people, and tax them heavily, for this supposed service. I hope this book mibht contribute to bringing that realization one day closer.

A SZASZIAN VIEW OF DEATH, OR THE MYTH OF DEATH

RICHARD E. VATZ   AND   LEE S. WEINBERG
Towson State University   *. University of Pittsburgh*
Baltimore, Maryland   *Pittsburgh, Pennsylvania*

We have been impressed by the humanistic writings of Thomas Szasz about the myth of mental illness (Szasz, 1961). It occurs to us that Szasz provides a paradigm for understanding other behavioral phenomena. A particularly poignant example is the behavior called "death."

What is "death"? In fact there is no objective reality to what we call "death." "Death" is simply the name we give to people whose behavior (typically lying down and doing nothing) we neither understand nor approve. By labeling it "death," we pretend that we understand it and enfranchise a panoply of actions to be taken ostensibly in the interest of the "dead" but, in fact, as we shall show, serving primarily to derrogate and persecute those we call "dead." We give no sustained care to "dead" people. We take away their vote (except in Cook County). We deprive them of food. "Death" therefore, is but a self-fulfilling prophecy.

The rhetoric of death serves to aggrandize and provide employment for those who "treat" the "dead." Surely, if there are "dead" people, we must train others to "take care of them." The harsh truth is that "alive" morticians need "dead" people more than "dead" people need morticians.

"Death" is a metaphor, despite the public's treatment of the term as reality. When we as a society see no purpose in behavior, we call the person or behavior "dead." The metaphor is now ubiquitous in lay usage. A party may be called "dead." We even have, as I. A. Richards (1936) explains in *The Philosophy of Rhetoric*, "dead metaphors." The metaphor of death is the prevailing ultimate term of derrogation. In short, any phenomenon not conforming to our standards may risk being labeled "dead."

The behavior we call "death" cannot be considered apart from the context within which it occurs. It is no coincidence that elderly people, who are singularly ignored or patronized in our society, are the ones who most frequently demonstrate the behavior we call "death." This is perhaps the ugliest aspect of the taxonomy of "death." It is a scheme of categori-

J. Humanistic Psychology, Vol. 17, No. 3, Summer 1977

zation superimposed upon those who can least well defend themselves; the old, the injured, and the critically ill.

Let us examine, now, from a new perspective the behavior that we have traditionally labeled "death." Let us consider "death" not as nonexistence, whatever that means, but as an iconic body sign. It is an expression of nondiscursive symbolism whose meaning lies within the "dead" person. "Death" is communication. Let us ask ourselves, therefore, the following question: Since "death," as all behavior, is learned, how does it function within its given psychosocial context?

A person who exhibits the behavior we call "death" has learned throughout his or her life that such behavior garners immediate attention and produces guilt and redemption-seeking from loved oves. "Death," therefore, as in the case of "mental illness," is a form of blackmail. The loved ones have virtually no choice but to attend to luxurious preparations for honoring the "dead" person. Once a person has been labeled "dead," he or she no longer can be held responsible for his or her actions. Furthermore, unlike prisoners or even the "mentally ill," this label is permanent.

In the preparation of the body and the burial itself, the "dead" person is never consulted. During the festivities of the funeral, the "dead" person is either covered up or set in a position from which he or she cannot even see what is happening, much less participate.

The rhetoric of burial, as in the rhetoric associated with justifying the involuntary incarceration in "mental institutions," is the language of doublethink. We imprison the dead in maximum security, no escape prisons which used to be called the "hole" in the old gangster movies, and we call it "burial." Relatives periodically come to the site of this "burial" and call it "visiting" or "paying respects." Visiting whom? They do not see their "dead" relative. They bring flowers and taunt the "dead," however innocently or naively, by putting their flowers outside of the smell of the one they are "visiting."

The rhetoric of "death," like that of "mental illness" is a rhetoric of mystification and disparagement, not of understanding. It is based upon the myth of the empirical reality of something called "death." In fact there is no such phenomenon. What we call "death" is simply symbolic behavior misunderstood and exploited by morticians, family, and society to benefit themselves while justifying their actions in the name of the interests of the "dead."

REFERENCES

RICHARDS, I. A. *The philosophy of rhetoric*. New York: Oxford University Press, 1936.
SZASZ, T. *The myth of mental illness*, New York: Hoeber-Harper, 1961.
VATZ, R., & MELIA, T. A bibliographic book review of Thomas Szasz. *Quarterly Journal of Speech*, February, 1977.
WEINBERG, L., & VATZ, R. Thomas Szasz and the law: An alternative view. *Journal of Psychiatry and the Law*, in press.

Reprint requests: Richard Vatz. Department of Communications. Towson State University. Baltimore. Maryland 21204.

UNIT ASSIGNMENT

Write a one or two page, typed (double spaced), answer to the following item.

Identify a situation either from personal knowledge or from the newspaper in which psychiatrists have been involved in diagnosing behavior. If you prefer, you may use the hypothetical news article. Analyze it from a Szaszian point of view making certain to include Szasz' ideas about mental illness, literalization of metaphor, the medical model, and, if applicable, the insanity defense, incompetency to stand trial, the right to treatment, and involuntary hospitalization.

Also, be sure to discuss how psychiatry is being used in your situation as a means of social control, i.e., to enforce rules of proper or desirable behavior.

Pittsburgh Man Found Incompetent to Stand Trial on 2nd Degree Murder Charge

PITTSBURGH, SEPTEMBER 10, 1978-Following extensive psychiatric testimony from three prominent Pittsburgh psychiatrists, Hugo Nutts was found incompetent to stand trial for the brutal slaying of his girl friend last summer. The psychiatrists told the court that Mr. Nutts was suffering from acute paranoid schizophrenia and was unable to understand the charges against him. Mr. Nutts is charged with strangling his girl friend and then soaking her body in paint thinner and igniting it following an argument at the Three Rivers Arts Festival.

Mr. Nutts was released only 6 months earlier from the county hospital for the criminally insane where he had been sent by criminal court Judge Hussein following an earlier finding of incompetency to stand trial in a previous murder charge. In that case, Nutts allegedly shot and killed the paperboy because Nutts believed that the boy was distributing newspapers which contained daily attacks on Nutts, his private life, his political beliefs, and his eating habits. He was at the time of that trial found incompetent as a result of severe schizophrenia. After spending 11 months in the hospital, psychiatrists told the court that Nutts' illness had gone into remission, and that he had regained sufficient competency to stand trial for the boys murder. He was, therefore, released.

It was while Nutts was awaiting his trial for the first murder that he allegedly committed the second. Nutts has been ordered back to the mental hospital to undergo treatment and further tests.

REFERENCES

Rosenhan, D.L. On being sane in insane places. Science, January 14, 1973.

Schoenfeld, C.G. An analysis of the views of Thomas S. Szasz. The Journal of Psychiatry and Law, Summer, 1976, pp. 245-263.

Schur, E.M. Law and society. New York: Random House, 1968.

Vatz, R.E., & Weinberg, L.S. A Szaszian view of death, or the myth of death. Journal of Humanistic Psychology, Summer, 1977, pp. 71-73.

Weinberg, L.S., & Vatz, R.E. Szasz and the law. The Journal of Psychiatry and Law, Winter, 1976, pp. 551-558.

Weinberg, L.S., & Vatz, R.E. Psychiatry and crime: the contribution of Thomas Szasz. Paper presented at Academy of Criminal Justice Sciences meeting, New Orleans, Match 10, 1978.

SUGGESTED READING

Allen, R.C. et al. Readings in law and psychiatry. Baltimore: Johns Hopkins University Press, 1975.

Brakel, S. & Rock, R. The mentally disabled and the law. Chicago: University of Chicago Press, 1971.

Ennis, B. Prisoners of psychiatry: mental patients, psychiatrists, and the law. New York: Harcourt, Brace, and Jovanovich, 1973.

Menninger, K. The crime of punishment. New York: Viking Press, 1968.

Schoenfeld, C.G. Psychoanalysis and the law. Springfield: Charles C. Thomas, 1973.

Szasz, T.S. Ceremonial chemistry. New York: Anchor Press, 1973.

Szasz, T.S. Heresies. Garden City: Anchor Press, 1976.

Szasz, T.S. Ideology and insanity. New York: Anchor Books, 1970.

Szasz, T.S. Law, liberty, and psychiatry. New York: Collier, 1963.

Szasz, T.S. The manufacture of madness. New York: Harper and Row, 1970.

Szasz, T.S. The second sin. Garden City: Anchor Press, 1973.

CASES

Baxtrom v. Herald, 383 U.S. 107 (1966).

Bolton v. Harris, 395 F. 2d 642 (1968).

Donaldson v. O'Connor, 95 S. Ct. 2846 (1975).

Durham v. United States, 214 F. 2d 862 (1954).

Jackson v. Indiana, 406 U.S. 715 (1972).

Knecht v. Gillman, 488 F. 2d 1136 (1973).

Lake v. Cameron, 364 F. 2d 657 (1966).

Lessard v. Schmidt, 349 F. Supp. 1078 (1972).

Pate v. Robinson, 383 U.S. 375 (1966).

Robinson v. California, 370 U.S. 660 (1962).

Rouse v. Cameron, 373 F. 3d 451 (1966).

Wyatt v. Stickney, 334 F. Supp. (1972).

UNIT 9

A Case Study: Regents Of The University Of California v. Allan Bakke

Rationale

One of the goals of this course has been to help you think in new ways about legal events around you. It's important, but often difficult, to gain some understanding of the technical and factual aspects of legal decisions in order to properly relate them to broader social and political ideas. In this unit you will read about the factual and legal dimensions of the famous case of Allan Bakke, and you will see how this case can be related to many of the central theories and concepts in the course. The Bakke case represents a major development in the civil rights area and has stimulated vigorous debate among politicians, lawyers, and the millions of Americans who have a stake in the problem of how to redress wrongs done to black Americans without treating white Americans unjustly.

Objectives

After you have completed this unit, you should be able to:

1. Describe the Court's standards for applying the "equal protection" clause of the Fourteenth Amendment.

2. Summarize the facts of the Bakke case.

3. Summarize the opinions of the Supreme Court Justices for the given case.

4. Analyze given aspects of the Bakke case in terms of concepts and ideas drawn from all preceeding units.

Overview

The mini-lecture briefly outlines the law which is involved in the Bakke case. Because the 'strict scrutiny' test is frequently referred to in the opinion of the Court, it is important for you to understand some basic constitutional law in order to understand the opinions in Bakke. The focus, therefore, in the mini-lecture is on the 'equal protection' clause of the Fourteenth Amendment. Next you will read a brief summary of the development of the Bakke case prior to the Supreme Court decision. The Bakke opinions have been excerpted for you and section by section comments are provided to assist you in your reading. These comments constitute, in effect, a Discussion of the opinions. Finally, you will read Schur's conclusions and then attempt to draw some conclusions of your own.

Study Task Checklist

☐ 1. A.   Read the Mini-Lecture #1, "Equal Protection of the Law."

☐ 1. B.   Answer the Study Questions and compare your answers with the Discussion of them.

☐ 2. A.   Read Reading #1, "Regents of the University of California v. Allan Bakke."

☐ 2. B.   Answer the Study Questions and compare your answers with the Discussion of them.

☐ 3. A.   Complete Unit Study Questions.

Mini-Lecture

EQUAL PROTECTION OF THE LAW

The Fourteenth Amendment to the Constitution says that no state shall deprive any person within its jurisdiction the "equal protection of the laws." This literally means that the states may not act in such a way as to treat some people differently from others. Of course it's clear that government must and should treat some people differently from others. In other words, there is no question that government can distribute food stamps to the poor and not the rich, or tax those with higher incomes at higher rates, or treat those with drivers licenses differently from those without licenses in terms of the motor vehicle code. The problem arises when courts are asked to decide on what basis states may treat some people differently from others. Put another away, the courts are not faced with the question of whether discrimination should be permitted. They are faced with the question of whom to discriminate against. It is necessary to treat rich and poor differently in some respects; this constitutes 'discrimination'. So the courts must wrestle with the justification for discrimination against various groups and decide which are violative of the 'equal protection' clause.

Over the year, the Supreme Court has developed two basic 'tests' which it applies to claims of discrimination.

The Rational Basis Test

The rational basis test is the traditional test applied to discrimination claims. A person claiming to be the victim of a state action which discriminates against him/her must prove that the state policy is irrational in the sense that it is not related to a legitimate goal of government. For example, if government seeks to promote road safety by denying drivers licenses to those with poor eyesight, the court would never find that such drivers had been discriminated against when their licenses were revoked. In other words, if the state policy is rational, the Court will uphold its constitutionality without further inquiry.

The Strict Scrutiny Test

In certain cases the Court has felt it necessary to require states to provide more than merely rational grounds for their discriminating policies. Two types of cases have been held to require a state to prove that it has a 'compelling state interest' in discriminating as it has and that no less drastic means were available to achieve its purpose. The two types of cases giving rise to this strict judicial scrutiny are those in which fundamental rights have been infringed or those based upon suspect classifications which the Court has enumerated.

Discrimination based upon racial classifications has been held to be inherently suspect, thus triggering the strict scrutiny test which is very difficult for the state to meet. Since Bakke involves racial classifications by a state university, the strict scrutiny test is applicable. Five of the Justices, as you will see, believe that the University of California did not adequately demonstrate that it was necessary to operate a two-track admissions program. Four of the Justices were satisfied that the admission program passed the strict scrutiny test.

It might interest you to know that sex-based classifications have not yet been held inherently suspect. Therefore, the strict scrutiny test is not applicable, though the Court has been demanding something more than a rational basis in sex discrimination cases.

MINI-LECTURE #1 QUESTIONS

1. Does the 'equal protection' clause prohibit all discrimination?

2. What are the two tests used to evaluate claims of discrimination?

3. When is the strict scrutiny test applied?

4. Why is strict scrutiny applied to the Bakke case?

1. While perhaps literally seeming to prohibit all discrimination, the 'equal protection' clause is interpreted as prohibiting only certain kinds of discrimination.

2. The <u>rational basic test</u> requires only that the state come forth with a reasonable justification for the discriminatory policy. The <u>strict scrutiny test</u> is a much more difficult standard to meet. The state must show a compelling interest and the unavailability of less offensive means to achieve it.

3. Strict scrutiny is applied when fundamental rights are affected or suspect classifications are used.

4. Since the University used a racial classification in its admissions process, it was immediately subject to strict scrutiny because race is a suspect classification.

THE ROUTE TO THE SUPREME COURT

Allan Bakke

1. Bakke files action claiming violation of Fourteenth Amendment occurs when University reserves places on basis of race.

2. Trial court denies Bakke's request to be admitted. It holds that he fails to show that he would have been admitted had there not been a special program for minorities.

3. Trial court said that burden of proof was on Bakke and that he failed to meet this burden.

4. Bakke appeals this to California Supreme Court.

5. California Supreme Court says that burden of proof shifts to University once Bakke succeeds in proving that the University has, in fact, discriminated on the basis of race in its admissions process.

6. Therefore, University must prove that Bakke would NOT have been admitted even in the absence of the discriminatory admissions policy.

7. University admits that it could not prove this, and, therefore, Bakke is entitled to an order to the University to admit him to medical school.

University of California

1. University files cross complaint seeking declaratory judgment approving the admissions policy.

2. Trial court finds that admissions program violates Fourteenth Amendment by setting racial quotas.

3. University appeals this decision to the California Supreme Court.

4. California Supreme Court agrees with trial court that this admissions program violates constitution because it uses racial quotas.

5. Therefore, trial court was right on this issue.

(continued on next page)

8. Supreme Court, therefore, has said that trial court was wrong on this issue.

9. Bakke does not appeal this decision. He has won his case in the Supreme Court of California.

6. University, therefore, appeals this decision to U.S. Supreme Court.

SUPREME COURT OF THE UNITED

No. 76-811

Regents of the University of
   California, Petitioner,   On Writ of Certiorari
          vs.   to the Supreme Court
   Allan Bakke.   of California.

[June 28, 1978]

Syllabus

The Medical School of the University of California at Davis (hereinafter Davis) had two admissions programs for the entering class of 100 students—the regular admissions program and the special admissions program. Under the regular procedure, candidates whose overall undergraduate grade point averages fell below 2.5 on a scale of 4.0 were summarily rejected. About one out of six applicants was then given an interview, following which he was rated on a scale of 1 to 100 by each of the committee members (five in 1973 and six in 1974), his rating being based on the interviewers' summaries, his overall grade point average, his science courses grade point average, and his Medical College Admissions Test (MCAT) scores, letters of recommendation, extracurricular activities, and other biographical data, all of which resulted in a total "benchmark score." The full admissions committee then made offers of admission on the basis of their review of the applicant's file and his score, considering and acting upon applications as they were received. The committee chairman was responsible for placing names on the waiting list and had discretion to include persons with "special skills." A separate committee, a majority of whom were members of minority groups, operated the special admissions program. The 1973 and 1974 application forms, respectively, asked candidates whether they wished to be considered as "economically and/or educationally disadvantaged" applicants and members of a "minority group" (blacks, Chicanos, Asians, American Indians). If an applicant of a minority group was found to be "disadvantaged," he would be rated in a manner similar to the one employed by the general admissions committee. Special candidates, however, did not have to meet the 2.5 grade point cut-off and were not ranked against candidates in the general admissions process. About one-fifth of the special applicants were invited for interviews in 1973 and 1974, following which they were given benchmark scores, and the top choices were then given to the general admissions committee, which could reject special candidates for failure to meet course requirements or other specific deficiencies. The special committee continued to recommend candidates until 16 special admission selections had been made. During a four-year period 63 minority students were admitted to Davis under the special program and 44 under the general program. No disadvantaged whites were admitted under the special program, though many applied. Respondent, a white male, applied to Davis in 1973 and 1974, in both years being considered only under the general admissions program. Though he had a 468 out of 500 score in 1973, he was rejected since no general applicants with scores less than 470 were being accepted after respondent's application, which was filed late in the year, had been processed and completed. At that time four special admission slots were still unfilled. In 1974 respondent applied early, and though he had a total score of 549 out of 600, he was again rejected. In neither year was his name placed on the discretionary waiting list. In both years special applicants were admitted with significantly lower scores than respondent's. After his second rejection, respondent filed this action in state court for mandatory injunctive and declaratory relief to compel his admission to Davis, alleging that the special admissions program operated to exclude him on the basis of his race in violation of the Equal Protection Clause of the Fourteenth Amendment, a provision of the California Constitution, and § 601 of Title VI of the Civil Rights Act of 1964, which provides, inter alia, that no person shall on the ground of race or color be excluded from participating in any program receiving federal financial assistance

The facts of this case are described in this section. Important to remember is that the University of California at Davis Medical School operated a dual admissions process. Members of minority groups who wished to be considered as disadvantaged applicants were considered separately for a small number of reserved seats in the incoming class. Allan Bakke, a white applicant for admission, claimed that his rejection was on the basis of race and that the special admissions program of the University violated the Fourteenth Amendment 'equal protection' clause and Section 601 of the 1964 Civil Rights Act.

The trial court held that the admissions process constituted a racial quota in violation of the Fourteenth Amendment and Section 601, but that Bakke was not to be admitted because he failed to prove that he would have been admitted in the absence of this special admissions process for disadvantaged minorities.

The California Supreme Court agreed that the admissions process violated the Fourteenth Amendment by setting racial quotas, but said that Bakke was entitled to admission because the University failed to prove he would not have been admitted even in the absence of the discriminatory process.

The U.S. Supreme Court in this divided opinion holds that while race may be considered in the admissions process, the particular system in use at the University of California at Davis did not meet the 'strict scrutiny' test and, therefore,

Petitioner cross-claimed for a declaration that its special admissions program was lawful. The trial court found that the special program operated as a racial quota, because minority applicants in that program were rated only against one another, and 16 places in the class of 100 were reserved for them. Declaring that petitioner could not take race into account in making admissions decisions, the program was held to violate the Federal and State Constitutions and Title VI. Respondent's admission was not ordered, however, for lack of proof that he would have been admitted but for the special program. The California Supreme Court, applying a strict-scrutiny standard, concluded that the special admissions program was not the least intrusive means of achieving the goals of the admittedly compelling state interests of integrating the medical profession and increasing the number of doctors willing to serve minority patients. Without passing on the state constitutional or federal statutory grounds the court held that petitioner's special admissions program violated the Equal Protection Clause. Since petitioner could not satisfy its burden of demonstrating that respondent, absent the special program, would not have been admitted, the court ordered his admission to Davis.

Held: The judgment below is affirmed insofar as it orders respondent's admission to Davis and invalidates petitioner's special admissions program, but is reversed insofar as it prohibits petitioner from taking race into account as a factor in its future admissions decisions.

18 Cal. 3d 34, 553 P. 2d 1152, affirmed in part and reversed in part.

MR. JUSTICE POWELL concluded:

1. Title VI proscribes only those racial classifications that would violate the Equal Protection Clause if employed by a State or its agencies. Pp. 12–18.

2. Racial and ethnic classifications of any sort are inherently suspect and call for the most exacting judicial scrutiny. While the goal of achieving a diverse student body is sufficiently compelling to justify consideration of race in admissions decisions under some circumstances, petitioner's special admissions program, which forecloses consideration to persons like respondent, is unnecessary to the achievement of this compelling goal and therefore invalid under the Equal Protection Clause. Pp. 18–49.

3. Since petitioner could not satisfy its burden of proving that respondent would not have been admitted even if there had been no special admissions program, he must be admitted. P. 49.

MR. JUSTICE BRENNAN, MR. JUSTICE WHITE, MR. JUSTICE MARSHALL, and MR. JUSTICE BLACKMUN concluded:

1. Title VI proscribes only those racial classifications that would violate the Equal Protection Clause if employed by a State or its agencies. Pp. 4–31.

2. Racial classifications call for strict judicial scrutiny. Nonetheless, the purpose of overcoming substantial, chronic minority underrepresentation in the medical profession is sufficiently important to justify petitioner's remedial use of race. Thus, the judgment below must be reversed in that it prohibits race from being used as a factor in university admissions. Pp. 31–55.

MR. JUSTICE STEVENS, joined by THE CHIEF JUSTICE, MR. JUSTICE STEWART, and MR. JUSTICE REHNQUIST, being of the view that whether race can ever be a factor in an admissions policy is not an issue here; that Title VI applies; and that respondent was excluded from Davis in violation of Title VI, concurs in the Court's judgment insofar as it affirms the judgment of the court below ordering respondent admitted to Davis.

POWELL, J., announced the Court's judgment and filed an opinion expressing his views of the case, in Parts I, III–A, and V–C of which WHITE, J., joined; and in Parts I and V–C of which BRENNAN, MARSHALL, and BLACKMUN, JJ., joined. BRENNAN, WHITE, MARSHALL, and BLACKMUN, JJ., filed an opinion concurring in the judgment in part and dissenting in part. WHITE, MARSHALL, and BLACKMUN, JJ., filed separate opinions. STEVENS, J., filed an opinion concurring in the judgment in part and dissenting in part, in which BURGER, C. J., and STEWART and REHNQUIST, JJ., joined.

violates Title VI and the Fourteenth Amendment, and, since the University failed to prove Bakke would not have been admitted in the absence of the minority program, he is entitled to admission now.

The court divided as follows: Brennan, White, Marshall, Blackmun:

a. race may be used.
b. the Davis plan is constitutional.
c. Bakke should not be admitted.

Powell:

a. admitted race may be used.
b. the Davis plan is NOT constitutional.
c. Bakke should be admitted.

Stevens, Burger, Stewart, Rehnquist: —

a. race may not be used.
b. the Davis plan is NOT acceptable because it violates Title VI.
c. Bakke should be admitted.

The effect of these divisions is to make two 5-4 decisions with Powell the swing judge in each.

It is decided, 5-4, that race may be used. It is decided, 5-4 that the Davis plan is NOT constitutional and that Bakke be admitted.

459

MR. JUSTICE POWELL announced the judgment of the Court.

This case presents a challenge to the special admissions program of the petitioner, the Medical School of the University of California at Davis, which is designed to assure the admission of a specified number of students from certain minority groups. The Superior Court of California sustained respondent's challenge, holding that petitioner's program violated the California Constitution, Title VI of the Civil Rights Act of 1964, 42 U. S. C. § 2000d, and the Equal Protection Clause of the Fourteenth Amendment. The court enjoined petitioner from considering respondent's race or the race of any other applicant in making admissions decisions. It refused, however, to order respondent's admission to the Medical School, holding that he had not carried his burden of proving that he would have been admitted but for the constitutional and statutory violations. The Supreme Court of California affirmed those portions of the trial court's judgment declaring the special admissions program unlawful and enjoining petitioner from considering the race of any applicant.* It modified that portion of the judgment denying respondent's requested injunction and directed the trial court to order his admission.

For the reasons stated in the following opinion, I believe that so much of the judgment of the California court as holds petitioner's special admissions program unlawful and directs that respondent be admitted to the Medical School must be affirmed. For the reasons expressed in a separate opinion, my Brothers THE CHIEF JUSTICE, MR. JUSTICE STEWART, MR. JUSTICE REHNQUIST, and MR. JUSTICE STEVENS concur in this judgment.

I also conclude for the reasons stated in the following opinion that the portion of the court's judgment enjoining petitioner from according any consideration to race in its admissions process must be reversed. For reasons expressed in separate opinions, my Brothers MR. JUSTICE BRENNAN, MR. JUSTICE WHITE, MR. JUSTICE MARSHALL, and MR. JUSTICE BLACKMUN concur in this judgment.

Affirmed in part and reversed in part.

Powell states that the Court upholds the California Supreme Court ruling that the Davis plan is unconstitutional and that Bakke is entitled to admission. (Burger, Stewart, Rehnquist, and Stevens agree.) The Court is reversing the California Supreme Court ruling that racial categories may not be used to help blacks. (Brennan, White, Marshall, and Blackmun agree.)

The language of § 601, like that of the Equal Protection Clause, is majestic in its sweep:

> "No person in the United States shall, on the ground of race, color, or national origin, be excluded from participation in, be denied the benefits of, or be subjected to discrimination under any program or activity receiving Federal financial assistance."

The concept of "discrimination," like the phrase "equal protection of the laws," is susceptible to varying interpretations, for as Mr. Justice Holmes declared, "[a] word is not a crystal, transparent and unchanged, it is the skin of a living thought and may vary greatly in color and content according to the circumstances and the time in which it is used." *Towne* v. *Eisner*, 245 U. S. 418, 425 (1918). We must, therefore, seek whatever aid is available in determining the precise meaning of the statute before us. *Train* v. *Colorado Public Interest Research Group*, 426 U. S. 1, 10 (1976), quoting *United States* v. *American Trucking Assns.*, 310 U. S. 534, 543–544 (1940). Examination of the voluminous legislative history of Title VI reveals a congressional intent to halt federal funding of entities that violate a prohibition of racial discrimination similar to that of the Constitution. Although isolated statements of various legislators, taken out of context, can be marshalled in support of the proposition that § 601 enacted a purely color-blind scheme,[19] without regard to the reach of the Equal Protection Clause, these comments must be read against the background of both the problem that Congress was addressing and the broader view of the statute that emerges from a full examination of the legislative debates.

The problem confronting Congress was discrimination against Negro citizens at the hands of recipients of federal moneys. Indeed, the color-blindness pronouncements cited in the margin at n. 19, generally occur in the midst of extended remarks dealing with the evils of segregation in federally funded programs. Over and over again, proponents of the bill detailed the plight of Negroes seeking equal treatment in such programs.[20] There simply was no reason for Congress to consider the validity of hypothetical preferences that might be accorded minority citizens; the legislators were dealing with the real and pressing problem of how to guarantee those citizens equal treatment.

In view of the clear legislative intent, Title VI must be held to proscribe only those racial classifications that would violate the Equal Protection Clause or the Fifth Amendment.

Powell argues here that the word 'discrimination' in Section 601 of the 1964 Civil Rights Act does not mean 'color blind'. Rather, based upon Congressional intent in enacting it, the language is interpreted as identical in meaning to the Fourteenth Amendment which only prohibits certain racial classifications, <u>not all</u>.

En route to this crucial battle over the scope of judicial review,[25] the parties fight a sharp preliminary action over the proper characterization of the special admissions program. Petitioner prefers to view it as establishing a "goal" of minority representation in the medical school. Respondent, echoing the courts below, labels it a racial quota.[26]

This semantic distinction is beside the point: the special admissions program is undeniably a classification based on race and ethnic background. To the extent that there existed a pool of at least minimally qualified minority applicants to fill the 16 special admissions seats, white applicants could compete only for 84 seats in the entering class, rather than the 100 open to minority applicants. Whether this limitation is described as a quota or a goal, it is a line drawn on the basis of race and ethnic status.[27]

The guarantees of the Fourteenth Amendment extend to persons. Its language is explicit: "No state shall . . . deny to any person within its jurisdiction the equal protection of the laws." It is settled beyond question that the "rights created by the first section of the Fourteenth Amendment are, by its terms, guaranteed to the individual. They are personal rights," *Shelley* v. *Kraemer*, *supra*, at 22. Accord, *Missouri ex rel. Gaines* v. *Canada*, *supra*, at 351; *McCabe* v. *Atchison, T. & S. F. R. Co.*, 235 U. S. 151, 161–162 (1914). The guarantee of equal protection cannot mean one thing when applied to one individual and something else when applied to a person of another color. If both are not accorded the same protection, then it is not equal.

Here Powell talks about the University's view that their program constitutes a racial 'goal' while Bakke says it is a racial 'quota'. Powell says the distinction is meaningless. Since whites were ineligible for the minority program, the program was based upon race. Therefore, if the race-based program unfairly discriminated against whites it violated the Fourteenth Amendment.

The Court has never questioned the validity of those pronouncements. Racial and ethnic distinctions of any sort are inherently suspect and thus call for the most exacting judicial examination.

Powell emphasizes that racial classifications are subject to strict judicial examination in all cases.

Petitioner urges us to adopt for the first time a more restrictive view of the Equal Protection Clause and hold that discrimination against members of the white "majority" cannot be suspect if its purpose can be characterized as "benign."[34] The clock of our liberties, however, cannot be turned back to 1868. *Brown* v. *Board of Education, supra,* at 492; accord, *Loving* v. *Virginia, supra,* at 9. It is far too late to argue that the guarantee of equal protection to *all* persons permits the recognition of special wards entitled to a degree of protection greater than that accorded others.[35] "The Fourteenth Amendment is not directed solely against discrimination due to a 'two-class theory'—that is, based upon differences between 'white' and Negro." *Hernandez, supra,* at 478.

Once the artificial line of a "two-class theory" of the Fourteenth Amendment is put aside, the difficulties entailed in varying the level of judicial review according to a perceived "preferred" status of a particular racial or ethnic minority are intractable. The concepts of "majority" and "minority" necessarily reflect temporary arrangements and political judgments. As observed above, the white "majority" itself is composed of various minority groups, most of which can lay claim to a history of prior discrimination at the hands of the state and private individuals. Not all of these groups can receive preferential treatment and corresponding judicial tolerance of distinctions drawn in terms of race and nationality, for then the only "majority" left would be a new minority of White Anglo-Saxon Protestants. There is no principled basis for deciding which groups would merit "heightened judicial solicitude" and which would not.[36] Courts would be asked to evaluate the extent of the prejudice and consequent harm suffered by various minority groups. Those whose societal injury is thought to exceed some arbitrary level of tolerability then would be entitled to preferential classifications at the expense of individuals belonging to other groups. Those classifications would be free from exacting judicial scrutiny. As these preferences began to have their desired effect, and the consequences of past discrimination were undone, new judicial rankings would be necessary. The kind of variable sociological and political analysis necessary to produce such rankings simply does not lie within the judicial competence—even if they otherwise were politically feasible and socially desirable.[37]

If it is the individual who is entitled to judicial protection against classifications based upon his racial or ethnic background because such distinctions impinge upon personal rights, rather than the individual only because of his membership in a particular group, then constitutional standards may be applied consistently. Political judgments regarding the necessity for the particular classification may be weighed in the constitutional balance, *Korematsu* v. *United States,* 323 U. S. 214 (1944), but the standard of justification will remain constant. This is as it should be, since those political judgments are the product of rough compromise struck by contending groups within the democratic process.[38] When they touch upon an individual's race or ethnic background, he is entitled to a judicial determination that the burden he is asked to bear on that basis is precisely tailored to serve a compelling governmental interest. The Constitution guarantees that right to every person regardless of his background.

On the issue of whether benign racial categories set up by a white majority are less subject to strict scrutiny, Powell says that the white majority is not monolithic, but a collection of white minorities and that there is no ground for deciding which racial categories should be reviewed as benign and which discriminatory. Therefore, no such distinction is recognized.

He argues that the individual is entitled to judicial protection because his/her rights are violated, not because of mere membership in a racial group. The State must prove a compelling interest to justify this type of impingement upon personal rights.

463

Petitioner contends that on several occasions this Court has approved preferential classifications without applying the most exacting scrutiny. Most of the cases upon which petitioner relies are drawn from three areas: school desegregation, employment discrimination, and sex discrimination. Each of the cases cited presented a situation materially different from the facts of this case.

The school desegregation cases are inapposite. Each involved remedies for clearly determined constitutional violations. *E. g., Swann* v. *Charlotte-Mecklenburg Board of Education,* 402 U. S. 1 (1971); *McDaniel* v. *Barresi,* 402 U. S. 39 (1971); *Green* v. *County School Board,* 391 U. S. 430 (1968). Racial classifications thus were designed as remedies for the vindication of constitutional entitlement.[39] Moreover, the scope of the remedies was not permitted to exceed the extent of the violations. *E. g., Dayton Board of Education* v. *Brinkman,* 433 U. S. 406 (1977); *Milliken* v. *Bradley,* 418 U. S. 717 (1974); see *Pasadena City Board of Education* v. *Spangler,* 427 U. S. 424 (1976). See also *Austin Indep. School Dist.* v. *United States,* 429 U. S. 990, 991–995 (1976) (POWELL, J., concurring). Here, there was no judicial determination of constitutional violation as a predicate for the formulation of a remedial classification.

We have held that in "order to justify the use of a suspect classification, a State must show that its purpose or interest is both constitutionally permissible and substantial, and that its use of the classification is 'necessary . . . to the accomplishment' of its purpose or the safeguarding of its interest." *In re Griffiths,* 413 U. S. 717, 722–723 (1973) (footnotes omitted); *Loving* v. *Virginia,* 388 U. S. 1, 11 (1967); *McLaughlin* v. *Florida,* 379 U. S. 184, 196 (1964). The special admissions program purports to serve the purposes of: (i) "reducing the historic deficit of traditionally disfavored minorities in medical schools and the medical profession," Brief for Petitioner 32; (ii) countering the effects of societal discrimination;[43] (iii) increasing the number of physicians who will practice in communities currently underserved; and (iv) obtaining the educational benefits that flow from an ethnically diverse student body. It is necessary to decide which, if any, of these purposes is substantial enough to support the use of a suspect classification.

Powell rejects the University's claim that prior decisions permitted racial categories to aid minorities. He says that in the school desegregation cases, employment discrimination cases, and sex discrimination cases, there were clear past violations for which the racial categories were the only remedies.

Invoking the standard that the State must demonstrate a compelling reason to use racial categories in pursuing a legitimate and important goal, Powell lists the University's stated purposes of reducing the historic deficit of minorities in the medical field, counterir the effects of social discrimination, increasing the number of doctors in underserved areas, and creating a diverse student body.

464

If petitioner's purpose is to assure within its student body some specified percentage of a particular group merely because of its race or ethnic origin, such a preferential purpose must be rejected not as insubstantial but as facially invalid. Preferring members of any one group for no reason other than race or ethnic origin is discrimination for its own sake. This the Constitution forbids.

Powell says that preference in the student body on the mere basis of race is invalid.

The State certainly has a legitimate and substantial interest in ameliorating, or eliminating where feasible, the disabling effects of identified discrimination. The line of school desegregation cases, commencing with *Brown*, attests to the importance of this state goal and the commitment of the judiciary to affirm all lawful means towards its attainment. In the school cases, the States were required by court order to redress the wrongs worked by specific instances of racial discrimination. That goal was far more focused than the remedying of the effects of "societal discrimination," an amorphous concept of injury that may be ageless in its reach into the past.

We have never approved a classification that aids persons perceived as members of relatively victimized groups at the expense of other innocent individuals in the absence of judicial, legislative, or administrative findings of constitutional or statutory violations.

While recognizing as legitimate the goal of removing the effects of social discrimination, Powell says that to hurt the innocent individual to help the group where no specific prior violations are shown is not acceptable. (Note that if such violations were shown, Powell's view may have changed.) The plan cannot be defended on this basis.

Hence, the purpose of helping certain groups whom the faculty of the Davis Medical School perceived as victims of "societal discrimination" does not justify a classification that imposes disadvantages upon persons like respondent, who bear no responsibility for whatever harm the beneficiaries of the special admissions program are thought to have suffered. To hold otherwise would be to convert a remedy heretofore reserved for violations of legal rights into a privilege that all institutions throughout the Nation could grant at their pleasure to whatever groups are perceived as victims of societal discrimination. That is a step we have never approved.

Therefore, since racially-based actions are only acceptable to remedy past discrimination, the University, never having itself discriminated, may not now use racial categories to remedy effects of general social discrimination. The plan cannot be defended on this basis.

Petitioner identifies, as another purpose of its program, improving the delivery of health care services to communities currently underserved. It may be assumed that in some situations a State's interest in facilitating the health care of its citizens is sufficiently compelling to support the use of a suspect classification. But there is virtually no evidence in the record indicating that petitioner's special admissions program is either needed or geared to promote that goal.[46]

No evidence suggests that the program would help to provide more doctors in needed areas. Thus, the plan cannot be defended on this basis.

The fourth goal asserted by petitioner is the attainment of a diverse student body. This clearly is a constitutionally permissible goal for an institution of higher education. Academic freedom, though not a specifically enumerated constitutional right, long has been viewed as a special concern of the First Amendment. The freedom of a university to make its own judgments as to education includes the selection of its student body.

This argument does support the University's plan since the University can seek a diverse student body if it likes. However, this is insufficient to support the plan in light of above arguments and the next argument.

It may be assumed that the reservation of a specified number of seats in each class for individuals from the preferred ethnic groups would contribute to the attainment of considerable ethnic diversity in the student body. But petitioner's argument that this is the only effective means of serving the interest of diversity is seriously flawed. In a most fundamental sense the argument misconceives the nature of the state interest that would justify consideration of race or ethnic background. It is not an interest in simple ethnic diversity, in which a specified percentage of the student body is in effect guaranteed to be members of selected ethnic groups, with the remaining percentage an undifferentiated aggregation of students. The diversity that furthers a compelling state interest encompasses a far broader array of qualifications and characteristics of which racial or ethnic origin is but a single though important element. Petitioner's special admissions program, focused *solely* on ethnic diversity, would hinder rather than further attainment of genuine diversity.[50]

Powell states that even if diversity is a valid objective, this plan is not designed to achieve it because, by definition, diversity means more than racial distributions. Other plans would far better work to achieve real diversity

The experience of other university admissions programs, which take race into account in achieving the educational diversity valued by the First Amendment, demonstrates that the assignment of a fixed number of places to a minority group is not a necessary means toward that end. An illuminating example is found in the Harvard College program:

Other programs achieve diversity without reserving places for minorities.

In such an admissions program,[51] race or ethnic background may be deemed a "plus" in a particular applicant's file, yet it does not insulate the individual from comparison with all other candidates for the available seats. The file of a particular black applicant may be examined for his potential contribution to diversity without the factor of race being decisive when compared, for example, with that of an applicant identified as an Italian-American if the latter is thought to exhibit qualities more likely to promote beneficial educational pluralism. Such qualities could include exceptional personal talents, unique work or service experience, leadership potential, maturity, demonstrated compassion, a history of overcoming disadvantage, ability to communicate with the poor, or other qualifications deemed important. In short, an admissions program operated in this way is flexible enough to consider all pertinent elements of diversity in light of the particular qualifications of each applicant, and to place them on the same footing for consideration, although not necessarily according them the same weight. Indeed, the weight attributed to a particular quality may vary from year to year depending upon the "mix" both of the student body and the applicants for the incoming class.

This kind of program treats each applicant as an individual in the admissions process. The applicant who loses out on the last available seat to another candidate receiving a "plus" on the basis of ethnic background will not have been foreclosed from all consideration for that seat simply because he was not the right color or had the wrong surname. It would mean only that his combined qualifications, which may have included similar nonobjective factors, did not outweigh those of the other applicant. His qualifications would have been weighed fairly and competitively, and he would have no basis to complain of unequal treatment under the Fourteenth Amendment.[52]

Harvard, for instance, flexibly looks at many characteristics of every individual, rather than looking only at race. They consider race among other qualities and characteristics, but exclude no one purely on that basis.

467

In summary, it is evident that the Davis special admission program involves the use of an explicit racial classification never before countenanced by this Court. It tells applicants who are not Negro, Asian, or "Chicano" that they are totally excluded from a specific percentage of the seats in an entering class. No matter how strong their qualifications, quantitative and extracurricular, including their own potential for contribution to educational diversity, they are never afforded the chance to compete with applicants from the preferred groups for the special admission seats. At the same time, the preferred applicants have the opportunity to compete for every seat in the class.

The fatal flaw in petitioner's preferential program is its disregard of individual rights as guaranteed by the Fourteenth Amendment. *Shelley* v. *Kraemer*, 334 U. S. 1, 22 (1948). Such rights are not absolute. But when a State's distribution of benefits or imposition of burdens hinges on the color of a person's skin or ancestry, that individual is entitled to a demonstration that the challenged classification is necessary to promote a substantial state interest. Petitioner has failed to carry this burden. For this reason, that portion of the California court's judgment holding petitioner's special admissions program invalid under the Fourteenth Amendment must be affirmed.

C

In enjoining petitioner from ever considering the race of any applicant, however, the courts below failed to recognize that the State has a substantial interest that legitimately may be served by a properly devised admissions program involving the competitive consideration of race and ethnic origin. For this reason, so much of the California court's judgment as enjoins petitioner from any consideration of the race of any applicant must be reversed.

VI

With respect to respondent's entitlement to an injunction directing his admission to the Medical School, petitioner has conceded that it could not carry its burden of proving that, but for the existence of its unlawful special admissions program, respondent still would not have been admitted. Hence, respondent is entitled to the injunction, and that portion of the judgment must be affirmed.[54]

Davis' plan excludes on the basis of race. The University fails to meet the strict scrutiny test in trying to justify this. Therefore, the plan is unconstitutional as the California Supreme Court said. However, race may be considered in the manner done at Harvard, and, therefore, the California Court's ban on such uses of race is reversed. Finally, Bakke is entitled to admission since the University failed to prove he would not have been admitted anyway.

Opinion of MR. JUSTICE BRENNAN, MR. JUSTICE WHITE, MR. JUSTICE MARSHALL, and MR. JUSTICE BLACKMUN, concurring in the judgment in part and dissenting.

The Court today, in reversing in part the judgment of the Supreme Court of California, affirms the constitutional power of Federal and State Government to act affirmatively to achieve equal opportunity for all. The difficulty of the issue presented—whether Government may use race-conscious programs to redress the continuing effects of past discrimination—and the mature consideration which each of our Brethren has brought to it have resulted in many opinions, no single one speaking for the Court. But this should not and must not mask the central meaning of today's opinions: Government may take race into account when it acts not to demean or insult any racial group, but to remedy disadvantages cast on minorities by past racial prejudice, at least when appropriate findings have been made by judicial, legislative, or administrative bodies with competence to act in this area.

THE CHIEF JUSTICE and our Brothers STEWART, REHNQUIST, and STEVENS, have concluded that Title VI of the Civil Rights Act of 1964, 78 Stat. 252, as amended, 42 U. S. C. § 2000d *et seq.* (1970 ed. and Supp. V), prohibits programs such as that at the Davis Medical School. On this statutory theory alone, they would hold that respondent Allan Bakke's rights have been violated and that he must, therefore, be admitted to the Medical School. Our Brother POWELL, reaching the Constitution, concludes that, although race may be taken into account in university admissions, the particular special admissions program used by petitioner, which resulted in the exclusion of respondent Bakke, was not shown to be necessary to achieve petitioner's stated goals. Accordingly, these Members of the Court form a majority of five affirming the judgment of the Supreme Court of California insofar as it holds that respondent Bakke "is entitled to an order that he be admitted to the University." *Bakke* v. *Regents of the University of California,* 18 Cal. 3d 34, 64, 132 Cal. Rptr. 680, 700, 553 P. 2d 1152, 1172 (1976).

We agree with MR. JUSTICE POWELL that, as applied to the case before us, Title VI goes no further in prohibiting the use of race than the Equal Protection Clause of the Fourteenth Amendment itself. We also agree that the effect of the California Supreme Court's affirmance of the judgment of the Superior Court of California would be to prohibit the University from establishing in the future affirmative action programs that take race into account. See *ante,* at 1 n.*. Since we conclude that the affirmative admissions program at the Davis Medical School is constitutional, we would reverse the judgment below in all respects. MR. JUSTICE POWELL agrees that some uses of race in university admissions are permissible and, therefore, he joins with us to make five votes reversing the judgment below insofar as it prohibits the University from establishing race-conscious programs in the future.[1]

Brennan (for himself, White, Stewart, and Marshall) agrees with Powell that race may at times be used. He disagrees with Powell (and Burger, Stewart, Rehnquist, and Stevens) that Bakke is entitled to admission. Burger, Stewart, Rehnquist, and Stevens base the order to admit Bakke on Section 601 which they believe to prohibit Davis' plan. Powell bases this decision to admit Bakke on the failure of Davis to meet the strict scrutiny test.

Our Nation was founded on the principle that "all men are created equal." Yet candor requires acknowledgment that the Framers of our Constitution, to forge the Thirteen Colonies into one Nation, openly compromised this principle of equality with its antithesis: slavery. The consequences of this compromise are well known and have aptly been called our "American Dilemma." Still, it is well to recount how recent the time has been, if it has yet come, when the promise of our principles has flowered into the actuality of equal opportunity for all regardless of race or color.

The Fourteenth Amendment, the embodiment in the Constitution of our abiding belief in human equality, has been the law of our land for only slightly more than half its 200 years. And for half of that half, the Equal Protection Clause of the Amendment was largely moribund so that, as late as 1927, Mr. Justice Holmes could sum up the importance of that Clause by remarking that it was "the last resort of constitutional arguments." *Buck* v. *Bell*, 274 U. S. 200, 208 (1927). Worse than desuetude, the Clause was early turned against those whom it was intended to set free, condemning them to a "separate but equal" [2] status before the law, a status always separate but seldom equal. Not until 1954—only 24 years ago—was this odious doctrine interred by our decision in *Brown* v. *Board of Education*, 347 U. S. 483 (1954) (*Brown I*), and its progeny,[3] which proclaimed that separate schools and public facilities of all sorts were inherently unequal and forbidden under our Constitution. Even then inequality was not eliminated with "all deliberate speed." *Brown* v. *Board of Education*, 349 U. S. 294, 301 (1955). In 1968 [4] and again in 1971,[5] for example, we were forced to remind school boards of their obligation to eliminate racial discrimination root and branch. And a glance at our docket [6] and at those of lower courts will show that even today officially sanctioned discrimination is not a thing of the past.

Against this background, claims that law must be "color-blind" or that the datum of race is no longer relevant to public policy must be seen as aspiration rather than as description of reality. This is not to denigrate aspiration; for reality rebukes us that race has too often been used by those who would stigmatize and oppress minorities. Yet we cannot—and as we shall demonstrate, need not under our Constitution or Title VI, which merely extends the constraints of the Fourteenth Amendment to private parties who receive federal funds—let color blindness become myopia which masks the reality that many "created equal" have been treated within our lifetimes as inferior both by the law and by their fellow citizens.

In our view, Title VI prohibits only those uses of racial criteria that would violate the Fourteenth Amendment if employed by a State or its agencies; it does not bar the preferential treatment of racial minorities as a means of remedying past societal discrimination to the extent that such action is consistent with the Fourteenth Amendment.

After reviewing the "American dilemma," Brennan concludes that to be blind to race is to be blind to the realities of American life.

He argues that Title VI (Section 601) prohibits only those racial preferences which the 14th amendment would prohibit—no more.

In sum, Congress' equating of Title VI's prohibition with the commands of the Fifth and Fourteenth Amendments, its refusal precisely to define that racial discrimination which it intended to prohibit, and its expectation that the statute would be administered in a flexible manner, compel the conclusion that Congress intended the meaning of the statute's prohibition to evolve with the interpretation of the commands of the Constitution. Thus any claim that the use of racial criteria is barred by the plain language of the statute must fail in light of the remedial purpose of Title VI and its legislative history. The cryptic nature of the language employed in Title VI merely reflects Congress' concern with the then prevalent use of racial standards as a means of excluding or disadvantaging Negroes and its determination to prohibit absolutely such discrimination,

A review of Congressional debate leads to the conclusion that Congress intended that section 601 be interpreted this way.

The assertion of human equality is closely associated with the proposition that differences in color or creed, birth or status, are neither significant nor relevant to the way in which persons should be treated. Nonetheless, the position that such factors must be "[c]onstitutionally an irrelevance," *Edwards v. California*, 314 U. S. 160, 185 (1941) (Jackson, J., concurring), summed up by the shorthand phrase "[o]ur Constitution is color-blind," *Plessy v. Ferguson*, 163 U. S. 537, 559 (1896) (Harlan, J., dissenting), has never been adopted by this Court as the proper meaning of the Equal Protection Clause. Indeed, we have expressly rejected this proposition on a number of occasions.

We conclude, therefore, that racial classifications are not *per se* invalid under the Fourteenth Amendment. Accordingly, we turn to the problem of articulating what our role should be in reviewing state action that expressly classifies by race.

The use of race has never been per se unconstitutional.

Unquestionably we have held that a government practice or statute which restricts "fundamental rights" or which contains "suspect classifications" is to be subjected to "strict scrutiny" and can be justified only if it furthers a compelling government purpose and, even then, only if no less restrictive alternative is available.[30]

In fact, where a fundamental right or a suspect category (like race) is used, the Court requires a compelling reason and a demonstration that nothing less would work. But it does not bar all such categories.

471

On the other hand, the fact that this case does not fit neatly into our prior analytic framework for race cases does not mean that it should be analyzed by applying the very loose rational-basis standard of review that is the very least that is always applied in equal protection cases.[34] " '[T]he mere recitation of a benign, compensatory purpose is not an automatic shield which protects against any inquiry into the actual purposes underlying a statutory scheme.' " *Califano* v. *Webster*, 430 U. S. 313, 317 (1977), quoting *Weinberger* v. *Weisenfeld*, 420 U. S. 636, 648 (1975). Instead, a number of considerations—developed in gender discrimination cases but which carry even more force when applied to racial classifications—lead us to conclude that racial classifications designed to further remedial purposes " 'must serve important governmental objectives and must be substantially related to achievement of those objectives.' "

A benign purpose is insufficient to lower the degree of judicial scrutiny required.

First, race, like, "gender-based classifications too often [has] been inexcusably utilized to stereotype and stigmatize politically powerless segments of society."

Race often has been used to hurt politically weak segments of society.

Second, race, like gender and illegitimacy, see *Weber* v. *Aetna Cas. & Surety Co.*, 406 U. S. 164 (1972), is an immutable characteristic which its possessors are powerless to escape or set aside. While a classification is not *per se* invalid because it divides classes on the basis of an immutable characteristic, see *supra*, pp. 31–32, it is nevertheless true that such divisions are contrary to our deep belief that "legal burdens should bear some relationship to individual responsibility or wrongdoing," *Weber, supra,* at 175; *Frontiero* v. *Richardson*, 411 U. S. 667, 686 (1973) (opinion of Brennan, White, and Marshall, JJ.), and that advancement sanctioned, sponsored, or approved by the State should ideally be based on individual merit or achievement, or at the least on factors within the control of an individual.

Race, being unchangeable, requires great justification as a basis for categorizing individuals.

In sum, because of the significant risk that racial classifications established for ostensibly benign purposes can be misused, causing effects not unlike those created by invidious classifications, it is inappropriate to inquire only whether there is any conceivable basis that might sustain such a classification. Instead, to justify such a classification an important and articulated purpose for its use must be shown. In addition, any statute must be stricken that stigmatizes any group or that singles out those least well represented in the political process to bear the brunt of a benign program. Thus our review under the Fourteenth Amendment should be strict—not " 'strict' in theory and fatal in fact," [36] because it is stigma that causes fatality—but strict and searching nonetheless.

Therefore, a strict standard of judicial scrutiny will be applied to the Davis admissions program.

Davis' articulated purpose of remedying the effects of past societal discrimination is, under our cases, sufficiently important to justify the use of race-conscious admissions programs where there is a sound basis for concluding that minority underrepresentation is substantial and chronic, and that the handicap of past discrimination is impeding access of minorities to the medical school

Davis' goal of remedying the effects of past social discrimination is a substantially important goal to meet the test.

Finally, the conclusion that state educational institutions may constitutionally adopt admissions programs designed to avoid exclusion of historically disadvantaged minorities, even when such programs explicitly take race into account, finds direct support in our cases construing congressional legislation designed to overcome the present effects of past discrimination. Congress can and has outlawed actions which have a disproportionately adverse and unjustified impact upon members of racial minorities and has required or authorized race-conscious action to put individuals disadvantaged by such impact in the position they otherwise might have enjoyed. See *Franks* v. *Bowman, supra; International Brotherhood of Teamsters* v. *United States,* 431 U. S. 324 (1977). Such relief does not require as a predicate proof that recipients of preferential advancement have been individually discriminated against; it is enough that each recipient is within a general class of persons likely to have been the victims of discrimination.

The goal of avoiding exclusion of minorities is also valid.

Moreover, the presence or absence of past discrimination by universities or employers is largely irrelevant to resolving respondent's constitutional claims. The claims of those burdened by the race-conscious actions of a university or employer who has never been adjudged in violation of an antidiscrimination law are not any more or less entitled to deference than the claims of the burdened nonminority workers in *Franks* v. *Bowman,* 424 U. S. 747 (1976), in which the employer had violated Title VII, for in each case the employees are innocent of past discrimination. And, although it might be argued that, where an employer has violated an antidiscrimination law, the expectations of nonminority workers are themselves products of discrimination and hence "tainted," see *Franks, supra,* at 776, and therefore more easily upset, the same argument can be made with respect to respondent. If it was reasonable to conclude—as we hold that it was—that the failure of minorities to qualify for admission at Davis under regular procedures was due principally to the effects of past discrimination, then there is a reasonable likelihood that, but for pervasive racial discrimination, respondent would have failed to qualify for admission even in the absence of Davis' special admissions program.[41]

The lack of past discrimination by Davis is irrelevant since the absence of blacks in the school was the result of past discrimination.

Davis' goal of admitting minority students disadvantaged by the effects of past discrimination is sufficiently important to justify use of race-conscious admissions criteria.

Therefore, the goal of remedying past discrimination justifies racial categories to assist minorities.

Properly construed, therefore, our prior cases unequivocally show that a state government may adopt race-conscious programs if the purpose of such programs is to remove the disparate racial impact its actions might otherwise have and if there is reason to believe that the disparate impact is itself the product of past discrimination, whether its own or that of society at large. There is no question that Davis' program is valid under this test.

Certainly, on the basis of the undisputed factual submissions before this Court, Davis had a sound basis for believing that the problem of underrepresentation of minorities was substantial and chronic and that the problem was attributable to handicaps imposed on minority applicants by past and present racial discrimination.

The Davis plan is a valid way to achieve their valid goals.

The second prong of our test—whether the Davis program stigmatizes any discrete group or individual and whether race is reasonably used in light of the program's objectives—is clearly satisfied by the Davis program.

It is not even claimed that Davis' program in any way operates to stigmatize or single out any discrete and insular, or even any identifiable, nonminority group. Nor will harm comparable to that imposed upon racial minorities by exclusion or separation on grounds of race be the likely result of the program. It does not, for example, establish an exclusive preserve for minority students apart from and exclusive of whites. Rather, its purpose is to overcome the effects of segregation by bringing the races together. True, whites are excluded from participation in the special admissions program, but this fact only operates to reduce the number of whites to be admitted in the regular admissions program in order to permit admission of a reasonable percentage—less than their proportion of the California population [57]—of otherwise underrepresented qualified minority applicants.[58]

Whites are not stigmatized by this plan. They are excluded from the special admissions, but not stigmatized as a group.

We disagree with the lower courts' conclusion that the Davis program's use of race was unreasonable in light of its objectives. First, as petitioner argues, there are no practical means by which it could achieve its ends in the foreseeable future without the use of race-conscious measures. With respect to any factor (such as poverty or family educational background) that may be used as a substitute for race as an indicator of past discrimination, whites greatly outnumber racial minorities simply because whites make up a far larger percentage of the total population and therefore far outnumber minorities in absolute terms at every socioeconomic level.[59]

Therefore, Brennan disagrees that the use of race was unreasonable. No other means of increasing minorities in medical schools is available.

Second, the Davis admissions program does not simply equate minority status with disadvantage. Rather, Davis considers on an individual basis each applicant's personal history to determine whether he or she has likely been disadvantaged by racial discrimination. The record makes clear that only minority applicants likely to have been isolated from the mainstream of American life are considered in the special program; other minority applicants are eligible only through the regular admissions program. True, the procedure by which disadvantage is detected is informal, but we have never insisted that educators conduct their affairs through adjudicatory proceedings, and such insistence here is misplaced.

The Davis plan examines minority applicants individually and only applies to disadvantaged individual minority members.

Finally, Davis' special admissions program cannot be said to violate the Constitution simply because it has set aside a predetermined number of places for qualified minority applicants rather than using minority status as a positive factor to be considered in evaluating the applications of disadvantaged minority applicants. For purposes of constitutional adjudication, there is no difference between the two approaches. In any admissions program which accords special consideration to disadvantaged racial minorities, a determination of the degree of preference to be given is unavoidable, and any given preference that results in the exclusion of a white candidate is no more or less constitutionally acceptable than a program such as that at Davis. Furthermore, the extent of the preference inevitably depends on how many minority applicants the particular school is seeking to admit in any particular year so long as the number of qualified minority applicants exceeds that number. There is no sensible, and certainly no constitutional, distinction between, for example, adding a set number of points to the admissions rating of disadvantaged minority applicants as an expression of the preference with the expectation that this will result in the admission of an approximately determined number of qualified minority applicants and setting a fixed number of places for such applicants as was done here.[63]

Brennan says that there is no difference between setting aside places for minorities and using race as a positive quality in assessing minority applicants.

The "Harvard" program, see *ante*, at 43–47, as those employing it readily concede, openly and successfully employs a racial criterion for the purpose of ensuring that some of the scarce places in institutions of higher education are allocated to disadvantaged minority students. That the Harvard approach does not also make public the extent of the preference and the precise workings of the system while the Davis program employs a specific, openly stated number, does not condemn the latter plan for purposes of Fourteenth Amendment adjudication. It may be that the Harvard plan is more acceptable to the public than is the Davis "quota." If it is, any State, including California, is free to adopt it in preference to a less acceptable alternative, just as it is generally free, as far as the Constitution is concerned, to abjure granting any racial preferences in its admissions program. But there is no basis for preferring a particular preference program simply because in achieving the same goals that the Davis Medical School is pursuing, it proceeds in a manner that is not immediately apparent to the public.

IV

Accordingly, we would reverse the judgment of the Supreme Court of California holding the Medical School's special admissions program unconstitutional and directing respondent's admission, as well as that portion of the judgment enjoining the Medical School from according any consideration to race in the admissions process.

Brennan states that the Harvard plan may be more acceptable to the public, but is no different in outcome or purpose. Therefore, Brennan would reverse the finding of unconstitutionality, reverse the order to admit Bakke, and reverse its ban on using race in admissions.

I agree with the judgment of the Court only insofar as it permits a university to consider the race of an applicant in making admissions decisions. I do not agree that petitioner's admissions program violates the Constitution. For it must be remembered that, during most of the past 200 years, the Constitution as interpreted by this Court did not prohibit the most ingenious and pervasive forms of discrimination against the Negro. Now, when a State acts to remedy the effects of that legacy of discrimination, I cannot believe that this same Constitution stands as a barrier.

Three hundred and fifty years ago, the Negro was dragged to this country in chains to be sold into slavery. Uprooted from his homeland and thrust into bondage for forced labor, the slave was deprived of all legal rights. It was unlawful to teach him to read; he could be sold away from his family and friends at the whim of his master; and killing or maiming him was not a crime. The system of slavery brutalized and dehumanized both master and slave.[1]

Marshall writes a separate opinion emphasizing his position that race may be used and that the Davis plan meets constitutional requirements.

The status of the Negro as property was officially erased by his emancipation at the end of the Civil War. But the long awaited emancipation, while freeing the Negro from slavery, did not bring him citizenship or equality in any meaningful way. Slavery was replaced by a system of "laws which imposed upon the colored race onerous disabilities and burdens, and curtailed their rights in the pursuit of life, liberty, and property to such an extent that their freedom was of little value." *Slaughter-House Cases*, 16 Wall. 36, 70 (1873). Despite the passage of the Thirteenth, Fourteenth, and Fifteenth Amendments, the Negro was systematically denied the rights those amendments were supposed to secure. The combined actions and inactions of the State and Federal Government maintained Negroes in a position of legal inferiority for another century after the Civil War.

The position of the Negro today in America is the tragic but inevitable consequence of centuries of unequal treatment. Measured by any benchmark of comfort or achievement, meaningful equality remains a distant dream for the Negro.

A Negro child today has a life expectancy which is shorter by more than five years than that of a white child.[2] The Negro child's mother is over three times more likely to die of complications in childbirth,[3] and the infant mortality rate for Negroes is nearly twice that for whites.[4] The median income of the Negro family is only 60% that of the median of a white family,[5] and the percentage of Negroes who live in families with incomes below the poverty line is nearly four times greater than that of whites.[6]

The tragic position of the American Negro today, says Marshall, is traceable to the actions of government in forcing Negroes into a position of inferior status.

In light of the sorry history of discrimination and its devastating impact on the lives of Negroes, bringing the Negro into the mainstream of American life should be a state interest of the highest order. To fail to do so is to ensure that America will forever remain a divided society.

III

I do not believe that the Fourteenth Amendment requires us to accept that fate. Neither its history nor our past cases lend any support to the conclusion that a University may not remedy the cumulative effects of society's discrimination by giving consideration to race in an effort to increase the number and percentage of Negro doctors.

It has been said that this case involves only the individual, Bakke, and this University. I doubt, however, that there is a computer capable of determining the number of persons and institutions that may be affected by the decision in this case. For example, we are told by the Attorney General of the United States that at least 27 federal agencies have adopted regulations requiring recipients of federal funds to take "*affirmative action* to overcome the effects of conditions which resulted in limiting participation . . . by persons of a particular race, color, or national origin." Supplemental Brief for the United States as *Amicus Curiae* 16 (emphasis added). I cannot even guess the number of state and local governments that have set up affirmative action programs, which may be affected by today's decision.

I fear that we have come full circle. After the Civil War our government started several "affirmative action" programs. This Court in the *Civil Rights Cases* and *Plessy* v. *Ferguson* destroyed the movement toward complete equality. For almost a century no action was taken, and this nonaction was with the tacit approval of the courts. Then we had *Brown* v. *Board of Education* and the Civil Rights Acts of Congress, followed by numerous affirmative action programs. *Now*, we have this Court again stepping in, this time to stop affirmative action programs of the type used by the University of California.

Therefore, the Fourteenth Amendment cannot be read to prohibit a State University from using race to remedy the effects of years of official discrimination.

Marshall argues that this case involves more than one white male's claim to a seat in one medical school. This case, by striking Davis' affirmative action plan, will cause many other affirmative action programs to be halted. It is this effect of the Court's decision which Marshall fears.

I participate fully, of course, in the opinion, *ante*, p. —, that bears the names of my Brothers Brennan, White, Marshall, and myself. I add only some general observations that hold particular significance for me, and then a few comments on equal protection.

Blackmun agrees with Brennan, Marshall, and White but adds his own personal thoughts concerning this case.

I yield to no one in my earnest hope that the time will come when an "affirmative action" program is unnecessary and is, in truth, only a relic of the past. I would hope that we could reach this stage within a decade at the most. But the story of *Brown* v. *Board of Education*, 347 U. S. 483 (1954), decided almost a quarter of a century ago, suggests that that hope is a slim one. At some time, however, beyond any period of what some would claim is only transitional inequality, the United States must and will reach a stage of maturity where action along this line is no longer necessary. Then persons will be regarded as persons, and discrimination of the type we address today will be an ugly feature of history that is instructive but that is behind us.

His hope is that affirmative action program will be made unnecessary within ten years.

It is somewhat ironic to have us so deeply disturbed over a program where race is an element of consciousness, and yet to be aware of the fact, as we are, that institutions of higher learning, albeit more on the undergraduate than the graduate level, have given conceded preferences up to a point to those possessed of athletic skills, to the children of alumni, to the affluent who may bestow their largess on the institutions, and to those having connections with celebrities, the famous, and the powerful.

Blackmun finds the concern over racial preferences ironic in light of all the other preferences commonly given to applicants to schools.

I am not convinced, as MR. JUSTICE POWELL seems to be, that the difference between the Davis program and the one employed by Harvard is very profound or constitutionally significant. The line between the two is a thin and indistinct one. In each, subjective application is at work. Because of my conviction that admission programs are primarily for the educators, I am willing to accept the representation that the Harvard program is one where good faith in its administration is practiced as well as professed. I agree that such a program, where race or ethnic background is only one of many factors, is a program better formulated than Davis' two-track system. The cynical, of course, may say that under a program such as Harvard's one may accomplish covertly what Davis concedes it does openly. I need not go that far, for despite its two-track aspect, the Davis program, for me, is within constitutional bounds, though perhaps barely so.

Unlike Powell, Blackmun sees no real difference between the Harvard plan and the Davis plan. He feels both are constitutional, though Harvard's may be a better plan.

I suspect that it would be impossible to arrange an affirmative action program in a racially neutral way and have it successful. To ask that this be so is to demand the impossible. In order to get beyond racism, we must first take account of race. There is no other way. And in order to treat some persons equally, we must treat them differently. We cannot—we dare not—let the Equal Protection Clause perpetrate racial supremacy.

In fact, he argues, a racially neutral plan would not work. Therefore, the equal protection clause must be interpreted in a way supportive of racially-based policies.

MR. JUSTICE STEVENS, with whom THE CHIEF JUSTICE, MR. JUSTICE STEWART, and MR. JUSTICE REHNQUIST join, concurring in the judgment in part and dissenting in part.

This is not a class action. The controversy is between two specific litigants. Allan Bakke challenged petitioner's special admissions program, claiming that it denied him a place in medical school because of his race in violation of the Federal and California Constitutions and of Title VI of the Civil Rights Act of 1964, 42 U.S.C. § 2000d *et seq.* The California Supreme Court upheld his challenge and ordered him admitted. If the state court was correct in its view that the University's special program was illegal, and that Bakke was therefore unlawfully excluded from the medical school because of his race, we should affirm its judgment, regardless of our views about the legality of admissions programs that are not now before the Court.

The judgment as originally entered by the trial court contained four separate paragraphs, two of which are of critical importance.[2] Paragraph 3 declared that the University's special admissions program violated the Fourteenth Amendment, the State Constitution, and Title VI. The trial court did not order the University to admit Bakke because it concluded that Bakke had not shown that he would have been admitted if there had been no special program. Instead, in paragraph 2 of its judgment it ordered the University to consider Bakke's application for admission without regard to his race or the race of any other applicant. The order did not include any broad prohibition against any use of race in the admissions process; its terms were clearly limited to the University's consideration

of *Bakke*'s application.[3]

The California Supreme Court, in a holding that is not challenged, ruled that the trial court incorrectly placed the burden on Bakke of showing that he would have been admitted in the absence of discrimination. The University then conceded: "that it [could] not meet the burden of proving that the special admission program did not result in Bakke's exclusion."[4] Accordingly, the California Supreme Court directed the trial court to enter judgment ordering Bakke's admission.[5] Whether the judgment of the state court is affirmed or reversed, in whole or in part, there is no outstanding injunction forbidding any consideration of racial criteria in processing applications.

It is therefore perfectly clear that the question whether race can ever be used as a factor in an admissions decision is not an issue in this case, and that discussion of that issue is inappropriate.[6]

Stevens, Burger, Stewart, and Rehnquist seek to narrow the ruling to the specific facts of Bakke's situation. They emphasize that the California trial court (upheld by California Supreme Court) ordered Davis to consider Bakke's application without reference to race. It did not prohibit the use of race in admissions processes generally.

The order by the California Supreme Court to admit Bakke was based only on the fact that the University failed to meet the burden of proving that Bakke would not have been admitted in the absence of the special program. The broader question of whether race can be used in the admissions process is not an issue in this case.

In this case, we are presented with a constitutional question of undoubted and unusual importance. Since, however, a dispositive statutory claim was raised at the very inception of this case, and squarely decided in the portion of the trial court judgment affirmed by the California Supreme Court, it is our plain duty to confront it. Only if petitioner should prevail on the statutory issue would it be necessary to decide whether the University's admissions program violated the Equal Protection Clause of the Fourteenth Amendment.

This case, the four Justices argue, should be decided upon the grounds of the Federal Civil Rights Act of 1964, NOT the constitution.

Petitioner contends, however, that exclusion of applicants on the basis of race does not violate Title VI if the exclusion carries with it no racial stigma. No such qualification or limitation of § 601's categorical prohibition of "exclusion" is justified by the statute or its history

The University's argument that their program does not violate Section 601 because it does not stigmatize whites is rejected because the statute prohibits all racial exclusions, not only those involving stigma.

In giving answers such as these, it seems clear that the proponents of Title VI assumed that the Constitution itself required a colorblind standard on the part of government,[17] but that does not mean that the legislation only codifies an existing constitutional prohibition. The Act's proponents plainly considered Title VI consistent with their view of the Constitution and they sought to provide an effective weapon to implement that view.[18]

The Civil Rights Act of 1964 was designed as a tool to implement the goal of color-blindness expressed in the Fourteenth Amendment.

In short, nothing in the legislative history justifies the conclusion that the broad language of § 601 should not be given its natural meaning. We are dealing with a distinct statutory prohibition, enacted at a particular time with particular concerns in mind; neither its language nor any prior interpretation suggests that its place in the Civil Rights Act, won after long debate, is simply that of a constitutional appendage.[21] In unmistakable terms the Act prohibits the exclusion of individuals from federally funded programs because of their race.[22] As succinctly phrased during the Senate debate, under Title VI it is not "permissible to say 'yes' to one person, but to say 'no' to another person, only because of the color of his skin." [23]

The University's special admissions program violated Title VI of the Civil Rights Act of 1964 by excluding Bakke from the medical school because of his race. It is therefore our duty to affirm the judgment ordering Bakke admitted to the University.

Accordingly, I concur in the Court's judgment insofar as it affirms the judgment of the Supreme Court of California. To the extent that it purports to do anything else, I respectfully dissent.

The plain language of Section 601 prohibits the exclusion on the basis of race of any people from programs receiving federal funds. Therefore, the Davis plan violated the constitution and Bakke is entitled to admission.

1. What were the basic facts in the <u>Bakke</u> case?

2. Summarize the opinions of:

    A. Justice Powell

    B. Justices Brennan, White, Marshall, Blackman

    C. Justices Stevens, Burger, Stewart, Rehnquist

DISCUSSION OF READING #1 QUESTIONS

1. The central facts involve the claim of a white male that the special admissions program at the University of California at Davis Medical School discriminated against him on the basis of race. Under the special program, minority applicants who were found to be disadvantaged were not compared to other applicants. Consequently, some applicants admitted under the special program had lower test scores than some applicants rejected under the general admissions program. Bakke was one of these rejected students.

2. A. Powell rejects the idea that the Civil Rights Act of 1964 and the Fourteenth Amendment require a "color blind" approach to solving racial problems. However, he says that Davis' goals were equivalent to quotas and, therefore, do not meet the "strict scrutiny" test of the Constitution. The result, he says along with four other justices, is that Bakke must be admitted.

   B. Brennan, White, Marshall, and Blackmun maintain that the historical reality of racial discrimination requires consideration of race today in public policy decisions. While rejecting the claim that 'benign' discrimination does not trigger the 'strict scrutiny test' these four justices believe that the Davis program does pass constitutional muster. The goal of remedying past social discrimination is sufficiently compelling. Bakke, in their view, must not be admitted because the admissions program was constitutional.

   C. Stevens, Burger, Stewart, and Rehnquist argue that this set of facts does not even present the general question of racial preferences. But even if it did, they maintain that the plain meaning of the Civil Rights Act of 1964 precludes all racial exclusions. Therefore, Bakke should be admitted.

<u>UNIT STUDY QUESTIONS</u>

For the final task in the course you are to try to "put it all toge-ther" by applying your knowledge to a discussion of the <u>Bakke</u> case which you have just studied. Before attempting to synthesize all of this material, you should review the Study Questions and Discussions in order to remind yourself of key issues. Below are some of the questions which you might want to think about in your analysis of the <u>Bakke</u> case in light of your learning. Follow-ing these questions is a discussion in which I have tried to illustrate for you the ways in which a social scientist might look at a Supreme Court deci-sion. Because you are now familiar with the <u>Bakke</u> case, it provides a good opportunity for you to begin to apply what you've studied in this course.

<u>Questions</u>

1. Once the facts of the <u>Bakke</u> case are established, why does the court find it a simple matter to compare the facts with the law and arrive at a proper result?

2. In what way do the Bakke opinions illustrate problems raised in the Speluncean Explorers Case in Unit 1?

3. Can you see in the Bakke opinions any traces of the philosophical positions studied in Unit 1? Specifically, are
there strains of historical jurisprudence or utilitarianism
in the arguments of the justices in Bakke?

4. Using what you have studied in Unit 2, what issues might
interest social scientists in the various disciplines?
Specifically, can Bakke be seen through the eyes of a
systems or stimulus-response theorist? What would political
scientists want to know about the make-up of the court?

5. Unit 3 suggested that law reflects social arrangements.
How does Bakke illustrate this relationship between law
and society?

6. Is the Bakke case a problem of social control as defined
    in Unit 5? What style of social control is predominant
    in this case?

7. The impact theory explained in Unit 6 hypothesized condi-
    tions which increase and decrease the court's impact. How
    might these hypotheses help us to predict the impact of
    Bakke?

8. Did the court undermine its legitimacy by making a poli-
    tical decision in Bakke? The politics of rights and the
    limits of adjudication (Unit 7) may suggest some inter-
    pretations to you.

These are questions which occur to me as I try to put it all together and examine Bakke as a case study of the role of law in society. In
the Discussion, therefore, I look at answers to these questions. You might
very likely have raised other questions or arrived at different answers to
these questions. It is the process of integrating and applying the material,
rather than the precise way in which you do it, that is important.

After you have thought about the Bakke case in light of this course,
jot down some of your ideas. Then read the Discussion and see if any of
these ideas have occurred to you.

DISCUSSION OF UNIT STUDY QUESTIONS:
"PUTTING IT ALL TOGETHER"

In order to summarize for you some of the major ideas in the course, indicate to you how they relate to one another, and encourage you to use these ideas to analyze current examples of the role of law, I have attempted to discuss here the <u>Bakke</u> case in light of the preceding nine units. While every topic covered in the course is not applicable to an analysis of the <u>Bakke</u> case, I have tried to show you some of the ways in which you can use the knowledge you have acquired. My analysis is neither exhaustive nor necessarily correct. It represents only one person's attempts to integrate the large amount of material you were asked to study. If you are unable to disagree, see omissions, or raise questions, the course has not been entirely successful!

Statuatory Interpretation

The Bakke decision which you have read (in part) illustrates many of the same dilemmas raised in the case of the Speluncean Explorers. When judges are faced with interpreting the law, <u>how</u> should they go about it? In <u>Bakke</u>, Justices Stevens, Burger, Stewart, and Rehnquist seem to agree with the Chief Justice in the Speluncean Explorers case: the law is to be technically read and literally applied. Section 601 of title 6 unambiguously states:

> No person in the United States shall, on the ground of race, color, or national origin, be excluded from participation in, be denied the benefits of, or be subjected to discrimination under any program or activity receiving Federal financial assistance. (Title VI, Civil Rights Act of 1964, 42 U.S.C. 2000d)

For these four justices this means that "In unmistakable terms the Act prohibits the exclusion of individuals from federally funded programs because of their race" (p. 10.34).

On the other hand, Justices Brennan, White, Marshall, and Blackmun take the common sense approach of Justice Handy in the Speluncean case. For them, it is obvious that the reality of black history in America requires that we cannot "...let color blindness become myopia which masks the reality that many 'created equal' have been treated within our lifetimes as inferior both by the law and by their fellow citizens" (p. 10.22).

The ambiguous nature of law, the unavoidability of making a decision, and the difficulties of interpretation which are highlighted in the Speluncean Explorers case are strikingly evident again as you read Bakke.

Jurisprudential Roots

In addition, the jurisprudential positions explored in Unit 1 are visible in the Bakke situation. For example, one senses a strain of historical jurisprudence in the way the court handled Bakke. Savigny argued that the validity of law depended upon its correspondence with the spirit of the people. Fearing that any unambiguous decision would produce a negative reaction and perhaps even a threat to the validity of its decision, the Court walked a fine line in its effort to antagonize no one.

On the other hand, we might see (in the portion of the decision upholding the use of race in admissions policies) some evidence that Maine's theory that progressive law moves from a status to contract basis is incorrect. For isn't it the very point of this part of the opinion that having a particular status in American society may legally be the basis for deciding who will attend professional schools?

From a utilitarian point of view we might ask whether the Bakke result tends to produce the greatest amount of good for the greatest number of Americans, and from a legal realist point of view we might assert that the Justices, in fact, applied neither the constitution, nor section 601 to decide Bakke, but rather used these legal arguments to produce a result consistent with their own preferences. In other words, it was a foregone conclusion that Justice Marshall would support the use of racial categories to assist blacks and Justice Rehnquist would oppose it.

Interdisciplinary Approaches to Bakke

Undoubtedly, representatives of the various disciplines you studied in Unit 2 will be writing about Bakke for years to come. Let's try to imagine, based upon Unit 2, what questions they will be aksing.

The normative sociologist of law will inquire as to whether or not Bakke does harm to the legal system's claim of legality. Since his concern is more with the system than the particular decision, he will likely see no threat to legality. For the scientific sociologist of law, the question is, what general proposition about law is illustrated in Bakke?

Conceptually, both systems and stimuli-response theorists will be studying the nature of the demands which led to the Bakke case and certainly will focus on the effect of the largest number of amicus briefs ever filed in the Supreme Court. Why did the gatekeepers let Bakke in while keeping DeFunis out? Who will next be allowed to reach the Supreme Court in seeking clarifications of Bakke? What will be the effect of the decision on subsequent litigation and on the perceptions and attitudes of Americans toward the court? Will blacks feel betrayed or supported? Certainly the rhetorician would want to study the effect of competing communications about the Bakke decision on these perceptions and attitudes.

Political scientists will want to know the effect of the backgrounds of these particular judges and will pay close attention to the reactions of political elites in Congress, the White House, and state and local decision makers. The particular blocs of Stevens, Burger, Stewart, and Rehnquist vs. Brennan, Marshall, Blackman and White with Powell partly on each side will be compared with past divisions on the court. How did the Nixon appointees (Burger, Blackman, Powell, Rehnquist) divide and what does that tell us about the ability of Presidents to have political impact long after the expiration of their terms?

Might a follower of cognitive legal development theory not find a rich task in attempting to evaluate the stages of reasoning to be found in the various opinions on the Bakke case?

Obviously I am merely suggesting approaches and questions which scholars of law and society from the various social sciences would likely ask.

Reverse Discrimination and Social Structure

If, as Unit 3 suggests, law is best understood as a reflection of the social structure, what interpretation might be placed upon the Bakke case? A Marxist view might be that the effect of the decision is to preserve the underlying social and economic advantages for whites while purporting to up-hold affirmative action. This accomplishes the goal of temporarily satisfying blacks while providing the means for whites to continue to dominate the economic structure.

Bakke might also be interpreted as reflecting the developing social arrangements in America which have, in recent years, brought more and more blacks into the mainstream of social life. A decision upholding racial considerations benefitting blacks would have been though utterly absurd only a few years ago. Law, we might argue, has indeed moved to reflect social structure.

The Bakke Dispute

Unit 4 is not as helpful in looking at Bakke because the Bakke dispute with the University of California at Davis is not the type of trivial issue which Unit 4 suggests might be resolved in a non-legal setting. The policy implications of Bakke are vast and this type of case probably is better judged than mediated.

Consider, however, that in fact a case like this might be settled by mediation if the parties did not define their dispute as a general resolution of a big issue. In fact, probably a large number of racial disputes are or could be resolved by a mediation process or a community moot. In fact, it might be argued that such a process would be preferable as it would not require the parties to adopt rigid positions which affect all future decisions.

Bakke as Social Control

Certainly the Supreme Court's decision in Bakke addresses the normative dimension of social life. It tells us what is right, what is wrong, and rough-ly how to proceed to handle this problem. The style was conciliatory in the sense that the disputants themselves sought a resolution of their conflict. But elements of the penal style appear when the claim is made by Bakke that the University violated a legal prohibition on using racially-based categories for admission.

Clearly Black's theory of the inverse relation of law and other social control can be seen as explaining why a court even is asked this question. If religious or other controls provided adequate answers, law would not likely have entered the picture in the first place.

The Bakke Decision and Social Change

The concerns of Unit 6 are closely related to the Bakke case. The basic question of whether law can bring about social changes is at the heart of Bakke. Can the court decision bring about further movement in integrating black Americans into the social system. Will Bakke produce a hostile reaction from whites or will Bakke's admission to medical school satisfy them?

The impact theory poses a number of problems for analysis. Will the unusual division (4-1-4) in the Court lessen the impact of its decision? Will the public even understand Bakke in light of the claims of victory and defeat by representatives on both sides of the issue? Will the lack of clear guidelines--beyond the Harvard example--mean that those schools which want to admit blacks preferentially will do so and those that wish to exclude them will do so? Undoubtedly, follow-up research should and will be done in an effort to measure the impact of Bakke on educational policy and on subsequent challenge in other areas, such as employment.

Law in American Society

Unit 7 is concerned with American attitudes toward and reliance on law. American legal culture includes a great faith in legal forms and legal solutions. Yet the dilemma of how to appear to make purely legal decisions while in fact making political decisions is painfully apparent in Bakke. Left only with section 601 and the Fourteenth Amendment, the Justices would be hard pressed to resolve the case of Allan Bakke. Yet to make a politically momentous decision would have undermined their very claim to legitimacy. Thus, the cautious opinion of the Court indicates their sensitivity to the problem.

The politics of rights notion is particularly applicable to Bakke. For Scheingold, the critical question becomes, how will the Court's decision be employed by those who favor and oppose 'reverse discrimination'. Horovitz's analysis of the inherent limitations of the process of adjudication is also informative here, for the Bakke decision is a small link in a chain of civil rights decisions. As such, it is necessarily isolated and discrete, and does little to answer the broader policy questions which are at stake. In Bakke, furthermore, we may see further evidence for Glazer's hypothesis that the permanently activist Court has taken one more step toward becoming the 'imperical judiciary'. Surely _Bakke_ will raise more legal questions than it has answered, and many will ultimately have to be answered by the Supreme Court.

Conclusion

While only a few of the many concerns of the course have been singled out here and applied to the _Bakke_ decision, you hopefully have been stimulated by the course to think further about this and other examples of the law and society relationship.

ABOUT THE AUTHORS

Lee S. Weinberg received his Ph.D. in Political Science and his J.D. degree at the University of Pittsburgh and currently is Associate Professor of Administration of Justice and Associate Director of the Legal Studies Program at the University of Pittsburgh. Judith W. Weinberg received her M.A. in Education and is a Doctoral Candidate in Curriculum and Supervision at the University of Pittsburgh.